SWEET & MAXWELL'S

EUROPEAN COMMUNITY TREATIES

Including the European Communities Act 1972

AUSTRALIA
The Law Book Company Ltd.
Sydney: Melbourne: Brisbane

CANADA AND U.S.A.
The Carswell Company Ltd.
Agincourt, Ontario

INDIA
N. M. Tripathi Private Ltd.
Bombay
and
Eastern Law House Private Ltd.
Calcutta
M.P.P. House
Bangalore

ISRAEL
Steimatzky's Agency Ltd.
Jerusalem: Tel Aviv: Haifa

MALAYSIA: SINGAPORE: BRUNEI
Malayan Law Journal (Pte.) Ltd.
Singapore

NEW ZEALAND
Sweet & Maxwell (N.Z.) Ltd.
Auckland

PAKISTAN
Pakistan Law House
Karachi

SWEET & MAXWELL'S

EUROPEAN COMMUNITY TREATIES

Including

THE EUROPEAN COMMUNITIES ACT 1972

FOURTH EDITION

Edited by

SWEET & MAXWELL'S
LEGAL EDITORIAL STAFF

Advisory Editor

K. R. SIMMONDS, M.A., D.PHIL. (OXON.)

Professor of International Law
in the University of London (Queen Mary College),
formerly Director of the British Institute
of International and Comparative Law

LONDON
SWEET & MAXWELL
1980

First Edition	1972
Second Edition	1975
Third Edition	1977
Second Impression	1979
Fourth Edition	1980

Published by
Sweet & Maxwell Limited of
11 New Fetter Lane, London.
Photoset by Promenade Graphics Ltd., Cheltenham.
Printed in Great Britain by
Page Bros. (Norwich) Ltd.

British Library Cataloguing in Publication Data

Sweet & Maxwell's European Community Treaties
—4th ed.
European Economic Community 2. European
Coal and Steel Community 3. Euratom
I. Simmonds, Kenneth Royston II. European
Community Treaties

341'. 0264'4 [Law]

ISBN 0-421-27210-4
ISBN 0-421-27220-1 Pbk

PREFACE

THIS is the fourth edition of *Sweet and Maxwell's European Community Treaties* which now appears in an expanded form. This will probably be the last edition to be published in one volume. Further expansion of the Communities will result in a commensurate expansion of this book to a size which we feel will no longer be practical for easy reference. However, this problem is not yet upon us and we hope that our readers will find this edition as useful as previous editions.

The principal reason for a new edition lies, of course, in the impending accession to membership of the European Communities of Greece on January 1, 1981. The Treaty of Accession of the Hellenic Republic, which was signed in Athens on May 28, 1979, is printed in Part V, together with the Act concerning the Conditions of Accession and the Adjustments to the Treaties and the principal Protocols and Declarations. Space, unfortunately, has dictated that we must omit the lengthier Annexes which we thought would be of limited appeal to our readers.

This edition follows the format of previous editions with the texts arranged in chronological order starting with the Treaty establishing the European Coal and Steel Community (Part I), the Treaty establishing the European Economic Community (Part II) and the Treaty establishing the European Atomic Energy Community (Part III). This is followed by Part IV—Community Texts in which are set out the materials common to the three Communities, including the Statutes of the Court of Justice, the Merger and both Budgetary Treaties and the Luxembourg Accords. The financial provisions of the Second Budgetary Treaty, 1975, which had to appear in the previous edition in a temporary form, have now been consolidated into the principal texts in this edition. This Treaty entered into force on June 1, 1977. The documents relating to the Accession of the United Kingdom, Denmark and Ireland and Greece form Part V and the European Communities Act in its up-to-date and amended form is contained in Part VI.

The official English language texts as issued by the Official Publications Office in Luxembourg have been used and all amendments, repeals and additions are indicated by square brackets in the text along with the citation of the amending authority.

We would like to express our sincere gratitude to our advisory editor, Professor K. R. Simmonds, for his continually cheerful assistance, support and enthusiasm during the planning and final stages of this edition.

London,
June 1980
                                                        SWEET & MAXWELL

v

CONTENTS

Part I

EUROPEAN COAL AND STEEL COMMUNITY

PAGE

Part II

EUROPEAN ECONOMIC COMMUNITY

Part III

EUROPEAN ATOMIC ENERGY COMMUNITY

Part IV

COMMUNITY TEXTS

Part V

ACCESSION

Part VI

EUROPEAN COMMUNITIES ACT

PROVISIONS OF THE TREATIES GOVERNING THE INSTITUTIONS AND OTHER BODIES

IT IS our policy to print in this collection the constituent Treaties as amended by subsequent Treaties. Wherever possible we have incorporated in this way the amendments to the constituent Treaties made by the provisions of the Act of Accession of the Hellenic Republic. However, in some instances, amendments will only be carried out after the accession has taken place on January 1, 1981. For ease of reference, therefore, we set out below the principal provisions governing the composition and voting procedures of the Institutions of the Communities and the major committees which will be affected by the accession of Greece.

THE ASSEMBLY
ECSC Treaty	EEC Treaty	Euratom Treaty
Art. 21	Art. 138	Art. 108

See also: Art. 10 of the Act of Accession of the Hellenic Republic.

THE COUNCIL
ECSC Treaty	EEC Treaty	Euratom Treaty	Merger Treaty
Arts. 28, 95	Art. 148(2)	Art. 118(2)	Art. 2

See also: Arts. 11–14 and 133 of the Act of Accession of the Hellenic Republic.

THE COMMISSION

Merger Treaty
Arts. 10(1), 14

See also: Arts. 15 and 134 of the Act of Accession of the Hellenic Republic.

THE COURT OF JUSTICE
ECSC Treaty	EEC Treaty	Euratom Treaty
Arts. 32, 32(a), 32(b)	Arts. 165–167	Arts. 137–139

See also: Art. 18 of the Statute of the Court of Justice of the ECSC, Art. 15 of the Statute of the Court of Justice of the EEC, and Art. 15 of the Statute of the Court of Justice of Euratom; and Arts. 16 and 135 of the Act of Accession of the Hellenic Republic.

THE ECONOMIC AND SOCIAL COMMITTEE
EEC Treaty	Euratom Treaty
Art. 194	Art. 166(1)

See also: Arts. 17 and 136 of the Act of Accession of the Hellenic Republic.

THE COURT OF AUDITORS
ECSC Treaty	EEC Treaty	Euratom Treaty
Art. 78e(2)	Art. 206(2)	Art. 180(2)

See also: Arts, 18 and 137 of the Act of Accession of the Hellenic Republic.

THE SCIENTIFIC AND TECHNICAL COMMITTEE
Euratom Treaty
Art. 134(2)
See also: Arts. 19 and 139 of the Act of Accession of the Hellenic Republic.

THE CONSULTATIVE COMMITTEE
ECSC Treaty
Art. 18(1)
See also: Art. 138 of the Act of Accession of the Hellenic Republic.

THE MONETARY COMMITTEE
EEC Treaty
Art. 105(2)
See also: Art. 140 of the Act of Accession of the Hellenic Republic.

Part I

EUROPEAN COAL AND STEEL COMMUNITY

TREATY

ESTABLISHING

THE EUROPEAN COAL AND STEEL COMMUNITY

(PARIS, 18 APRIL 1951)

THE PRESIDENT OF THE FEDERAL REPUBLIC OF GERMANY, HIS ROYAL HIGHNESS THE PRINCE ROYAL OF BELGIUM, THE PRESIDENT OF THE FRENCH REPUBLIC, THE PRESIDENT OF THE ITALIAN REPUBLIC, HER ROYAL HIGHNESS THE GRAND DUCHESS OF LUXEMBOURG, HER MAJESTY THE QUEEN OF THE NETHERLANDS,

CONSIDERING that world peace can be safeguarded only be creative efforts commensurate with the dangers that threaten it,

CONVINCED that the contribution which an organised and vital Europe can make to civilisation is indispensable to the maintenance of peaceful relations,

RECOGNISING that Europe can be built only through practical achievements which will first of all create real solidarity, and through the establishment of common bases for economic development,

ANXIOUS to help, by expanding their basic production, to raise the standard of living and further the works of peace,

RESOLVED to substitute for age-old rivalries the merging of their essential interests; to create, by establishing an economic community, the basis for a broader and deeper community among peoples long divided by bloody conflicts; and to lay the foundations of institutions which will give direction to a destiny henceforward shared,

HAVE DECIDED to create a European Coal and Steel Community and to this end have designated as their plenipotentiaries:

THE PRESIDENT OF THE FEDERAL REPUBLIC OF GERMANY:
Dr. Konrad ADENAUER, Chancellor and
Minister for Foreign Affairs;

HIS ROYAL HIGHNESS THE PRINCE ROYAL OF BELGIUM:
Mr. Paul VAN ZEELAND, Minister for Foreign Affairs,
Mr. Joseph MEURICE, Minister for Foreign Trade;

THE PRESIDENT OF THE FRENCH REPUBLIC:
Mr. Robert SCHUMAN, Minister for Foreign Affairs;

THE PRESIDENT OF THE ITALIAN REPUBLIC:
Mr. Carlo SFORZA, Minister for Foreign Affairs;

HER ROYAL HIGHNESS THE GRAND DUCHESS OF LUXEMBOURG:
Mr. Joseph BECH, Minister for Foreign Affairs;

HER MAJESTY THE QUEEN OF THE NETHERLANDS:
Mr. D. U. STIKKER, Minister for Foreign Affairs,
Mr. J. R. M. VAN DEN BRINK, Minister for Economic Affairs;

WHO, having exchanged their Full Powers, found in good and due form, HAVE AGREED as follows:

Title One

THE EUROPEAN COAL AND STEEL COMMUNITY

ARTICLE 1

By this Treaty, the High Contracting Parties establish among themselves a EUROPEAN COAL AND STEEL COMMUNITY, founded upon a common market, common objectives and common institutions.

ARTICLE 2

The European Coal and Steel Community shall have as its task to contribute, in harmony with the general economy of the Member States and through the establishment of a common market as provided in Article 4, to economic expansion, growth of employment and a rising standard of living in the Member States.

The Community shall progressively bring about conditions which will of themselves ensure the most rational distribution of production at the highest possible level of productivity, while safeguarding continuity of employment and taking care not to provoke fundamental and persistent disturbances in the economies of Member States.

ARTICLE 3

The institutions of the Community shall, within the limits of their respective powers, in the common interest:

(a) ensure an orderly supply to the common market, taking into account the needs of third countries;

(b) ensure that all comparably placed consumers in the common market have equal access to the sources of production;

(c) ensure the establishment of the lowest prices under such conditions that these prices do not result in higher prices charged by the same undertakings in other transactions or in a higher general price level at another time, while allowing necessary amortization and normal return on invested capital;

(d) ensure the maintenance of conditions which will encourage undertakings to expand and improve their production potential and to promote a policy of using natural resources rationally and avoiding their unconsidered exhaustion;

(e) promote improved working conditions and an improved standard of living for the workers in each of the industries for which it is responsible, so as to make possible their harmonisation while the improvement is being maintained;

(f) promote the growth of international trade and ensure that equitable limits are observed in export pricing;

(g) promote the orderly expansion and modernisation of production, and the improvement of quality, with no protection against competing industries that is not justified by improper action on their part or in their favour.

ARTICLE 4

The following are recognised as incompatible with the common market for coal and steel and shall accordingly be abolished and prohibited within the Community, as provided in this Treaty:

(a) import and export duties, or charges having equivalent effect, and quantitative restrictions on the movement of products;

(b) measures or practices which discriminate between producers, between purchasers or between consumers, especially in prices and delivery terms or transport rates and conditions, and measures or practices which interfere with the purchaser's free choice of supplier;

(c) subsidies or aids granted by States, or special charges imposed by States, in any form whatsoever;

(d) restrictive practices which tend towards the sharing or exploiting of markets.

ARTICLE 5

The Community shall carry out its task in accordance with this Treaty, with a limited measure of intervention.

To this end the Community shall:

—provide guidance and assistance for the parties concerned, by obtaining information, organising consultations and laying down general objectives;

—place financial resources at the disposal of undertakings for their investment and bear part of the cost of readaptation;

—ensure the establishment, maintenance and observance of normal competitive conditions and exert direct influence upon production or upon the market only when circumstances so require;

—publish the reasons for its actions and take the necessary measures to ensure the observance of the rules laid down in this Treaty.

The institutions of the Community shall carry out these activities with a minimum of administrative machinery and in close co-operation with the parties concerned.

ARTICLE 6

The Community shall have legal personality.

In international relations, the Community shall enjoy the legal capacity it requires to perform its functions and attain its objectives.

In each of the Member States, the Community shall enjoy the most extensive legal capacity accorded to legal persons constituted in that State; it may, in particular, acquire or dispose of movable and immovable property and may be a party to legal proceedings.

The Community shall be represented by its institutions, each within the limits of its powers.

Title Two

THE INSTITUTIONS OF THE COMMUNITY

ARTICLE 7

The institutions of the Community shall be:
a High Authority, assisted by a Consultative Committee;
a Common Assembly (hereinafter called the " Assembly ");
a Special Council of Ministers (hereinafter called the " Council ");
a Court of Justice (hereinafter called the " Court ");
[The audit shall be carried out by a Court of Auditors acting within the limits of the powers conferred upon it by this Treaty.]

AMENDMENT
The second paragraph of this article was added by the second Budgetary Treaty of July 22, 1975, Art. 1.

CHAPTER I—THE HIGH AUTHORITY

ARTICLE 8

It shall be the duty of the High Authority to ensure that the objectives set out in this Treaty are attained in accordance with the provisions thereof.

ARTICLES 9 TO 13

[*Arts. 9 to 13 were repealed by the Merger Treaty, Art. 19. See now ibid., Arts. 10 to 15 and 17.*]

ARTICLE 14

In order to carry out the tasks assigned to it the High Authority shall, in accordance with the provisions of this Treaty, take decisions, make recommendations or deliver opinions.
Decisions shall be binding in their entirety.
Recommendations shall be binding as to the aims to be pursued but shall leave the choice of the appropriate methods for achieving these aims to those to whom the recommendations are addressed.
Opinions shall have no binding force.
In cases were the High Authority is empowered to take a decision, it may confine itself to making a recommendation.

ARTICLE 15

Decisions, recommendations and opinions of the High Authority shall state the reasons on which they are based and shall refer to any opinions which were required to be obtained.
Where decisions and recommendations are individual in character, they shall become binding upon being notified to the party concerned.
In all other cases, they shall take effect by the mere fact of publication.
The High Authority shall determine the manner in which this Article is to be implemented.

Article 16

The High Authority shall make all appropriate administrative arrangements for the operation of its departments.

It may set up study committees, including an economic study committee.

[. . .].

AMENDMENT

The third paragraph of this Article was repealed by the Merger Treaty, Art. 19. See now *ibid.*, Art. 16.

Article 17

[*Repealed by the Merger Treaty, Art.* 19. *See now ibid., Art.* 18.]

Article 18

[A Consultative Committee shall be attached to the High Authority. It shall consist of not less than sixty and not more than eight-four members and shall comprise equal numbers of producers, of workers and of consumers and dealers.]

The members of the Consultative Committee shall be appointed by the Council.

In the case of the producers and workers, the Council shall designate representative organisations among which it shall allocate the seats to be filled. Each organisation shall be required to draw up a list containing twice as many names as there are seats allotted to it. Appointments shall be made from this list.

The members of the Consultative Committee shall be appointed in their personal capacity for two years. They shall not be bound by any mandate or instructions from the organisations which nominated them.

The Consultative Committee shall elect its chairman and officers from among its members for a term of one year. The Committee shall adopt its rules of procedure.

[. . .].

AMENDMENTS

The first paragraph of this Article was substituted by the Act of Accession, Art. 22.

The sixth paragraph of this Article was repealed by the Merger Treaty, Art. 19. See now *ibid.*, Art. 6.

Article 19

The High Authority may consult the Consultative Committee in all cases in which it considers this appropriate. It must do so whenever such consultation is prescribed by this Treaty.

The High Authority shall submit to the Consultative Committee the general objectives and the programmes drawn up under Article 46 and shall keep the Committee informed of the broad lines of its action under Articles 54, 65 and 66.

Should the High Authority consider it necessary, it may set the Consultative Committee a time limit for the submission of its opinion. The period allowed may not be less than ten days from the date on which the chairman receives notification to this effect.

The Consultative Committee shall be convened by its chairman, either at the request of the High Authority or at the request of a majority of its members, for the purpose of discussing a specific question.

The minutes of the proceedings shall be forwarded to the High Authority and to the Council at the same time as the opinions of the Committee.

CHAPTER II—THE ASSEMBLY

ARTICLE 20

The Assembly, which shall consist of representatives of the peoples of the States brought together in the Community, shall exercise the supervisory powers which are conferred upon it by this Treaty.

ARTICLE 21

[1. The Assembly shall consist of delegates who shall be designated by the respective Parliaments from among their members in accordance with the procedure laid down by each Member State.]

[2. The number of these delegates shall be as follows:

Belgium	14
Denmark	10
Germany	36
France	36
Ireland	10
Italy	36
Luxembourg	6
Netherlands	14
United Kingdom	36]

[3. The Assembly shall draw up proposals for elections by direct universal suffrage in accordance with a uniform procedure in all Members States.

The Council shall, acting unanimously, lay down the appropriate provisions, which it shall recommend to Member States for adoption in accordance with their respective constitutional requirements.]

AMENDMENTS
The original Article 21 was substituted by the Convention on Certain Institutions Common to the European Communities, Art. 2.
Para. (2) has since been substituted by the Act of Accession, Art. 10, as amended by the Adaption Decision, Art. 4.

ARTICLE 22

[The Assembly shall hold an annual session. It shall meet, without requiring to be convened, on the second Tuesday in March.]

The Assembly may be convened in extraordinary session at the request of the Council in order to deliver an opinion on such questions as may be put to it by the Council.

It may also meet in extraordinary session at the request of a majority of its members or of the High Authority.

AMENDMENT
The words in square brackets were substituted by the Merger Treaty, Art. 27 (1).

ARTICLE 23

The Assembly shall elect its President and its officers from among its members.

Members of the High Authority may attend all meetings. The President of the High Authority or such of its members as it may designate shall be heard at their request.

The High Authority shall reply orally or in writing to questions put to it by the Assembly or by its members.

The members of the Council may attend all meetings and shall be heard at their request.

Article 24

The Assembly shall discuss in open session the general report submitted to it by the High Authority.

[If a motion of censure on the activities of the High Authority is tabled before it, the Assembly shall not vote thereon until at least three days after the motion has been tabled and only by open vote.]

If the motion of censure is carried by a two-thirds majority of the votes cast, representing a majority of the Members of the Assembly, the members of the High Authority shall resign as a body. They shall continue to deal with current business until they are replaced in accordance with Article 10.

AMENDMENT
The words in square brackets were substituted by the Merger Treaty, Art. 27 (2).

Article 25

The Assembly shall adopt its rules of procedure, acting by a majority of its members.

The proceedings of the Assembly shall be published in the manner laid down in its rules of procedure.

CHAPTER III—THE COUNCIL

Article 26

The Council shall exercise its powers in the cases provided for and in the manner set out in this Treaty, in particular in order to harmonise the action of the High Authority and that of the Governments, which are responsible for the general economic policies of their countries.

To this end, the Council and the High Authority shall exchange information and consult each other.

The Council may request the High Authority to examine any proposals or measures which the Council may consider appropriate or necessary for the attainment of the common objectives.

Article 27

[Repealed by the Merger Treaty, Art. 7. See now ibid., Art. 2.]

Article 28

[When the Council is consulted by the High Authority, it shall consider the matter without necessarily taking a vote. The minutes of its proceedings shall be forwarded to the High Authority.

Wherever this Treaty requires that the assent of the Council be given, that assent shall be considered to have been given if the proposal submitted by the High Authority receives the approval:

—of an absolute majority of the representatives of the Member States, including the votes of the representatives of two Member States which each produce at least one eighth of the total value of the coal and steel output of the Community; or

—in the event of an equal division of votes and if the High Authority maintains its proposal after a second discussion, of the representatives of three Member States which each produce at least one eighth of the total value of the coal and steel output of the Community.

Wherever this Treaty requires a unanimous decision or unanimous assent, such decision or assent shall have been duly given if all the members of the Council vote in favour. However, for the purposes of applying Articles 21, 32, 32a, 78d and 78f of this Treaty, and Article 16, the third paragraph of Article 20, the fifth paragraph of Article 28 and Article 44 of the Protocol on the Statute of the Court of Justice, abstention by members present in person or represented shall not prevent the adoption by the Council of acts which require unanimity.

[Decisions of the Council, other than those for which a qualified majority or unanimity is required, shall be taken by a vote of the majority of its members; this majority shall be considered to be attained if it represents an absolute majority of the representatives of the Member States, including the votes of the representatives of two Member States which each produce at least one eighth of the total value of the coal and steel output of the Community. However, for the purpose of applying those provisions of Articles 78, 78b and 78d of this Treaty which require a qualified majority, the votes of the members of the Council shall be weighted as follows: Belgium 5, Denmark 3, Germany 10, Greece 5, France 10, Ireland 3, Italy 10, Luxembourg 2, Netherlands 5, United Kingdom 10. For their adoption, acts shall require at least 45 votes in favour, cast by not less than six members.]

Where a vote is taken, any member of the Council may act on behalf of not more than one other member.

The Council shall deal with the Member States through its President.

The acts of the Council shall be published in such a manner as it may decide.]

AMENDMENTS

This article was substituted by the Act of Accession, Art. 12, as amended by the Adaptation Decision, Art. 6.

The fourth paragraph was substituted by the Act of Accession of the Hellenic Republic of May 28, 1979, Art. 12.

ARTICLE 29

[*Repealed by the Merger Treaty, Art.* 7. *See now ibid., Art.* 6.]

ARTICLE 30

[*Repealed by the Merger Treaty, Art.* 7. *See now ibid., Art.* 5.]

CHAPTER IV—THE COURT

ARTICLE 31

The Court shall ensure that in the interpretation and application of this Treaty, and of rules laid down for the implementation thereof, the law is observed.

ARTICLE 32

[The Court of Justice shall consist of nine Judges.]

[The Court shall sit in plenary session. It may, however, form chambers, each consisting of three or five Judges, either to undertake certain preparatory inquiries or to adjudicate on particular categories of cases in accordance with rules laid down for these purposes.

[Whenever the Court of Justice hears cases brought before it by a Member State or by one of the institutions of the Community or, to the extent that the chambers of the court do not have the requisite jurisdiction under the Rules of Procedure, has to give preliminary rulings on questions submitted to it pursuant to Article 41, it shall sit in plenary session.]

Should the Court so request, the Council may, acting unanimously, increase the number of Judges and make the necessary adjustments to the second and third paragraphs of this Article and to the second paragraph of Article 32 (*b*).]

AMENDMENTS

Article 32 was substituted by the Convention on Certain Institutions Common to the European Communities, Art. 4.

The first paragraph has since been substituted by the Act of Accession, Art. 17, as amended by the Adaptation Decision, Art. 9.

The third paragraph was replaced by Dec. 74/584, Art. 1 (O.J. 1974, L318/22).

[ARTICLE 32 (*a*)

[The Court of Justice shall be assisted by four Advocates-General.]

It shall be the duty of the Advocate-General acting with complete impartiality and independence, to make, in open court, reasoned submissions on cases brought before the Court, in order to assist the Court in the performance of the task assigned to it in Article 31.

Should the Court so request, the Council may, acting unanimously, increase the number of Advocates-General and make the necessary adjustments to the third paragraph of Article 32 (*b*).]

AMENDMENTS

Art. 32 (*a*) was added by the Convention on Certain Institutions Common to the European Communities, Art. 4.

The first paragraph has since been substituted by the Council Decision of January 1, 1973, increasing the number of Advocates-General, Art. 1.

[ARTICLE 32 (*b*)

The Judges and Advocates-General shall be chosen from persons whose independence is beyond doubt and who possess the qualifications required for appointment to the highest judicial offices in their respective countries or who are jurisconsults of recognised competence; they shall be appointed by common accord of the Governments of the Member States for a term of six years.

[Every three years there shall be a partial replacement of the Judges. Five and four Judges shall be replaced alternately.]

[Every three years there shall be a partial replacement of the Advocates-General. Two Advocates-General shall be replaced on each occasion.]

Retiring Judges and Advocates-General shall be eligible for reappointment.

The Judges shall elect the President of the Court from among their number for a term of three years. He may be re-elected.]

AMENDMENTS

Art. 32 (*b*) was added by the Convention on Certain Institutions Common to the European Communities, Art. 4.

The second and third paragraphs were substituted by the Act of Accession, Art. 19. The second paragraph was subsequently substituted by the Adaptation Decision, Art. 10, and the third para. by the Council Decision of January 1, 1973, increasing the number of Advocates-General, Art. 2.

[ARTICLE 32 (c)

The Court shall appoint its Registrar and lay down the rules governing his service.]

AMENDMENT

Article 32 (c) was added by the Convention on Certain Institutions Common to the European Communities, Art. 4.

ARTICLE 33

The Court shall have jurisdiction in actions brought by a Member State or by the Council to have decisions or recommendations of the High Authority declared void on grounds of lack of competence, infringement of an essential procedural requirement, infringement of this Treaty or of any rule of law relating to its application, or misuse of powers. The Court may not, however, examine the evaluation of the situation, resulting from economic facts or circumstances, in the light of which the High Authority took its decisions or made its recommendations, save where the High Authority is alleged to have misused its powers or to have manifestly failed to observe the provisions of this Treaty or any rule of law relating to its application.

Undertakings or the associations referred to in Article 48 may, under the same conditions, institute proceedings against decisions or recommendations concerning them which are individual in character or against general decisions or recommendations which they consider to involve a misuse of powers affecting them.

The proceedings provided for in the first two paragraphs of this Article shall be instituted within one month of the notification or publication, as the case may be, of the decision or recommendation.

ARTICLE 34

If the Court declares a decision or recommendation void, it shall refer the matter back to the High Authority. The High Authority shall take the necessary steps to comply with the judgment. If direct and special harm is suffered by an undertaking or group of undertakings by reason of a decision or recommendation held by the Court to involve a fault of such a nature as to render the Community liable, the High Authority shall, using the powers conferred upon it by this Treaty, take steps to ensure equitable redress for the harm resulting directly from the decision or recommendation declared void and, where necessary, pay appropriate damages.

If the, High Authority fails to take within a reasonable time the necessary steps to comply with the judgment, proceedings for damages may be instituted before the Court.

ARTICLE 35

Wherever the High Authority is required by this Treaty, or by rules laid down for the implementation thereof, to take a decision or make a recommendation and fails to fulfil this obligation, it shall be for States, the Council, undertakings or associations, as the case may be, to raise the matter with the High Authority.

The same shall apply if the High Authority, where empowered by this Treaty, or by rules laid down for the implementation thereof, to take a decision or make a recommendation, abstains from doing so and such abstention constitutes a misuse of powers.

If at the end of two months the High Authority has not taken any decision or made any recommendation, proceedings may be instituted before the Court within one month against the implied decision of refusal which is to be inferred from the silence of the High Authority on the matter.

Article 36

Before imposing a pecuniary sanction or ordering a periodic penalty payment as provided for in this Treaty, the High Authority must give the party concerned the opportunity to submit its comments.

The Court shall have unlimited jurisdiction in appeals against pecuniary sanctions and periodic penalty payments imposed under this Treaty.

In support of its appeal, a party may, under the same conditions as in the first paragraph of Article 33 of this Treaty, contest the legality of the decision or recommendation which that party is alleged not to have observed.

Article 37

If a Member State considers that in a given case action or failure to act on the part of the High Authority is of such a nature as to provoke fundamental and persistent disturbances to its economy, it may raise the matter with the High Authority.

The High Authority, after consulting the Council, shall, if there are grounds for so doing, recognise the existence of such a situation and decide on the measures to be taken to end it, in accordance with the provisions of this treaty, while at the same time safeguarding the essential interests of the Community.

When proceedings are instituted in the Court under this Article against such a decision or against an express or implied decision refusing to recognise the existence of the situation referred to above, it shall be for the Court to determine whether it is well founded.

If the Court declares the decision void, the High Authority shall, within the terms of the judgment of the Court, decide on the measures to be taken for the purposes indicated in the second paragraph of this Article.

Article 38

The Court may, on application by a Member State or the High Authority, declare an act of the Assembly or of the Council to be void.

Application shall be made within one month of the publication of the act of the Assembly or the notification of the act of the Council to the Member States or to the High Authority.

The only grounds for such application shall be lack of competence or infringement of an essential procedural requirement.

Article 39

Actions brought before the Court shall not have suspensory effect.

The Court may, however, if it considers that circumstances so require, order that application of the contested decision or recommendation be suspended.

The Court may prescribe any other necessary interim measures.

Article 40

Without prejudice to the first paragraph of Article 34, the Court shall have jurisdiction to order pecuniary reparation from the Community, on application by the injured party, to make good any injury caused in carrying out this Treaty by a wrongful act or omission on the part of the Community in the performance of its functions.

[The Court shall also have jurisdiction to order the Community to make good any injury caused by a personal wrong by a servant of the Community in the performance of his duties. The personal liability of its servants towards the Community shall be governed by the provisions laid down in their Staff Regulations or the Conditions of Employment applicable to them.]

All other disputes between the Community and persons other than its servants to which the provisions of this Treaty or the rules laid down for the implementation thereof do not apply shall be brought before national courts or tribunals.

AMENDMENT
The words in square brackets were substituted by the Merger Treaty, Art. 26.

ARTICLE 41

The Court shall have sole jurisdiction to give preliminary rulings on the validity of acts of the High Authority and of the Council where such validity is in issue in proceedings brought before a national court or tribunal.

ARTICLE 42

The Court shall have jurisdiction to give judgment pursuant to any arbitration clause contained in a contract concluded by or on behalf of the Community, whether that contract be governed by public or private law.

ARTICLE 43

The Court shall have jurisdiction in any other case provided for by a provision supplementing this Treaty.

It may also rule in all cases which relate to the subject matter of this Treaty where jurisdiction is conferred upon it by the law of a Member State.

ARTICLE 44

The judgments of the Court shall be enforceable in the territory of Member States under the conditions laid down in Article 92.

ARTICLE 45

The Statute of the Court is laid down in a Protocol annexed to this Treaty.

Title Three

ECONOMIC AND SOCIAL PROVISIONS

CHAPTER I—GENERAL PROVISIONS

ARTICLE 46

The High Authority may at any time consult Governments, the various parties concerned (undertakings, workers, consumers and dealers) and their associations, and any experts.

Undertakings, workers, consumers and dealers, and their associations, shall be entitled to present any suggestions or comments to the High Authority on questions affecting them.

To provide guidance, in line with the tasks assigned to the Community, on the course of action to be followed by all concerned, and to determine its own course of action, in accordance with the provisions of this Treaty, the High Authority shall, in consultation as provided above:

(1) conduct a continuous study of market and price trends;

(2) periodically draw up programmes indicating foreseeable developments in production, consumption, exports and imports;

(3) periodically lay down general objectives for modernisation, long-term planning of manufacture and expansion of productive capacity;

(4) take part, at the request of the Governments concerned, in studying the possibilities for re-employing, in existing industries or through the creation of new activities, workers made redundant by market developments or technical changes;

(5) obtain the information it requires to assess the possibilities for improving working conditions and living standards for workers in the industries within its province, and the threats to those standards.

The High Authority shall publish the general objectives and the programmes after submitting them to the Consultative Committee.

It may publish the studies and information mentioned above.

Article 47

The High Authority may obtain the information it requires to carry out its tasks. It may have any necessary checks made.

The High Authority must not disclose information of the kind covered by the obligation of professional secrecy, in particular information about undertakings, their business relations or their cost components. Subject to this reservation, it shall publish such data as could be useful to Governments or to any other parties concerned.

The High Authority may impose fines or periodic penalty payments on undertakings which evade their obligations under decisions taken in pursuance of this Article or which knowingly furnish false information. The maximum amount of such fines shall be 1 per cent. of the annual turnover, and the maximum amount of such penalty payments shall be 5 per cent. of the average daily turnover for each day's delay.

Any breach of professional secrecy by the High Authority which has caused damage to an undertaking may be the subject of an action for compensation before the Court, as provided in Article 40.

Article 48

The right of undertakings to form associations shall not be affected by this Treaty. Membership of such associations must be voluntary. Associations may engage in any activity which is not contrary to the provisions of this Treaty or to the decisions or recommendations of the High Authority.

Where this Treaty requires the Consultative Committee to be consulted, any association shall have the right to submit to the High Authority, within such time as the latter may set, the comments of its members on the proposed course of action.

To obtain information which it requires, or to facilitate the performance of the tasks entrusted to it, the High Authority shall normally call upon producers' associations on condition either that they provide for accredited representatives of workers and consumers to sit on their governing bodies or on advisory committees attached to them, or that they make satisfactory provision in some other way in their organisation for the interests of workers and consumers to be voiced.

The associations referred to in the preceding paragraphs shall furnish the High Authority with such information on their activities as it may consider necessary. The comments referred to in the second paragraph of this Article and the information furnished in pursuance of this paragraph shall also be forwarded by those associations to the Government concerned.

CHAPTER II—FINANCIAL PROVISIONS

Article 49

The High Authority is empowered to procure the funds it requires to carry out its tasks:
—by imposing levies on the production of coal and steel;
—by contracting loans.
It may receive gifts.

Article 50

1. The levies are intended to cover:
—the administrative expenditure provided for in Article 78;
—the non-repayable aid towards readaptation provided for in Article 56;
—in the case of the financing arrangements provided for in Articles 54 and 56, and after recourse to the reserve fund, any portion of the amounts required for servicing loans raised by the High Authority which may not be covered by receipts from the servicing of loans granted by it, and any payments to be made under guarantees granted by the High Authority on loans contracted directly by undertakings;
—expenditure on the promotion of technical and economic research as provided for in Article 55 (2).

2. The levies shall be assessed annually on the various products according to their average value; the rate thereof shall not, however, exceed 1 per cent. unless previously authorised by the Council, acting by a two-thirds majority. The mode of assessment and collection shall be determined by a general decision of the High Authority taken after consulting the Council; cumulative imposition shall be avoided as far as possible.

3. The High Authority may impose upon undertakings which do not comply with decisions taken by it under this Article surcharges of not more than 5 per cent. for each quarter's delay.

Article 51

1. The High Authority may not use the funds obtained by borrowing except to grant loans.

The issue of loans by the High Authority on the markets of Member States shall be subject to the rules and regulations in force on these markets.

If the High Authority considers the guarantee of Member States necessary in order to contract certain loans, it shall approach the Government or Governments concerned after consulting the Council; no State shall be obliged to give its guarantee.

2. The High Authority may, as provided in Article 54, guarantee loans granted direct to undertakings by third parties.

3. The High Authority may so determine its conditions for loans or guarantees as to enable a reserve fund to be built up for the sole purpose of reducing whatever amounts may have to be paid out of the levies in accordance with the third subparagraph of Article 50 (1); the sums thus accumulated must not, however, be used for any form of lending to undertakings.

4. The High Authority shall not itself engage in the banking operations which its financial tasks entail.

ARTICLE 52

Member States shall make all appropriate arrangements to enable transfers of funds derived from the levies, from pecuniary sanctions and periodic penalty payments and from the reserve fund to be effected within the territories referred to in the first paragraph of Article 79 in accordance with the procedure for commercial payments, to the extent necessary to make it possible for them to be used for the purposes intended by this Treaty.

The procedure for effecting transfers, both between Member States and to third countries, arising out of other financial operations carried out or guaranteed by the High Authority, shall be determined by agreement between the High Authority and the Member States concerned or the appropriate agencies; there shall, however, be no obligation upon any Member State which applies exchange controls to permit transfers where it has not expressly undertaken to do so.

ARTICLE 53

Without prejudice to the provisions of Article 58 or of Chapter V of Title III, the High Authority may:

(a) after consulting the Consultative Committee and the Council, authorise the making, on conditions which it shall determine and under its supervision, of any financial arrangements common to several undertakings which it recognises to be necessary for the performance of the tasks set out in Article 3 and compatible with this Treaty, and in particular with Article 65;

(b) with the unanimous assent of the Council, itself make any financial arrangements serving the same purposes.

Similar arrangements made or maintained by Member States shall be notified to the High Authority, which, after consulting the Consultative Committee and the Council, shall make the necessary recommendations to the States concerned where such arrangements are inconsistent, in whole or in part, with the application of this Treaty.

CHAPTER III—INVESTMENT AND FINANCIAL AID

ARTICLE 54

The High Authority may facilitate the carrying out of investment programmes by granting loans to undertakings or by guaranteeing other loans which they may contract.

With the unanimous assent of the Council, the High Authority may by the same means assist the financing of works and installations which contribute directly and primarily to increasing the production, reducing the production costs or facilitating the marketing of products within its jurisdiction.

In order to encourage co-ordinated development of investment, the High Authority may, in accordance with Article 47, require undertakings to inform it of individual programmes in advance, either by a special request addressed to the undertaking concerned or by a decision stating what kind and scale of programme must be communicated.

The High Authority may, after giving the parties concerned full opportunity to submit their comments, deliver a reasoned opinion on such programmes within the framework of the general objectives provided for in Article 46. If application is made by the undertaking concerned, the High Authority must deliver a reasoned opinion. The High Authority shall notify the opinion to the undertaking concerned and shall bring the opinion to the attention of its Government. Lists of such opinions shall be published.

If the High Authority finds that the financing of a programme or the operation of the installations therein planned would involve subsidies, aids, protection or discrimination contrary to this Treaty, the adverse opinion delivered by it on these grounds shall have the force of a decision within the meaning of Article 14 and the effect of prohibiting the undertaking concerned from drawing on resources other than its own funds to carry out the programme.

The High Authority may impose on undertakings which disregard the prohibition referred to in the preceding paragraph fines not exceeding the amounts improperly devoted to carrying out the programme in question.

ARTICLE 55

1. The High Authority shall promote technical and economic research relating to the production and increased use of coal and steel and to occupational safety in the coal and steel industries. To this end it shall organise all appropriate contacts among existing research bodies.

2. After consulting the Consultative Committee, the High Authority may initiate and facilitate such research:

   (a) by inducing joint financing by the undertakings concerned; or
   (b) by allotting for that purpose any funds received as gifts; or
   (c) with the assent of the Council, by allotting for that purpose funds derived from the levies provided for in Article 50; the limit laid down in paragraph 2 of that Article must not, however, be exceeded.

The results of research financed as provided in subparagraphs (b) and (c) shall be made available to all concerned in the Community.

3. The High Authority shall deliver any opinions which serve to make technical improvements more widely known, particularly with regard to the exchange of patents and the granting of licences for using them.

ARTICLE 56

1. If the introduction, within the framework of the general objectives of the High Authority, of new technical processes or equipment should lead to an exceptionally large reduction in labour requirements in the coal or the steel industry, making it particularly difficult in one or more areas to re-employ redundant workers, the High Authority, on application by the Governments concerned:

   (a) shall obtain the opinion of the Consultative Committee;
   (b) may facilitate, in the manner laid down in Article 54, either in the industries within its jurisdiction or, with the assent of the Council, in any other industry, the financing of such programmes as it may approve for the creation of new and economically sound activities capable of reabsorbing the redundant workers into productive employment;

(c) shall provide non-repayable aid towards:
—the payment of tideover allowances to workers;
—the payment of resettlement allowances to workers;
—the financing of vocational retraining for workers having to change their employment.

The High Authority shall make the provision of non-repayable aid conditional upon payment by the State concerned of a special contribution of not less than the amount of that aid, unless an exception is authorised by the Council, acting by a two-thirds majority.

[2. If fundamental changes, not directly connected with the establishment of the common market, in market conditions for the coal or the steel industry should compel some undertakings permanently to discontinue, curtail or change their activities, the High Authority, on application by the Governments concerned:

(a) may facilitate, in the manner laid down in Article 54, either in the industries within its jurisdiction or, with the assent of the Council, in any other industry, the financing of such programmes as it may approve for the creation of new and economically sound activities or for the conversion of existing undertakings capable of reabsorbing the redundant workers into productive employment;

(b) may provide non-repayable aid towards:
—the payment of tideover allowances to workers;
—the payment of allowances to undertakings to enable them to continue paying such of their workers as may have to be temporarily laid off as a result of the undertakings' change of activity;
—the payment of resettlement allowances to workers;
—the financing of vocational retraining for workers having to change their employment.

The High Authority shall make the provision of non-repayable aid conditional upon payment by the State concerned of a special contribution of not less than the amount of that aid, unless an exception is authorised by the Council, acting by a two-thirds majority.]

AMENDMENT
Para. 2 was added by an amendment made by Special Council of Ministers and published in the *Official Journal of the European Communities*, No. 33, 16 May 1960, p. 781 (see *European Communities Treaties and Related Instruments*, Vol. I, HMSO, 1972).

CHAPTER IV—PRODUCTION

ARTICLE 57

In the sphere of production, the High Authority shall give preference to the indirect means of action at its disposal, such as:
—co-operation with Governments to regularise or influence general consumption, particularly that of the public services;
—intervention in regard to prices and commercial policy as provided for in this Treaty.

ARTICLE 58

1. In the event of a decline in demand, if the High Authority considers that the Community is confronted with a period of manifest crisis and that the means of action provided for in Article 57 are not sufficient to deal with this, it shall, after consulting the Consultative Committee and with the assent of the

Council, establish a system of production quotas, accompanied to the necessary extent by the measures provided for in Article 74.

If the High Authority fails to act, a Member State may bring the matter before the Council, which may, acting unanimously, require the High Authority to establish a system of quotas.

2. The High Authority shall, on the basis of studies made jointly with undertakings and associations of undertakings, determine the quotas on an equitable basis, taking account of the principles set out in Articles 2, 3 and 4. It may in particular regulate the level of activity of undertakings by appropriate levies on tonnages exceeding a reference level set by a general decision.

The funds thus obtained shall be used to support undertakings whose rate of production has fallen below that envisaged, in order, in particular, to maintain employment in these undertakings as far as possible.

3. The system of quotas shall be ended on a proposal made to the Council by the High Authority after consulting the Consultative Committee, or by the Government of a Member State, unless the Council decides otherwise, acting unanimously if the proposal emanates from the High Authority or by a simple majority if the proposal emanates from a Government. An announcement on the ending of the quota system shall be made by the High Authority.

4. The High Authority may impose upon undertakings which do not comply with decisions taken by it under this Article fines not exceeding the value of the tonnages produced in disregard thereof.

ARTICLE 59

1. If, after consulting the Consultative Committee, the High Authority finds that the Community is confronted with a serious shortage of any or all of the products within its jurisdiction, and that the means of action provided for in Article 57 are not sufficient to deal with this, it shall bring the situation to the attention of the Council and shall, unless the Council, acting unanimously, decides otherwise, propose to it the necessary measures.

If the High Authority fails to act, a Member State may bring the matter before the Council, which may, acting unanimously, recognise that the situation in question does in fact exist.

2. The Council shall, acting unanimously on a proposal from and in consultation with the High Authority, establish consumption priorities and determine the allocation of the coal and steel resources fo the Community to the industries within its jurisdiction, to export and to other sectors of consumption.

On the basis of the consumption priorities thus established, the High Authority shall, after consulting the undertakings concerned, draw up the production programmes with which the undertakings shall be required to comply.

3. If the Council does not reach a unanimous decision on the measures referred to in paragraph 2, the High Authority shall itself allocate the resources of the Community among the Member States on the basis of consumption and exports, irrespective of the place of production.

Within each of the Member States allocation of the resources assigned by the High Authority shall be carried out on the responsibility of the Government, provided that the deliveries scheduled to be supplied to other Member States are not affected and that the High Authority is consulted concerning the portions to be allotted to export and to the operation of the coal and steel industries.

If the portion allotted by a Government to export is less than the amount taken as the basis for calculating the total tonnage to be assigned to the Member State concerned, the High Authority shall, to the necessary extent, at the next allocation, redivide among the Member States the resources thus made available for consumption.

If the portion allotted by a Government to the operation of the coal and steel industries is similarly less and the result is a decrease in Community production of one of these, the tonnage assigned to the Member State concerned shall, at the next allocation, be reduced by the amount of the decrease in production so caused.

4. In all cases, the High Authority shall be responsible for allocating equitably among undertakings the quantities assigned to the industries within its jurisdiction, on the basis of studies made jointly with under-takings and association of undertakings.

5. Should the situation provided for in paragraph 1 of this Article arise, the High Authority may, in accordance with Article 57, after consulting the Consultative Committee and with the assent of the Council, decide that restrictions on exports to third countries shall be imposed in all the Member States, or, if the High Authority fails to act, the Council may, acting unanimously, so decide on a proposal from a Government.

6. The High Authority may end the arrangements made under this Article after consulting the Consultative Committee and the Council. It shall not do so if the Council unanimously dissents.

If the High Authority fails to act, the Council may, acting unanimously, itself end the arrangements.

7. The High Authority may impose upon undertakings which do not comply with decisions taken under this Article fines not exceeding twice the value of prescribed production or deliveries either not effected or diverted from their proper use.

CHAPTER V—PRICES

ARTICLE 60

1. Pricing practices contrary to Articles 2, 3 and 4 shall be prohibited, in particular:

—unfair competitive practices, especially purely temporary or purely local price reductions tending towards the acquisition of a monopoly position within the common market;

—discriminatory practices involving, with the common market, the application by a seller of dissimilar conditions to comparable transactions, especially on grounds of the nationality of the buyer.

The High Authority may define the practices covered by this prohibition by decisions taken after consulting the Consultative Committee and the Council.

2. For these purposes:

(a) the price lists and conditions of sale applied by undertakings within the common market must be made public to the extent and in the manner prescribed by the High Authority after consulting the Consultative Committee. If the High Authority finds that an undertaking's choice of point on which it bases its price lists is abnormal and in particular makes it possible to evade the provisions of subparagraph (b), it shall make appropriate recommendations to that undertaking;

(b) the methods of quotation used must not have the effect that prices charged by an undertaking in the common market, when reduced to their equivalent at the point chosen for its price lists, result in:

—increases over the price shown in the price list in question for a comparable transaction; or

—reductions below that price the amount of which exceeds either:

—the extent enabling the quotation to be aligned on the price list, based on another point which secures the buyer the most advantageous delivered terms; or

—the limits fixed, by the decision of the High Authority after the Consultative Committee has delivered its opinion, for each category of product, with due regard, where appropriate, for the origin and destination of products.

Such decisions shall be taken when found necessary to avoid disturbances in the whole or any part of the common market or disequilibria resulting from a difference between the methods of quotation used for a product and for materials involved in making it. Such decisions shall not preclude undertakings from aligning their quotations on those of undertakings outside the Community, on condition that the transactions are notified to the High Authority, which may, in the event of abuse, restrict or abrogate the right of the undertakings concerned to take advantage of this exception.

ARTICLE 61

On the basis of studies made jointly with undertakings and associations of undertakings, in accordance with the first paragraph of Article 46 and the third paragraph of Article 48, and after consulting the Consultative Committee and the Council as to the advisability of so doing and the price level to be so determined, the High Authority may, for one or more of the products within its jurisdiction:

(a) fix maximum prices within the common market, if it finds that such a decision is necessary to attain the objectives set out in Article 3, and particularly in paragraph (c) thereof;

(b) fix minimum prices within the common market, if it finds that a manifest crisis exists or is imminent and that such a decision is necessary to attain the objectives set out in Article 3;

(c) after consulting the associations to which the undertakings concerned belong, or the undertakings themselves, fix, by methods appropriate to the nature of the export markets, minimum or maximum export prices, if such an arrangement can be effectively supervised and is necessary both in view of the dangers to the undertakings resulting from the state of the market and in order to secure the acceptance in international economic relations of the objectives set out in Article 3 (f); any fixing of minimum prices shall be without prejudice to the measures provided for in the last subparagraph of Article 60 (2).

In fixing prices, the High Authority shall take into account the need to ensure that the coal and steel industries and the consumer industries remain competitive, in accordance with the principles laid down in Article 3 (c).

If in these circumstances the High Authority fails to act, the Government of a Member State may bring the matter before the Council, which may, acting unanimously, call upon the High Authority to fix such maximum or minimum prices.

ARTICLE 62

If the High Authority considers this the most appropriate way of preventing coal from being priced at the level of the production costs of the minutes which have the highest costs but which it is recognised should be temporarily maintained in service in order that the tasks laid down in Article 3 may be performed, it may, after consulting the Consultative Committee, authorise equalisation payments:

—between undertakings in the same coalfield to which the same price lists apply;

—after consulting the Council, between undertakings in different coalfields.

These equalisation payments may, moreover, be instituted as provided in Article 53.

Article 63

1. If the High Authority finds that discrimination is being systematically practised by purchasers, in particular under provisions governing contracts entered into by bodies dependent on a public authority, it shall make appropriate recommendations to the Governments concerned.

2. Where the High Authority considers it necessary, it may decide that:

(a) undertakings must frame their conditions of sale in such a way that their customers and commission agents acting on their behalf shall be under an obligation to comply with the rules made by the High Authority in application of this Chapter;

(b) undertakings shall be held responsible for infringements of this obligation by their direct agents or by commission agents acting on their behalf.

In the event of an infringement of this obligatign by a purchaser, the High Authority may restrict or, should the infringement be repeated, temporarily prohibit dealings with that purchaser by Community undertakings. If this is done, the purchaser shall have the right, without prejudice to Article 33, to bring an action before the Court.

3. In addition, the High Authority is empowered to make to the Member States concerned any appropriate recommendations to ensure that the rules laid down for the application of Article 60 (1) are duly observed by all distributive undertakings and agencies in the coal and steel sectors.

Article 64

The High Authority may impose upon undertakings which infringe the provisions of this Chapter or decisions taken thereunder fines not exceeding twice the value of the sales effected in disregard thereof. If the infringement is repeated, the maximum shall be doubled.

CHAPTER VI—AGREEMENTS AND CONCENTRATIONS

Article 65

1. All agreements between undertakings, decisions by associations of undertakings and concerted practices tending directly or indirectly to prevent, restrict or distort normal competition within the common market shall be prohibited, and in particular those tending:

(a) to fix or determine prices;

(b) to restrict or control production, technical development or investments;

(c) to share markets, products, customers or sources of supply.

2. However, the High Authority shall authorise specialisation agreements or joint-buying or joint-selling agreements in respect of particular products, if it finds that:

    (*a*) such specialisation or such joint-buying or-selling will make for a substantial improvement in the production or distribution of those products;

    (*b*) the agreement in question is essential in order to achieve these results and is not more restrictive than is necessary for that purpose; and

    (*c*) the agreement is not liable to give the undertakings concerned the power to determine the prices, or to control or restrict the production or marketing, of a substantial part of the products in question within the common market, or to shield them against effective competition from other undertakings within the common market.

If the High Authority finds that certain agreements are strictly analogous in nature and effect to those referred to above, having particular regard to the fact that this paragraph applies to distributive undertakings, it shall authorise them also when satisfied that they meet the same requirements.

Authorisations may be granted subject to specified conditions and for limited periods. In such cases the High Authority shall renew an authorisation once or several times if it finds that the requirements of subparagraphs (*a*) to (*c*) are still met at the time of renewal.

The High Authority shall revoke or amend an authorisation if it finds that as a result of a change in circumstances the agreement no longer meets these requirements, or that the actual results of the agreement or of the application thereof are contrary to the requirements for its authorisation.

Decisions granting, renewing, amending, refusing or revoking an authorisation shall be published together with the reasons therefor; the restrictions imposed by the second paragraph of Article 47 shall not apply thereto.

3. The High Authority may, as provided in Article 47, obtain any information needed for the application of this Article, either by making a special request to the parties concerned or by means of regulations stating the kinds of agreement, decision or practice which must be communicated to it.

4. Any agreement or decision prohibited by paragraph 1 of this Article shall be automatically void and may not be relied upon before any court or tribunal in the Member States.

The High Authority shall have sole jurisdiction, subject to the right to bring actions before the Court, to rule whether any such agreement or decision is compatible with this Article.

5. On any undertaking which has entered into an agreement which is automatically void, or has enforced or attempted to enforce, by arbitration, penalty, boycott or any other means, an agreement or decision which is automatically void or an agreement for which authorisation has been refused or revoked, or has obtained an authorisation by means of information which it knew to be false or misleading, or has engaged in practices prohibited by paragraph 1 of this Article, the High Authority may impose fines or periodic penalty payments not exceeding twice the turnover on the products which were the subject of the agreement, decision or practice prohibited by this Article; if, however, the purpose of the agreement, decision or practice is to restrict production, technical development or investment, this maximum may be raised to 10 per cent. of the annual turnover of the undertakings in question in the case of fines, and 20 per cent. of the daily turnover in the case of periodic penalty payments.

Article 66

1. Any transaction shall require the prior authorisation of the High Authority, subject to the provisions of paragraph 3 of this Article, if it has in itself the direct or indirect effect of bringing about within the territories referred to in the first paragraph of Article 79, as a result of action by any person or undertaking or group of persons or undertakings, a concentration between undertakings at least one of which is covered by Article 80, whether the transaction concerns a single product or a number of different products, and whether it is effected by merger, acquisition of shares or parts of the undertaking or assets, loan, contract or any other means of control. For the purpose of applying these provisions, the High Authority shall, be regulations made after consulting the Council, define what constitutes control of an undertaking.

2. The High Authority shall grant the authorisation referred to in the preceding paragraph if it finds that the proposed transaction will not give to the persons or undertakings concerned the power, in respect of the product or products within its jurisdiction:

—to determine prices, to control or restrict production or distribution or to hinder effective competition in a substantial part of the market for those products; or

—to evade the rules of competition instituted under this Treaty, in particular by establishing an artificially privileged position involving a substantial advantage in access to supplies or markets.

In assessing whether this is so, the High Authority shall, in accordance with the principle of non-discrimination laid down in Article 4 (*b*), take account of the size of like undertakings in the Community, to the extent it considers justified in order to avoid or correct disadvantages resulting from unequal competitive conditions.

The High Authority may make its authorisation subject to any conditions which it considers appropriate for the purposes of this paragraph.

Before ruling on a transaction concerning undertakings at least one of which is not subject to Article 80, the High Authority shall obtain the comments of the Governments concerned.

3. The High Authority shall exempt from the requirement of prior authorisation such classes of transactions as it finds should, in view of the size of the assets or undertakings concerned, taken in conjunction with the kind of concentration to be effected, be deemed to meet the requirements of paragraph 2. Regulations made to this effect, with the assent of the Council, shall also lay down the conditions governing such exemption.

4. Without prejudice to the application of Article 47 to undertakings within its jurisdiction, the High Authority may, either by regulations made after consultation with the Council stating the kind of transaction to be communicated to it or by a special request under these regulations to the parties concerned, obtain from the natural or legal persons who have acquired or regrouped or are intending to acquire or regroup the rights or assets in question any information needed for the application of this Article concerning transactions liable to produce the effect referred to in paragraph 1.

5. If a concentration should occur which the High Authority finds has been effected contrary to the provisions of paragraph 1 but which nevertheless meets the requirements of paragraph 2, the High Authority shall make its approval of that concentration subject to payment by the persons who have acquired or regrouped the rights or assets in question of the fine provided for in the second subparagraph of paragraph 6; the amount of the fine shall not be less than half

of the maximum determined in that subparagraph should it be clear that authorisation ought to have been applied for. If the fine is not paid, the High Authority shall take the steps hereinafter provided for in respect of concentrations found to be unlawful.

If a concentration should occur which the High Authority finds cannot fulfil the general or specific conditions to which an authorisation under paragraph 2 would be subject, the High Authority shall, by means of a reasoned decision, declare the concentration unlawful and, after giving the parties concerned the opportunity to submit their comments, shall order separation of the undertakings or assets improperly concentrated or cessation of joint control, and any other measures which it considers appropriate to return the undertakings or assets in question to independent operation and restore normal conditions of competition. Any person directly concerned may institute proceedings against such decisions, as provided in Article 33. By way of derogation from Article 33, the Court shall have unlimited jurisdiction to assess whether the transaction effected is a concentration within the meaning of paragraph 1 and of regulations made in application thereof. The institution of proceedings shall have suspensory effect. Proceedings may not be instituted until the measures provided for above have been ordered, unless the High Authority agrees to the institution of separate proceedings against the decision declaring the transaction unlawful.

The High Authority may at any time, unless the third paragraph of Article 39 is applied, take or cause to be taken such interim measures of protection as it may consider necessary to safeguard the interests of competing undertakings and of third parties, and to forestall any step which might hinder the implementation of its decisions. Unless the Court decides otherwise, proceedings shall not have suspensory effect in respect of such interim measures.

The High Autority shall allow the parties concerned a reasonable period in which to comply with its decisions, on expiration of which it may impose daily penalty payments not exceeding one tenth of one per cent. of the value of the rights or assets in question.

Furthermore, if the parties concerned do not fulfil their obligations, the High Authority shall itself take steps to implement its decision; it may in particular suspend the exercise, in undertakings within its jurisdiction, of the rights attached to the assets acquired irregularly, obtain the appointment by the judicial authorities of a receiver of such assets, organise the forced sale of such assets subject to the protection of the legitimate interests of their owners, and annul with respect to natural or legal persons who have acquired the rights or assets in question through the unlawful transaction, the acts, decisions, resolutions or proceedings of the supervisory and managing bodies or undertakings over which control has been obtained irregularly.

The High Authority is also empowered to make such recommendations to the Member States concerned as may be necessary to ensure that the measures provided for in the preceding subparagraphs are implemented under their own law.

In the exercise of its powers, the High Authority shall take account of the rights of third parties which have been acquired in good faith.

6. The High Authority may impose fines not exceeding:
    —3 per cent. of the value of the assets acquired or regrouped or to be acquired or regrouped, on natural or legal persons who have evaded the obligations laid down in paragraph 4;
    —10 per cent. of the value of the assets acquired or regrouped, on natural or legal persons who have evaded the obligations laid down in

paragraph 1; this maximum shall be increased by one twenty-fourth for each month which elapses after the end of the twelfth month following completion of the transaction until the High Authority establishes that there has been an infringement;

—10 per cent. of the value of the assets acquired or regrouped or to be acquired or regrouped, on natural or legal persons who have obtained or attempted to obtain authorisation under paragraph 2 by means of false or misleading information;

—15 per cent. of the value of the assets acquired or regrouped, on undertakings within its jurisdiction which have engaged in or been party to transactions contrary to the provisions of this Article.

Persons fined under this paragraph may appeal to the Court as provided in Article 36.

7. If the High Authority finds that public or private undertakings which, in law or in fact, hold or acquire in the market for one of the products within its jurisdiction a dominant position shielding them against effective competition in a substantial part of the common market are using that position for purposes contrary to the objectives of this Treaty, it shall make to them such recommendations as may be appropriate to prevent the position from being so sued. If these recommendations are not implemented satisfactorily within a reasonable time, the High Authority shall, by decisions taken in consultation with the Government concerned, determine the prices and conditions of sale to be applied by the undertaking in question or draw up production or delivery programmes with which it must comply, subject to liability to the penalties provided for in Articles 58, 59 and 64.

CHAPTER VII—INTERFERENCE WITH CONDITIONS OF COMPETITION

ARTICLE 67

1. Any action by a Member State which is liable to have appreciable repercussions on conditions of competition in the coal or the steel industry shall be brought to the knowledge of the High Authority by the Government concerned.

2. If the action is liable, by substantially increasing differences in production costs otherwise than through changes in productivity, to provoke a serious disequilibrium, the High Authority, after consulting the Consultative Committee and the Council, may take the following steps:

If the action taken by that State is having harmful effects on the coal or steel undertakings within the jurisdiction of that State, the High Authority may authorise it to grant aid to these undertakings, the amount, conditions and duration of which shall be determined in agreement with the High Authority. The same shall apply in the case of any change in wages and working conditions which would have the same effects, even if not resulting from any action by that State.

If the action taken by that State is having harmful effects on the coal or steel undertakings within the jurisdiction of other Member States, the High Authority shall make a recommendation to that State with a view to remedying these effects by such measures as that State may consider most compatible with its own economic equilibrium.

3. If the action taken by that State reduces differences in production costs by allowing special benefits to or imposing special charges on the coal or steel

undertakings within its jurisdiction in comparison with the other industries in the same country, the High Authority is empowered to make the necessary recommendations to that State after consulting the Consultative Committee and the Council.

CHAPTER VIII—WAGES AND MOVEMENT OF WORKERS

ARTICLE 68

1. The methods used for fixing wages and welfare benefits in the several Member States shall not, in the case of the coal and steel industries, be affected by this Treaty, subject to the following provisions.

2. If the High Authority finds that one or more undertakings are charging abnormally low prices because they are paying abnormally low wages compared with the wage level in the same area, it shall, after consulting the Consultative Committee, make appropriate recommendations to them. If the abnormally low wages are the result of governmental decisions, the High Authority shall confer with the Government concerned, and failing agreement it may, after consulting the Consultative Committee, make a recommendation to that Government.

3. If the High Authority finds that wage reduction entails a lowering of the standard of living of workers and at the same time is being used as a means for the permanent economic adjustment of undertakings or as a means of competition between them, it shall, after consulting the Consultative Committee, make a recommendation to the undertaking or Government concerned with a view to securing, at the expense of the undertakings, benefits for the workers in order to compensate for the reductions.

This provision shall not apply to:
   (a) overall measures taken by a Member State to restore its external equilibrium, without prejudice in such case to any action under Article 67;
   (b) wage reductions resulting from the application of a sliding scale established by law or by contract;
   (c) wage reductions resulting from a fall in the cost of living;
   (d) wage reductions to correct abnormal increases that occurred previously in exceptional circumstances which no longer obtain.

4. Save in the cases referred to in paragraph 3 (a) and (b), any wage reduction affecting all or a substantial number of the workers in an undertaking shall be notified to the High Authority.

5. The recommendations provided for in the preceding paragraphs may be made by the High Authority only after consulting the Council, unless they are addressed to undertakings smaller than a minimum size to be defined by the High Authority in agreement with the Council.

If in one of the Member States a change in the arrangements for the financing of social security or for dealing with unemployment and its effects, or a change in wages, produces the effects referred to in Article 67 (2) or (3), the High Authority is empowered to take the steps provided for in that Article.

6. The High Authority may impose upon undertakings which do not comply with the recommendations made to them under this Article fines and periodic penalty payments not exceeding twice the amount of the saving in labour costs improperly effected.

Article 69

1. Member States undertake to remove any restriction based on nationality upon the employment in the coal and steel industries of workers who are nationals of Member States and have recognised qualifications in a coalmining or steelmaking occupation, subject to the limitations imposed by the basic requirements of health and public policy.

2. For the purpose of applying this provision, Member States shall draw up common definitions of skilled trades and qualifications therefor, shall determine by common accord the limitations provided for in paragraph 1, and shall endeavour to work out arrangements on a Community-wide basis for bringing offers of employment into touch with applications for employment.

3. In addition, with regard to workers not covered by paragraph 2, they shall, should growth of coal or steel production be hampered by a shortage of suitable labour, adjust their immigration rules to the extent needed to remedy this state of affairs; in particular, they shall facilitate the re-employment of workers from the coal and steel industries of other Member States.

4. They shall prohibit any discrimination in remuneration and working conditions between nationals and migrant workers, without prejudice to special measures concerning frontier workers; in particular, they shall endeavour to settle among themselves any matters remaining to be dealt with in order to ensure that social security arrangements do not inhibit labour mobility.

5. The High Authority shall guide and facilitate action by Member States in applying this Article.

6. This Article shall not affect the international obligations of Member States.

CHAPTER IX—TRANSPORT

Article 70

It is recognised that the establishment of the common market necessitates the application of such rates and conditions for the carriage of coal and steel as will afford comparable price conditions to comparably placed consumers.

Any discrimination in rates and conditions of carriage of every kind which is based on the country of origin or destination of products shall be prohibited in traffic between Member States. For the purpose of eliminating such discrimination it shall in particular be obligatory to apply to the carriage of coal and steel to or from another country of the Community the scales, rates and all other tariff rules of every kind which are applicable to the internal carriage of the same goods on the same route.

The scales, rates and all other tariff rules of every kind applied to the carriage of coal and steel within each Member State and between Member States shall be published or brought to the knowledge of the High Authority.

The application of special internal rates and conditions in the interest of one or more coal- or steel-producing undertakings shall require the prior agreement of the High Authority, which shall verify that they are in accordance with the principles of this Treaty; it may make its agreement temporary or conditional.

Subject to the provisions of this Article, and to the other provisions of this Treaty, transport policy, including the fixing and altering of rates and conditions of carriage of every kind and the making of rates on a basis calculated to secure for the transport undertakings concerned a properly balanced financial position, shall continue to be governed by the laws or regulations of the individual Member States, as shall measures relating to co-ordination or competition between different modes of transport or different routes.

CHAPTER X—COMMERCIAL POLICY

Article 71

The powers of the Governments of Member States in matters of commercial policy shall not be affected by this Treaty, save as otherwise provided therein.

The powers conferred on the Community by this Treaty in matters of commercial policy towards third countries may not exceed those accorded to Member States under international agreements to which they are parties, subject to the provisions of Article 75.

The Governments of Member States shall afford each other such mutual assistance as is necessary to implement measures recognised by the High Authority as being in accordance with this Treaty and with existing international agreements. The High Authority is empowered to propose to the Member States concerned the methods by which this mutual assistance may be provided.

Article 72

Minimum rates below which Member States undertake not to lower their customs duties on coal and steel as against third countries, and maximum rates above which they undertake not to raise them, may be fixed by decision of the Council, acting unanimously on a proposal from the High Authority made on the latter's own initiative or at the request of a Member State.

Within the limits so fixed, each Government shall determine its tariffs according to its own national procedure. The High Authority may, on its own initiative or at the request of a Member State, deliver an opinion suggesting amendment of the tariffs of that State.

Article 73

The administration of import and export licences for trade with third countries shall be a matter for the Government in whose territory the place of destination for imports or the place of origin for exports is situated.

The High Authority is empowered to supervise the administration and verification of these licences with respect to coal and steel. Where necessary it shall, after consulting the Council, make recommendations to Member States to ensure that the arrangements in this connection are not more restrictive than the circumstances governing their adoption or retention require, and to secure the co-ordination of measures taken under the third paragraph of Article 71 or under Article 74.

Article 74

In the cases set out below, the High Authority is empowered to take any measures which is in accordance with this Treaty, and in particular with the objectives set out in Article 3, and to make to Governments any recommendation which is in accordance with the second paragraph of Article 71:

    (1) if it is found that countries not members of the Community or undertakings situated in such countries are engaging in dumping or other practices condemned by the Havana Charter;

    (2) if a difference between quotations by undertakings outside and by undertakings within the jurisdiction of the Community is due solely to the fact that those of the former are based on conditions of competition contrary to this Treaty;

(3) if one of the products referred to in Article 81 of this Treaty is imported into the territory of one or more Member States in relatively increased quantities and under such conditions that these imports cause or threaten to cause serious injury to production within the common market of like or directly competing products.

However, recommendations for the introduction of quantitative restrictions under subparagraph 2 may be made only with the assent of the Council, and under subparagraph 3 only under the conditions laid down in Article 58.

Article 75

The Member States undertake to keep the High Authority informed of proposed commercial agreements or arrangements having similar effect where these relate to coal and steel or to the importation of other raw materials and specialised equipment needed for the production of coal and steel in Member States.

If a proposed agreement or arrangement contains clauses which would hinder the implementation of this Treaty, the High Authority shall make the necessary recommendations to the State concerned within ten days of receiving notification of the communication addressed to it; in any other case it may deliver opinions.

Title Four

GENERAL PROVISIONS

Article 76

[*Repealed by the Merger Treaty, Art. 28, para. 2. See now ibid., Art. 28, para. 1.*]

Article 77

The seat of the institutions of the Community will be determined by common accord of the Government of the Member States.

Article 78

[1. The financial year shall run from 1 January to 31 December.

The administrative expenditure of the Community shall comprise the expenditure of the High Authority, including that relating to the functioning of the Consultative Committee, and that of the Assembly, the Council, and of the Court of Justice.

2. Each institution of the Community shall, before 1 July, draw up estimates of its administrative expenditure. The High Authority shall consolidate these estimates in a preliminary draft administrative budget. It shall attach thereto an opinion which may contain different estimates.

The preliminary draft budget shall contain an estimate of revenue and an estimate of expenditure.

3. The High Authority shall place the preliminary draft administrative budget before the Council not later than 1 September of the year preceding that in which the budget is to be implemented.

The Council shall consult the High Authority and, where appropriate, the other institutions concerned whenever it intends to depart from the preliminary draft budget.

The Council shall, acting by a qualified majority, establish the draft administrative budget and forward it to the Assembly.

4. The draft administrative budget shall be placed before the Assembly not later than 5 October of the year preceding that in which the budget is to be implemented.

The Assembly shall have the right to amend the draft administrative budget, acting by a majority of its members and to propose to the Council, acting by an absolute majority of the votes cast, modifications to the draft budget relating to expenditure necessarily resulting from this Treaty or from acts adopted in accordance therewith.

If, within forty-five days of the draft administrative budget being placed before it, the Assembly has given its approval, the administrative budget shall stand as finally adopted. If within this period the Assembly has not amended the draft administrative budget nor proposed any modifications thereto, the administrative budget shall be deemed to be finally adopted.

If within this period the Assembly has adopted amendments or proposed modifications, the draft administrative budget together with the amendments or proposed modifications shall be forwarded to the Council.

5. After discussing the draft administrative budget with the High Authority and, where appropriate, with the other institutions concerned, the Council shall act under the following conditions:

(a) The Council may, acting by a qualified majority, modify any of the amendments adopted by the Assembly;

(b) With regard to the proposed modifications:

—where a modification proposed by the Assembly does not have the effect of increasing the total amount of the expenditure of an institution, owing in particular to the fact that the increase in expenditure which it would involve would be expressly compensated by one or more proposed modifications correspondingly reducing expenditure, the Council may, acting by a qualified majority, reject the proposed modification. In the absence of a decision to reject it, the proposed modification shall stand as accepted;

—where a modification proposed by the Assembly has the effect of increasing the total amount of the expenditure of an institution, the Council may, acting by a qualified majority, accept this proposed modification. In the absence of a decision to accept it, the proposed modification shall stand as rejected;

—where, in pursuance of one of the two preceding subparagraphs, the Council has rejected a proposed modification, it may, acting by a qualified majority, either retain the amount shown in the draft administrative budget or fix another amount.

The draft administrative budget shall be modified on the basis of the proposed modifications accepted by the Council.

If, within fifteen days of the draft administrative budget being placed before it, the Council has not modified any of the amendments adopted by the Assembly and if the modifications proposed by the latter have been accepted, the administrative budget shall be deemed to be finally adopted. The Council shall inform the Assembly that it has not modified any of the amendments and that the proposed modifications have been accepted.

If, within this period the Council has modified one or more of the amendments adopted by the Assembly or if the modifications proposed by the latter have been rejected or modified, the modified draft administrative budget shall again be forwarded to the Assembly. The Council shall inform the Assembly of the results of its deliberations.

6. Within fifteen days of the draft administrative budget being placed before it, the Assembly, which shall have been notified of the action taken on its proposed modification, may, acting by a majority of its members and three fifths of the votes cast, amend or reject the modifications to its amendments made by the Council and shall adopt the administrative budget accordingly. If within this period the Assembly has not acted, the administrative budget shall be deemed to be finally adopted.

7. When the procedure provided for in this Article has been completed, the President of the Assembly shall declare that the administrative budget has been finally adopted.

8. However, the Assembly, acting by a majority of its members and two thirds of the votes cast, may, if there are important reasons, reject the draft administrative budget and ask for a new draft to be submitted to it.

9. A maximum rate of increase in relation to the expenditure of the same type to be incurred during the current year shall be fixed annually for the total expenditure other than that necessarily resulting from this Treaty or from acts adopted in accordance therewith.

The High Authority shall, after consulting the Economic Policy Committee, declare what this maximum rate is as it results from:
—the trend, in terms of volume, of the gross national product within the Community;
—the average variation in the budgets of the Member States; and
—the trend of the cost of living during the preceding financial year.

The maximum rate shall be communicated, before 1 May, to all the institutions of the Community. The latter shall be required to conform to this during the budgetary procedure, subject to the provisions of the fourth and fifth subparagraphs of this paragraph.

If, in respect of expenditure other than that necessarily resulting from this Treaty or from acts adopted in accordance therewith, the actual rate of increase in the draft administrative budget established by the Council is over half the maximum rate, the Assembly may, exercising its right of amendment, further increase the total amount of that expenditure to a limit not exceeding half the maximum rate.

Where the Assembly, the Council or the High Authority considers that the activities of the Communities require that the rate determined according to the procedure laid down in this paragraph should be exceeded, another rate may be fixed by agreement between the Council, acting by a qualified majority, and the Assembly, acting by a majority of its members and three fifths of the votes cast.

10. Each institution shall exercise the powers conferred upon it by this Article, with due regard for the provisions of this Treaty and for acts adopted in accordance therewith, in particular those relating to the Communities' own resources and to the balance between revenue and expenditure.

11. Final adoption of the administrative budget shall have the effect of authorising and requiring the High Authority to collect the corresponding revenue in accordance with the provisions of Article 49.]

AMENDMENTS
This article was repealed and replaced first by the Merger Treaty, Art. 21, and then by the Budgetary Treaty, Art. 1.
It was subsequently replaced by the Second Budgetary Treaty of July 22, 1975, Art. 2.

[ARTICLE 78A

By way of derogation from the provisions of Article 78, the following provisions shall apply to budgets for financial years preceding the financial year 1975:

1. The financial year shall run from 1 January to 31 December.

The administrative expenditure of the Community shall comprise the expenditure of the High Authority, including that relating to the functioning of the Consultative Committee, and that of the Court, the Assembly and the Council.

2. Each institution of the Community shall, before 1 July, draw up estimates of its administrative expenditure. The High Authority shall consolidate these estimates in a preliminary draft administrative budget. It shall attach thereto an opinion which may contain different estimates.

The preliminary draft budget shall contain an estimate of revenue and an estimate of expenditure.

3. The High Authority shall place the preliminary draft administrative budget before the Council not later than 1 September of the year preceding that in which the budget is to be implemented.

The Council shall consult the High Authority and, where appropriate, the other institutions concerned whenever it intends to depart from the preliminary draft budget.

The Council shall, acting by a qualified majority, establish the draft administrative budget and forward it to the Assembly.

4. The draft administrative budget shall be placed before the Assembly not later than 5 October of the year preceding that in which the budget is to be implemented.

The Assembly shall have the right to propose to the Council modifications to the draft administrative budget.

If, within forty-five days of the draft administrative budget being placed before it, the Assembly has given its approval or has not proposed any modifications to the draft budget, the administrative budget shall be deemed to be finally adopted.

If within this period the Assembly has proposed modifications, the draft administrative budget together with the proposed modifications shall be forwarded to the Council.

5. The Council shall, after discussing the draft administrative budget with the High Authority and, where appropriate, with the other institutions concerned, adopt the administrative budget, within thirty days of the draft budget being placed before it, under the following conditions.

Where a modification proposed by the Assembly does not have the effect of increasing the total amount of the expenditure of an institution, owing in particular to the fact that the increase in expenditure which it would involve would be expressly compensated by one or more proposed modifications correspondingly reducing expenditure, the Council may, acting by a qualified majority, reject the proposed modification. In the absence of a decision to reject it, the proposed modification shall stand as accepted.

Where a modification proposed by the Assembly has the effect of increasing the total amount of the expenditure of an institution, the Council must act by a qualified majority in accepting the proposed modification.

Where, in pursuance of the second or third subparagraph of this paragraph, the Council has rejected or has not accepted a proposed modification, it may, acting by a qualified majority, either retain the amount shown in the draft administrative budget or fix another amount.

6. When the procedure provided for in this Article has been completed, the President of the Council shall declare that the administrative budget has been finally adopted.

7. Each institution shall exercise the powers conferred upon it by this Article, with due regard for the provisions of this Treaty and for acts adopted in accordance therewith, in particular those relating to the Communities' own resources and to the balance between revenue and expenditure.

8. Final adoption of the administrative budget shall have the effect of authorising and requiring the High Authority to collect the corresponding revenue in accordance with the provisions of Article 49.]

AMENDMENT
This article was added by the Budgetary Treaty, Art. 2.

[Article 78a

The administrative budget shall be drawn up in the unit of account determined in accordance with the provisions of the regulations made pursuant to Article [78h].

The expenditure shown in the budget shall be authorised for one financial year, unless the regulations made pursuant to Article [78h] provide otherwise.

In accordance with conditions to be laid down pursuant to Article [78h], any appropriations, other than those relating to staff expenditure, that are unexpended at the end of the financial year may be carried forward to the next financial year only.

Appropriations shall be classified under different chapters grouping items of expenditure according to their nature or purpose and sub-divided, as far as may be necessary, in accordance with the regulations made pursuant to Article [78h].

The expenditure of the Assembly, the Council, the High Authority and the Court shall be set out in separate parts of the administrative budget, without prejudice to special arrangements for certain common items of expenditure.]

AMENDMENTS
This article was added by the Merger Treaty, Art. 21.
The figures in square brackets were replaced by the Second Budgetary Treaty of July 22, 1975, Art. 3.

[Article 78b

[1. If, at the beginning of a financial year, the administrative budget has not yet been voted, a sum equivalent to not more than one twelfth of the budget appropriations for the preceding financial year may be spent each month in respect of any chapter or other subdivision of the administrative budget in accordance with the provisions of the regulations made pursuant to Article 78h; this arrangement shall not, however, have the effect of placing at the disposal of the High Authority appropriations in excess of one twelfth of those provided for in the draft administrative budget in course of preparation.

The High Authority is authorised and required to impose the levies up to the amount of the appropriations for the preceding financial year, but shall not thereby exceed the amount which would have resulted from the adoption of the draft administrative budget.

2. The Council may, acting by a qualified majority, provided that the other conditions laid down in paragraph 1 are observed, authorise expenditure in excess of one twelfth. The authorisation and requirement to impose the levies may be adjusted accordingly.

If the decision relates to expenditure which does not necessarily result from this Treaty or from acts adopted in accordance therewith, the Council shall forward it immediately to the Assembly; within thirty days the Assembly, acting by a majority of its members and three fifths of the votes cast, may adopt a different decision on the expenditure in excess of the one twelfth referred to in paragraph 1. This part of the decision of the Council shall be suspended until the Assembly has taken its decision. If within the said period the Assembly has not taken a decision which differs from the decision of the Council, the latter shall be deemed to be finally adopted.]

AMENDMENTS
This article was added by the Merger Treaty, Art. 21.
It was subsequently replaced by the Second Budgetary Treaty of July 22, 1975, Art. 4.

[ARTICLE 78c

The High Authority shall implement the administrative budget, in accordance with the provisions of the regulations made pursuant to Article [78h], on its own responsibility and within the limits of the approriations.

The regulations shall lay down detailed rules for each institution concerning its part in effecting its own expenditure.

With the administrative budget, the High Authority may, subject to the limits and conditions laid down in the regulations made pursuant to Article [78h], transfer appropriations from one chapter to another or from one subdivision to another.]

AMENDMENTS
This article was added by the Merger Treaty, Art. 21.
The figures in square brackets were replaced by the Second Budgetary Treaty of July 22, 1975, Art. 5.

[ARTICLE 78d

[The High Authority shall submit annually to the Council and to the Assembly the accounts of the preceding financial year relating to the implementation of the administrative budget. The High Authority shall also forward to them a financial statement of the assets and liabilities of the Community in the field covered by that Budget.]]

AMENDMENTS
This article was added by the Merger Treaty, Art. 21.
It was subsequently replaced by the Second Budgetary Treaty of July 22, 1975, Art. 6.

[ARTICLE 78e

[1. A Court of Auditors is hereby established.
[2. The Court of Auditors shall consist of ten members.]
3. The members of the Court of Auditors shall be chosen from among persons who belong or have belonged in their respective countries to external

audit bodies or who are especially qualified for this office. Their independence must be beyond doubt.

4. The members of the Court of Auditors shall be appointed for a term of six years by the Council, acting unanimously after consulting the Assembly.

However, when the first appointments are made, four members of the Court of Auditors, chosen by lot, shall be appointed for a term of office of four years only.

The members of the Court of Auditors shall be eligible for reappointment.

They shall elect the President of the Court of Auditors from among their number for a term of three years. The President may be re-elected.

5. The members of the Court of Auditors shall, in the general interest of the Community, be completely independent in the performance of their duties.

In the performance of these duties, they shall neither seek nor take instructions from any Government or from any other body. They shall refrain from any action incompatible with their duties.

6. The members of the Court of Auditors may not, during their term of office, engage in any other occupation, whether gainful or not. When entering upon their duties they shall give a solemn undertaking that, both during and after their term of office, they will respect the obligations arising therefrom and in particular their duty to behave with integrity and discretion as regards the acceptance, after they have ceased to hold office, of certain appointments or benefits.

7. Apart from normal replacement, or death, the duties of a member of the Court of Auditors shall end when he resigns, or is compulsorily retired by a ruling of the Court of Justice pursuant to paragraph 8.

The vacancy thus caused shall be filled for the remainder of the member's term of office.

Save in the case of compulsory retirement, members of the Court of Auditors shall remain in office until they have been replaced.

8. A member of the Court of Auditors may be deprived of his office or of his right to a pension or other benefits in its stead only if the Court of Justice, at the request of the Court of Auditors, finds that he no longer fulfils the requisite conditions or meets the obligations arising from his office.

9. The Council, acting by a qualified majority, shall determine the conditions of employment of the President and the members of the Court of Auditors and in particular their salaries, allowances and pensions. It shall also, by the same majority, determine any payment to be made instead of remuneration.

10. The provisions of the Protocol on the Privileges and Immunities of the European Communities applicable to the Judges of the Court of Justice shall also apply to the members of the Court of Auditors.]]

Amendments
    This article was added by the Merger Treaty, Art. 21.
    It was subsequently replaced by the Second Budgetary Treaty of July 22, 1975, Art. 7.
    Para. (2) was substituted by the Act of Accession of the Hellenic Republic of May 28, 1979, Art. 18.

[Article 78f

[1. The Court of Auditors shall examine the account of all administrative expenditure and administrative revenue of the Community, including the revenue from the tax for the benefit of the Community levied on the salaries, wages and emoluments of officials and other servants of the latter. It shall also examine the accounts of all revenue and expenditure of all bodies set up by the Community insofar as the relevant constituent instrument does not preclude such examination.

2. The Court of Auditors shall examine whether all revenue referred to in paragraph 1 has been received and all expenditure referred to in that paragraph has been incurred in a lawful and regular manner and whether the financial management has been sound.

The audit of revenue shall be carried out on the basis both of the amounts established as due and the amounts actually paid to the Community.

The audit of expenditure shall be carried out on the basis both of commitments undertaken and payments made.

These audits may be carried out before the closure of accounts for the financial year in question.

3. The audit shall be based on records and, if necessary, performed on the spot in the institutions of the Community and in the Member States. In the Member States the audit shall be carried out in liaison with the national audit bodies or, if these do not have the necessary powers, with the competent national departments. These bodies or departments shall inform the Court of Auditors whether they intend to take part in the audit.

The institutions of the Community and the national audit bodies or, if these do not have the necessary powers, the competent national departments, shall forward to the Court of Auditors, at its request, any document or information necessary to carry out its task.

4. The Court of Auditors shall draw up an annual report after the close of each financial year. It shall be forwarded to the institutions of the Community and shall be published, together with the replies of these institutions to the observations of the Court of Auditors, in the Official Journal of the European Communities.

The Court of Auditors may also, at any time, submit observations on specific questions and deliver opinions at the request of one of the insitutions of the Community.

It shall adopt its annual reports or opinions by a majority of its members.

It shall assist the Assembly and the Council in exercising their powers of control over the implementation of the budget.

5. The Court of Auditors shall also draw up a separate annual report stating whether the accounting other than that for the expenditure and revenue referred to in paragraph 1 and the financial management by the High Authority relating thereto have been effected in a regular manner. It shall draw up this report within six months of the end of the financial year to which the accounts refer and shall submit it to the High Authority and the Council. The High Authority shall forward it to the Assembly.]]

AMENDMENTS
This article was added by the Merger Treaty, Art. 21.
It was subsequently replaced by the Second Budgetary Treaty of July 22, 1975, Art. 8.

[ARTICLE 78g

The Assembly, acting on a recommendation from the Council which shall Act by a qualified majority, shall give a discharge to the High Authority in respect of the implementation of the administrative budget. To this end, the Council and the Assembly in turn shall examine the accounts and the financial statement referred to in Article 78d, and the annual report by the Court of Auditors together with the replies of the institutions under audit to the observations of the Court of Auditors.]

AMENDMENT
This article was added by the Second Budgetary Treaty of July 22, 1975, Art. 9.

[Article 78h

The Council, acting unanimously on a proposal from the High Authority and after consulting the Assembly and obtaining the opinion of the Court of Auditors, shall:

(a) make financial regulations specifying in particular the procedure to be adopted for establishing and implementing the administrative budget and for presenting and auditing accounts;

(b) lay down rules concerning the responsibility of authorising officers and accounting officers and concerning appropriate arrangements for inspection.]

AMENDMENT
This article was added by the Second Budgetary Treaty of July 22, 1975, Art. 10.

Article 79

This Treaty shall apply to the European territories of the High Contracting Parties. It shall also apply to European territories for whose external relations a signatory State is responsible; as regards the Saar, an exchange of letters between the Government of the Federal Republic of Germany and the Government of the French Republic is annexed to this Treaty.

[Notwithstanding the preceding paragraph:

(a) This Treaty shall not apply to the Faroe Islands. The Government of the Kingdom of Denmark may, however, give notice, by a declaration deposited by 31 December 1975 at the latest with the Government of the French Republic, which shall transmit a certified copy thereof to each of the Governments of the other Member States, that this Treaty shall apply to those Islands. In that event, this Treaty shall apply to those Islands from the first day of the second month following the deposit of the declaration.

(b) This Treaty shall not apply to the Sovereign Base Areas of the United Kingdom of Great Britain and Northern Ireland in Cyprus.

(c) This Treaty shall apply to the Channel Islands and the Isle of Man only to the extent necessary to ensure the implementation of the arrangements for those Islands set out in the Decision of the Council of the European Communities of 22 January 1972 concerning the accession of new Member States to the European Coal and Steel Community.]

Each High Contracting Party undertakes to extend to the other Member States the preferential treatment which it enjoys with respect to coal and steel in the non-European territories under its jurisdiction.

AMENDMENTS
The second paragraph was added by the Act of Accession, Art. 25, as amended by the Adaptation Decision, Art. 14.

Article 80

For the purposes of this Treaty, " undertaking " means any undertaking engaged in production in the coal or the steel industry within the territories referred to in the first paragraph of Article 79, and also, for the purposes of

Articles 65 and 66 and of information required for their application and proceedings in connection with them, any undertaking or agency regularly engaged in distribution other than sale to domestic consumers or small craft industries.

ARTICLE 81

The expressions " coal " and " steel " are defined in Annex I to this Treaty.
Additions to the lists in that Annex may be made by the Council, acting unanimously.

ARTICLE 82

The turnover taken as the basis for calculating any fines and periodic penalty payments imposed on undertakings under this Treaty shall be the turnover on products within the jurisdiction of the High Authority.

ARTICLE 83

The establishment of the Community shall in no way prejudice the system of ownership of the undertakings to which this Treaty applies.

ARTICLE 84

For the purposes of this Treaty, the words " this Treaty " mean the provisions of the Treaty and its Annexes, of the Protocols annexed thereto and of the Convention on the Transitional Provisions.

ARTICLE 85

The initial and transitional measures agreed by the High Contracting Parties to enable the provisions of this Treaty to be applied are laid down in a Convention annexed to this Treaty.

ARTICLE 86

Member States undertake to take all appropriate measures, whether general or particular, to ensure fulfilment of the obligations resulting from decisions and recommendations of the institutions of the Community and to facilitate the performance of the Community's tasks.

Member States undertake to refrain from any measures incompatible with the common market referred to in Articles 1 and 4.

They shall make all appropriate arrangements, as far as lies within their powers, for the settlement of international accounts arising out of trade in coal and steel within the common market and shall afford each other mutual assistance to facilitate such settlements.

Officials of the High Authority entrusted by it with tasks of inspection shall enjoy in the territories of Member States, to the full extent required for the performance of their duties, such rights and powers as are granted by the laws of these States to their own revenue officials. Forthcoming visits of inspection and the status of the officials shall be duly notified to the State concerned. Officials of that State may, at its request or at that of the High Authority, assist the High Authority's officials in the performance of their task.

ARTICLE 87

The High Contracting Parties undertake not to avail themselves of any treaties, conventions or declarations made between them for the purpose of submitting a dispute concerning the interpretation or application of this Treaty to any method of settlement other than those provided for therein.

Article 88

If the High Authority considers that a State has failed to fulfil an obligation under this Treaty, it shall record this failure in a reasoned decision after giving the State concerned the opportunity to submit its comments. It shall set the State a time limit for the fulfilment of its obligation.

The State may institute proceedings before the Court within two months of notification of the decision; the Court shall have unlimited jurisdiction in such cases.

If the State has not fulfilled its obligation by the time limit set by the High Authority, or if it brings an action which is dismissed, the High Authority may, with the assent of the Council acting by a two-thirds majority:

(a) suspend the payment of any sums which it may be liable to pay to the State in question under this Treaty;

(b) take measures, or authorise the other Member States to take measures, by way of derogation from the provisions of Article 4, in order to correct the effects of the infringement of the obligation.

Proceedings may be instituted before the Court against decisions taken under subparagraphs (a) and (b) within two months of their notification; the Court shall have unlimited jurisdiction in such cases.

If these measures prove ineffective, the High Authority shall bring the matter before the Council.

Article 89

Any dispute between Member States concerning the application of this Treaty which cannot be settled by another procedure provided for in this Treaty may be submitted to the Court on application by one of the States which are parties to the dispute.

The Court shall also have jurisdiction in any dispute between Member States which relates to the subject matter of this Treaty, if the Dispute is submitted to it under a special agreement between the parties.

Article 90

If failure to fulfil an obligation under this Treaty on the part of an undertaking also constitutes an infringement of its obligations under the law of its State and judicial or administrative action is being taken under that law against the undertaking, the State in question shall so inform the High Authority, which may defer its decision.

If the High Authority defers its decision, it shall be kept informed of the progress of the action taken by national authorities and shall be permitted to produce all relevant documents and expert and other evidence. It shall also be informed of the final decision on the case and shall take account of this decision in determining any penalty it may itself impose.

Article 91

If an undertaking does not pay by the time limit set a sum which it is liable to pay to the High Authority either under this Treaty or rules laid down for the implementation thereof or in discharge of a pecuniary sanction or periodic penalty payment imposed by the High Authority, the High Authority may suspend payment of sums which it is liable to pay to that undertaking, up to the amount of the outstanding payment.

ARTICLE 92

Decisions of the High Authority which impose a pecuniary obligation shall be enforceable.

Enforcement in the territory of Member States shall be carried out by means of the legal procedure in force in each State, after the order for enforcement in the form in use in the State in whose territory the decision is to be enforced has been appended to the decision, without other formality than verification of the authenticity of the decision. This formality shall be carried out at the instance of a Minister designated for this purpose by each of the Governments.

Enforcement may be suspended only by a decision of the Court.

ARTICLE 93

The High Authority shall maintain all appropriate relations with the United Nations and the Organisation for European Economic Co-operation and shall keep these organisations regularly informed of the activities of the Community.

ARTICLE 94

Relations shall be maintained between the institutions of the Community and the Council of Europe as provided in a Protocol annexed to this Treaty.

ARTICLE 95

In all cases not provided for in this Treaty where it becomes apparent that a decision or recommendation of the High Authority is necessary to attain, within the common market in coal and steel and in accordance with Article 5, one of the objectives of the Community set out in Articles 2, 3 and 4, the decision may be taken or the recommendation made with the unanimous assent of the Council and after the Consultative Committee has been consulted.

Any decision so taken or recommendation so made shall determine what penalties, if any, may be imposed.

If, after the end of the transitional period provided in the Convention on the Transitional Provisions, unforeseen difficulties emerging in the light of experience in the application of this Treaty, or fundamental economic or technical changes directly affecting the common market in coal and steel, make it necessary to adapt the rules for the High Authority's exercise of its powers, appropriate amendments may be made; they must not, however, conflict with the provisions of Articles 2, 3 and 4 or interfere with the relationship between the powers of the High Authority and those of the other institutions of the Community.

[These amendments shall be proposed jointly by the High Authority and the Council, acting by a nine-tenths majority of its members, and shall be submitted to the Court for its opinion. In considering them, the Court shall have full power to assess all points of fact and of law. If as a result of such consideration it finds the proposals compatible with the provisions of the preceding paragraph, they shall be forwarded to the Assembly and shall enter into force if approved by a majority of three quarters of the votes cast and two thirds of the members of the Assembly.]

AMENDMENTS

The fourth paragraph was substituted by the Act of Accession, Art. 13, and subsequently by the Act of Accession of the Hellenic Republic, Art. 13.

ARTICLE 96

After the end of the transitional period, the Government of any Member State or the High Authority may propose amendments to this Treaty. Such proposals shall be submitted to the Council. If the Council, acting by a two-thirds majority, delivers an opinion in favour of calling a conference of representatives of the Governments of the Member States, the conference shall be convened forthwith by the President of the Council for the purpose of determining by common accord the amendments to be made to the Treaty.

Such amendments shall enter into force after being ratified by all the Member States in accordance with their respective constitutional requirements.

ARTICLE 97

This Treaty is concluded for a period of fifty years from its entry into force.

ARTICLE 98

Any European State may apply to accede to this Treaty. It shall address its application to the Council, which shall act unanimously after obtaining the opinion of the High Authority; the Council shall also determine the terms of accession, likewise acting unanimously. Accession shall take effect on the day when the instrument of accession is received by the Government acting as depositary of this Treaty.

ARTICLE 99

This Treaty shall be ratified by all the Member States in accordance with their respective constitutional requirements; the instruments of ratification shall be deposited with the Government of the French Republic.

This Treaty shall enter into force on the date of deposit of the instrument of ratification by the last signatory State to take this step.

If all the instruments of ratification have not been deposited within six months of the signature of this Treaty, the Governments of the States which have deposited their instruments shall consult each other on the measures to be taken.

ARTICLE 100

This Treaty, drawn up in a single original, shall be deposited in the archives of the Government of the French Republic, which shall transmit a certified copy thereof to each of the Governments of the other signatory States.

IN WITNESS WHEREOF, the undersigned plenipotentiaries have signed this Treaty and affixed thereto their seals.

Done at Paris this eighteenth day of April in the year one thousand nine hundred and fifty-one.

ADENAUER

Paul VAN ZEELAND
J. MEURICE

SCHUMAN

SFORZA

JOS. BECH

STIKKER
VAN DEN BRINK

ANNEXES

ANNEX I

DEFINITION OF THE EXPRESSIONS " COAL " AND " STEEL "

1. The expressions " coal " and " steel " cover the products listed below.

2. In the exercise of its functions in relation to special steels, coke and scrap the High Authority shall take account of the special features of production of these materials or of trade in them.

3. The High Authority shall exercise its functions in relation to gas coke and to brown coal other than for the making of briquettes and semi-coke, only where this is necessary by reason of appreciable disturbances caused by these products on the market in fuels.

4. The High Authority shall take account of the fact that the production of some of the products listed is directly linked with the production of by-products which are not listed but whose selling prices may influence those of the principal products.

OEEC Code No. (for reference)	*Product*
3000	FUELS
3100	Hard coal
3200	Hard coal briquettes
3300	Coke, excluding electrode and petroleum coke
	Semi-coke derived from hard coal
3400	Brown coal briquettes
3500	Run-of-mine brown coal
	Semi-coke derived from brown coal
4000	IRON AND STEEL
4100	Raw materials for iron and steel production [1]
	Iron ore (except pyrites)
	[Sponge iron and steel [1a]]
	Ferrous scrap
	Manganese ore
4200	Pig iron and ferro-alloys
	Pig iron for steelmaking
	Foundry and other pig iron
	Spiegeleisen and high-carbon ferro-manganese [2]
4300	Crude and semi-finished products of iron, ordinary steel or special steel, including products of re-use and re-rolling.
	Liquid steel cast or not cast into ingots, including ingots for forging [3]
	Semi-finished products: blooms, billets and slabs; sheet bars and tinplate bars; hot-rolled wide coils (other than coils classed as finished products)

---

[1] Not including the raw materials under OEEC Code No. 4190 (" Other Raw Materials not elsewhere classified for Iron and Steel Production ") which are not contained in this list. Not including refractories.

[1a] Including sponge iron proper or in briquetted form, Renn balls and similar products.

[2] Not including other ferro-alloys.

[3] The High Authority shall concern itself with production of liquid steel for castings only where this is to be regarded as an activity of the steel industry proper.

Any other production of liquid steel for castings, such as that at small and medium-sized independent foundries, shall be subject to statistical coverage only, such coverage not to give rise to any discriminatory action in respect thereof.

OEEC Code No. (for reference)	Product
4400	Hot finished products of iron, ordinary steel or special steel [4]
	Rails, sleepers, fishplates, soleplates, joists, heavy sections 80 mm and over, sheet piling
	Bars and sections of less than 80 mm and flats of less than 150 mm
	Wire rod
	Tube rounds and squares
	Hot-rolled hoop and strip (including tube strip)
	Hot-rolled sheets under 3 mm (coated or uncoated)
	Plates and sheets of 3 mm thickness and over, universal plates of 150 mm and over
4500	End products of iron, ordinary steel or special steel [5]
	Tinplate, terneplate, blackplate, galvanized sheets, other coated sheets
	Cold-rolled sheets under 3 mm
	Electrical sheets
	Strip for tinplate

AMENDMENT

The words in square brackets and footnote 1a were added by Council Decision published in the *Official Journal of the European Communities*, No. 129, 6 December 1962, p. 2810.

ANNEX II SCRAP

The provisions of this Treaty shall apply to ferrous scrap, but account shall be taken of the following practical arrangements necessitated by the special features of the recovery of and trade in scrap:

(a) any prices fixed by the High Authority under Chapter V of Title III shall apply to purchases by Community undertakings; Members States shall cooperate with the High Authority in ensuring that sellers comply with the decisions taken;

(b) Article 59 shall not apply to:
cast iron scrap usable only in foundries outside the jurisdiction of the Community;
undertakings' own arisings, availabilities of which shall, however, be taken into account in calculating the bases for allocations of bought scrap;

(c) for the application of Article 59 to bought scrap, the High Authority shall, in cooperation with the Governments of Member States, obtain the necessary information on availabilities and requirements, including exports to third countries.

On the basis of the information thus obtained the High Authority shall allocate availabilities among Member States in accordance with Article 59, in such a way as to enable the most efficient use to be made of them and taking into account all the operating and supply conditions in the different parts of the steel industry within its jurisdiction.

To ensure that shipments of scrap so allocated from one Member State to another, or purchases by undertakings in one Member State of the tonnages to which they are entitled on the market of another Member State, will not involve discrimination harmful to undertakings in either State, the following measures shall be taken:

1. Each Member State shall authorise the shipment from its territory to other Member States of tonnages in accordance with the allocation made by the High Authority; in return, each Member State shall be authorised to effect the necessary checks to establish that outgoing shipments are not in excess of the amounts provided for. The High Authority is empowered to ensure that the arrangements made are not more restrictive than is necessary for this purpose.

---

[4] Not including steel castings, forgings and powder metallurgy products.
[5] Not including steel tubes (seamless or welded), cold-rolled strip less than 500 mm in width (other than for tinplating), wire and wire products, bright bars and iron castings (tubes, pipes, and fittings, and other iron castings).

2. The allocation among Member States shall be reviewed at as frequent intervals as may be necessary to maintain a relation fair both to local purchasers and to purchasers from other Member States between the recorded availabilities in each Member State and the tonnages it is required to ship to other Member States.
3. The High Authority shall ensure that the regulations made by each Member State concerning sellers within its jurisdiction do not lead to the application of dissimilar conditions to comparable transactions, especially on grounds of the nationality of the buyers.

ANNEX III SPECIAL STEELS

Special steels and high carbon steels, as defined in the draft European customs nomenclature finalised by the Tariff Committee at its meeting in Brussels on 15 July 1950, shall be treated according to which of the following groups they fall within:

(a) special steels commonly called structural steels, containing less than 0·6 per cent of carbon and not more than 8 per cent of two or more alloying elements taken together or 5 per cent of a single alloying element;[1]

(b) high carbon steels, containing between 0·6 and 1·6 per cent of carbon; special steels other than those defined in (a) above, containing less than 40 per cent of two or more alloying elements taken together or 20 per cent of a single alloying element;[1]

(c) special steels not covered by (a) or (b).

Products in groups (a) and (b) shall come within the jursidiction of the High Authority, but to enable study to be made of appropriate arrangements for the application of this Treaty to them, given the special features of their production and of trade in them, the date for the abolition of import and export duties or equivalent charges and of all quantitative restrictions on their movement within the Community shall be deferred until one year after the date of the establishment of the common market in steel.

As to products in group (c), the High Authority shall, upon taking up its duties, enter into a series of studies to determine appropriate arrangements for the application of the Treaty to them, taking into account the special features of their production and of trade in them; as and when the findings are forthcoming, and within three years of the establishment of the common market at the latest, the arrangements suggested for each of the products in question shall be submitted by the High Authority to the Council, which shall pronounce upon them in accordance with Article 81. During this period products in group (c) shall be subject only to statistical checks by the High Authority.

[1] Sulphur, phosphorus, silicon and manganese in the amounts normally accepted in ordinary steels are not counted as alloying elements.

PROTOCOL ON RELATIONS WITH THE COUNCIL OF EUROPE

THE HIGH CONTRACTING PARTIES,

FULLY AWARE of the need to establish ties as close as possible between the European Coal and Steel Community and the Council of Europe, particularly between the two Assemblies.

TAKING NOTE of the recommendations of the Assembly of the Council of Europe,

HAVE AGREED upon the following provisions:

ARTICLE 1

The Governments of the Member States are invited to recommend to their respective Parliaments that the members of the Assembly whom these Parliaments are called upon to designate should preferably be chosen from among the representatives to the Consultative Assembly of the Council of Europe.

ARTICLE 2

The Assembly of the Community shall forward each year to the Consultative Assembly of the Council of Europe a report on its activities.

ARTICLE 3

The High Authority shall communicate each year to the Committee of Ministers and to the Consultative Assembly of the Council of Europe the general report provided for in Article 17 of this Treaty.

ARTICLE 4

The High Authority shall inform the Council of Europe of the action which it has been able to take on any recommendations that may have been sent to it by the Committee of Ministers of the Council of Europe under Article 15 (*b*) of the Statute of the Council of Europe.

ARTICLE 5

The present Treaty establishing the European Coal and Steel Community and the Annexes thereto shall be registered with the Secretariat of the Council of Europe.

ARTICLE 6

Agreements between the Community and the Council of Europe may, among other things, provide for any other type of mutual assistance and cooperation between the two organisations and indicate the appropriate forms thereof.

Done at Paris this eighteenth day of April in the year one thousand nine hundred and fifty-one.

ADENAUER

Paul VAN ZEELAND
J. MEURICE

SCHUMAN

SFORZA

JOS. BECH

STIKKER
VAN DEN BRINK

EXCHANGE OF LETTERS BETWEEN THE GOVERNMENT OF THE FEDERAL REPUBLIC OF GERMANY AND THE GOVERNMENT OF THE FRENCH REPUBLIC CONCERNING THE SAAR

(Translation)

The Federal Chancellor
and
Minister for Foreign Affairs

Paris, 18 April 1951

His Excellency President Robert Schuman,
Minister for Foreign Affairs,
Paris

Sir,

The representatives of the Federal Government have several times declared in the course of the negotiations on the European Coal and Steel Community that the status of the Saar can be finally settled only by the Peace Treaty or a similar Treaty. Furthermore, they have declared in the course of the negotiations that in signing the Treaty the Federal Government is not expressing recognition of the present status of the Saar.

I would repeat this declaration and would ask you to confirm that the French Government agrees with the Federal Government that the status of the Saar can be finally settled only by the Peace Treaty or a similar Treaty and that the French Government does not view the Federal Government's signature of the European Coal and Steel Community Treaty as recognition by the Federal Government of the present status of the Saar.

I am, Sir,
(Signed) ADENAUER

(Translation)

Paris, 18 April 1951

Sir,

In reply to your letter of 18 April 1951, the French Government notes that the Federal Government in signing the Treaty establishing the European Coal and Steel Community does not intend recognition of the present status of the Saar.

The French Government declares, in accordance with its own point of view, that it is acting on behalf of the Saar by virtue of the present status of the latter but does not view the Federal Government's signature of the Treaty as recognition by the Federal Government of the present status of the Saar. It is not its understanding that the Treaty establishing the European Coal and Steel Community prejudges the final status of the Saar, which is a matter for the Peace Treaty or a Treaty in place thereof.

I am, Sir,
(Signed) SCHUMAN

Dr. Konrad ADENAUER,
Chancellor and Minister for Foreign Affairs
of the Federal Republic of Germany

CONVENTION ON THE TRANSITIONAL PROVISIONS

THE HIGH CONTRACTING PARTIES,

DESIRING to draw up the Convention on the Transitional Provisions provided for in Article 85 of the Treaty,

HAVE AGREED as follows:

PURPOSE OF THE CONVENTION

ARTICLE 1

1. The purpose of this Convention, drawn up in pursuance of Article 85 of the Treaty, is to provide for the measures required in order to establish the common market and enable production to be progressively adapted to the new conditions, while helping to eliminate disequilibria arising out of the former conditions.

2. To this end, the implementation of the Treaty shall be effected in two stages—a preparatory period and a transitional period.

3. The preparatory period shall extend from the date of entry into force of the Treaty to the date of the establishment of the common market.

During this period:

(a) all the institutions of the Community shall be set up and contacts established between them and undertakings and associations of undertakings, trade unions, and associations of consumers and dealers, in order to place the functioning of the Community on a basis of regular consultation and to develop a common approach and mutual understanding among all concerned;

(b) the High Authority shall conduct:

(1) studies and consultations;

(2) negotiations with third countries.

The purpose of the studies and consultations shall be to enable an overall survey to be drawn up, in regular contact with Governments, with undertakings and associations of undertakings, with workers and with consumers and dealers, of the situation of the coal and steel industries in the Community and the problems arising therefrom, and the way to be prepared for the actual measures which will have to be taken to deal with these during the transitional period.

The purpose of the negotiations with third countries shall be:

—first, to lay the foundations for cooperation between the Community and these countries;

—second, to obtain, before the elimination of customs duties and quantitative restrictions within the Community, the necessary derogations from:

—most-favoured-nation treatment under the General Agreement on Tariffs and Trade and under bilateral agreements;

—the principle of non-discrimination in liberalisation of trade within the Organisation for European Cooperation.

4. The transitional period shall begin on the date of the establishment of the common market and shall end five years after the establishment of the common market in coal.

5. Upon the entry into force of the Treaty in accordance with Article 99, the provisions thereof shall apply subject to the derogations allowed by this Convention and without prejudice to the supplementary provisions contained in this Convention for the ends set out above.

Save where this Convention expressly provides otherwise, these derogations and supplementary provisions shall cease to apply, and measures taken to implement them shall cease to have effect, at the end of the transitional period.

Part One

IMPLEMENTATION OF THE TREATY

CHAPTER 1—SETTING UP OF THE INSTITUTIONS OF THE COMMUNITY

THE HIGH AUTHORITY

ARTICLE 2

1. The High Authority shall take office upon the appointment of its members.

2. In order to perform the tasks assigned to it by Article 1 of this Convention, the High Authority shall exercise forthwith the information and study functions assigned to it by the Treaty, in the manner and with the powers provided in Articles 46, 47 and 48 and the third paragraph of Article 54. Once the High Authority has taken office, the Governments shall notify it in accordance with Article 67 of any action liable to have repercussions on conditions of competitions and in accordance with Article 75 of any provisions in trade agreements or arrangements having similar effect where these relate to coal and steel.

On the basis of information obtained concerning facilities existing and planned, the High Authority shall determine the date from which the provisions of Article 54 other than those referred to in the preceding subparagraph shall apply to investment programmes and to projects already in process of execution on that date. The penultimate paragraph of Article 54 shall not apply, however, to projects for which orders were placed before 1 March 1951.

Once the High Authority has taken office, it shall exercise where necessary, in consultation with the Governments, the powers provided in Article 59 (3).

It shall not exercise the other functions assigned to it by the Treaty until the opening date of the transitional period for each of the products in question.

3. On each of the opening dates referred to in the preceding paragraph, the High Authority shall notify Member States that it is ready to assume the functions concerned. Until such notification the relevant powers shall continue to be exercised by Member States.

However, from a date which the High Authority shall appoint on taking office, prior consultations shall be held between it and Member States concerning any laws or regulations which Member States may be planning to introduce on matters assigned to the jurisdiction of the High Authority by the Treaty.

4. Without prejudice to the provisions of Article 67 relating to the effect of new measures, the High Authority shall examine with the Governments concerned the effect on the coal and steel industries of existing laws and regulations, including any which fix prices for by-products not coming within its jurisdiction, and of such contractual social security schemes as are equivalent in effect to regulations. If it finds that some of these, by reason either of their own effects or of differences in them between two or more Member States, are liable seriously to distort conditions of competition in the coal or the steel industry, whether in the market of the country in question or in the rest of the common market or in export markets, it shall, after consulting the Council propose to the Governments concerned any action which it considers will correct them or offset their effects.

5. In order to have a working basis which is independent of the practices of the various undertakings, the High Authority shall seek to establish, in consultation with Governments, undertakings and associations of undertakings, workers, and consumers and dealers, by what means it will be possible to make comparable:

—the price ranges for different qualities relative to the average price for the products, or for the successive stages of their production;

—the calculation of provision for depreciation.

6. During the preparatory period the main task of the High Authority shall be to establish relations with undertakings and associations of undertakings, trade unions, and associations of consumers and dealers, in order to obtain practical knowledge of the general situation and of particular situations in the Community.

In the light of the information it obtains on markets, supplies, the production conditions of undertakings, the living conditions of workers, and modernisation and equipment programmes, the High Authority shall, in contact with all concerned, draw up an overall survey of the situation of the Community to guide their work together.

On the basis of these consultations and the overall picture thus formed, the measures shall be prepared which will be needed to establish the common market and facilitate the adaptation of production.

THE COUNCIL

ARTICLE 3

The Council shall meet within one month after the High Authority takes office.

THE CONSULTATIVE COMMITTEE

ARTICLE 4

To enable the Consultative Committee to be set up as provided in Article 18 of the Treaty, Governments shall forward to the High Authority upon its taking office all information on the producers', workers' and consumers' organisations for coal and steel in each country, particularly on their membership geographical coverage, statutes, powers and functions.

On the basis of this information, the High Authority shall, within two months of taking office, obtain a decision of the Council designating the producers' and workers' associations which are to put forward candidates.

The Consultative Committee shall be set up within one month of this decision.

THE COURT

ARTICLE 5

The Court shall take office upon the appointment of its members. Its first President shall be appointed in the same manner as the President of the High Authority.

The Court shall adopt its rules of procedure within three months.

No matter may be brought before the Court until its rules of procedure have been published. The imposition of periodic penalty payments and the collection of fines shall be suspended until the date of that publication.

The time within which an action must be brought shall run only from the same date.

THE ASSEMBLY

ARTICLE 86

The Assembly shall meet, having been convened by the President of the High Authority, one month after the High Authority takes office, in order to elect its officers and draw up its rules of procedure. Pending the election of its officers, the oldest member shall take the chair.

The Assembly shall hold a second meeting five months after the High Authority takes office in order to consider a general report on the situation of the Community, together with the first budget estimates.

ADMINISTRATIVE AND FINANCIAL PROVISIONS

ARTICLE 7

The first financial year shall run from the date on which the High Authority takes office to 30 June of the following year.

The levy provided for in Article 50 of the Treaty may be collected upon the adoption of the first budget estimates. As a transitional measure to meet initial administrative expenditure, Member States shall make repayable interest-free advances, the amount of which shall be calculated in proportion to their contributions to the Organisation for European Economic Co-operation. [. . .].

AMENDMENT
The third paragraph of this Article was repealed by the Merger Treaty, Art. 24 (2).

CHAPTER 2—ESTABLISHMENT OF THE COMMON MARKET

ARTICLE 8

The common market will be established as effect is given to Article 4 of the Treaty, once all the institutions of the Community have been set up and the High Authority has consulted Governments, undertakings and associations of undertakings, workers and consumers, and an overall picture of the situation in the Community has been established on the basis of the information thus obtained.

This shall be done, without prejudice to the special provisions contained in this Convention:

(a) in the case of coal, upon notification by the High Authority that the equalisation machinery provided for in Chapter 2 of Part Three of this Convention has been set up;
(b) in the case of iron ore and scrap, on the same date as for coal;
(c) in the case of steel, two months after that date.

The equalisation machinery for coal provided for in Part Three of this Convention shall be set up within six months after the High Authority takes office.

If more time should be needed, revised dates shall be fixed by the Council acting on a proposal from the High Authority.

ELIMINATION OF CUSTOMS DUTIES AND QUANTITATIVE RESTRICTIONS

ARTICLE 9

Subject to the special provisions contained in this Convention, Member States shall abolish all import and export duties or charges having equivalent effect and all quantitative restrictions on the movement of coal and steel within the Community on the dates appointed for the establishment of the common market in coal, iron ore and scrap, and the common market in steel, as provided in Article 8.

PART I—EUROPEAN COAL AND STEEL COMMUNITY

TRANSPORT

ARTICLE 10

A Committee of Experts designated by the Governments of the Member States shall be convened forthwith by the High Authority to study the arrangements to be proposed to the Governments for the carriage of coal and steel, in order to attain the objectives set out in Article 70 of the Treaty.

The negotiations required to obtain the agreement of the Governments concerning the various measures proposed shall, without prejudice to the last paragraph of Article 70, be initiated by the High Authority, as shall any necessary negotiations with third countries concerned.

The Committee of Experts shall study:

(1) measures to eliminate discriminatory practices contrary to the second paragraph of Article 70;

(2) measures to establish through international tariffs incorporating a degressive factor taking account of total distance for carriage within the Community, without prejudice to the apportionment of the receipts among the carriers concerned;

(3) examination of the rates and conditions of every kind for the carriage of coal and steel by the different modes of transport, with a view to their harmonisation on a Community-wide basis to the extent necessary to the proper functioning of the common market, taking account *inter alia* of transport costs.

The Committee of Experts shall have not more than:

—three months for its studies of the measures referred to under (1);

—two years for its studies of the measures referred to under (2) and (3).

The measures referred to under (1) shall enter into force on the date of the establishment of the common market in coal at the latest.

The measures referred to under (2) and (3) shall enter into force simultaneously as soon as the Governments are agreed. If, however, two and a half years after the High Authority is set up the Governments of Member States are still not agreed concerning the measures referred to under (3), the measures referred to under (2) shall enter into force separately on a date to be determined by the High Authority. In that case the High Authority shall, on a proposal from the Committee of Experts, make such recommendations as it considers necessary to avoid any serious disturbances in the transport sector.

The rates and conditions referred to in the fourth paragraph of Article 70 which are in force when the High Authority is set up shall be notified to the High Authority, which shall allow such time for their modification as may be necessary to avoid any serious economic disturbance.

The Committee of Experts shall work out and propose to the Governments concerned the derogations which they will authorise the Luxembourg Government to make from the measures and principles set out above so as to take account of the special position of Luxembourg Railways.

The Governments concerned shall, after consulting the Committee of Experts, authorise the Luxembourg Government, in so far as the special position of Luxembourg Railways makes it necessary, to continue after the transitional period to operate the arrangements adopted.

Until such time as agreement is reached among the Governments concerned on the measures referred to in the preceding paragraphs, the Luxembourg Government shall be authorised not to give effect to the principles set out in Article 70 of the Treaty and in this Article.

SUBSIDIES, DIRECT OR INDIRECT AIDS, SPECIAL CHARGES

ARTICLE 11

The Governments of the Member States shall notify the High Authority upon its taking office of all aids and subsidies to or special charges on the coal and steel industries in their respective countries. Unless the High Authority agrees to the continuance of such aids, subsidies or special charges and to the terms on which they are to be continued, they shall be withdrawn, when and in the manner which the High Authority shall determine after consulting the Council, though it shall not be mandatory to withdraw them until the opening date of the transitional period for the products in question.

RESTRICTIVE AGREEMENTS AND ARRANGEMENTS

ARTICLE 12

All information concerning agreements or arrangements coming under Article 65 shall be communicated to the High Authority as provided in Article 65 (3).

Where the High Authority does not grant authorisation under Article 65 (2), it shall set reasonable time limits after which the prohibitions contained in this Article shall apply.

To facilitate the winding-up of arrangements prohibited by Article 65, the High Authority may appoint liquidators, who shall be responsible to it and shall act under its instructions.

With the assistance of these liquidators, the High Authority shall study the problems involved and the means to be employed:

—to ensure the most economic distribution and use of the products, and particularly of the different grades and qualities of coal;

—in the event of a fall in demand, to avoid any cutback in production capacity, and particularly in colliery capacity, which is needed to keep the common market supplied in times of normal or high demand;

—to avoid inequitable distribution among workers of any reductions in employment arising out of a fall in demand.

On the basis of these studies the High Authority shall, in accordance with the tasks assigned to it, establish such procedures or bodies to which it is authorised to have recourse under the Treaty as it considers appropriate for the purpose of solving the problems through the exercise of its powers, in particular under Articles 53, 57 and 58, and Chapter V of Title III; recourse to these procedures or bodies need not be confined to the transitional period.

ARTICLE 13

The provisions of Article 65 (5) shall apply from the entry into force of the Treaty. They may also be applied to transactions bringing about concentrations effected between the signature and the entry into force of the Treaty if the High Authority can show that they were effected in order to evade the application of Article 66.

Until the regulations provided for in paragraph 1 of Article 66 have been made, transactions of the kind referred to in that paragraph shall not automatically require prior authorisation. The High Authority shall not be obliged to rule immediately on applications for authorisation submitted to it.

Until the regulations provided for in paragraph 4 of Article 66 have been made, the information referred to in that paragraph may be required only from undertakings within the jurisdiction of the High Authority in accordance with the provisions of Article 47.

The regulations provided for in Article 66 (1) and (4) shall be made within four months after the High Authority takes office.

The High Authority shall obtain from Governments, from associations of producers and from undertakings all information relevant to the application of Article 66 (2) and (7) concerning the situation in the different areas of the Community.

The provisions of Article 66 (6) shall apply from the entry into force of the provisions in the case of which legal sanctions are provided for non-compliance.

The provisions of Article 66 (7) shall apply from the date of the establishment of the common market as provided in Article 8 of this Convention.

Part Two

RELATIONS BETWEEN THE COMMUNITY AND THIRD COUNTRIES

CHAPTER 1—NEGOTIATIONS WITH THIRD COUNTRIES

ARTICLE 14

Once the High Authority has taken office, Member States shall open negotiations with the Governments of third countries, and in particular with the British Government, on the whole range of economic and commercial relations concerning coal and steel between the Community and these countries. In these negotiations the High Authority shall act, upon instructions unanimously agreed by the Council, for the Member States jointly. Representatives of Member States may be present at the negotiations.

ARTICLE 15

In order to leave Member States entirely free to negotiate concessions from third countries, including in particular concessions in return for a lowering of customs duties on steel so as to harmonise with the least protective tariffs in the Community, Member States agree to the following arrangements, to take effect upon the establishment of the common market in steel:

The Benelux countries shall continue to charge on products which are imported from third countries under tariff quotas and are bound for their own home markets the duties which they are charging at the date of entry into force of the Treaty.

On imports in excess of the quota which are deemed to be bound for other community countries, they shall charge duties equal to the lowest duty being applied in the other Member States, by reference to the Brussels Nomenclature of 1950, at the date of entry into force of the Treaty.

The tariff quota for each heading of the Benelux customs tariff shall be fixed by the Governments of the Benelux countries, in agreement with the High Authority, for a year at a time subject to quarterly revision, taking into account·movements in demand and in trade flows. The initial quotas shall be fixed on the basis of the average imports of the Benelux countries from third countries over an appropriate reference period, account being taken where necessary of any intended change from importation to home production as newly installed capacity comes into service. Any imports in excess of the quota in response to unforeseen demand shall be notified forthwith to the High Authority, which, should it find that shipments from the Benelux countries to other Member States show a substantial increase accounted for entirely by the importation of tonnages in excess of the quota, may prohibit such importation unless temporary controls are imposed on these shipments. Benelux importers shall be entitled to pay the lowest rate of duty only if they undertake not to re-export the products in question to other Community countries.

The undertaking by the Benelux countries to operate a tariff quota shall cease to apply as provided in the agreement concluding the negotiations with Great Britain, and at latest at the end of the transitional period.

If the High Authority finds, at the end of the transitional period or on the abolition of the tariff quota in advance of that date, that one or more Member States are justified in charging on imports from third countries customs duties above the rates which would be chargeable if harmonised with the least protective tariffs in the Community, it shall, as provided in Article 29, authorise these States to take appropriate steps of their own to afford their indirect imports through Member States with lower tariffs the same degree of protection as that afforded by their own tariffs to their direct imports.

To facilitate the harmonisation of the tariffs, the Benelux countries agree, where the High Authority in consultation with their Governments finds it necessary, to raise their present duties on steel by up to two points. They shall not be bound to do so until the tariff quotas provided for in the second, third and fourth paragraphs of this Article have been abolished and until one or more of the Member States bordering on the Benelux countries forgo the corresponding arrangements provided for in the preceding paragraph.

ARTICLE 16

Save with the agreement of the High Authority, the undertaking given under Article 72 of the Treaty shall debar Member States from binding by international agreements the customs duties in force at the date of entry into force of the Treaty.

Earlier bindings under bilateral or multilateral agreements shall be notified to the High Authority, which shall examine whether their retention is compatible with the proper functioning of the common arrangements and may if necessary make to Member State the appropriate recommendations for terminating the bindings by the procedure provided in the agreements containing them.

ARTICLE 17

Trade agreements which still have more than one year to run at the date of entry into force of the Treaty, or which contain a clause for tacit extension, shall be notified to the High Authority, which may make to the Member State concerned appropriate recommendations for bringing the provisions of these agreements into line where necessary with Article 75 under the procedure provided in these agreements.

CHAPTER 2—EXPORTS

ARTICLE 18

Until such time as the provisions of the exchange control regulations of the various Member States concerning foreign currency left at the disposal of exporters have been made uniform, special measures must be taken to ensure that the elimination of customs duties and quantitative restrictions between Member States does not have the effect of depriving some of them of the foreign currency which is earned when their undertakings export to a third country.

In application of this principle, the Member States undertake not to give exporters of coal or steel, under the regulations referred to above, greater advantages in the use of foreign currency than those accorded under the regulations of the Member State in which the products originate.

The High Authority is empowered to see to it that this is done by making recommendations to Governments after consulting the Council.

ARTICLE 19

If the High Authority finds that the establishing of the common market, by causing a change from direct exporting to re-exporting, is leading to a shift in the pattern of trade with third countries which causes substantial injury to one of the Member States, it may, at the request of the Government concerned, require producers in that State to insert a destination clause in their sales contracts.

CHAPTER 3—
EXCEPTIONS FROM MOST-FAVOURED-NATION TREATMENT

ARTICLE 20

1. As regards the countries entitled to most-favoured-nation treatment under Article 1 of the General Agreement on Tariffs and Trade, Member States shall jointly approach the Contracting Parties to the Agreement to arrange that the provisions of that Article shall not be a bar to the application of the provisions of the Treaty. If necessary, a special session of the GATT shall be requested for this purpose.

2. As regards countries not parties to the General Agreement on Tariffs and Trade but entitled nevertheless to most-favoured-nation treatment under bilateral agreements in force, negotiations shall be opened once the Treaty has been signed. Should the countries concerned not consent, the agreements shall be amended or denounced as provided therein.

If any country refuses its consent to Member States or to any one of them, the other Member States undertake to give each other effective assistance, which may extend to the denunciation by all Member States of agreements with the country in question.

CHAPTER 4—LIBERALISATION OF TRADE

ARTICLE 21

The member States of the Community recognise that they constitute a special customs system such as is referred to in Article 5 of the Code of Liberalisation of Trade of the Organisation for European Economic Co-operation as in force on the date of the signature of the Treaty. They therefore agree to notify the Organisation accordingly in due course.

CHAPTER 5—SPECIAL PROVISION

ARTICLE 22

Notwithstanding the expiry of the transitional period, trade in coal and steel between the Federal Republic of Germany and the Soviet Zone of Occupation shall be regulated, as far as the Federal Republic is concerned, by the Federal Government in agreement with the High Authority.

Part Three

GENERAL SAFEGUARDS

CHAPTER 1—GENERAL PROVISIONS

READAPTATION

ARTICLE 23

1. If in consequence of the establishment of the common market some undertakings or parts of undertakings should be compelled to discontinue or alter their activities during the transitional period defined in Article 1 of this Convention, the High Authority shall, on application by the

Governments concerned, assist as provided below in ensuring that the workers do not have to bear the brunt of the readaptation and in affording them productive employment, and may provide non-repayable aid to some undertakings.

2. On application by the Governments concerned, the High Authority shall take part, as provided in Article 46, in studying the possibilities for re-employing redundant workers in existing undertakings or through the creation of new activities.

3. The High Authority shall facilitate, in the manner laid down in Article 54, the financing of programmes submitted by the Governments concerned and approved by itself for the conversion of undertakings or for the creation, either in the industries within its jurisdiction or, with the assent of the Council, in any other industry, of new and economically sound activities capable of reabsorbing the redundant workers into productive employment. Subject to the approval of the Government concerned, the High Authority shall give preference to programmes submitted by undertakings which have to close as a result of the establishment of the common market.

4. The High Authority shall provide non-repayable aid towards:

    (a) the payment of tideover allowances to workers, where undertakings are closing altogether or in part;

    (b) the payment of allowances to undertakings to enable them to continue paying such of their workers as may have to be temporarily laid off as a result of the undertakings' change of activity;

    (c) the payment of resettlement allowances to workers;

    (d) the financing of vocational retraining for workers having to change their employment.

5. The High Authority may also provide non-repayable aid to undertakings which have to close as a result of the establishment of the common market, provided that this state of affairs is directly and solely due to the fact that the common market is confined to the coal and steel sectors, and is leading to a relative increase in the production of other Community undertakings. The aid shall be limited to the amount required to enable the undertakings to meet their immediate liabilities.

The undertakings concerned must make all applications for aid through their Governments. The High Authority may decline to provide any aid to an undertaking which has not informed its Government and the High Authority that a situation was developing which might lead it to close or change its activity.

6. The High Authority shall make the provision of non-repayable aid under paragraphs 4 and 5 conditional upon payment by the State concerned of a special contribution at least equal in amount, unless an exception is authorised by the Council, acting by a two-thirds majority.

7. The financing arrangements laid down for the application of Article 56 shall apply to this Article.

8. Assistance under this Article may be provided during the two years following the end of the transitional period by decision of the High Authority with the assent of the Council.

CHAPTER 2—SPECIAL PROVISIONS FOR COAL

ARTICLE 24

It is agreed that, during the transitional period, safeguards will be necessary to avoid sudden and harmful shifts in production levels. The safeguards shall take account of the position as it is when the common market is established.

Furthermore, if it should become apparent that in one or more areas some price increases are liable to be so sudden and of such extent as to be harmful, precautions will have to be taken to ensure that they do not occur.

To deal with these problems, the High Authority shall, to the necessary extent, authorise during the transitional period, under its supervision:

    (a) practices referred to in Article 60 (2) (b) and zone prices in cases not covered by Chapter V of Title III;

    (b) the retention or institution of national equalisation schemes or arrangements financed by a levy on home production, without prejudice to the exceptional expedients provided for below.

ARTICLE 25

The High Authority shall impose an equalisation levy per saleable metric ton, fixed at a uniform percentage of producers' receipt, on the coal production of those countries whose average costs are below the weighted average of the Community.

The ceiling of the equalisation levy shall be 1·5 per cent. of these receipts for the first year that the common market is operating and shall be regularly lowered each year by 20 per cent. of the initial ceiling.

Taking into account needs recognised by it, in accordance with Articles 26 and 27 below and excluding any special charges in connection with exports to third countries, the High Authority shall periodically determine the amount of the levy to be actually charged and of the Government subsidies related to it in accordance with the following rules:

(1) Within the ceiling defined above, it shall calculate the amount to be actually levied in such a way that the Government subsidies to be actually paid shall be at least equal to that amount;

(2) It shall fix the maximum permitted amount of the Government subsidies, on the understanding that:
   —the Governments may, but need not, grant subsidies up to that amount;
   —aid received from outside may in no circumstances exceed the amount of the subsidy actually paid.

Extra charges in connection with exports to third countries shall be allowed for neither in calculating the equalisation payments required nor in assessing the offsetting subsidies.

BELGIUM

ARTICLE 26

1. It is agreed that net Belgian coal production:
   —need not be reduced each year by more than 3 per cent. as compared with the level of the preceding year if total Community production is the same or is above the level of the preceding year; or
   —if total Community production is below the level of the preceding year, need not be lower than the figure obtained by applying to the level of Belgian production in the preceding year less 3 per cent. the same coefficient of decrease as that in total Community production.[1]

The High Authority, as the body responsible for ensuring that the Community is kept regularly supplied, shall make an assessment of the long-term production and sales prospects and, after consulting the Consultative Committee and the Council, shall make to the Belgian Government, for as long as the Belgian market is insulated under paragraph 3 of this Article, a recommendation as to the shifts in production levels which it finds possible on the basis of this assessment. The Belgian Government shall decide, in agreement with the High Authority, what arrangements are to be made to cause these possible shifts to come about within the limits defined above.

2. The equalisation arrangements shall be designed, from the beginning of the transitional period:

(a) to enable all consumers of Belgian coal within the common market to be charged prices more nearly in line with the ruling common market prices, reducing Belgian prices to the approximate figure of the estimated production costs at the end of the transitional period. The price list so fixed shall not be changed without the agreement of the High Authority;

(b) to ensure that the Belgian steel industry is not prevented by the special arrangements for Belgian coal from being integrated into the common market in steel and reducing its prices accordingly to the level ruling in that market.
   The High Authority shall periodically fix the amount of such additional equalisation payments in respect of Belgian coal sold to the Belgian steel industry as it considers necessary for this purpose in view of all the operational factors involved for that industry, taking care, however, that these equalisation payments do not bear unfairly on the steel industries of the neighbouring countries. Also, having regard to the price of the coke used by the Belgian steel industry to below the delivered price it could obtain if supplied with coke from the Ruhr;

(c) to allow, in respect of exports of Belgian coal within the common market considered by the High Authority to be necessary in view of the production and demand prospects in the Community, additional equalisation payments to cover 80 per cent. of the difference which the High Authority finds to exist between the pithead price plus carriage to destination of Belgian coal and of coal from other Community countries.

3. The Belgian Government may, by way of derogation from the provisions of Article 9 of this Convention, retain or institute, under the supervision of the High Authority, machinery for insulating the Belgian market from the common market.

Imports of coal from third countries shall require the approval of the High Authority.
These special arrangements shall end as provided below.

4. The Belgian Government undertakes to remove the machinery for insulating the Belgian market under paragraph 3 of this Article by the end of the transitional period at the latest. If the High Authority considers it necessary by reason of exceptional circumstances not now foreseeable, it may, after consulting the Consultative Committee and with the assent of the Council, allow the Belgian Government an additional year which may be extended by a further year.

The integration thus provided for shall take place after consultation between the Belgian Government and the High Authority, which shall both determine the ways and means therefor; these may include allowing the Belgian Government, notwithstanding Article 4 (c) of the Treaty, to grant subsidies covering the extra operating costs due to the natural conditions of the coalfields, taking into account any charges due to manifest disequilibria which add to these costs. The procedure for granting of subsidies and their maximum amount shall require the approval of the High Authority, which shall see to it that the maximum amount of subsidies and the tonnage subsidised are lowered as quickly as possible, taking into account the facilities for readaptation and the extension of the common market to products other than coal and steel, and ensuring that the scale of such production cutbacks as may be made does not give rise to fundamental disturbances in the Belgian economy.

The High Authority shall every two years submit to the Council for approval proposals as to the tonnage which may be subsidised.

ITALY

ARTICLE 27

1. The Sulcis mines shall be entitled to equalisation payments under Article 25 to enable them to meet competition in the common market pending completion of the plant installation operations now in progress; the High Authority shall periodically determine the amount of aid required, but outside aid may not be continued for more than two years.

2. In view of the special position of the Italian coking plants, the High Authority is empowered to authorise the Italian Government to continue, to the necessary extent during the transitional period defined in Article 1 of this Convention, to charge customs duties on coke from other Member States; however, in the first year of the transitional period these may not exceed the rates of duty under Presidential Decree No. 442 of 7 July 1950, this ceiling being reduced by 10 per cent. in the second year, 25 per cent. in the third, 45 per cent. in the fourth and 70 per cent. in the fifth, and the duties being abolished altogether at the end of the transitional period.

FRANCE

ARTICLE 28

1. It is agreed that coal production in the French mines:
   —need not be reduced each year by more than one million metric tons as compared with the level of the preceding year if total Community production is the same or is above the level of the preceding year; or
   —if total Community production is below the level of the preceding year, need not be lower than the figure obtained by applying to the level of French production in the preceding year less one million metric tons the same coefficient of decrease as that in total Community production.

2. To ensure that shifts in production levels are kept within these limits, the arrangements referred to in Article 24 of this Convention may be supplemented by the exceptional expedient of a special levy imposed by the High Authority on increases in the net deliveries from other collieries as shown in French customs statistics, to the extent that these increases represent shifts in production levels.

Accordingly, the levy shall be chargeable on the amounts by which net deliveries in each period exceed those in 1950, up to the amount of the decrease in the coal production of French mines since 1950 or, if total Community production is also down, to the figure obtained by applying to that amount the same coefficient of decrease as that in total Community production. The special levy shall be fixed at a maximum of 10 per cent. of the producers' receipts on the amounts in question and shall be used, in agreement with the High Authority, to reduce, in the appropriate zones, the price for certain coals produced by the French mines.

CHAPTER 3—SPECIAL PROVISIONS FOR THE STEEL INDUSTRY

ARTICLE 29

1. It is agreed that, during the transitional period, special safeguards may be necessary in the case of the steel industry to ensure that shifts in production levels due to the establishment of the common market neither create difficulties for undertakings which would be in a position to meet competition following the adaptation provided for in Article 1 of this Convention, nor lead to more redundancies than can benefit under Article 23. Where the High Authority finds that the provisions of the Treaty, and in particular Articles 57, 58, 59 and 60 (2) (*b*), cannot be applied, it is empowered, in the following order of preference:

(*a*) after consulting the Consultative Committee and the Council, to limit by direct or indirect means the net increase in deliveries from one area to another within the common market;

(*b*) after consulting the Consultative Committee and with the assent of the Council both as to the advisability and the details of the proposed action, to use the powers of intervention provided in Article 61 (*b*), but, by way of derogation from that Article, without the requirement that a manifest crisis should exist or be imminent;

(*c*) after consulting the Consultative Committee and with the assent of the Council, to establish a system of production quotas, which shall not, however, affect production for export;

(*d*) after consulting the Consultative Committee and with the assent of the Council, to authorise a Member State to take the steps referred to in the sixth paragraph of Article 15 of this Convention, in the manner provided therein.

2. For the purpose of applying these provisions, the High Authority shall during the preparatory period defined in Article 1 of this Convention, in consultation with associations of producers, the Consultative Committee and the Council, fix the technical details for the application of the safeguard arrangements.

3. If during part of the transitional period, either because of a shortage, or because the funds earned by undertakings or placed at their disposal are insufficient, or because of exceptional circumstances not now foreseeable, it has not been possible to effect the necessary adaptation of or alterations in production conditions, the provisions of this Article may, after the Consultative Committee has been consulted and the assent of the Council obtained, be applied after the end of the transitional period for as long as, but no longer than, this state of affairs continues, up to a maximum of two years.

ITALY

ARTICLE 30

1. In view of the special position of the Italian steel industry, the High Authority is empowered to authorise the Italian Government to continue, to the necessary extent during the transitional period defined in Article 1 of this Convention, to charge customs duties on steel products from other Member States; however, in the first year of the transitional period these may not exceed the rates of duty under the Annecy Convention of 10 October 1949, this ceiling being reduced by 10 per cent. in the second year, 25 per cent. in the third, 45 per cent. in the fourth and 70 per cent. in the fifth, and the duties being abolished altogether at the end of the transitional period.

2. The prices charged by undertakings for sales of steel on the Italian market, when reduced to their equivalents at the point chosen for their price lists, may not be lower than the prices shown in the lists in question for comparable transactions, save where authorised by the High Authority in agreement with the Italian Government, without prejudice to the last subparagraph of Article 60 (2) (*b*).

LUXEMBOURG

ARTICLE 31

In the operation of the safeguards provided for in Article 29 of this Convention, the High Authority shall take account of the exceptional importance of the steel industry to the general economy of Luxembourg and the need to avoid serious disturbances in the marketing of Luxembourg steel, given the special conditions under which this is effected by reason of the Belgo-Luxembourg Economic Union.

Failing other action, the High Authority may if necessary draw on the funds at its disposal under Article 49 of the Treaty up to the amount needed to deal with any repercussions on the Luxembourg steel industry of the arrangements provided for in Article 26 of this Convention.

Done at Paris this eighteenth day of April in the year one thousand nine hundred and fifty-one.

ADENAUER

Paul VAN ZEELAND
J. MEURICE

SCHUMAN

SFORZA

JOS. BECH

STIKKER
VAN DEN BRINK

Part II

EUROPEAN ECONOMIC COMMUNITY

TREATY

ESTABLISHING

THE EUROPEAN ECONOMIC COMMUNITY

(Rome, 25 March 1957)

HIS MAJESTY THE KING OF THE BELGIANS, THE PRESIDENT OF THE FEDERAL REPUBLIC OF GERMANY, THE PRESIDENT OF THE FRENCH REPUBLIC, THE PRESIDENT OF THE ITALIAN REPUBLIC, HER ROYAL HIGHNESS THE GRAND DUCHESS OF LUXEMBOURG, HER MAJESTY THE QUEEN OF THE NETHER-LANDS,

DETERMINED to lay the foundations of an ever closer union among the peoples of Europe,

RESOLVED to ensure the economic and social progress of their countries by common action to eliminate the barriers which divide Europe,

AFFIRMING as the essential objective of their efforts the constant improvement of the living and working conditions of their peoples,

RECOGNISING that the removal of existing obstacles calls for concerted action in order to guarantee steady expansion, balanced trade and fair competition,

ANXIOUS to strengthen the unity of their economies and to ensure their harmonious development by reducing the differences existing between the various regions and the backwardness of the less favoured regions,

DESIRING to contribute, by means of a common commercial policy, to the progressive abolition of restrictions on international trade,

INTENDING to confirm the solidarity which binds Europe and the over-seas countries and desiring to ensure the development of their prosperity, in accordance with the principles of the Charter of the United Nations,

RESOLVED by thus pooling their resources to preserve and strengthen peace and liberty, and calling upon the other peoples of Europe who share their ideal to join in their efforts,

HAVE DECIDED to create a European Economic Community and to this end have designated as their Plenipotentiaries:

HIS MAJESTY THE KING OF THE BELGIANS:

Mr. Paul-Henri SPAAK, Minister for Foreign Affairs,

Baron J. Ch. SNOY et d'OPPUERS, Secretary-General of the Ministry of Economic Affairs, Head of the Belgian Delegation to the Intergovernmental Conference;

THE PRESIDENT OF THE FEDERAL REPUBLIC OF GERMANY:

Dr. Konrad ADENAUER, Federal Chancellor,

Professor Dr. Walter HALLSTEIN, State Secretary of the Federal Foreign Office;

THE PRESIDENT OF THE FRENCH REPUBLIC
  Mr. Christian PINEAU, Minister for Foreign Affairs,
  Mr. Maurice FAURE, Under-Secretary of State for Foreign Affairs;

THE PRESIDENT OF THE ITALIAN REPUBLIC:
  Mr. Antonio SEGNI, President of the Council of Ministers,
  Professor Gaetano MARTINO, Minister for Foreign Affairs;

HER ROYAL HIGHNESS THE GRAND DUCHESS OF LUXEM-
BOURG:
  Mr. Joseph BECH, President of the Government, Minister for Foreign
  Affairs,
  Mr. Lambert SCHAUS, Ambassador, Head of the Luxembourg Delegation
  to the Intergovernmental Conference;

HER MAJESTY THE QUEEN OF THE NETHERLANDS:
  Mr. Joseph LUNS, Minister for Foreign Affairs,
  Mr. J. LINTHORST HOMAN, Head of the Netherlands Delegation to the
  Intergovernmental Conference;
  WHO, having exchanged their Full Powers, found in good and due form,
HAVE AGREED as follows:

Part One

PRINCIPLES

Article 1

By this Treaty, the High Contracting Parties establish among themselves a
EUROPEAN ECONOMIC COMMUNITY.

Article 2

The Community shall have as its task, by establishing a common market
and progressively approximating the economic policies of Member States, to
promote throughout the Community a harmonious development of economic
activities, a continuous and balanced expansion, an increase in stability, an
accelerated raising of the standard of living and closer relations between the
States belonging to it.

Article 3

For the purposes set out in Article 2, the activities of the Community shall
include, as provided in this Treaty and in accordance with the timetable set out
therein:
  (a) the elimination, as between Member States, of customs duties and
      of quantitative restrictions on the import and export of goods, and
      of all other measures having equivalent effect;
  (b) the establishment of a common customs tariff and of a common
      commercial policy towards third countries;
  (c) the abolition, as between Member States, of obstacles to freedom of
      movement for persons, services and capital;

(*d*) the adoption of a common policy in the sphere of agriculture;

(*e*) the adoption of a common policy in the sphere of transport;

(*f*) the institution of a system ensuring that competition in the common market is not distorted;

(*g*) the application of procedures by which the economic policies of Member States can be coordinated and disequilibria in their balances of payments remedied;

(*h*) the approximation of the laws of Member States to the extent required for the proper functioning of the common market;

(*i*) the creation of a European Social Fund in order to improve employment opportunities for workers and to contribute to the raising of their standard of living;

(*j*) the establishment of a European Investment Bank to facilitate the economic expansion of the Community by opening up fresh resources;

(*k*) the association of the overseas countries and territories in order to increase trade and to promote jointly economic and social development.

Article 4

1. The tasks entrusted to the Community shall be carried out by the following institutions:

an ASSEMBLY
a COUNCIL,
a COMMISSION,
a COURT OF JUSTICE.

Each institution shall act within the limits of the powers conferred upon it by this Treaty.

2. The Council and the Commission shall be assisted by an Economic and Social Committee acting in an advisory capacity.

[3. The audit shall be carried out by a Court of Auditors acting within the limits of the powers conferred upon it by this Treaty.]

Amendment
Paragraph (3) was added by the second Budgetary Treaty of July 22, 1975, Article 11.

Article 5

Member States shall take all appropriate measures; whether general or particular, to ensure fulfilment of the obligations arising out of this Treaty or resulting from action taken by the institutions of the Community. They shall facilitate the achievement of the Community's tasks.

They shall abstain from any measure which could jeopardise the attainment of the objectives of this Treaty.

Article 6

1. Member States shall, in close cooperation with the institutions of the Community, coordinate their respective economic policies to the extent necessary to attain the objectives of this Treaty.

2. The institutions of the Community shall take care not to prejudice the internal and external financial stability of the Member States.

ARTICLE 7

Within the scope of application of this Treaty, and without prejudice to any special provisions contained therein; any discrimination on grounds of nationality shall be prohibited.

The Council may, on a proposal from the Commission and after consulting the Assembly, adopt, by a qualified majority, rules designed to prohibit such discrimination.

ARTICLE 8

1. The common market shall be progressively established during a transitional period of twelve years.

This transitional period shall be divided into three stages of four years each; the length of each stage may be altered in accordance with the provisions set out below.

2. To each stage there shall be assigned a set of actions to be initiated and carried through concurrently.

3. Transition from the first to the second stage shall be conditional upon a finding that the objectives specifically laid down in this Treaty for the first stage have in fact been attained in substance and that, subject to the exceptions and procedures provided for in this Treaty the obligations have been fulfilled.

This finding shall be made at the end of the fourth year by the Council, acting unanimously on a report from the Commission. A Member State may not, however, prevent unanimity by relying upon the non-fulfilment of its own obligations. Failing unanimity, the first stage shall automatically be extended for one year.

At the end of the fifth year, the Council shall make its finding under the same conditions. Failing unanimity, the first stage shall automatically be extended for a further year.

At the end of the sixth year, the Council shall make its finding, acting by a qualified majority on a report from the Commission.

4. Within one month of the last-mentioned vote any Member State which voted with the minority or, if the required majority was not obtained, any Member State shall be entitled to call upon the Council to appoint an arbitration board whose decision shall be binding upon all Member States and upon the institutions of the Community. The arbitration board shall consist of three members appointed by the Council acting unanimously on a proposal from the Commission.

If the Council has not appointed the members of the arbitration board within one month of being called upon to do so, they shall be appointed by the Court of Justice within a further period of one month.

The arbitration board shall elect its own Chairman.

The board shall make its award within six months of the date of the Council vote referred to in the last subparagraph of paragraph 3.

5. The second and third stages may not be extended or curtailed except by a decision of the Council, acting unanimously on a proposal from the Commission.

6. Nothing in the preceding paragraphs shall cause the transitional period to last more than fifteen years after the entry into force of this Treaty.

7. Save for the exceptions or derogations provided for in this Treaty, the expiry of the transitional period shall constitute the latest date by which all the rules laid down must enter into force and all the measures required for establishing the common market must be implemented.

Part Two

FOUNDATIONS OF THE COMMUNITY

TITLE I—FREE MOVEMENT OF GOODS

Article 9

1. The Community shall be based upon a customs union which shall cover all trade in goods and which shall involve the prohibition between Member States of customs duties on imports and exports and of all charges having equivalent effect, and the adoption of a common customs tariff in their relations with third countries.

2. The provisions of Chapter 1, Section 1, and of Chapter 2 of this Title shall apply to products originating in Member States and to products coming from third countries which are in free circulation in Member States.

Article 10

1. Products coming from a third country shall be considered to be in free circulation in a Member State if the import formalities have been complied with and any customs duties or charges having equivalent effect which are payable have been levied in that Member State, and if they have not benefited from a total or partial drawback of such duties or charges.

2. The Commission shall, before the end of the first year after the entry into force of this Treaty, determine the methods of administrative cooperation to be adopted for the purpose of applying Article 9 (2), taking into account the need to reduce as much as possible formalities imposed on trade.

Before the end of the first year after the entry into force of this Treaty, the Commission shall lay down the provisions applicable, as regards trade between Member States, to goods originating in another Member State in whose manufacture products have been used on which the exporting Member State has not levied the appropriate customs duties or charges having equivalent effect, or which have benefited from a total or partial drawback of such duties or charges.

In adopting these provisions, the Commission shall take into account the rules for the elimination of customs duties within the Community and for the progressive application of the common customs tariff.

Article 11

Member States shall take all appropriate measures to enable Governments to carry out, within the periods of time laid down, the obligations with regard to customs duties which devolve upon them pursuant to this Treaty.

CHAPTER 1—THE CUSTOMS UNION

Section 1

Elimination of Customs Duties Between Member States

Article 12

Member States shall refrain from introducing between themselves any new customs duties on imports or exports or any charges having equivalent effect, and from increasing those which they already apply in their trade with each other.

ARTICLE 13

1. Customs duties on imports in force between Member States shall be progressively abolished by them during the transitional period in accordance with Articles 14 and 15.

2. Charges having an effect equivalent to customs duties on imports, in force between Member States, shall be progessively abolished by them during the transitional period. The Commission shall determine by means of directives the timetable for such abolition. It shall be guided by the rules contained in Article 14 (2) and (3) and by the directives issued by the Council pursuant to Article 14 (2).

ARTICLE 14

1. For each product, the basic duty to which the successive reductions shall be applied shall be the duty applied on 1 January 1957.

2. The timetable for the reductions shall be determined as follows:

(a) during the first stage, the first reduction shall be made one year after the date when this Treaty enters into force; the second reduction, eighteen months later; the third reduction, at the end of the fourth year after the date Treaty enters into force;

(b) during the second stage, a reduction shall be made eighteen months after that stage begins; a second reduction, eighteen months after the preceding one; a third reduction, one year later;

(c) any remaining reductions shall be made during the third stage; the Council shall, acting by a qualified majority on a proposal from the Commission, determine the timetable therefor by means of directives.

3. At the time of the first reduction, Member States shall introduce between themselves a duty on each product equal to the basic duty minus 10 per cent.

At the time of each subsequent reduction, each Member State shall reduce its customs duties as a whole in such manner as to lower by 10 per cent. its total customs receipts as defined in paragraph 4 and to reduce the duty on each product by at least 5 per cent. of the basic duty.

In the case, however, of products on which the duty is still in excess of 30 per cent., each reduction must be at least 10 per cent. of the basic duty.

4. The total customs receipts of each Member State, as referred to in paragraph 3, shall be calculated by multiplying the value of its imports from other Member States during 1956 by the basic duties.

5. Any special problems raised in applying paragraphs 1 to 4 shall be settled by directives issued by the Council acting by a qualified majority on a proposal from the Commission.

6. Member States shall report to the Commission on the Manner in which effect has been given to the preceding rules for the reduction of duties. They shall endeavour to ensure that the reduction made in the duties on each product shall amount:

—at the end of the first stage, to at least 25 per cent. of the basic duty;

—at the end of the second stage, to at least 50 per cent. of the basic duty.

If the Commission finds that there is a risk that the objectives laid down in Article 13, and the percentages laid down in this paragraph, cannot be attained, it shall make all appropriate recommendations to Member States.

7. The provisions of this Article may be amended by the Council, acting unanimously on a proposal from the Commission and after consulting the Assembly.

Article 15

1. Irrespective of the provisions of Article 14, any Member State may, in the course of the transitional period, suspend in whole or in part the collection of duties applied by it to products imported from other Member States. It shall inform the other Member States and the Commission thereof.

2. The Member States declare their readiness to reduce customs duties against the other Member States more rapidly than is provided for in Article 14 if their general economic situation and the situation of the economic sector concerned so permit.

To this end, the Commission shall make recommendations to the Member States concerned.

Article 16

Member States shall abolish between themselves customs duties on exports and charges having equivalent effect by the end of the first stage at the latest.

Article 17

1. The provisions of Articles 9 to 15 (1) shall also apply to customs duties of a fiscal nature. Such duties shall not, however, be taken into consideration for the purpose of calculating either total customs receipts or the reduction of customs duties as a whole as referred to in Article 14 (3) and (4).

Such duties shall, at each reduction, be lowered by not less than 10 per cent. of the basic duty. Member States may reduce such duties more rapidly than is provided for in Article 14.

2. Member States shall, before the end of the first year after the entry into force of this Treaty, inform the Commission of their customs duties of a fiscal nature.

3. Member States shall retain the right to substitute for these duties an internal tax which complies with the provisions of Article 95.

4. If the Commission finds that substitution for any customs duty of a fiscal nature meets with serious difficulties in a Member State, it shall authorise that State to retain the duty on condition that it shall abolish it not later than six years after the entry into force of this Treaty. Such authorisation must be applied for before the end of the first year after the entry into force of this Treaty.

Section 2

Setting up of The Common Customs Tariff

Article 18

The Member States declare their readiness to contribute to the development of international trade and the lowering of barriers to trade by entering into agreements designed, on a basis of reciprocity and mutual advantage, to reduce customs duties below the general level of which they could avail themselves as a result of the establishment of a customs union between them.

Article 19

1. Subject to the conditions and within the limits provided for hereinafter, duties in the common customs tariff shall be at the level of the arithmetical average of the duties applied in the four customs territories comprised in the Community.

2. The duties taken as the basis for calculating this average shall be those applied by Member States on 1 January 1957.

In the case of the Italian tariff, however, the duty applied shall be that without the temporary 10 per cent. reduction. Furthermore, with respect to items on which the Italian tariff contains a conventional duty, this duty shall be substituted for the duty applied as defined above, provided that it does not exceed the latter by more than 10 per cent. Where the conventional duty exceeds the duty applied as defined above by more than 10 per cent., the latter duty plus 10 per cent. shall be taken as the basis for calculating the arithmetical average.

With regard to the tariff headings in List A, the duties shown in that List shall, for the purpose of calculating the arithmetical average, be substituted for the duties applied.

3. The duties in the common customs tariff shall not exceed:
- (a) 3 per cent. for products within the tariff headings in List B;
- (b) 10 per cent. for products within the tariff headings in List C;
- (c) 15 per cent. for products within the tariff headings in List D;
- (d) 25 per cent. for products within the tariff headings in List E; where, in respect of such products, the tariff of the Benelux countries contains a duty not exceeding 3 per cent., such duty shall, for the purpose of calculating the arithmetical average, be raised to 12 per cent.

4. List F prescribes the duties applicable to the products listed therein.

5. The Lists of tariff headings referred to in this Article and in Article 20 are set out in Annex I to this Treaty.

ARTICLE 20

The duties applicable to the products in List G shall be determined by negotiation between the Member States. Each Member State may add further products to this List to a value not exceeding 2 per cent. of the total value of its imports from third countries in the course of the year 1956.

The Commission shall take all appropriate steps to ensure that such negotiations shall be undertaken before the end of the second year after the entry into force of this Treaty and be concluded before the end of the first stage.

If, for certain products, no agreement can be reached within these periods, the Council shall, on a proposal from the Commission, acting unanimously until the end of the second stage and by a qualified majority thereafter, determine the duties in the common customs tariff.

ARTICLE 21

1. Technical difficulties which may arise in applying Articles 19 and 20 shall be resolved, within two years of the entry into force of this Treaty, by directives issued by the Council acting by a qualified majority on a proposal from the Commission.

2. Before the end of the first stage, or at latest when the duties are determined, the Council shall, acting by a qualified majority on a proposal from the Commission, decide on any adjustments required in the interests of the internal consistency of the common customs tariff as a result of applying the rules set out in Articles 19 and 20, taking account in particular of the degree of processing undergone by the various goods to which the common tariff applies.

ARTICLE 22

The Commission shall, within two years of the entry into force of this Treaty, determine the extent to which the customs duties of a fiscal nature referred to in Article 17 (2) shall be taken into account in calculating the arithmetical average provided for in Article 19 (1). The Commission shall take account of any protective character which such duties may have.

Within six months of such determination, any Member State may request that the procedure provided for in Article 20 should be applied to the product in question, but in this event the percentage limit provided in that Article shall not be applicable to that State.

ARTICLE 23

1. For the purpose of the progressive introduction of the common customs tariff, Member States shall amend their tariffs applicable to third countries as follows:

 (*a*) in the case of tariff headings on which the duties applied in practice on 1 January 1957 do not differ by more than 15 per cent. in either direction from the duties in the common customs tariff, the latter duties shall be applied at the end of the fourth year after the entry into force of this Treaty;

 (*b*) in any other case, each Member State shall, as from the same date, apply a duty reducing by 30 per cent. the difference between the duty applied in practice on 1 January 1957 and the duty in the common customs tariff;

 (*c*) at the end of the second stage this difference shall again be reduced by 30 per cent.;

 (*d*) in the case of tariff headings for which the duties in the common customs tariff are not yet available at the end of the first stage, each Member State shall, within six months of the Council's action in accordance with Article 20, apply such duties as would result from application of the rules contained in this paragraph.

2. Where a Member State has been granted an authorisation under Article 17 (4), it need not, for as long as that authorisation remains valid, apply the preceding provisions to the tariff headings to which the authorisation applies. When such authorisation expires; the Member State concerned shall apply such duty as would have resulted from application of the rules contained in paragraph 1.

3. The common customs tariff shall be applied in its entirety by the end of the transitional period at the latest.

ARTICLE 24

Member States shall remain free to change their duties more rapidly than is provided for in Article 23 in order to bring them into line with the common customs tariff.

ARTICLE 25

1. If the Commission finds that the production in Member States of particular products contained in Lists B, C and D is insufficient to supply the demands of one of the Member States, and that such supply traditionally depends to a considerable extent on imports from third countries, the Council

shall, acting by a qualified majority on a proposal from the commission, grant the Member State concerned tariff quotas at a reduced rate of duty or duty free.

Such quotas may not exceed the limits beyond which the risk might arise of activities being transferred to the detriment of other Member States.

2. In the case of the products in List E, and of those in List G for which the rates of duty have been determined in accordance with the procedure provided for in the third paragraph of Article 20, the Commission shall, where a change in sources of supply or a shortage of supplies within the Community is such as to entail harmful consequences for the processing industries of a Member State, at the request of that Member State, grant it tariff quotas at a reduced rate of duty or duty free.

Such quotas may not exceed the limits beyond which the risk might arise of activities being transferred to the detriment of other Member States.

3. In the case of the products listed in Annex II to this Treaty, the Commission may authorise any Member State to suspend, in whole or in part, collection of the duties applicable or may grant such Member State tariff quotas at a reduced rate of duty or duty free, provided that no serious disturbance of the market of the products concerned results therefrom.

4. The Commission shall periodically examine tariff quotas granted pursuant to this Article.

Article 26

The Commission may authorise any Member State encountering special difficulties to postpone the lowering or raising of duties provided for in Article 23 in respect of particular headings in its tariff.

Such authorisation may only be granted for a limited period and in respect of tariff headings which, taken together, represent for such State not more than 5 per cent. of the value of its imports from third countries in the course of the latest year for which statistical data are available.

Article 27

Before the end of the first stage, Member States shall, in so far as may be necessary, take steps to approximate their provisions laid down by law, regulation or administrative action in respect of customs matters. To this end, the Commission shall make all appropriate recommendations to Member States.

Article 28

Any autonomous alteration or suspension of duties in the common customs tariff shall be decided unanimously by the Council. After the transitional period has ended, however, the Council may, acting by a qualified majority on a proposal from the Commission, decide on alterations or suspensions which shall not exceed 20 per cent. of the rate in the case of any one duty for a maximum period of six months. Such alterations or suspensions may only be extended, under the same conditions, for one further period of six months.

Article 29

In carrying out the tasks entrusted to it under this Section the Commission shall be guided by:

 (a) the need to promote trade between Member States and third countries;

(b) developments in conditions of competition within the Community in so far as they lead to an improvement in the competitive capacity of undertakings;

(c) the requirements of the Community as regards the supply of raw materials and semi-finished goods; in this connection the Commission shall take care to avoid distorting conditions of competition between Member States in respect of finished goods;

(d) the need to avoid serious disturbances in the economies of Member States and to ensure rational development of production and an expansion of consumption within the Community.

CHAPTER 2—ELIMINATION OF QUANTITATIVE RESTRICTIONS BETWEEN MEMBER STATES

ARTICLE 30

Quantitative restrictions on imports and all measures having equivalent effect shall, without prejudice to the following provisions, be prohibited between Member States.

ARTICLE 31

Member States shall refrain from introducing between themselves any new quantitative restrictions or measures having equivalent effect.

This obligation shall, however, relate only to the degree of liberalisation attained in pursuance of the decisions of the Council of the Organisation for European Economic Cooperation of 14 January 1955. Member States shall supply the Commission, not later than six months after the entry into force of this Treaty, with lists of the products liberalised by them in pursuance of these decisions. These lists shall be consolidated between Member States.

ARTICLE 32

In their trade with one another Member States shall refrain from making more restrictive the quotas and measures having equivalent effect existing at the date of the entry into force of this Treaty.

These quotas shall be abolished by the end of the transitional period at the latest. During that period, they shall be progressively abolished in accordance with the following provisions.

ARTICLE 33

1. One year after the entry into force of this Treaty, each Member State shall convert any bilateral quotas open to any other Member States into global quotas open without discrimination to all other Member States.

On the same date, Member States shall increase the aggregate of the global quotas so established in such a manner as to bring about an increase of not less than 20 per cent. in their total value as compared with the preceding year. The global quota for each product, however, shall be increased by not less than 10 per cent.

The quotas shall be increased annually in accordance with the same rules and in the same proportions in relation to the preceding year.

The fourth increase shall take place at the end of the fourth year after the entry into force of this Treaty; the fifth, one year after the beginning of the second stage.

2. Where, in the case of a product which has not been liberalised, the global quota does not amount to 3 per cent. of the national production of the State concerned, a quota equal to not less than 3 per cent. of such national production shall be introduced not later than one year after the entry into force of this Treaty. This quota shall be raised to 4 per cent. at the end of the second year, and to 5 per cent, at the end of the third. Thereafter, the Member State concerned shall increase the quota by not less than 15 per cent. annually.

Where there is no such national production, the Commission shall take a decision establishing an appropriate quota.

3. At the end of the tenth year, each quota shall be equal to not less than 20 per cent. of the national production.

4. If the Commission finds by means of a decision that during two successive years the imports of any products have been below the level of the quota opened, this global quota shall not be taken into account in calculating the total value of the global quotas. In such case, the Member State shall abolish quota restrictions on the product concerned.

5. In the case of quotas representing more than 20 per cent. of the national production of the product concerned, the Council may, acting by a qualified majority on a proposal from the Commission, reduce the minimum percentage of 10 per cent. laid down in paragraph 1. This alteration shall not, however, affect the obligation to increase the total value of global quotas by 20 per cent. annually.

6. Member States which have exceeded their obligations as regards the degree of liberalisation attained in pursuance of the decisions of the Council of the Organisation for European Economic Cooperation of 14 January 1955 shall be entitled, when calculating the annual total increase of 20 per cent. provided for in paragraph 1, to take into account the amount of imports liberalised by autonomous action. Such calculation shall be submitted to the Commission for its prior approval.

7. The Commission shall issue directives establishing the procedure and timetable in accordance with which Member States shall abolish, as between themselves, any measures in existence when this Treaty enters into force which have an effect equivalent to quotas.

8. If the Commission finds that the application of the provisions of this Article, and in particular of the provisions concerning percentages, makes it impossible to ensure that the abolition of quotas provided for in the second paragraph of Article 32 is carried out progressively, the Council may, on a proposal from the Commission, acting unanimously during the first stage and by a qualified majority thereafter, amend the procedure laid down in this Article and may, in particular, increase the percentages fixed.

ARTICLE 34

1. Quantitative restrictions on exports, and all measures having equivalent effect, shall be prohibited between Member States.

2. Member States shall, by the end of the first stage at the latest, abolish all quantitative restrictions on exports and any measures having equivalent effect which are in existence when this Treaty enters into force.

Article 35

The Member States declare their readiness to abolish quantitative restrictions on imports from and exports to other Member States more rapidly than is provided for in the preceding Articles, if their general economic situation and the situation of the economic sector concerned so permit.

To this end, the Commission shall make recommendations to the States concerned.

Article 36

The provisions of Articles 30 to 34 shall not preclude prohibitions or restrictions on imports, exports or goods in transit justified on grounds of public morality, public policy or public security; the protection of health and life of humans, animals or plants; the protection of national treasures possessing artistic, historic or archaeological value; or the protection of industrial and commercial property. Such prohibitions or restrictions shall not, however, constitute a means of arbitrary discrimination or a disguised restriction on trade between Member States.

Article 37

1. Member States shall progressively adjust any State monopolies of a commercial character so as to ensure that when the transitional period has ended no discrimination regarding the conditions under which goods are procured and marketed exists between nationals of Member States.

The provisions of this Article shall apply to any body through which a Member State, in law or in fact, either directly or indirectly supervises, determines or appreciably influences imports or exports between Member States. These provisions shall likewise apply to monopolies delegated by the State to others.

2. Member States shall refrain from introducing any new measure which is contrary to the principles laid down in paragraph 1 or which restricts the scope of the Articles dealing with the abolition of customs duties and quantitative restrictions between Member States.

3. The timetable for the measures referred to in paragraph 1 shall be harmonised with the abolition of quantitative restrictions on the same products provided for in Articles 30 to 34.

If a product is subject to a State monopoly of a commercial character in only one or some Member States, the Commission may authorise the other Member States to apply protective measures until the adjustment provided for in paragraph 1 has been effected; the Commission shall determine the conditions and details of such measures.

4. If a State monopoly of a commercial character has rules which are designed to make it easier to dispose of agricultural products or obtain for them the best return, steps should be taken in applying the rules contained in this Article to ensure equivalent safeguards for the employment and standard of living of the producers concerned, account being taken of the adjustments that will be possible and the specialisation that will be needed with the passage of time.

5. The obligations on Member States shall be binding only in so far as they are compatible with existing international agreements.

6. With effect from the first stage the Commission shall make recommendations as to the manner in which and the timetable according to which the adjustment provided for in this Article shall be carried out.

TITLE II—AGRICULTURE

ARTICLE 38

1. The common market shall extend to agriculture and trade in agricultural products. "Agricultural products" means the products of the soil, of stockfarming and of fisheries and products of first-stage processing directly related to these products.

2. Save as otherwise provided in Articles 39 to 46, rules laid down for the establishment of the common market shall apply to agricultural products.

3. The products subject to the provisions of Articles 39 to 46 are listed in Annex II to this Treaty. Within two years of the entry into force of this Treaty, however, the Council shall, acting by a qualified majority on a proposal from the Commission, decide what products are to be added to this list.

4. The operation and development of the common market for agricultural products must be accompanied by the establishment of a common agricultural policy among the Member States.

ARTICLE 39

1. The objectives of the common agricultural policy shall be:
   (a) to increase agricultural productivity by promoting technical progress and by ensuring the rational development of agricultural production and the optimum utilisation of the factors of production, in particular labour;
   (b) thus to ensure a fair standard of living for the agricultural community, in particular by increasing the individual earnings of persons engaged in agriculture;
   (c) to stabilise markets;
   (d) to assure the availability of supplies;
   (e) to ensure that supplies reach consumers at reasonable prices.

2. In working out the common agricultural policy and the special methods for its application, account shall be taken of:
   (a) the particular nature of agricultural activity, which results from the social structure of agriculture and from structural and natural disparities between the various agricultural regions;
   (b) the need to effect the appropriate adjustments by degrees;
   (c) the fact that in the Member States agriculture constitutes a sector closely linked with the economy as a whole.

ARTICLE 40

1. Member States shall develop the common agricultural policy by degrees during the transitional period and shall bring it into force by the end of that period at the latest.

2. In order to attain the objectives set out in Article 39 a common organisation of agricultural markets shall be established.

This organisation shall take one of the following forms, depending on the product concerned:
   (a) common rules on competition;
   (b) compulsory coordination of the various national market organisations;
   (c) a European market organisation.

3. The common organisation established in accordance with paragraph 2 may include all measures required to attain the objectives set out in Article 39, in particular regulation of prices, aids for the production and marketing of the various products, storage and carry-over arrangements and common machinery for stabilising imports or exports.

The common organisation shall be limited to pursuit of the objectives set out in Article 39 and shall exclude any discrimination between producers or consumers within the Community.

Any common price policy shall be based on common criteria and uniform methods of calculation.

4. In order to enable the common organisation referred to in paragraph 2 to attain its objectives, one or more agricultural guidance and guarantee funds may be set up.

Article 41

To enable the objectives set out in Article 39 to be attained, provision may be made within the framework of the common agricultural policy for measures such as:

(a) an effective coordination of efforts in the spheres of vocational training, of research and of the dissemination of agricultural knowledge; this may include joint financing of projects or institutions;

(b) joint measures to promote consumption of certain products.

Article 42

The provisions of the Chapter relating to rules on competition shall apply to production of and trade in agricultural products only to the extent determined by the Council within the framework of Article 43 (2) and (3) and in accordance with the procedure laid down therein, account being taken of the objectives set out in Article 39.

The Council may, in particular, authorise the granting of aid:

(a) for the protection of enterprises handicapped by structural or natural conditions;

(b) within the framework of economic development programmes.

Article 43

1. In order to evolve the broad lines of a common agricultural policy, the Commission shall, immediately this Treaty enters into force, convene a conference of the Member States with a view to making a comparison of their agricultural policies, in particular by producing a statement of their resources and needs.

2. Having taken into account the work of the conference provided for in paragraph 1, after consulting the Economic and Social Committee and within two years of the entry into force of this Treaty, the Commission shall submit proposals for working out and implementing the common agricultural policy, including the replacement of the national organisations by one of the forms of common organisation provided for in Article 40 (2), and for implementing the measures specified in this Title.

These proposals shall take account of the interdependence of the agricultural matters mentioned in this Title.

The Council shall, on a proposal from the Commission and after consulting the Assembly, acting unanimously during the first two stages and by a qualified majority thereafter make regulations, issue directives, or take decisions, without prejudice to any recommendations it may also make.

3. The Council may, acting by a qualified majority and in accordance with paragraph 2, replace the national market organisations by the common organisation provided for in Article 40 (2) if:

(a) the common organisation offers Member States which are opposed to this measure and which have an organisation of their own for the production in question equivalent safeguards for the employment and standard of living of the producers concerned, account being taken of the adjustments that will be possible and the specialisation that will be needed with the passage of time;

(b) such an organisation ensures conditions for trade within the Community similar to those existing in a national market.

4. If a common organisation for certain raw materials is established before a common organisation exists for the corresponding processed products, such raw materials as are used for processed products intended for export to third countries may be imported from outside the Community.

ARTICLE 44

1. In so far as progressive abolition of customs duties and quantitative restrictions between Member States may result in prices likely to jeopardise the attainment of the objectives set out in Article 39, each Member State shall during the transitional period, be entitled to apply to particular products, in a non-discriminatory manner and in substitution for quotas and to such an extent as shall not impede the expansion of the volume of trade provided for in Article 45 (2), a system of minimum prices below which imports may be either:
—temporarily suspended or reduced; or
—allowed, but subjected to the condition that they are made at a price higher than the minimum price for the product concerned.
In the latter case the minimum prices shall not include customs duties.

2. Minimum prices shall neither cause a reduction of the trade existing between Member States when this Treaty enters into force nor form an obstacle to progressive expansion of this trade. Minimum prices shall not be applied so as to form an obstacle to the development of a natural preference between Member States.

3. As soon as this Treaty enters into force the Council shall, on a proposal from the Commission, determine objective criteria for the establishment of minimum price systems and for the fixing of such prices.

These criteria shall in particular take account of the average national production costs in the Member State applying the minimum price, of the position of the various undertakings concerned in relation to such average production costs, and of the need to promote both the progressive improvement of agricultural practice and the adjustments and specialisation needed within the common market.

The Commission shall further propose a procedure for revising these criteria in order to allow for and speed up technical progress and to approximate prices progressively within the common market.

These criteria and the procedure for revising them shall be determined by the Council acting unanimously within three years of the entry into force of this Treaty.

4. Until the decision of the Council takes effect, Member States may fix minimum prices on condition that these are communicated beforehand to the Commission and to the other Member States so that they may submit their comments.

Once the Council has taken its decision, Member States shall fix minimum prices on the basis of the criteria determined as above.

The Council may, acting by a qualified majority on a proposal from the Commission, rectify any decisions taken by Member States which do not conform to the criteria defined above.

5. If it does not prove possible to determine the said objective criteria for certain products by the beginning of the third stage, the Council may, acting by a qualified majority on a proposal from the Commission, vary the minimum prices applied to these products.

6. At the end of the transitional period, a table of minimum prices still in force shall be drawn up. The Council shall, acting on a proposal from the Commission and by a majority of nine votes in accordance with the weighting laid down in the first subparagraph of Article 148 (2), determine the system to be applied within the framework of the common agricultural policy.

ARTICLE 45

1. Until national market organisations have been replaced by one of the forms of common organisation referred to in Article 40 (2), trade in products in respect of which certain Member States:

—have arrangements designed to guarantee national producers a market for their products; and

—are in need of imports,

shall be developed by the conclusion of long-term agreements or contracts between importing and exporting Member States.

These agreements or contracts shall be directed towards the progressive abolition of any discrimination in the application of these arrangements to the various producers within the Community.

Such agreements or contracts shall be concluded during the first stage; account shall be taken of the principle of reciprocity.

2. As regards quantities, these agreements or contracts shall be based on the average volume of trade between Member States in the products concerned during the three years before the entry into force of this Treaty and shall provide for an increase in the volume of trade within the limits of existing requirements, account being taken of traditional patterns of trade.

As regards prices, these agreements or contracts shall enable producers to dispose of the agreed quantities at prices which shall be progressively approximated to those paid to national producers on the domestic market of the purchasing country.

This approximation shall proceed as steadily as possible and shall be completed by the end of the transitional period at the latest.

Prices shall be negotiated between the parties concerned within the framework of directives issued by the Commission for the purpose of implementing the two preceding subparagraphs.

If the first stage is extended, these agreements or contracts shall continue to be carried out in accordance with the conditions applicable at the end of the fourth year after the entry into force of this Treaty, the obligation to increase quantities and to approximate prices being suspended until the transition to the second stage.

Member States shall avail themselves of any opportunity open to them under their legislation, particularly in respect of import policy, to ensure the conclusion and carrying out of these agreements or contracts.

3. To the extent that Member States require raw materials for the manufacture of products to be exported outside the Community in competition with products of third countries, the above agreements or contracts shall not form an obstacle to the importation of raw materials for this purpose from third countries. This provision shall not, however, apply if the Council unanimously decides to make provision for payments required to compensate for the higher price paid on goods imported for this purpose on the basis of these agreements or contracts in relation to the delivered price of the same goods purchased on the world market.

ARTICLE 46

Where in a Member State a product is subject to a national market organisation or to internal rules having equivalent effect which affect the competitive position of similar production in another Member State, a countervailing charge shall be applied by Member States to imports of this product coming from the Member State where such organisation or rules exist, unless that State applies a countervailing charge on export.

The Commission shall fix the amount of these charges at the level required to redress the balance; it may also authorise other measures, the conditions and details of which it shall determine.

ARTICLE 47

As to the functions to be performed by the Economic and Social Committee in pursuance of this Title, its agricultural section shall hold itself at the disposal of the Commission to prepare, in accordance with the provisions of Articles 197 and 198, the deliberations of the Committee.

TITLE III—FREE MOVEMENT OF PERSONS, SERVICES AND CAPITAL

CHAPTER 1—WORKERS

ARTICLE 48

1. Freedom of movement for workers shall be secured within the Community by the end of the transitional period at the latest.

2. Such freedom of movement shall entail the abolition of any discrimination based on nationality between workers of the Member States as regards employment, remuneration and other conditions of work and employment.

3. It shall entail the right, subject to limitations justified on grounds of public policy, public security or public health:

    (a) to accept offers of employment actually made;

    (b) to move freely within the territory of Member States for this purpose;

    (c) to stay in a Member State for the purpose of employment in accordance with the provisions governing the employment of nationals of that State laid down by law, regulation or administrative action;

(*d*) to remain in the territory of a Member State after having been employed in that State, subject to conditions which shall be embodied in implementing regulations to be drawn up by the Commission.

4. The provisions of this Article shall not apply to employment in the public service.

Article 49

As soon as this Treaty enters into force, the Council shall, acting on a proposal from the Commission and after consulting the Economic and Social Committee, issue directives or make regulations setting out the measures required to bring about by progressive stages, freedom of movement for workers, as defined in Article 48, in particular:

(*a*) by ensuring close cooperation between national employment services;

(*b*) by systematically and progressively abolishing those administrative procedures and practices and those qualifying periods in respect of eligibility for available employment, whether resulting from national legislation or from agreements previously concluded between Member States, the maintenance of which would form an obstacle to liberalisation of the movement of workers;

(*c*) by systematically and progressively abolishing all such qualifying periods and other restrictions provided for either under national legislation or under agreements previously concluded between Member States as imposed on workers of other Member States conditions regarding the free choice of employment other than those imposed on workers of the State concerned;

(*d*) by setting up appropriate machinery to bring offers of employment into touch with applications for employment and to facilitate the achievement of a balance between supply and demand in the employment market in such a way as to avoid serious threats to the standard of living and level of employment in the various regions and industries.

Article 50

Member States shall, within the framework of a joint programme, encourage the exchange of young workers.

Article 51

The Council shall, acting unanimously on a proposal from the Commission, adopt such measures in the field of social security as are necessary to provide freedom of movement for workers; to this end, it shall make arrangements to secure for migrant workers and their dependants:

(*a*) aggregation, for the purpose of acquiring and retaining the right to benefit and of calculating the amount of benefit, of all periods taken into account under the laws of the several countries;

(*b*) payment of benefits to persons resident in the territories of Member States.

CHAPTER 2—RIGHT OF ESTABLISHMENT

ARTICLE 52

Within the framework of the provisions set out below, restrictions on the freedom of establishment of nationals of a Member State in the territory of another Member State shall be abolished by progressive stages in the course of the transitional period. Such progressive abolition shall also apply to restrictions on the setting up of agencies, branches or subsidiaries by nationals of any Member State established in the territory of any Member State.

Freedom of establishment shall include the right to take up and pursue activities as self-employed persons and to set up and manage undertakings, in particular companies or firms within the meaning of the second paragraph of Article 58, under the conditions laid down for its own nationals by the law of the country where such establishment is effected, subject to the provisions of the Chapter relating to capital.

ARTICLE 53

Member States shall not introduce any new restrictions on the right of establishment in their territories of nationals of other Member States, save as otherwise provided in this Treaty.

ARTICLE 54

1. Before the end of the first stage, the Council shall, acting unanimously on a proposal from the Commission and after consulting the Economic and Social Committee and the Assembly, draw up a general programme for the abolition of existing restrictions on freedom of establishment within the Community. The Commission shall submit its proposal to the Council during the first two years of the first stage.

The programme shall set out the general conditions under which freedom of establishment is to be attained in the case of each type of activity and in particular the stages by which it is to be attained.

2. In order to implement this general programme or, in the absence of such programme, in order to achieve a stage in attaining freedom of establishment as regards a particular activity, the Council shall, on a proposal from the Commission and after consulting the Economic and Social Committee and the Assembly, issue directives, acting unanimously until the end of the first stage and by qualified majority thereafter.

3. The Council and the Commission shall carry out the duties devolving upon them under the preceding provisions, in particular:

(a) by according, as a general rule, priority treatment to activities where freedom of establishment makes a particularly valuable contribution to the development of production and trade;

(b) by ensuring close cooperation between the competent authorities in the Member States in order to ascertain the particular situation within the Community of the various activities concerned;

(c) by abolishing those administrative procedures and practices, whether resulting from national legislation or from agreements previously concluded between Member States, the maintenance of which would form an obstacle to freedon of establishment;

(d) by ensuring that workers of one Member State employed in the territory of another Member State may remain in that territory for the purpose of taking up activities therein as self-employed persons, where they satisfy the conditions which they would be required to satisfy if they were entering that State at the time when they intended to take up such activities;

(*e*) by enabling a national of one Member State to acquire and use land and buildings situated in the territory of another Member State, in so far as this does not conflict with the principles laid down in Article 39 (2);

(*f*) by effecting the progressive abolition of restrictions on freedom of establishment in every branch of activity under consideration, both as regards the conditions for setting up agencies, branches or subsidiaries in the territory of a Member State and as regards the conditions governing the entry of personnel belonging to the main establishment into managerial or supervisory posts in such agencies, branches or subsidiaries;

(*g*) by coordinating to the necessary extent the safeguards which, for the protection of the interests of members and others, are required by Member States of companies or firms within the meaning of the second paragraph of Article 58 with a view to making such safeguards equivalent throughout the Community;

(*h*) by satisfying themselves that the conditions of establishment are not distorted by aids granted by Member States.

Article 55

The provisions of this Chapter shall not apply, so far as any given Member State is concerned, to activities which in that State are connected, even occasionally, with the exercise of official authority.

The Council may, acting by qualified majority on a proposal from the Commission, rule that the provisions of this Chapter shall not apply to certain activities.

Article 56

1. The provisions of this Chapter and measures taken in pursuance thereof shall not prejudice the applicability of provisions laid down by law, regulation or administrative action providing for special treatment for foreign nationals on grounds of public policy, public security or public health.

2. Before the end of the transitional period, the Council shall, acting unanimously on a proposal from the Commission and after consulting the Assembly, issue directives for the coordination of the aforementioned provisions laid down by law, regulation or administrative action. After the end of the second stage, however, the Council shall, acting by a qualified majority on a proposal from the Commission, issue directives for the coordination of such provisions as, in each Member State, are a matter for regulation or administrative action.

Article 57

1. In order to make it easier for persons to take up and pursue activities as self-employed persons, the Council shall, on a proposal from the Commission and after consulting the Assembly, acting unanimously during the first stage and by a qualified majority thereafter, issue directives for the mutual recognition of diplomas, certificates and other evidence of formal qualifications.

2. For the same purpose, the Council shall, before the end of the transitional period, acting on a proposal from the Commission and after consulting the Assembly, issue directives for the coordination of the provisions laid down by law, regulation or administrative action in Member States concerning the taking up and pursuit of activities as self-employed persons. Unanimity shall be required on matters which are the subject of legislation in at least one Member State and measures concerned with the protection of savings, in particular the granting of credit and the exercise of the banking profession, and with the conditions governing the exercise of the medical and allied, and pharmaceutical professions in the various Member States. In other cases, the Council shall act unanimously during the first stage and by a qualified majority thereafter.

3. In the case of the medical and allied, and pharmaceutical professions, the progressive abolition of restrictions shall be dependent upon coordination of the conditions for their exercise in the various Member States.

Article 58

Companies or firms formed in accordance with the law of a Member State and having their registered office, central administration or principal place of business within the Community shall, for the purposes of this Chapter, be treated in the same way as natural persons who are nationals of Member States.

" Companies or firms " means companies or firms constituted under civil or commercial law, including cooperative societies, and other legal persons governed by public or private law, save for those which are non-profit-making.

CHAPTER 3—SERVICES

Article 59

Within the framework of the provisions set out below, restrictions on freedom to provide services within the Community shall be progressively abolished during the transitional period in respect of nationals of Member States who are established in a State of the Community other than that of the person for whom the services are intended.

The Council may, acting unanimously on a proposal from the Commission, extend the provisions of this Chapter to nationals of a third country who provide services and who are established within the Community.

Article 60

Services shall be considered to be " services " within the meaning of this Treaty where they are normally provided for remuneration, in so far as they are not governed by the provisions relating to freedom of movement for goods, capital and persons.

" Services " shall in particular include:
  (a) activities of an industrial character,
  (b) activities of a commercial character;
  (c) activities of craftsmen;
  (d) activities of the professions.

Without prejudice to the provisions of the Chapter relating to the right of establishment, the person providing a service may, in order to do so, temporarily pursue his activity in the State where the service is provided, under the same conditions as are imposed by that State on its own nationals.

ARTICLE 61

1. Freedom to provide services in the field of transport shall be governed by the provisions of the Title relating to transport.

2. The liberalisation of banking and insurance services connected with movements of capital shall be effected in step with the progressive liberalisation of movement of capital.

ARTICLE 62

Save as otherwise provided in this Treaty, Member States shall not introduce any new restrictions on the freedom to provide services which has in fact been attained at the date of the entry into force of this Treaty.

ARTICLE 63

1. Before the end of the first stage, the Council shall, acting unanimously on a proposal from the Commission and after consulting the Economic and Social Committee and the Assembly, draw up a general programme for the abolition of existing restrictions on freedom to provide services within the Community. The Commission shall submit its proposal to the Council during the first two years of the first stage.

The programme shall set out the general conditions under which and the stages by which each type of service is to be liberalised.

2. In order to implement this general programme or, in the absence of such programme, in order to achieve a stage in the liberalisation of a specific service, the Council shall, on a proposal from the Commission and after consulting the Economic and Social Committee and the Assembly, issue directives, acting unanimously until the end of the first stage and by a qualified majority thereafter.

3. As regards the proposals and decisions referred to in paragraphs 1 and 2, priority shall as a general rule be given to those services which directly affect production costs or the liberalisation of which helps to promote trade in goods.

ARTICLE 64

The Member States declare their readiness to undertake the liberalisation of services beyond the extent required by the directives issued pursuant to Article 63 (2), if their general economic situation and the situation of the economic sector concerned so permit.

To this end, the Commission shall make recommendations to the Member States concerned.

ARTICLE 65

As long as restrictions on freedom to provide services have not been abolished, each Member State shall apply such restrictions without distinction on grounds of nationality or residence to all persons providing services within the meaning of the first paragraph of Article 59.

ARTICLE 66

The provisions of Articles 55 to 58 shall apply to the matters covered by this Chapter.

CHAPTER 4—CAPITAL

ARTICLE 67

1. During the transitional period and to the extent necessary to ensure the proper functioning of the common market, Member States shall progressively abolish between themselves all restrictions on the movement of capital belonging to persons resident in Member States and any discrimination based on the nationality or on the place of residence of the parties or on the place where such capital is invested.

2. Current payments connected with the movement of capital between Member States shall be freed from all restrictions by the end of the first stage at the latest.

ARTICLE 68

1. Member States shall, as regards the matters dealt with in this Chapter, be as liberal as possible in granting such exchange authorisations as are still necessary after the entry into force of this Treaty.

2. Where a Member State applies to the movements of capital liberalised in accordance with the provisions of this Chapter the domestic rules governing the capital market and the credit system, it shall do so in a non-discriminatory manner.

3. Loans for the direct or indirect financing of a Member State or its regional or local authorities shall not be issued or placed in other Member States unless the States concerned have reached agreement thereon. This provision shall not preclude the application of Article 22 of the Protocol on the Statute of the European Investment Bank.

ARTICLE 69

The Council shall, on a proposal from the Commission, which for this purpose shall consult the Monetary Committee provided for in Article 105, issue the necessary directives for the progressive implementation of the provisions of Article 67, acting unanimously during the first two stages and by a qualified majority thereafter.

ARTICLE 70

1. The Commission shall propose to the Council measures for the progressive coordination of the exchange policies of Member States in respect of the movement of capital between those States and third countries. For this purpose the Council shall issue directives, acting unanimously. It shall endeavour to attain the highest possible degree of liberalisation.

2. Where the measures taken in accordance with paragraph 1 do not permit the elimination of differences between the exchange rules of Member States and where such differences could lead persons resident in one of the Member States to use the freer transfer facilities within the Community which are provided for in Article 67 in order to evade the rules of one of the Member States concerning the movement of capital to or from third countries, that State may, after consulting the other Member States and the Commission, take appropriate measures to overcome these difficulties.

Should the Council find that these measures are restricting the free movement of capital within the Community to a greater extent than is required for the purpose of overcoming the difficulties, it may, acting by a qualified majority on a proposal from the Commission, decide that the State concerned shall amend or abolish these measures.

Article 71

Member States shall endeavour to avoid introducing within the Community any new exchange restrictions on the movement of capital and current payments connected with such movements, and shall endeavour not to make existing rules more restrictive.

They declare their readiness to go beyond the degree of liberalisation of capital movements provided for in the preceding Articles in so far as their economic situation, in particular the situation of their balance of payments, so permits.

The Commission may, after consulting the Monetary Committee, make recommendations to Member States on this subject.

Article 72

Member States shall keep the Commission informed of any movements of capital to and from third countries which come to their knowledge. The Commission may deliver to Member States any opinions which it considers appropriate on this subject.

Article 73

1. If movements of capital lead to disturbances in the functioning of the capital market in any Member State, the Commission shall, after consulting the Monetary Committee, authorise that State to take protective measures in the field of capital movements, the conditions and details of which the Commission shall determine.

The Council may, acting by a qualified majority, revoke this authorisation or amend the conditions or details thereof.

2. A Member State which is in difficulties may, however, on grounds of secrecy or urgency, take the measures mentioned above, where this proves necessary, on its own initiative. The Commission and the other Member States shall be informed of such measures by the date of their entry into force at the latest. In this event the Commission may, after consulting the Monetary Committee, decide that the State concerned shall amend or abolish the measures.

TITLE IV—TRANSPORT

Article 74

The objectives of this Treaty shall, in matters governed by this Title, be pursued by Member States within the framework of a common transport policy.

Article 75

1. For the purpose of implementing Article 74, and taking into account the distinctive features of transport, the Council shall, acting unanimously until the end of the second stage and by a qualified majority thereafter, lay down, on a proposal from the Commission and after consulting the Economic and Social Committee and the Assembly:

(*a*) common rules applicable to international transport to or from the territory of a Member State or passing across the territory of one or more Member States;

(*b*) the conditions under which non-resident carriers may operate transport services within a Member State;

(*c*) any other appropriate provisions.

2. The provisions referred to in (a) and (b) of paragraph 1 shall be laid down during the transitional period.

3. By way of derogation from the procedure provided for in paragraph 1, where the application of provisions concerning the principles of the regulatory system for transport would be liable to have a serious effect on the standard of living and on employment in certain areas and on the operation of transport facilities, they shall be laid down by the Council acting unanimously. In so doing, the Council shall take into account the need for adaptation to the economic development which will result from establishing the common market.

ARTICLE 76

Until the provisions referred to in Article 75 (1) have been laid down, no Member State may, without the unanimous approval of the Council, make the various provisions governing the subject when this Treaty enters into force less favourable in their direct or indirect effect on carriers of other Member States as compared with carriers who are nationals of that State.

ARTICLE 77

Aids shall be compatible with this Treaty if they meet the needs of coordination of transport or if they represent reimbursement for the discharge of certain obligations inherent in the concept of a public service.

ARTICLE 78

Any measures taken within the framework of this Treaty in respect of transport rates and conditions shall take account of the economic circumstances of carriers.

ARTICLE 79

1. In the case of transport within the Community, discrimination which takes the form of carriers charging different rates and imposing different conditons for the carriage of the same goods over the same transport links on grounds of the country of origin or of destination of the goods in question, shall be abolished, at the latest, before the end of the second stage.

2. Paragraph 1 shall not prevent the Council from adopting other measures in pursuance of Article 75 (1).

3. Within two years of the entry into force of this Treaty, the Council shall, acting by a qualified majority on a proposal from the Commission and after consulting the Economic and Social Committee, lay down rules for implementing the provisions of paragraph1.

The Council may in particular lay down the provisions needed to enable the institutions of the Community to secure compliance with the rule laid down in paragraph 1 and to ensure that users benefit from it to the full.

4. The Commission shall, acting on its own initiative or on application by a Member State, investigate any cases of discrimination falling within paragraph

1 and, after consulting any Member State concerned, shall take the necessary decisions within the framework of the rules laid down in accordance with the provisions of paragraph 3.

ARTICLE 80

1. The imposition by a Member State, in respect of transport operations carried out within the Community, of rates and conditions involving any element of support or protection in the interest of one or more particular undertakings or industries shall be prohibited as from the beginning of the second stage, unless authorised by the Commission.

2. The Commission shall, acting on its own initiative or on application by a Member State, examine the rates and conditions referred to in paragraph 1, taking account in particular of the requirements of an appropriate regional economic policy, the needs of underdeveloped areas and the problems of areas seriously affected by political circumstances on the one hand, and of the effects of such rates and conditions on competition between the different modes of transport on the other.

After consulting each Member State concerned, the Commission shall take the necessary decisions.

3. The prohibition provided for in paragraph 1 shall not apply to tariffs fixed to meet competition.

ARTICLE 81

Charges or dues in respect of the crossing of frontiers which are charged by a carrier in addition to the transport rates shall not exceed a reasonable level after taking the costs actually incurred thereby into account.

Member States shall endeavour to reduce these costs progressively.

The Commission may make recommendations to Member States for the application of this Article.

ARTICLE 82

The provisions of this Title shall not form an obstacle to the application of measures taken in the Federal Republic of Germany to the extent that such measures are required in order to compensate for the economic disadvantages caused by the division of Germany to the economy of certain areas of the Federal Republic affected by that division.

ARTICLE 83

An Advisory Committee consisting of experts designated by the Governments of Member States, shall be attached to the Commission. The Commission, whenever it considers it desirable, shall consult the Committee on transport matters without prejudice to the powers of the transport section of the Economic and Social Committee.

ARTICLE 84

1. The provisions of this Title shall apply to transport by rail, road and inland waterway.

2. The Council may, acting unanimously, decide whether, to what extent and by what procedure appropriate provisions may be laid down for sea and air transport.

Part Three

POLICY OF THE COMMUNITY

TITLE I—COMMON RULES

CHAPTER 1—RULES ON COMPETITION

SECTION 1

RULES APPLYING TO UNDERTAKINGS

ARTICLE 85

1. The following shall be prohibited as incompatible with the common market: all agreements between undertakings, decisions by associations of undertakings and concerted practices which may affect trade between Member States and which have as their object or effect the prevention, restriction or distortion of competition within the common market, and in particular those which:

   (*a*) directly or indirectly fix purchase or selling prices for any other trading conditions;

   (*b*) limit or control production, markets, technical development, or investment;

   (*c*) share markets or sources of supply;

   (*d*) apply dissimilar conditions to equivalent transactions with other trading parties, thereby placing them at a competitive disadvantage;

   (*e*) make the conclusion of contracts subject to acceptance by the other parties of supplementary obligations which, by their nature or according to commercial usage, have no connection with the subject of such contracts.

2. Any agreements or decisions prohibited pursuant to this Article shall be automatically void.

3. The provisions of paragraph 1 may, however, be declared inapplicable in the case of:

—any agreement or category of agreements between undertakings;

—any decision or category of decisions by associations of undertakings;

—any concerted practice or category of concerted practices;

which contributes to improving the production or distribution of goods or to promoting technical or economic progress, while allowing consumers a fair share of the resulting benefit, and which does not:

   (*a*) impose on the undertakings concerned restrictions which are not indispensable to the attainment of these objectives;

   (*b*) afford such undertakings the possibility of eliminating competition in respect of a substantial part of the products in question.

ARTICLE 86

Any abuse by one or more undertakings of a dominant position within the common market or in a substantial part of it shall be prohibited as incompatible with the common market in so far as it may affect trade between Member States. Such abuse may, in particular, consist in:

(a) directly or indirectly imposing unfair purchase or selling prices or other unfair trading conditions;
(b) limiting production, markets or technical development to the prejudice of consumers;
(c) applying dissimilar conditions to equivalent transactions with other trading parties, thereby placing them at a competitive disadvantage;
(d) making the conclusion of contracts subject to acceptance by the other parties of supplementary obligations which, by their nature or according to commercial usage, have no connection with the subject of such contracts.

Article 87

1. Within three years of the entry into force of this Treaty the Council shall, acting unanimously on a proposal from the Commission and after consulting the Assembly, adopt any appropriate regulations or directives to give effect to the principles set out in Articles 85 and 86.

If such provisions have not been adopted within the period mentioned, they shall be laid down by the Council, acting by a qualified majority on a proposal from the Commission and after consulting the Assembly.

2. The regulations or directives referred to in paragraph 1 shall be designed, in particular:

(a) to ensure compliance with the prohibitions laid down in Article 85 (1) and in Article 86 by making provision for fines and periodic penalty payments;
(b) to lay down detailed rules for the application of Article 85 (3), taking into account the need to ensure effective supervision on the one hand, and to simplify administration to the greatest possible extent on the other;
(c) to define, if need be, in the various branches of the economy, the scope of the provisions of Articles 85 and 86;
(d) to define the respective functions of the Commission and of the Court of Justice in applying the provisions laid down in this paragraph;
(e) to determine the relationship between national laws and the provisions contained in this Section or adopted pursuant to this Article.

Article 88

Until the entry into force of the provisions adopted in pursuance of Article 87, the authorities in Member States shall rule on the admissibility of agreements, decisions and concerted practices and on abuse of a dominant position in the common market in accordance with the law of their country and with the provisions of Article 85 in particular paragraph 3, and of Article 86.

Article 89

1. Without prejudice to Article 88, the Commission shall, as soon as it takes up its duties, ensure the application of the principles laid down in Articles 85 and 86. On application by a Member State or on its own initiative, and in cooperation with the competent authorities in the Member States, who shall give it their assistance, the Commission shall investigate cases of suspected infringement of these principles. If it finds that there has been an infringement, it shall propose appropriate measures to bring it to an end.

2. If the infringement is not brought to an end, the Commission shall record such infringement of the principles in a reasoned decision. The Commission may publish its decision and authorise Member States to take the measures, the conditions and details of which it shall determine, needed to remedy the situation.

ARTICLE 90

1. In the case of public undertakings and undertakings to which Member States grant special or exclusive rights, Member States shall neither enact nor maintain in force any measure contrary to the rules contained in this Treaty, in particular to those rules provided for in Article 7 and Articles 85 to 94.

2. Undertakings entrusted with the operation of services of general economic interest or having the character of a revenue-producing monopoly shall be subject to the rules contained in this Treaty, in particular to the rules on competition, in so far as the application of such rules does not obstruct the performance, in law or in fact, of the particular tasks assigned to them. The development of trade must not be affected to such an extent as would be contrary to the interests of the Community.

3. The Commission shall ensure the application of the provisions of this Article and shall, where necessary, address appropriate directives or decisions to Member States.

SECTION 2

DUMPING

ARTICLE 91

1. If, during the transitional period, the Commission, on application by a Member State or by any other interested party, finds that dumping is being practised within the common market, it shall address recommendations to the person or persons with whom such practices originate for the purpose of putting an end to them.

Should the practices continue, the Commission shall authorise the injured Member State to take protective measures, the conditions and details of which the Commission shall determine.

2. As soon as this Treaty enters into force, products which originate in or are in free circulation in one Member State and which have been exported to another Member State shall, on reimportation, be admitted into the territory of the first-mentioned State free of all customs duties, quantitative restrictions or measures having equivalent effect. The Commission shall lay down appropriate rules for the application of this paragraph.

SECTION 3

AIDS GRANTED BY STATES

ARTICLE 92

1. Save as otherwise provided in this Treaty, any aid granted by a Member State or through State resources in any form whatsoever which distorts or threatens to distort competition by favouring certain undertakings or the production of certain goods shall, in so far as it affects trade between Member States, be incompatible with the common market.

2. The following shall be compatible with the common market:
  (a) aid having a social character, granted to individual consumers, provided that such aid is granted without discrimination related to the origin of the products concerned;
  (b) aid to make good the damage caused by natural disasters or exceptional occurrences;
  (c) aid granted to the economy of certain areas of the Federal Republic of Germany affected by the division of Germany, in so far as such aid is required in order to compensate for the economic disadvantages caused by that division.

3. The following may be considered to be compatible with the common market:
  (a) aid to promote the economic development of areas where the standard of living is abnormally low or where there is serious underemployment;
  (b) aid to promote the execution of an important project of common European interest or to remedy a serious disturbance in the economy of a Member State;
  (c) aid to facilitate the development of certain economic activities or of certain economic areas, where such aid does not adversely affect trading conditions to an extent contrary to the common interest. However, the aids granted to shipbuilding as of 1 January 1957 shall, in so far as they serve only to compensate for the absence of customs protection, be progressively reduced under the same conditions as apply to the elimination of customs duties, subject to the provisions of this Treaty concerning common commercial policy towards third countries;
  (d) such other categories of aid as may be specified by decision of the Council acting by a qualified majority on a proposal from the Commission.

Article 93

1. The Commission shall, in cooperation with Member States, keep under constant review all systems of aid existing in those States. It shall propose to the latter any appropriate measures required by the progressive development or by the functioning of the common market.

2. If, after giving notice to the parties concerned to submit their comments, the Commission finds that aid granted by a State or through State resources is not compatible with the common market having regard to Article 92, or that such aid is being misused, it shall decide that the State concerned shall abolish or alter such aid within a period of time to be determined by the Commission.

If the State concerned does not comply with this decision within the prescribed time, the Commission or any other interested State may, in derogation from the provisions of Articles 169 and 170, refer the matter to the Court of Justice direct.

On application by a Member State, the Council, may, acting unanimously, decide that aid which that State is granting or intends to grant shall be considered to be compatible with the common market, in derogation from the provisions of Article 92 or from the regulations provided for in Article 94, if such a decision is justified by exceptional circumstances. If, as regards the aid in question, the Commission has already initiated the procedure provided for in the first subparagraph of this paragraph, the fact that the State concerned has made its application to the Council shall have the effect of suspending that procedure until the Council has made its attitude known.

If, however, the council has not made its attitude known within three months of the said application being made, the Commission shall give its decision on the case.

3. The Commission shall be informed, in sufficient time to enable it to submit its comments, of any plans to grant or alter aid. If it considers that any such plan is not compatible with the common market having regard to Article 92, it shall without delay initiate the procedure provided for in paragraph 2. The Member State concerned shall not put its proposed measures into effect until this procedure has resulted in a final decision.

ARTICLE 94

The Council may, acting by a qualified majority on a proposal from the Commission, make any appropriate regulations for the application of Articles 92 and 93 and may in particular determine the conditions in which Article 93 (3) shall apply and the categories of aid exempted from this procedure.

CHAPTER 2—TAX PROVISIONS

ARTICLE 95

No Member State shall impose, directly or indirectly, on the products of other Member States any internal taxation of any kind in excess of that imposed directly or indirectly on similar domestic products.

Furthermore, no Member State shall impose on the products of other Member States any internal taxation of such a nature as to afford indirect protection to other products.

Member States shall, not later than at the beginning of the second stage, repeal or amend any provisions existing when this Treaty enters into force which conflict with the preceding rules.

ARTICLE 96

Where products are exported to the territory of any Member State, any repayment of internal taxation shall not exceed the internal taxation imposed on them, whether directly or indirectly.

ARTICLE 97

Member States which levy a turnover tax calculated on a cumulative multi-stage tax system may, in the case of internal taxation imposed by them on imported products or of repayments allowed by them on exported products, establish average rates for products or groups of products, provided that there is no infringement of the principles laid down in Articles 95 and 96.

Where the average rates established by a Member State do not conform to these principles, the Commission shall address appropriate directives or decisions to the State concerned.

ARTICLE 98

In the case of charges other than turnover taxes, excise duties and other forms of indirect taxation, remissions and repayments in respect of exports to other Member States may not be granted and countervailing charges in respect of imports from Member States may not be imposed unless the measures contemplated have been previously approved for a limited period by the Council acting by a qualified majority on a proposal from the Commission.

ARTICLE 99

The Commission shall consider how the legislation of the various Member States concerning turnover taxes, excise duties and other forms of indirect taxation, including countervailing measures applicable to trade between Member States, can be harmonised in the interest of the common market.

The Commission shall submit proposals to the Council, which shall act unanimously without prejudice to the provisions of Articles 100 and 101.

CHAPTER 3—APPROXIMATION OF LAWS

ARTICLE 100

The Council shall, acting unanimously on a proposal from the Commission, issue directives for the approximation of such provisions laid down by law, regulation or administrative action in Member States as directly affect the establishment or functioning of the common market.

The Assembly and the Economic and Social Committee shall be consulted in the case of directives whose implementation would, in one or more Member States, involve the amendment of legislation.

ARTICLE 101

Where the Commission finds that a difference between the provisions laid down by law, regulation or administrative action in Member States is distorting the conditions of competition in the common market and that the resultant distortion needs to be eliminated, it shall consult the Member States concerned.

If such consultation does not result in an agreement eliminating the distortion in question, the Council shall, on a proposal from the Commission, acting unanimously during the first stage and by a qualified majority thereafter, issue the necessary directives. The Commission and the Council may take any other appropriate measures provided for in this Treaty.

ARTICLE 102

1. Where there is reason to fear that the adoption or amendment of a provision laid down by law, regulation or administrative action may cause distortion within the meaning of Article 101, a Member State desiring to proceed therewith shall consult the Commission. After consulting the Member States, the Commission shall recommend to the States concerned such measures as may be appropriate to avoid the distortion in question.

2. If a State desiring to introduce or amend its own provisions does not comply with the recommendation addressed to it by the Commission, other Member States shall not be required, in pursuance of Article 101, to amend their own provisions in order to eliminate such distortion. If the Member State which has ignored the recommendation of the Commission causes distortion detrimental only to itself, the provisions of Article 101 shall not apply.

TITLE II—ECONOMIC POLICY
CHAPTER 1—CONJUNCTURAL POLICY
Article 103

1. Member States shall regard their conjunctural policies as a matter of common concern. They shall consult each other and the Commission on the measures to be taken in the light of the prevailing circumstances.

2. Without prejudice to any other procedures provided for in this Treaty, the Council may, acting unanimously on a proposal from the Commission, decide upon the measures appropriate to the situation.

3. Acting by a qualified majority on a proposal from the Commission, the Council shall, where required, issue any directives needed to give effect to the measures decided upon under paragraph 2.

4. The procedures provided for in this Article shall also apply if any difficulty should arise in the supply of certain products.

CHAPTER 2—BALANCE OF PAYMENTS

Article 104

Each Member State shall pursue the economic policy needed to ensure the equilibrium of its overall balance of payments and to maintain confidence in its currency, while taking care to ensure a high level of employment and a stable level of prices.

Article 105

1. In order to facilitate attainment of the objectives set out in Article 104, Member States shall coordinate their economic policies. They shall for this purpose provide for cooperation between their appropriate administrative departments and between their central banks.

The Commission shall submit to the Council recommendations on how to achieve such cooperation.

2. In order to promote coordination of the policies of Member States in the monetary field to the full extent needed for the functioning of the common market, a Monetary Committee with advisory status is hereby set up. It shall have the following tasks:
— to keep under review the monetary and financial situation of the Member States and of the Community and the general payments system of the Member States and to report regularly thereon to the Council and to the Commission;
— to deliver opinions at the request of the Council or of the Commission or on its own initiative, for submission to these institutions.

The Member States and the Commission shall each appoint two members of the Monetary Committee.

Article 106

1. Each Member State undertakes to authorise, in the currency of the Member State in which the creditor or the beneficiary resides, any payments connected with the movement of goods, services or capital, and any transfers of capital and earnings, to the extent that the movement of goods, services, capital and persons between Member States has been liberalised pursuant to this Treaty.

The Member States declare their readiness to undertake the liberalisation of payments beyond the extent provided in the preceding subparagraph, in so far as their economic situation in general and the state of their balance of payments in particular so permit.

2. In so far as movements of goods, services, and capital are limited only by restrictions on payments connected therewith, these restrictions shall be progressively abolished by applying, *mutatis mutandis*, the provisions of the Chapters relating to the abolition of quantitative restrictions, to the liberalisation of services and to the free movement of capital.

3. Member States undertake not to introduce between themselves any new restrictions on transfers connected with the invisible transactions listed in Annex III to this Treaty.

The progressive abolition of existing restrictions shall be effected in accordance with the provisions of Article 63 to 65, in so far as such abolition is not governed by the provisions contained in paragraphs 1 and 2 or by the Chapter relating to the free movement of capital.

4. If need be, Member States shall consult each other on the measures to be taken to enable the payments and transfers mentioned in this Article to be effected; such measures shall not prejudice the attainment of the objectives set out in this Chapter.

ARTICLE 107

1. Each Member State shall treat its policy with regard to rates of exchange as a matter of common concern.

2. If a Member State makes an alteration in its rate of exchange which is inconsistent with the objectives set out in Article 104 and which seriously distorts conditions of competition, the Commission may, after consulting the Monetary Committee, authorise other Member States to take for a strictly limited period the necessary measures, the conditions and details of which it shall determine, in order to counter the consequences of such alteration.

ARTICLE 108

1. Where a Member State is in difficulties or is seriously threatened with difficulties as regards its balance of payments either as a result of an overall disequilibrium in its balance of payments, or as a result of the type of currency at its disposal, and where such difficulties are liable in particular to jeopardise the functioning of the common market or the progressive implementation of the common commercial policy, the Commission shall immediately investigate the position of the State in question and the action which, making use of all the means at its disposal, that State has taken or may take in accordance with the provisions of Article 104. The Commission shall state what measures it recommends the State concerned to take.

If the action taken by a Member State and the measures suggested by the Commission do not prove sufficient to overcome the difficulties which have arisen or which threaten, the Commission shall after consulting the Monetary Committee. recommend to the Council the granting of mutual assistance and appropriate methods therefor.

The Commission shall keep the Council regularly informed of the situation and of how it is developing.

2. The Council, acting by a qualified majority, shall grant such mutual assistance; it shall adopt directives or decisions laying down the conditions and details of such assistance, which may take such forms as:

    (a) a concerted approach to or within any other international organisa-
tions to which Member States may have recourse;

    (b) measures needed to avoid deflection of trade where the State which
is in difficulties maintains or reintroduces quantitative restrictions
against third countries;

    (c) the granting of limited credits by other Member States, subject to
their agreement.

During the transitional period, mutual assistance may also take the form of
special reductions in customs duties or enlargements of quotas in order to
facilitate and increase in imports from the State which is in difficulties, subject
to the agreement of the States by which such measures would have to be taken.

3. If the mutual assistance recommended by the Commission is not granted
by the Council or if the mutual assistance granted and the measures taken are
insufficient, the Commission shall authorise the State which is in difficulties to
take protective measures, the conditions and details of which the Commission
shall determine.

Such authorisation may be revoked and such conditions and details may be
changed by the Council acting by a qualified majority.

ARTICLE 109

1. Where a sudden crisis in the balance of payments occurs and a decision
within the meaning of Article 108 (2) is not immediately taken, the Member
State concerned may, as a precaution, take the necessary protective measures.
Such measures must cause the least possible disturbance in the functioning of
the common market and must not be wider in scope than is strictly necessary
to remedy the sudden difficulties which have arisen.

2. The Commission and the other Member States shall be informed of such
protective measures not later than when they enter into force. The Commission
may recommend to the Council the granting of mutual assistance under Article
108.

3. After the Commission has delivered an opinion and the Monetary Committee has been consulted, the Council may, acting by a qualified majority,
decide that the State concerned shall amend, suspend or abolish the protective
measures referred to above.

CHAPTER 3—COMMERCIAL POLICY

ARTICLE 110

By establishing a customs union between themselves Member States aim to
contribute, in the common interest, to the harmonious development of world
trade, the progressive abolition of restrictions on international trade and the
lowering of customs barriers.

The common commercial policy shall take into account the favourable effect
which the abolition of customs duties between Member States may have on the
increase in the competitive strength of undertakings in those States.

ARTICLE 111

The following provisions shall, without prejudice to Articles 115 and 116,
apply during the transitional period:

1. Member States shall coordinate their trade relations with third countries
so as to bring about, by the end of the transitional period, the conditions
needed for implementing a common policy in the field of external trade.

The Commission shall submit to the Council proposals regarding the procedure for common action to be followed during the transitional period and regarding the achievement of uniformity in their commercial policies.

2. The Commission shall submit to the Council recommendations for tariff negotiations with third countries in respect of the common customs tariff.

The Council shall authorise the Commission to open such negotiations.

The Commission shall conduct these negotiations in consultation with a special committee appointed by the Council to assist the Commission in this task and within the framework of such directives as the Council may issue to it.

3. In exercising the powers conferred upon it by this Article, the Council shall act unanimously during the first two stages and by a qualified majority thereafter.

4. Member States shall, in consultation with the Commission, take all necessary measures, particularly those designed to bring about an adjustment of tariff agreements in force with third countries, in order that the entry into force of the common customs tariff shall not be delayed.

5. Member States shall aim at securing as high a level of uniformity as possible between themselves as regards their liberalisation lists in relation to third countries or groups of third countries. To this end, the Commission shall make all appropriate recommendations to Member States.

If Member States abolish or reduce quantitative restrictions in relation to third countries, they shall inform the Commission beforehand and shall accord the same treatment to other Member States.

Article 112

1. Without prejudice to obligations undertaken by them within the framework of other international organisations, Member States shall, before the end of the transitional period, progressively harmonise the systems whereby they grant aid for exports to third countries, to the extent necessary to ensure that competition between undertakings of the Community is not distorted.

On a proposal from the Commission, the Council shall, acting unanimously until the end of the second stage and by a qualified majority thereafter, issue any directives needed for this purpose.

2. The preceding provisions shall not apply to such drawback of customs duties or charges having equivalent effect nor to such repayment of indirect taxation including turnover taxes, excise duties and other indirect taxes as is allowed when goods are exported from a Member State to a third country, in so far as such drawback or repayment does not exceed the amount imposed, directly or indirectly, on the products exported.

Article 113

1. After the transitional period has ended, the common commercial policy shall be based on uniform principles, particularly in regard to changes in tariff rates, the conclusion of tariff and trade agreements, the achievement of uniformity in measures of liberalisation, export policy and measures to protect trade such as those to be taken in case of dumping or subsidies.

2. The Commission shall submit proposals to the Council for implementing the common commercial policy.

3. Where agreements with third countries need to be negotiated, the Commission shall make recommendations to the Council, which shall authorise the Commission to open the necessary negotiations.

The Commission shall conduct these negotiations in consultation with a special committee appointed by the Council to assist the Commission in this task and within the framework of such directives as the Council may issue to it.

4. In exercising the powers conferred upon it by this Article, the Council shall act by a qualified majority.

ARTICLE 114

The agreements referred to in Article 111 (2) and in Article 113 shall be concluded by the Council on behalf of the Community, acting unanimously during the first two stages and by a qualified majority thereafter.

ARTICLE 115

In order to ensure that the execution of measures of commercial policy taken in accordance with this Treaty by any Member State is not obstructed by deflection of trade, or where differences between such measures lead to economic difficulties in one or more of the Member States, the Commission shall recommend the methods for the requisite cooperation between Member States. Failing this, the Commission shall authorise Member States to take the necessary protective measures, the conditions and details of which it shall determine.

In case of urgency during the transitional period, Member States may themselves take the necessary measures and shall notify them to the other Member States and to the Commission, which may decide that the States concerned shall amend or abolish such measures.

In the selection of such measures, priority shall be given to those which cause the least disturbance to the functioning of the common market and which take into account the need to expedite, as far as possible, the introduction of the common customs tariff.

ARTICLE 116

From the end of the transitional period onwards, Member States shall, in respect of all matters of particular interest to the common market, proceed within the framework of international organisations of an economic character only by common action. To this end, the Commission shall submit to the Council, which shall act by a qualified majority, proposals concerning the scope and implementation of such common action.

During the transitional period, Member States shall consult each other for the purpose of concerting the action they take and adopting as far as possible a uniform attitude.

TITLE III—SOCIAL POLICY

CHAPTER 1—SOCIAL PROVISIONS

ARTICLE 117

Member States agree upon the need to promote improved working conditions and an improved standard of living for workers, so as to make possible their harmonisation while the improvement is being maintained.

They believe that such a development will ensue not only from the functioning of the common market, which will favour the harmonisation of social systems, but also from the procedures provided for in this Treaty and from the approximation of provisions laid down by law, regulation or administrative action.

ARTICLE 118

Without prejudice to the other provisions of this Treaty and in conformity with its general objectives, the Commission shall have the task of promoting close cooperation between Member States in the social field, particularly in matters relating to:

—employment;

—labour law and working conditions;

—basic and advanced vocational training;

—social security;

—prevention of occupational accidents and diseases;

—occupational hygiene;

—the right of association, and collective bargaining between employers and workers.

To this end, the Commission shall act in close contact with Member States by making studies, delivering opinions and arranging consultations both on problems arising at national level and on those of concern to international organisations.

Before delivering the opinions provided for in this Article, the Commission shall consult the Economic and Social Committee,

ARTICLE 119

Each Member State shall during the first stage ensure and subsequently maintain the application of the principle that men and women should receive equal pay for equal work.

For the purpose of this Article, " pay " means the ordinary basic or minimum wage or salary and any other consideration, whether in cash or in kind, which the worker receives, directly or indirectly, in respect of his employment from his employer.

Equal pay without discrimination based on sex means:

(a) that pay for the same work at piece rates shall be calculated on the basis of the same unit of measurement;

(b) that pay for work at time rates shall be the same for the same job.

ARTICLE 120

Member States shall endeavour to maintain the existing equivalence between paid holiday schemes.

ARTICLE 121

The Council may, acting unanimously and after consulting the Economic and Social Committee, assign to the Commission tasks in connection with the implementation of common measures, particularly as regards social security for the migrant workers referred to in Articles 48 to 51.

ARTICLE 122

The Commission shall include a separate chapter on social developments within the Community in its annual report to the Assembly.

The Assembly may invite the Commission to draw up reports on any particular problems concerning social conditions.

CHAPTER 2—THE EUROPEAN SOCIAL FUND

ARTICLE 123

In order to improve employment opportunities for workers in the common market and to contribute thereby to raising the standard of living, a European Social Fund is hereby established in accordance with the provisions set out below; it shall have the task of rendering the employment of workers easier and of increasing their geographical and occupational mobility within the Community.

ARTICLE 124

The Fund shall be administered by the Commission.

The Commission shall be assisted in this task by a Committee presided over by a member of the Commission and composed of representatives of Governments, trade unions and employers' organisations.

ARTICLE 125

1. On application by a Member State the Fund shall, within the framework of the rules provided for in Article 127, meet 50 per cent. of the expenditure incurred after the entry into force of this Treaty by that State or by a body governed by public law for the purposes of:
    (a) ensuring productive re-employment of workers by means of:
        vocational retraining;
        resettlement allowances;
    (b) granting aid for the benefit of workers whose employment is reduced or temporarily suspended, in whole or in part, as a result of the conversion of an undertaking to other production, in order that they may retain the same wage level pending their full re-employment.
2. Assistance granted by the Fund towards the cost of vocational retraining shall be granted only if the unemployed workers could not be found employment except in a new occupation and only if they have been in productive employment for at least six months in the occupation for which they have been retrained.

Assistance towards resettlement allowances shall be granted only if the unemployed workers have been caused to change their home within the Community and have been in productive employment for at least six months in their new place of residence.

Assistance for workers in the case of the conversion of an undertaking shall be granted only if:
    (a) the workers concerned have again been fully employed in that undertaking for at least six months;
    (b) the Government concerned has submitted a plan beforehand, drawn up by the undertaking in question, for that particular conversion and for financing it;
    (c) the Commission has given its prior approval to the conversion plan.

ARTICLE 126

When the transitional period has ended, the Council, after receiving the opinion of the Commission and after consulting the Economic and Social Committee and the Assembly, may:

(a) rule, by a qualified majority, that all or part of the assistance referred to in Article 125 shall no longer be granted; or

(b) unanimously determine what new tasks may be entrusted to the Fund within the framework of its terms of reference as laid down in Article 123.

ARTICLE 127

The Council shall, acting by a qualified majority on a proposal from the Commission and after consulting the Economic and Social Committee and the Assembly, lay down the provisions required to implement Articles 124 to 126; in particular it shall determine in detail the conditions under which assistance shall be granted by the Fund in accordance with Article 125 and the classes of undertakings whose workers shall benefit from the assistance provided for in Article 125 (1) (b).

ARTICLE 128

The Council shall, acting on a proposal from the Commission and after consulting the Economic and Social Committee, lay down general principles for implementing a common vocational training policy capable of contributing to the harmonious development both of the national economies and of the common market.

TITLE IV—THE EUROPEAN INVESTMENT BANK

ARTICLE 129

A European Investment Bank is hereby established; it shall have legal personality.

The members of the European Investment Bank shall be the Member States.

The Statute of the European Investment Bank is laid down in a Protocol annexed to this Treaty.

ARTICLE 130

The task of the European Investment Bank shall be to contribute, by having recourse to the capital market and utilising its own resources, to the balanced and steady development of the common market in the interest of the Community. For this purpose the Bank shall, operating on a non-profit-making basis, grant loans and give guarantees which facilitate the financing of the following projects in all sectors of the economy:

(a) projects for developing less developed regions;

(b) projects for modernising or converting undertakings or for developing fresh activities called for by the progressive establishment of the common market, where these projects are of such a size or nature that they cannot be entirely financed by the various means available in the individual Member States;

(c) projects of common interest to several Member States which are of such a size or nature that they cannot be entirely financed by the various means available in the individual Member States.

Part Four

ASSOCIATION OF THE OVERSEAS COUNTRIES AND TERRITORIES

ARTICLE 131

The Member States agree to associate with the Community the non-European countries and territories which have special relations with Belgium, France, Italy, Netherlands [and the United Kingdom]. These countries and territories (hereinafter called the " countries and territories ") are listed in Annex IV to this Treaty.

The purpose of association shall be to promote the economic and social development of the countries and territories and to establish close economic relations between them and the Community as a whole.

In accordance with the principles set out in the Preamble to this Treaty, association shall serve primarily to further the interests and prosperity of the inhabitants of these countries and territories in order to lead them to the economic, social and cultural development to which they aspire.

AMENDMENT
The words in square brackets were added by the Act of Accession, Art 24 (1), as amended by the Adaptation Decision, Art.13.

ARTICLE 132

Association shall have the following objectives:

1. Member States shall apply to their trade with the countries and territories the same treatment as they accord each other pursuant to this Treaty.

2. Each country or territory shall apply to its trade with Member States and with the other countries and territories the same treatment as that which it applies to the European State with which it has special relations.

3. The Member States shall contribute to the investments required for the progressive development of these countries and territories.

4. For investments financed by the Community, participation in tenders and supplies shall be open on equal terms to all natural and legal persons who are nationals of a Member State or of one of the countries and territories.

5. In relations between Member States and the countries and territories the right of establishment of nationals and companies or firms shall be regulated in accordance with the provisions and procedures laid down in the Chapter relating to the right of establishment and on a nondiscriminatory basis, subject to any special provisions laid down pursuant to Article 136.

ARTICLE 133

1. Customs duties on imports into the Member States of goods originating in the countries and territories shall be completely abolished in conformity with the progressive abolition of customs duties between Member States in accordance with the provisions of this Treaty.

2. Customs duties on imports into each country or territory from Member States or from the other countries or territories shall be progressively abolished in accordance with the provisions of Articles 12, 13, 14, 15 and 17.

3. The countries and territories may, however, levy customs duties which meet the needs of their development and industrialisation or produce revenue for their budgets.

The duties referred to in the preceding subparagraph shall nevertheless be progressively reduced to the level of those imposed on imports of products from the Member State with which each country or territory has special relations. The percentages and the timetable of the reductions provided for under this Treaty shall apply to the difference between the duty imposed on a product coming from the Member State which has special relations with the country or territory concerned and the duty imposed on the same product coming from within the Community on entry into the importing country or territory.

4. Paragraph 2 shall not apply to countries and territories which, by reason of the particular international obligations by which they are bound, already apply a non-discriminatory customs tariff when this Treaty enters into force.

5. The introduction of or any change in customs duties imposed on goods imported into the countries and territories shall not, either in law or in fact, give rise to any direct or indirect discrimination between imports from the various Member States.

Article 134

If the level of the duties applicable to goods from a third country on entry into a country or territory is liable, when the provisions of Article 133 (1) have been applied, to cause deflections of trade to the detriment of any Member State, the latter may request the Commission to propose to the other Member States the measures needed to remedy the situation.

Article 135

Subject to the provisions relating to public health, public security or public policy, freedom of movement within Member States for workers from the countries and territories, and within the countries and territories for workers from Member States, shall be governed by agreements to be concluded subsequently with the unanimous approval of Member States.

Article 136

For an initial period of five years after the entry into force of this Treaty, the details of and procedure for the association of the countries and territories with the Community shall be determined by an Implementing Convention annexed to this Treaty.

Before the Convention referred to in the preceding paragraph expires, the Council shall, acting unanimously, lay down provisions for a furhter period, on the basis of the experience acquired and of the principles set out in this Treaty.

Part Five

INSTITUTIONS OF THE COMMUNITY

TITLE I—PROVISIONS GOVERNING THE INSTITUTIONS

CHAPTER 1—THE INSTITUTIONS

Section 1

The Assembly

Article 137

The Assembly, which shall consist of representatives of the peoples of the States brought together in the Community, shall exercise the advisory and supervisory powers which are conferred upon it by this Treaty.

ARTICLE 138

1. The Assembly shall consist of delegates who shall be designated by the respective Parliaments from among their members in accordance with the procedure laid down by each Member State.

2. [The number of these delegates shall be as follows:

Belgium	... 14
Denmark	... 10
Germany	... 36
France	... 36
Ireland	... 10
Italy	... 36
Luxembourg	... 6
Netherlands	... 14
United Kingdom	... 36]

3. The Assembly shall draw up proposals for elections by direct universal suffrage in accordance with a uniform procedure in all Member States.

The Council shall, acting unanimously, lay down the appropriate provisions, which it shall recommend to Member States for adoption in accordance with their respective constitutional requirements.

AMENDMENT
Para. (2) was substituted by the Act of Accession, Art. 10, as amended by the Adaptation Decision, Art. 4.

ARTICLE 139

[The Assembly shall hold an annual session. It shall meet, without requiring to be convened, on the second Tuesday in March.]

The Assembly may meet in extraordinary session at the request of a majority of its members or at the request of the Council or of the Commission.

AMENDMENT
The first paragraph was repealed and substituted by the Merger Treaty, Art. 27.

ARTICLE 140

The Assembly shall elect its President and its officers from among its members.

Members of the Commission may attend all meetings and shall, at their request, be heard on behalf of the Commission.

The Commission shall reply orally or in writing to questions put to it by the Assembly or by its members.

The Council shall be heard by the Assembly in accordance with the conditions laid down by the Council in its rules of procedure.

ARTICLE 141

Save as otherwise provided in this Treaty, the Assembly shall act by an absolute majority of the votes cast.

The rules of procedure shall determine the quorum.

ARTICLE 142

The Assembly shall adopt its rules of procedure, acting by a majority of its members.

The proceedings of the Assembly shall be published in the manner laid down in its rules of procedure.

Article 143

The Assembly shall discuss in open session the annual general report submitted to it by the Commission.

Article 144

If a motion of censure on the activities of the Commission is tabled before it, the Assembly shall not vote thereon until at least three days after the motion has been tabled and only by open vote.

If the motion of censure is carried by a two-thirds majority of the votes cast, representing a majority of the members of the Assembly, the members of the Commission shall resign as a body. They shall continue to deal with current business until they are replaced in accordance with Article 158.

Section 2

The Council

Article 145

To ensure that the objectives set out in this Treaty are attained, the Council shall, in accordance with the provisions of this Treaty:
—ensure coordination of the general economic policies of the Member States;
—have power to take decisions.

Article 146

[*Repealed by the Merger Treaty, Art. 7. See now ibid., Art. 2.*]

Article 147

[*Repealed by the Merger Treaty, Art. 7. See now ibid., Art. 3.*]

Article 148

1. Save as otherwise provided in this Treaty, the Council shall act by a majority of its members.

2. [Where the Council is required to act by a qualified majority, the votes of its members shall be weighted as follows:

Belgium	5
Denmark	3
Germany	10
Greece	5
France	10
Ireland	3
Italy	10
Luxembourg	2
Netherlands	5
United Kingdom	10

For their adoption, acts of the Council shall require at least:
— forty-five votes in favour where this Treaty requires them to be adopted on a proposal from the Commission.
— forty-five votes in favour, cast by at least six members, in other cases.]

3. Abstentions by members present in person or represented shall not prevent the adoption by the Council of acts which require unanimity.

AMENDMENTS
Para. (2) was substituted by the Act of Accession, Art. 14, as amended by the Adaptation Decision, Art. 8. It was subsequently substituted by the Act of Accession of the Hellenic Republic of May 28, 1979, Art. 14.

ARTICLE 149

Where, in pursuance of this Treaty, the Council acts on a proposal from the Commission, unanimity shall be required for an act constituting an amendment to that proposal.

As long as the Council has not acted, the Commission may alter its original proposal, in particular where the Assembly has been consulted on that proposal.

ARTICLE 150

Where a vote is taken, any member of the Council may also act on behalf of not more than one other member.

ARTICLE 151

[Repealed by the Merger Treaty, Art. 7. See now ibid., Arts. 4 and 5.]

ARTICLE 152

The Council may request the Commission to undertake any studies which the Council considers desirable for the attainment of the common objectives, and to submit to it any appropriate proposals.

ARTICLE 153

The Council shall, after receiving an opinion from the Commission, determine the rules governing the committees provided for in this Treaty.

ARTICLE 154

[Repealed by the Merger Treaty, Art. 7. See now ibid., Art. 6.]

SECTION 3

THE COMMISSION

ARTICLE 155

In order to ensure the proper functioning and development of the common market, the Commission shall:
—ensure that the provisions of this Treaty and the measures taken by the institutions pursuant thereto are applied;
—formulate recommendations or deliver opinions on matters dealt with in this Treaty, if it expressly so provides or if the Commission considers it necessary;
—have its own power of decision and participate in the shaping of measures taken by the Council and by the Assembly in the manner provided for in this Treaty;
—exercise the powers conferred on it by the Council for the implementation of the rules laid down by the latter.

ARTICLE 156

[*This article was repealed by the Merger Treaty, Art. 19. See now ibid., Art.* 18.]

ARTICLE 157

[*This article was repealed by the Merger Treaty, Art. 19. See now ibid., Art.* 10, *as modified by the Adaptation Decision.*]

ARTICLE 158

[*This article was repealed by the Merger Treaty, Art. 19. See now ibid., Art.* 11.]

ARTICLE 159

[*This article was repealed by the Merger Treaty, Art. 19. See now ibid., Art.* 12.]

ARTICLE 160

[*This article was repealed by the Merger Treaty, Art. 19. See now ibid., Art.* 13.]

ARTICLE 161

[*This article was repealed by the Merger Treaty, Art. 19. See now ibid., Art.* 14.]

ARTICLE 162

[*This article was repealed by the Merger Treaty, Art. 19. See now ibid., Arts.* 15 *and* 16.]

ARTICLE 163

[*This article was repealed by the Merger Treaty, Art. 19. See now ibid., Art.* 17.]

SECTION 4

THE COURT OF JUSTICE

ARTICLE 164

The Court of Justice shall ensure that in the interpretation and application of this Treaty the law is observed.

ARTICLE 165

[The Court of Justice shall consist of nine Judges.]

The Court of Justice shall sit in plenary session. It may, however, form chambers, each consisting of three or five Judges, either to undertake certain preparatory inquiries or to adjudicate on particular categories of cases in accordance with rules laid down for these purposes.

[Whenever the Court of Justice hears cases brought before it by a Member State or by one of the institutions of the Community or, to the extent that the chambers of the court do not have the requisite jurisdiction under the Rules of Procedure, has to give preliminary rulings on questions submitted to it pursuant to Article 177, it shall sit in plenary session.]

Should the Court of Justice so request, the Council may, acting unanimously, increase the number of Judges and make the necessary adjustments to the second and third paragraphs of this Article and to the second paragraph of Article 167.

AMENDMENTS
The first paragraph was substituted by the Act of Accession, Art. 17, as amended by the Adaptation Decision, Art. 9.
The third paragraph was replaced by Dec. 74/584, Art. 1 (O.J. 1974, L318/22).

ARTICLE 166

[The Court of Justice shall be assisted by four Advocates-General.]

It shall be the duty of the Advocate-General, acting with complete impartiality and independence, to make, in open court, reasoned submissions on cases brought before the Court of Justice, in order to assist the Court in the performance of the task assigned to it in Article 164.

Should the Court of Justice so request, the Council may, acting unanimously, increase the number of Advocates-General and make the necessary adjustments to the third paragraph of Article 167.

AMENDMENT
The first paragraph was substituted by the Council Decision of January 1, 1973, increasing the number of Advocates-General, Art. 1.

ARTICLE 167

The Judges and Advocates-General shall be chosen from persons whose independence is beyond doubt and who possess the qualifications required for appointment to the highest judicial offices in their respective countries or who are jurisconsults of recognised competence; they shall be appointed by common accord of the Governments of the Member States for a term of six years.

[Every three years there shall be a partial replacement of the Judges. Five and four Judges shall be replaced alternately.]

[Every three years there shall be a partial replacement of the Advocates-General. Two Advocates-General shall be replaced on each occasion.]

Retiring Judges and Advocates-General shall be eligible for reappointment.

The Judges shall elect the President of the Court of Justice from among their number for a term of three years. He may be re-elected.

AMENDMENTS
The second and third paragraphs were substituted by the Act of Accession, Art. 19. The second paragraph was subsequently substituted by the Adaptation Decision, Art. 10, and the third paragraph by the Council Decision of January 1, 1973, increasing the number of Advocates-General, Art. 2.

ARTICLE 168

The Court of Justice shall appoint its Registrar and lay down the rules governing his service.

ARTICLE 169

If the Commission considers that a Member State has failed to fulfil an obligation under this Treaty, it shall deliver a reasoned opinion on the matter after giving the State concerned the opportunity to submit its observations.

If the State concerned does not comply with the opinion within the period laid down by the Commission, the latter may bring the matter before the Court of Justice.

ARTICLE 170

A Member State which considers that another Member State has failed to fulfil an obligation under this Treaty may bring the matter before the Court of Justice.

Before a Member State brings an action against another Member State for an alleged infringement of an obligation under this Treaty, it shall bring the matter before the Commission.

The Commission shall deliver a reasoned opinion after each of the States concerned has been given the opportunity to submit its own case and its observations on the other party's case both orally and in writing.

If the Commission has not delivered an opinion within three months of the date on which the matter was brought before it, the absence of such opinion shall not prevent the matter from being brought before the Court of Justice.

ARTICLE 171

If the Court of Justice finds that a Member State has failed to fulfil an obligation under this Treaty, the State shall be required to take the necessary measures to comply with the judgment of the Court of Justice.

ARTICLE 172

Regulations made by the Council pursuant to the provisions of this Treaty may give the Court of Justice unlimited jurisdiction in regard to the penalties provided for in such regulations.

ARTICLE 173

The Court of Justice shall review the legality of acts of the Council and the Commission other than recommendations or opinions. It shall for this purpose have jurisdiction in actions brought by a Member State, the Council or the Commission on grounds of lack of competence, infringement of an essential procedural requirement, infringement of this Treaty or of any rule of law relating to its application, or misuse of powers.

Any natural or legal person may, under the same conditions, institute proceedings against a decision addressed to that person or against a decision which, although in the form of a regulation or a decision addressed to another person, is of direct and individual concern to the former.

The proceedings provided for in this Article shall be instituted within two months of the publication of the measure, or of its notification to the plaintiff, or, in the absence thereof, of the day on which it came to the knowledge of the latter, as the case may be.

ARTICLE 174

If the action is well founded, the Court of Justice shall declare the act concerned to be void.

In the case of a regulation, however, the Court of Justice shall, if it considers this necessary, state which of the effects of the regulation which it has declared void shall be considered as definitive.

ARTICLE 175

Should the Council or the Commission, in infringement of this Treaty, fail to act, the Member States and the other institutions of the Community may bring an action before the Court of Justice to have the infringement established.

The action shall be admissible only if the institution concerned has first been called upon to act. If, within two months of being so called upon, the institution concerned has not defined its position, the action may be brought within a further period of two months.

Any natural or legal person may, under the conditions laid down in the preceding paragraphs, complain to the Court of Justice that an institution of the Community has failed to address to that person any act other than a recommendation or an opinion.

Article 176

The institution whose act has been declared void or whose failure to act has been declared contrary to this Treaty shall be required to take the necessary measures to comply with the judgment of the Court of Justice.

This obligation shall not affect any obligation which may result from the application of the second paragraph of Article 215.

Article 177

The Court of Justice shall have jurisdiction to give preliminary rulings concerning:

(a) the interpretation of this Treaty;

(b) the validity and interpretation of acts of the institutions of the Community;

(c) The interpretation of the statutes of bodies established by an act of the Council, where those statutes so provide.

Where such a question is raised before any court or tribunal of a Member State, that court or tribunal may, if it considers that a decision on the question is necessary to enable it to give judgment, request the Court of Justice to give a ruling thereon.

Where any such question is raised in a case pending before a court or tribunal of a Member State, against whose decisions there is no judicial remedy under national law, that court or tribunal shall bring the matter before the Court of Justice.

Article 178

The Court of Justice shall have jurisdiction in disputes relating to compensation for damage provided for in the second paragraph of Article 215.

Article 179

The Court of Justice shall have jurisdiction in any dispute between the Community and its servants within the limits and under the conditions laid down in the Staff Regulations or the Conditions of Employment.

Article 180

The Court of Justice shall, within the limits hereinafter laid down, have jurisdiction in disputes concerning:

(a) the fulfilment by Member States of obligations under the Statute of the European Investment Bank. In this connection, the Board of Directors of the Bank shall enjoy the powers conferred upon the Commission by Article 169;

112

(b) measures adopted by the Board of Governors of the Bank. In this connection, any Member State, the Commission or the Board of Directors of the Bank may institute proceedings under the conditions laid down in Article 173;

(c) measures adopted by the Board of Directors of the Bank. Proceedings against such measures may be instituted only by Member States or by the Commission, under the conditions laid down in Article 173, and solely on the grounds of non-compliance with the procedure provided for in Article 21 (2), (5), (6) and (7) of the Statute of the Bank.

Article 181

The Court of Justice shall have jurisdiction to give judgment pursuant to any arbitration clause contained in a contract concluded by or on behalf of the Community, whether that contract be governed by public or private law.

Article 182

The Court of Justice shall have jurisdiction in any dispute between Member States which relates to the subject matter of this Treaty if the dispute is submitted to it under a special agreement between the parties.

Article 183

Save where jurisdiction is conferred on the Court of Justice by this Treaty, disputes to which the Community is a party shall not on that ground be excluded from the jurisdiction of the courts or tribunals of the Member States.

Article 184

Notwithstanding the expiry of the period laid down in the third paragraph of Article 173, any party may, in proceedings in which a regulation of the Council or of the Commission is in issue, plead the grounds specified in the first paragraph of Article 173, in order to invoke before the Court of Justice the inapplicability of that regulation.

Article 185

Actions brought before the Court of Justice shall not have suspensory effect. The Court of Justice may, however, if it considers that circumstances so require, order that application of the contested act be suspended.

Article 186

The Court of Justice may in any cases before it prescribe any necessary interim measures.

Article 187

The judgments of the Court of Justice shall be enforceable under the conditions laid down in Article 192.

Article 188

The Statute of the Court of Justice is laid down in a separate Protocol.

The Court of Justice shall adopt its rules of procedure. These shall require the unanimous approval of the Council.

CHAPTER 2—PROVISIONS COMMON TO SEVERAL INSTITUTIONS

ARTICLE 189

In order to carry out their task the Council and the Commission shall, in accordance with the provisions of this Treaty, make regulations, issue directives, take decisions, make recommendations or deliver opinions.

A regulation shall have general application. It shall be binding in its entirety and directly applicable in all Member States.

A directive shall be binding, as to the result to be achieved, upon each Member State to which it is addressed, but shall leave to the national authorities the choice of form and methods.

A decision shall be binding in its entirety upon those to whom it is addressed.

Recommendations and opinions shall have no binding force.

ARTICLE 190

Regulations, directives and decisions of the Council and of the Commission shall state the reasons on which they are based and shall refer to any proposals or opinions which were required to be obtained pursuant to this Treaty.

ARTICLE 191

Regulations shall be published in the Official Journal of the Community. They shall enter into force on the date specified in them or, in the absence thereof, on the twentieth day following their publication.

Directives and decisions shall be notified to those to whom they are addressed and shall take effect upon such notification.

ARTICLE 192

Decisions of the Council or of the Commission which impose a pecuniary obligation on persons other than States shall be enforceable.

Enforcement shall be governed by the rules of civil procedure in force in the State in the territory of which it is carried out. The order for its enforcement shall be appended to the decision, without other formality than verification of the authenticity of the decision, by the national authority which the Government of each Member State shall designate for this purpose and shall make known to the Commission and to the Court of Justice.

When these formalities have been completed on application by the party concerned, the latter may proceed to enforcement in accordance with the national law, by bringing the matter directly before the competent authority.

Enforcement may be suspended only by a decision of the Court of Justice. However, the courts of the country concerned shall have jurisdiction over complaints that enforcement is being carried out in an irregular manner.

CHAPTER 3—THE ECONOMIC AND SOCIAL COMMITTEE

ARTICLE 193

An Economic and Social Committee is hereby established. It shall have advisory status.

The Committee shall consist of representatives of the various categories of economic and social activity, in particular, representatives of producers, farmers, carriers, workers, dealers, craftsmen, professional occupations and representatives of the general public.

ARTICLE 194

[The number of members of the Committee shall be as follows:

Belgium	... 12
Denmark	... 9
Germany	... 24
Greece	... 12
France	... 24
Ireland	... 9
Italy	... 24
Luxembourg	... 6
Netherlands	... 12
United Kingdom	... 24.]

The members of the Committee shall be appointed by the Council, acting unanimously, for four years. Their appointments shall be renewable.

The members of the Committee shall be appointed in their personal capacity and may not be bound by any mandatory instructions.

AMENDMENTS

The first paragraph was substituted by the Act of Accession, Art. 21, as amended by the Adaptation Decision, Art. 11. It was subsequently substituted by the Act of Accession of the Hellenic Republic of May 28, 1979, Art. 17.

ARTICLE 195

1. For the appointment of the members of the Committee, each Member State shall provide the Council with a list containing twice as many candidates as there are seats allotted to its nationals.

The composition of the Committee shall take account of the need to ensure adequate representation of the various categories of economic and social activity.

2. The Council shall consult the Commission. It may obtain the opinion of European bodies which are representative of the various economic and social sectors to which the activities of the Community are of concern.

ARTICLE 196

The Committee shall elect its chairman and officers from among its members for a term of two years.

It shall adopt its rules of procedure and shall submit them to the Council for its approval, which must be unanimous.

The Committee shall be convened by its chairman at the request of the Council or of the Commission.

ARTICLE 197

The Committee shall include specialised sections for the principal fields covered by this Treaty.

In particular, it shall contain an agricultural section and a transport section, which are the subject of special provisions in the Titles relating to agriculture and transport.

These specialised sections shall operate within the general terms of reference of the Committee. They may not be consulted independently of the Committee.

Sub-committees may also be established within the Committee to prepare, on specific questions or in specific fields, draft opinions to be submitted to the Committee for its consideration.

The rules of procedure shall lay down the methods of composition and the terms of reference of the specialised sections and of the sub-committees.

ARTICLE 198

The Committee must be consulted by the Council or by the Commission where this Treaty so provides. The Committee may be consulted by these institutions in all cases in which they consider it appropriate.

The Council or the Commission shall, if it considers it necessary, set the Committee, for the submission of its opinion, a time limit which may not be less than ten days from the date on which the chairman receives notification to this effect. Upon expiry of the time limit, the absence of an opinion shall not prevent further action.

The opinion of the Committee and that of the specialised section, together with a record of the proceedings, shall be forwarded to the Council and to the Commission.

TITLE II—FINANCIAL PROVISIONS

ARTICLE 199

All items of revenue and expenditure of the Community, including those relating to the European Social Fund, shall be included in estimates to be drawn up for each financial year and shall be shown in the budget.

The revenue and expenditure shown in the budget shall be in balance.

ARTICLE 200

1. The budget revenue shall include, irrespective of any other revenue, financial contributions of Member States on the following scale:

[Belgium]	7.9
Germany	28
France	28
Italy	28
Luxembourg	0.2
Netherlands	7.9

2. The financial contributions of Member States to cover the expenditure of the European Social Fund, however, shall be determined on the following scale:

Belgium	8.8
Germany	32
France	32
Italy	20
Luxembourg	0.2
Netherlands	7

3. The scales may be modified by the Council, acting unanimously.

GENERAL NOTE

In para. (1) the word in square brackets is not printed in the official Text but is to be found in the Miscellaneous Treaties Series, H.M.S.O. Cmnd. 5179–II.

Article 201

The Commission shall examine the conditions under which the financial contributions of Member States provided for in Article 200 could be replaced by the Community's own resources, in particular by revenue accruing from the common customs tariff when it has been finally introduced.

To this end, the Commission shall submit proposals to the Council.

After consulting the Assembly on these proposals the Council may, acting unanimay down the appropriate provisions, which it shall recommend to the Member States for adoption in accordance with their respective constitutional requirements.

Article 202

The expenditure shown in the budget shall be authorised for one financial year, unless the regulations made pursuant to Article 209 provide otherwise.

In accordance with conditions to be laid down pursuant to Article 209, any appropriations, other than those relating to staff expenditure, that are unexpended at the end of the financial year may be carried forward to the next financial year only.

Appropriations shall be classified under different chapters grouping items of expenditure according to their nature or purpose and subdivided, as far as may be necessary, in accordance with the regulations made pursuant to Article 209.

The expenditure of the Assembly, the Council, the Commission and the Court of Justice shall be set out in separate parts of the budget, without prejudice to special arrangements for certain common items of expenditure.

Article 203

[1. The financial year shall run from 1 January to 31 December.

2. Each institution of the Community shall, before 1 July, draw up estimates of its expenditure. The Commission shall consolidate these estimates in a preliminary draft budget. It shall attach thereto an opinion which may contain different estimates.

The preliminary draft budget shall contain an estimate of revenue and an estimate of expenditure.

3. The Commission shall place the preliminary draft budget before the Council not later than 1 September of the year preceding that in which the budget is to implemented.

The Council shall consult the Commission and, where appropriate, the other institutions concerned whenever it intends to depart from the preliminary draft budget.

The Council shall, acting by a qualified majority, establish the draft budget and forward it to the Assembly.

4. The draft budget shall be placed before the Assembly not later than 5 October of the year preceding that in which the budget is to be implemented.

The Assembly shall have the right to amend the draft budget, acting by a majority of its members and to propose to the Council, acting by an absolute majority of the votes cast, modifications to the draft budget relating to expenditure necessarily resulting from this Treaty or from acts adopted in accordance therewith.

If, within forty-five days of the draft budget being placed before it, the Assembly has given its approval, the budget shall stand as finally adopted. If within this period the Assembly has not amended the draft budget nor proposed any modifications thereto, the budget shall be deemed to be finally adopted.

If within this period the Assembly has adopted amendments or proposed modifications, the draft budget together with the amendments or proposed modifications shall be forwarded to the Council.

5. After discussing the draft budget with the commission and, where appropriate, with the other institutions concerned, the Council shall act under the following conditions:

(a) The Council may, acting by a qualified majority, modify any of the amendments adopted by the Assembly;

(b) With regard to the proposed modifications:

—where a modification proposed by the Assembly does not have the effect of increasing the total amount of the expenditure of an institution, owing in particular to the fact that the increase in expenditure which it would involve would be expressly compensated by one or more proposed modifications correspondingly reducing expenditure, the Council may, acting by a qualified majority, reject the proposed modification. In the absence of a decision to reject it, the proposed modification shall stand as accepted;

—where a modification proposed by the Assembly has the effect of increasing the total amount of the expenditure of an institution, the Council may, acting by a qualified majority, accept this proposed modification. In the absence of a decision to accept it, the proposed modification shall stand as rejected;

—where, in pursuance of one of the two preceding sub-paragraphs, the Council has rejected a proposed modification, it may, acting by a qualified majority, either retain the amount shown in the draft budget or fix another amount.

The draft budget shall be modified on the basis of the proposed modifications accepted by the Council.

If within fifteen days of the draft budget being placed before it, the Council has not modified any of the amendments adopted by the Assembly and if the modifications proposed by the latter have been accepted, the budget shall be deemed to be finally adopted. The Council shall inform the Assembly that it has not modified any of the amendments and that the proposed modifications have been accepted.

If within this period the Council has modified one or more of the amendments adopted by the Assembly or if the modifications proposed by the latter have been rejected or modified, the modified draft budget shall again be forwarded to the Assembly. The Council shall inform the Assembly of the results of its deliberations.

6. Within fifteen days of the draft budget being placed before it, the Assembly, which shall have been notified of the action taken on its proposed modifications, may, acting by a majority of its members and three-fifths of the votes cast, amend or reject the modifications to its amendments made by the Council and shall adopt the budget accordingly. If within this period the Assembly has not acted, the budget shall be deemed to be finally adopted.

7. When the procedure provided for in this Article has been completed, the President of the Assembly shall declare that the budget has been finally adopted.

8. However, the Assembly, acting by a majority of its members and two-thirds of the votes cast, may if there are important reasons reject the draft budget and ask for a new draft to be submitted to it.

9. A maximum rate of increase in relation to the expenditure of the same type to be incurred during the current year shall be fixed annually for the total expenditure other than that necessarily resulting from this Treaty or from acts adopted in accordance therewith.

The Commission shall, after consulting the Economic Policy Committee, declare what this maximum rate is as it results from:

—the trend in terms of volume, of the gross national product within the community;

—the average variation in the budgets of the Member States; and

—the trend of the cost of living during the preceding financial year.

The maximum rate shall be communicated, before 1 May, to all the institutions of the Community. The latter shall be required to conform to this during the budgetary procedure, subject to the provisions of the fourth and fifth sub-paragraphs of this paragraph.

If, in respect of expenditure other than that necessarily resulting from this Treaty or from acts adopted in accordance therewith, the actual rate of increase in the draft budget established by the Council is over half of the maximum rate, the Assembly may, exercising its right of amendment, further increase the total amount of that expenditure to a limit not exceeding half the maximum rate.

Where the Assembly, the Council or the Commission consider that the activities of the Communities require that the rate determined according to the procedure laid down in this paragraph should be exceeded, another rate may be fixed by agreement between the Council, acting by a qualified majority, and the Assembly, acting by a majority of its members and three-fifths of the votes cast.

10. Each institution shall exercise the powers conferred upon it by this Article, with due regard for the provisions of the Treaty and for acts adopted in accordance therewith, in particular those relating to the Communities' own resources and to the balance between revenue and expenditure.]

Amendments

This article was substituted by the Budgetary Treaty, Art. 4. It was subsequently substituted by the Second Budgetary Treaty of July 22, 1975, Art. 12.

[Article 203a

By way of derogation from the provisions of Article 203, the following provisions shall apply to budgets for financial years preceding the financial year 1975:

1. The financial year shall run from 1 January to 31 December.

2. Each institution of the Community shall, before 1 July, draw up estimates of its expenditure. The Commission shall consolidate these estimates in a preliminary draft budget. It shall attach thereto an opinion which may contain different estimates.

The preliminary draft budget shall contain an estimate of revenue and an estimate of expenditure.

3. The Commission shall place the preliminary draft budget before the Council not later than 1 September of the year preceding that in which the budget is to be implemented.

The Council shall consult the Commission and, where appropriate, the other institutions concerned whenever it intends to depart from the preliminary draft budget.

The Council shall, acting by a qualified majority, establish the draft budget and forward it to the Assembly.

4. The draft budget shall be placed before the Assembly not later than 5 October of the year preceding that in which the budget is to be implemented.

The Assembly shall have the right to propose to the Council modifications to the draft budget.

If, within forty-five days of the draft budget being placed before it, the Assembly has given its approval or has not proposed any modifications to the draft budget, the budget shall be deemed to be finally adopted.

If within this period the Assembly has proposed modifications, the draft budget together with the proposed modifications shall be forwarded to the Council.

5. The Council shall, after discussing the draft budget with the Commission and, where appropriate, with the other institutions concerned, adopt the budget, within thirty days of the draft budget being placed before it, under the following conditions.

Where a modification proposed by the Assembly does not have the effect of increasing the total amount of the expenditure of an institution, owing in particular to the fact that the increase in expenditure which it would involve would be expressly compensated by one or more proposed modifications correspondingly reducing expenditure, the Council may, acting by a qualified majority, reject the proposed modification. In the absence of a decision to reject it, the proposed modification shall stand as accepted.

Where a modification proposed by the Assembly has the effect of increasing the total amount of the expenditure of an institution, the Council must act by a qualified majority in accepting the proposed modification.

Where, in pursuance of the second or third subparagraph of this paragraph, the Council has rejected or has not accepted a proposed modification, it may, acting by a qualified majority, either retain the amount shown in the draft budget or fix another amount.

6. When the procedure provided for in this Article has been completed, the President of the Council shall declare that the budget has been finally adopted.

7. Each institution shall exercise the powers conferred upon it by this Article, with due regard for the provisions of this Treaty and for acts adopted in accordance therewith, in particular those relating to the Communities' own resources and to the balance between revenue and expenditure.]

AMENDMENT
This article was added by the Budgetary Treaty, Art. 5.

ARTICLE 204

[If, at the beginning of a financial year, the budget has not yet been voted, a sum equivalent to not more than one twelfth of the budget appropriations for the preceding financial year may be spent each month in respect of any chapter or other subdivision of the budget in accordance with the provisions of the regulations made pursuant to Article 209; this arrangement shall not, however, have the effect of placing at the disposal of the Commission appropriations in excess of one twelfth of those provided for in the draft budget in course of preparation.

The Council may, acting by a qualified majority, provided that the other conditions laid down in the first subparagraph are observed, authorise expenditure in excess of one twelfth.

If the decision relates to expenditure which does not necessarily result from this Treaty or from acts adopted in accordance therewith, the Council shall forward it immediately to the Assembly; within thirty days the Assembly, acting by a majority of its members and three fifths of the votes cast, may adopt a different decision on the expenditure in excess of the one twelfth referred to in the first subparagraph. This part of the decision of the Council shall be suspended until the Assembly has taken its decision. If within the period the Assembly has not taken a decision which differs from the decision of the Council, the latter shall be deemed to be finally adopted.

The decisions referred to in the second and third subparagraphs shall lay down the necessary measures relating to resources to ensure application of this Article.]

AMENDMENT
This article was replaced by the Second Budgetary Treaty of July 22, 1975, Art. 13.

ARTICLE 205

The Commission shall implement the budget, in accordance with the provisions of the regulations made pursuant to Article 209, on its own responsibility and within the limits of the appropriations.

The regulations shall lay down detailed rules for each institution concerning its part in effecting its own expenditure.

Within the budget, the Commission may, subject to the limits and conditions laid down in the regulations made pursuant to Article 209, transfer appropriation from one chapter to another or from one subdivision to another.

[ARTICLE 205a

The Commission shall submit annually to the Council and to the Assembly the accounts of the preceding financial year relating to the implementation of the budget. The Commission shall also forward to them a financial statement of the assets and liabilities of the Community.]

AMENDMENT
This article was added by the Second Budgetary Treaty of July 22, 1975, Art. 14.

ARTICLE 206

[1. A Court of Auditors is hereby established.

[2. The Court of Auditors shall consist of ten members.]

3. The members of the Court of Auditors shall be chosen from among persons who belong or have belonged in their respective countries to external audit bodies or who are especially qualified for this office. Their independence must be beyond doubt.

4. The members of the Court of Auditors shall be appointed for a term of six years by the Council, acting unanimously after consulting the Assembly.

However, when the first appointments are made four members of the Court of Auditors, chosen by lot, shall be appointed for a term of office of four years only.

The members of the Court of Auditors shall be eligible for reappointment.

They shall elect the President of the Court of Auditors from among their number for a term of three years. The President may be re-elected.

5. The members of the Court of Auditors shall, in the general interest of the Community, be completely independent in the performance of their duties.

In the performance of these duties, they shall neither seek nor take instructions from any Government or from any other body. They shall refrain from any action incompatible with their duties.

6. The members of the Court of Auditors may not, during their term of office, engage in any other occupation, whether gainful or not. When entering upon their duties they shall give a solemn undertaking that, both during and after their term of office, they will respect the obligations arising therefrom and in particular their duty to behave with integrity and discretion as regards the acceptance, after they have ceased to hold office, of certain appointments or benefits.

7. Apart from normal replacement, or death, the duties of a member of the Court of Auditors shall end when he resigns, or is compulsorily retired by a ruling of the Court of Justice pursuant to paragraph 8.

The vacancy thus caused shall be filled for the remainder of the member's term of office.

Save in the case of compulsory retirement, mambers of the Court of Auditors shall remain in office until they have been replaced.

8. A member of the Court of Auditors may be deprived of his office or of his right to a pension or other benefits in its stead only if the Court of Justice, at the request of the Court of Auditors, finds that he no longer fulfils the requisite conditions or meets the obligations arising from his office.

9. The Council, acting by a qualified majority, shall determine the conditions of employment of the President and the members of the Court of Auditors and in particular their salaries, allowances and pensions. It shall also, by the same majority, determine any payment to be made instead of remuneration.

10. The provisions of the Protocol on the Privileges and Immunities of the European Communities applicable to the Judges of the Court of Justice shall also apply to the members of the Court of Auditors.]

AMENDMENTS
This article was amended by the Budgetary Treaty, Art. 6 and subsequently replaced by the Second Budgetary Treaty of July 22, 1975, Art. 15.

Para. (2) was substituted by the Act of Accession of the Hellenic Republic of May 28, 1979, Art. 18.

[ARTICLE 206a

1. The Court of Auditors shall examine the accounts of all revenue and expenditure of the Community. It shall also examine the accounts of all revenue and expenditure of all bodies set up by the Community insofar as the relevant constituent instrument dòes not preclude such examination.

2. The Court of Auditors shall examine whether all revenue has been received and all expenditure incurred in a lawful and regular manner and whether the financial management has been sound.

The audit of revenue shall be carried out on the basis both of the amounts established as due and the amounts actually paid to the Community.

The audit of expenditure shall be carried out on the basis both of commitments undertaken and payments made.

These audits may be carried out before the closure of accounts for the financial year in question.

3. The audit shall be based on records and, if necessary, performed on the spot in the institutions of the Community and in the Member States. In the Member States the audit shall be carried out in liaison with the national audit bodies or, if these do not have the necessary powers, with the competent national departments. These bodies or departments shall inform the Court of Auditors whether they intend to take part in the audit.

The institutions of the Community and the national audit bodies or, if these do not have the necessary powers, the competent national departments, shall forward to the Court of Auditors, at its request any document or information necessary to carry out its task.

4. The Court of Auditors shall draw up an annual report after the close of each financial year. It shall be forwarded to the institutions of the Community and shall be published, together with the replies of these institutions to the observations of the Court of Auditors, in the Official Journal of the European Communities.

The Court of Auditors may also, at any time submit observations on specific questions and deliver opinions at the request of one of the institutions of the Community.

It shall adopt its annual reports or opinions by a majority of its members.

It shall assist the Assembly and the Council in exercising their powers of control over the implementation of the budget.]

AMENDMENT
This article was added by the Second Budgetary Treaty of July 22, 1975, Art. 16.

[Article 206b

The Assembly, acting on a recommendation from the Council which shall act by a qualified majority, shall give a discharge to the Commission in respect of the implementation of the budget. To this end, the Council and the Assembly in turn shall examine the accounts and the financial statement referred to in Article 206a and the annual report by the Court of Auditors together with the replies of the institutions under audit to the observations of the Court of Auditors.]

AMENDMENT
This article was added by the Second Budgetary Treaty of July 22, 1975, Art. 17.

Article 207

The budget shall be drawn up in the unit of account determined in accordance with the provisions of the regulations made pursuant to Article 209.

The financial contributions provided for in Article 200 (1) shall be placed at the disposal of the Community by the Member States in their national currencies.

The available balances of these contributions shall be deposited with the Treasuries of Member States or with bodies designated by them. While on deposit, such funds shall retain the value corresponding to the parity, at the date of deposit, in relation to the unit of account referred to in the first paragraph.

The balances may be invested on terms to be agreed between the Commission and the Member State concerned.

The regulations made pursuant to Article 209 shall lay down the technical conditions under which financial operations relating to the European Social Fund shall be carried out.

Article 208

The Commission may, provided it notifies the competent authorities of the Member States concerned, transfer into the currency of one of the Member States its holdings in the currency of another Member State, to the extent necessary to enable them to be used for purposes which come within the scope of this Treaty. The Commission shall as far as possible avoid making such transfers if it possesses cash or liquid assets in the currencies which it needs.

The Commission shall deal with each Member State through the authority designated by the State concerned. In carrying out financial operations the Commission shall employ the services of the bank of issue of the Member State concerned or of any other financial institution approved by that State.

Article 209

[The Council, acting unanimously on a proposal from the Commission and after consulting the Assembly and obtaining the opinion of the Court of Auditors, shall:

  (a) make financial regulations specifying in particular the procedure to be adopted for establishing and implementing the budget and for presenting and auditing accounts;

  (b) determine the methods and procedure whereby the budget revenue provided under the arrangements relating to the Communities' own resources shall be made available to the Commission, and determine the measures to be applied, if need be, to meet cash requirements;

  (c) lay down rules concerning the responsibility of authorising officers and accounting officers and concerning appropriate arrangements for inspection.]

AMENDMENT
This article was replaced by the Second Budgetary Treaty of July 22, 1975, Art. 18.

Part Six

GENERAL AND FINAL PROVISIONS

Article 210

The Community shall have legal personality.

Article 211

In each of the Member States, the Community shall enjoy the most extensive legal capacity accorded to legal persons under their laws; it may, in particular, acquire or dispose of movable and immovable property and may be a party to legal proceedings. To this end, the Community shall be represented by the Commission.

Article 212

[*Repealed by the Merger Treaty, Art. 24 (2). See now ibid., Art. 24 (1).*]

Article 213

The Commission may, within the limits and under the conditions laid down by the Council in accordance with the provisions of this Treaty, collect any information and carry out any checks require for the performance of the tasks entrusted to it.

Article 214

The members of the institutions of the Community, the members of committees, and the officials and other servants of the Community shall be required, even after their duties have ceased, not to disclose information of the kind covered by the obligation of professional secrecy, in particular information about undertakings, their business relations or their cost components.

Article 215

The contractual liability of the Community shall be governed by the law applicable to the contract in question.

In the case of non-contractual liability, the Community shall, in accordance with the general principles common to the laws of the Member States, make good any damage caused by its institutions or by its servants in the performance of their duties.

The personal liability of its servants towards the Community shall be governed by the provisions laid down in their Staff Regulations or in the Conditions of Employment applicable to them.

Article 216

The seat of the institutions of the Community shall be determined by common accord of the Governments of the Member States.

Article 217

The rules governing the languages of the institutions of the Community shall, without prejudice to the provisions contained in the rules of procedure of the Court of Justice, be determined by the Council, acting unanimously.

Article 218

[*Repealed by the Merger Treaty, Art. 28, second para. See now ibid., Art. 28, first para.*]

Article 219

Member States undertake not to submit a dispute concerning the interpretation or application of this Treaty to any method of settlement other than those provided for therein.

Article 220

Member States shall, so far as is necessary, enter into negotiations with each other with a view to securing for the benefit of their nationals:
—the protection of persons and the enjoyment and protection of rights under the same conditions as those accorded by each State to its own nationals;
—the abolition of double taxation within the Community;

—the mutual recognition of companies or firms within the meaning of the second paragraph of Article 58, the retention of legal personality in the event of transfer of their seat from one country to another, and the possibility of mergers between companies of firms governed by the laws of different countries;

—the simplification of formalities governing the reciprocal recognition and enforcement of judgments of courts or tribunals and of arbitration awards.

ARTICLE 221

Within three years of the entry into force of this Treaty, Member States shall accord nationals of the other Member States the same treatment as their own nationals as regards participation in the capital of companies of firms within the meaning of Article 58, without prejudice to the application of the other provisions of this Treaty.

ARTICLE 222

This Treaty shall in no way prejudice the rules in Member States governing the system of property ownership.

ARTICLE 223

1. The provisions of this Treaty shall not preclude the application of the following rules:

   (a) No Member State shall be obliged to supply information the disclosure of which it considers contrary to the essential interests of its security;

   (b) Any Member State may take such measures as it considers necessary for the protection of the essential interests of its security which are connected with the production of or trade in arms, munitions and war material; such measures shall not adversely affect the conditions of competition in the common market regarding products which are not intended for specifically military purposes.

2. During the first year after the entry into force of this Treaty, the Council shall, acting unanimously, draw up a list of products to which the provisions of paragraph 1 (b) shall apply.

3. The Council may, acting unanimously on a proposal from the Commission, make changes in this list.

ARTICLE 224

Member States shall consult each other with a view to taking together the steps needed to prevent the functioning of the common market being affected by measures which a Member State may be called upon to take in the event of serious internal disturbances affecting the maintenance of law and order, in the event of war or serious international tension constituting a threat of war, or in order to carry out obligations it has accepted for the purpose of maintaining peace and international security.

ARTICLE 225

If measures taken in the circumstances referred to in Articles 223 and 224 have the effect of distorting the conditions of competition in the common market, the Commission shall, together with the State concerned, examine how these measures can be adjusted to the rules laid down in this Treaty.

By way of derogation from the procedure laid down in Articles 169 and 170, the Commission or any Member State may bring the matter directly before the Court of Justice if it considers that another Member State is making improper use of the powers provided for in Articles 223 and 224. The Court of Justice shall give its ruling *in camera*.

ARTICLE 226

1. If, during the transitional period, difficulties arise which are serious and liable to persist in any sector of the economy of which could bring about serious deterioration in the economic situation of a given area, a Member State may apply for authorisation to take protective measures in order to rectify the situation and adjust the sector concerned to the economy of the common market.

2. On application by the State concerned, the Commission shall, by emergency procedure, determine without delay the protective measures which it considers necessary, specifying the circumstances and the manner in which they are to be put into effect.

3. The measures authorised under paragraph 2 may involve derogations from the rules of this Treaty, to such an extent and for such periods as are strictly necessary in order to attain the objectives referred to in paragraph 1. Priority shall be given to such measures as will least disturb the functioning of the common market.

ARTICLE 227

[1. This Treaty shall apply to the Kingdom of Belgium, the Kingdom of Denmark, the Federal Republic of Germany, the Hellenic Republic, the French Republic, Ireland, the Italian Republic, the Grand Duchy of Luxembourg, the Kingdom of the Netherlands and the United Kingdom of Great Britain and Northern Ireland.]

2. With regard to Algeria and the French overseas departments, the general and particular provisions of this Treaty relating to:
—the free movement of goods;
—agriculture, save for Article 40 (4);
—the liberalisation of services;
—the rules on competition;
—the protective measures provided for in Articles 108, 109 and 226;
—the institutions,
shall apply as soon as this Treaty enters into force.

The conditions under which the other provisions of this Treaty are to apply shall be determined, within two years of the entry into force of this Treaty, by decisions of the Council, acting unanimously on a proposal from the Commission.

The institutions of the Community will, within the framework of the procedures provided for in this Treaty, in particular Article 226, take care that the economic and social development of these areas is made possible.

3. The special arrangements for association set out in Part Four of this Treaty shall apply to the overseas countries and territories listed in Annex IV to this Treaty.

[This Treaty shall not apply to those overseas countries and territories having special relations with the United Kingdom of Great Britain and Northern Ireland which are not included in the aforementioned list.]

4. The provisions of this Treaty shall apply to the European territories for whose external relations a Member State is responsible.

[5. Notwithstanding the preceding paragraphs:

    (a) This Treaty shall not apply to the Faroe Islands. The Government of the Kingdom of Denmark may, however, give notice, by a declaration deposited by 31 December 1975 at the latest with the Government of the Italian Republic, which shall transmit a certified copy thereof to each of the Governments of the other Member States, that this Treaty shall apply to those Islands. In that event, this Treaty shall apply to those Islands from the first day of the second month following the deposit of the declaration.

    (b) This Treaty shall not apply to the Sovereign Base Areas of the United Kingdom of Great Britain and Northern Ireland in Cyprus.

    (c) This Treaty shall apply to the Channel Islands and the Isle of Man only to the extent necessary to ensure the implementation of the arrangements for those islands set out in the Treaty concerning the accession of new Member States to the European Economic Community and to the European Atomic Energy Community signed on 22 January 1972.]

AMENDMENTS

Para. (1) was substituted by the Act of Accession, Art. 26 (1), as amended by the Adaptation Decision, Art. 15 (1). It was subsequently substituted by the Act of Accession of the Hellenic Republic of May 28, 1979, Art. 20.

In para. (3) the words in square brackets were added by the Act of Accession, Art. 26 (2).

Para. (5) was added by the Act of Accession, Art. 26 (3), as amended by the Adaptation Decision, Art. 15 (2).

ARTICLE 228

1. Where this Treaty provides for the conclusion of agreements between the Community and one or more States or an international organisation, such agreements shall be negotiated by the Commission. Subject to the powers vested in the Commission in this field, such agreements shall be concluded by the Council, after consulting the Assembly where required by this Treaty.

The Council, the Commission or a Member State may obtain beforehand the opinion of the Court of Justice as to whether an agreement envisaged is compatible with the provisions of this Treaty. Where the opinion of the Court of Justice is adverse, the agreement may enter into force only in accordance with Article 236.

2. Agreements concluded under these conditions shall be binding on the institutions of the Community and on Member States.

ARTICLE 229

It shall be for the Commission to ensure the maintenance of all appropriate relations with the organs of the United Nations, of its specialised agencies and of the General Agreement on Tariffs and Trade.

The Commission shall also maintain such relations as are appropriate with all international organisations.

ARTICLE 230

The Community shall establish all appropriate forms of co-operation with the Council of Europe.

Article 231

The Community shall establish close co-operation with the Organisation for European Economic Co-operation, the details to be determined by common accord.

Article 232

1. The provisions of this Treaty shall not affect the provisions of the Treaty establishing the European Coal and Steel Community, in particular as regards the rights and obligations of Member States, the powers of the institutions of that Community and the rules laid down by that Treaty for the functioning of the common market in coal and steel.

2. The provisions of this Treaty shall not derogate from those of the Treaty establishing the European Atomic Energy Community.

Article 233

The provisions of this Treaty shall not preclude the existence or completion of regional unions between Belgium and Luxembourg, or between Belgium, Luxembourg and the Netherlands, to the extent that the objectives of these regional unions are not attained by application of this Treaty.

Article 234

The rights and obligations arising from agreements concluded before the entry into force of this Treaty between one or more Member States on the one hand, and one or more third countries on the other, shall not be affected by the provisions of this Treaty.

To the extent that such agreements are not compatible with this Treaty, the Member State or States concerned shall take all appropriate steps to eliminate the incompatibilities established. Member States shall, where necessary, assist each other to this end and shall, where appropriate, adopt a common attitude.

In applying the agreements referred to in the first paragraph, Member States shall take into account the fact that the advantages accorded under this Treaty by each Member State form an integral part of the establishment of the Community and are thereby inseparably linked with the creation of common institutions, the conferring of powers upon them and the granting of the same advantages by all the other Member States.

Article 235

If action by the Community should prove necessary to attain, in the course of the operation of the common market, one of the objectives of the Community and this Treaty has not provided the necessary powers, the Council shall, acting unanimously on a proposal from the Commission and after consulting the Assembly, take the appropriate measures.

Article 236

The Government of any Member State or the Commission may submit to the Council proposals for the amendment of this Treaty.

If the Council, after consulting the Assembly and, where appropriate, the Commission, delivers an opinion if favour of calling a conference of representatives of the Governments of the Member States, the conference shall be convened by the President of the Council for the purpose of determining by common accord the amendments to be made to this Treaty.

The amendments shall enter into force after being ratified by all the Member States in accordance with their respective constitutional requirements.

ARTICLE 237

Any European State may apply to become a member of the Community. It shall address its application to the Council, which shall act unanimously after obtaining the opinion of the Commission.

The conditions of admission and the adjustments to this Treaty necessitated thereby shall be the subject of an agreement between the Member States and the applicant State. This agreement shall be submitted for ratification by all the Contracting States in accordance with their respective constitutional requirements.

ARTICLE 238

The Community may conclude with a third State, a union of States or an international organisation agreements establishing an association involving reciprocal rights and obligations, common action and special procedures.

These agreements shall be concluded by the Council, acting unanimously after consulting the Assembly.

Where such agreements call for amendments to this Treaty, these amendments shall first be adopted in accordance with the procedure laid down in Article 236.

ARTICLE 239

The Protocols annexed to this Treaty by common accord of the Member States shall form an integral part thereof.

ARTICLE 240

This Treaty is concluded for an unlimited period.

SETTING UP OF THE INSTITUTIONS

ARTICLE 241

The Council shall meet within one month of the entry into force of this Treaty.

ARTICLE 242

The Council shall, within three months of its first meeting, take all appropriate measures to constitute the Economic and Social Committee.

ARTICLE 243

The Assembly shall meet within two months of the first meeting of the Council, having been convened by the President of the Council, in order to elect its officers and draw up its rules of procedure. Pending the election of its officers, the oldest member shall take the chair.

ARTICLE 244

The Court of Justice shall take up its duties as soon as its members have been appointed. Its first President shall be appointed for three years in the same manner as its members.

The Court of Justice shall adopt its rules of procedure within three months of taking up its duties.

No matter may be brought before the Court of Justice until its rules of procedure have been published. The time within which an action must be brought shall run only from the date of this publication.

Upon his appointment, the President of the Court of Justice shall exercise the powers conferred upon him by this Treaty.

ARTICLE 245

The Commission shall take up its duties and assume the responsibilities conferred upon it by this Treaty as soon as its members have been appointed.

Upon taking up its duties, the Commission shall undertake the studies and arrange the contacts needed for making an overall survey of the economic situation of the Community.

ARTICLE 246

1. The first financial year shall run from the date on which this Treaty enters into force until 31 December following. Should this Treaty, however, enter into force during the second half of the year, the first financial year shall run until 31 December of the following year.

2. Until the budget for the first financial year has been established, Member States shall make the Community interest-free advances which shall be deducted from their financial contributions to the implementation of the budget.

3. Until the Staff Regulations of officials and the Conditions of Employment of other servants of the Community provided for in Article 212 have been laid down, each institution shall recruit the Staff it needs and to this end conclude contracts of limited duration.

Each institution shall examine together with the Council any question concerning the number, remuneration and distribution of posts.

FINAL PROVISIONS

ARTICLE 247

This Treaty shall be ratified by the High Contracting Parties in accordance with their respective constitutional requirements. The instruments of ratification shall be deposited with the Government of the Italian Republic.

This Treaty shall enter into force on the first day of the month following the deposit of the instrument of ratification by the last signatory State to take this step. If, however, such deposit is made less than fifteen days before the beginning of the following month, this Treaty shall not enter into force until the first day of the second month after the date of such deposit.

ARTICLE 248

This Treaty, drawn up in a single original in the Dutch, French, German and Italian languages, all four texts being equally authentic, shall be deposited in the archives of the Government of the Italian Republic, which shall transmit a certified copy to each of the Governments of the other signatory States.

IN WITNESS WHEREOF, the undersigned Plenipotentiaries have signed this Treaty.

DONE at Rome this twenty-fifth day of March in the year one thousand nine hundred and fifty-seven.

P. H. SPAAK	J. Ch. SNOY et d'OPPUERS
ADENAUER	HALLSTEIN
PINEAU	M. FAURE
Antonio SEGNI	Gaetano MARTINO
BECH	Lambert SCHAUS
J. LUNS	J. LINTHORST HOMAN

ANNEX IV—OVERSEAS COUNTRIES AND TERRITORIES

to which the provisions of Part Four of this Treaty apply

French West Africa: Senegal, French Sudan, French Guinea, Ivory Coast, Dahomey, Mauritania, Niger and Upper Volta;

French Equatorial Africa: Middle Congo, Ubangi-Shari, Chad and Gabon;

Saint Pierre and Miquelon, the Comoro Archipelago, Madagascar and dependencies, French Somaliland, New Caledonia and dependencies, French Settlements in Oceania, Southern and Antarctic Territories;

The Autonomous Republic of Togoland;

The Trust Territory of the Cameroons under French administration;

The Belgian Congo and Ruanda-Urundi;

The Trust Territory of Somaliland under Italian administration;

Netherlands New Guinea;

[The Netherlands Antilles];

[Anglo-French Condominium of the New Hebrides;

The Bahamas;

Bermuda;

British Antarctic Territory;

British Honduras;

British Indian Ocean Territory;

British Solomon Islands;

British Virgin Islands;

Brunei;

Associated States in the Caribbean: Antigua, Dominica, Grenada, St. Lucia, St. Vincent, St. Kitts-Nevis-Anguilla;

Cayman Islands;

Central and Southern Line Islands;

Falkland Islands and Dependencies;

Gilbert and Ellice Islands;

Montserrat;

Pitcairn;

St. Helena and Dependencies;

The Seychelles;

Turks and Caicos Islands.]

AMENDMENTS

The Dutch West Indies were added to this list by the Convention of 13 November 1962, amending the EEC Treaty.

The countries listed within the square brackets were added by the Act of Accession, Art. 24 (2), as amended by the Adaptation Decision, Art. 13.

PROTOCOL ON THE STATUTE OF THE EUROPEAN INVESTMENT BANK

See the Appendix for amending provisions.

THE HIGH CONTRACTING PARTIES,

DESIRING to lay down the Statute of the European Investment Bank provided for in Article 129 of this Treaty,

HAVE AGREED upon the following provisions, which shall be annexed to this Treaty:

ARTICLE 1

The European Investment Bank established by Article 129 of this Treaty (hereinafter called the " Bank ") is hereby constituted; it shall perform its functions and carry on its activities in accordance with the provisions of this Treaty and of this Statute.

The seat of the Bank shall be determined by common accord of the Governments of the Member States.

ARTICLE 2

The task of the Bank shall be that defined in Article 130 of this Treaty.

ARTICLE 3

[In accordance with Article 129 of this Treaty, the following shall be members of the Bank:
—the Kingdom of Belgium;
—the Kingdom of Denmark;
—the Federal Republic of Germany;
—the Hellenic Republic;
—the French Republic;
—Ireland;
—the Italian Republic;
—the Grand Duchy of Luxembourg;
—the Kingdom of the Netherlands;
—the United Kingdom of Great Britain and Northern Ireland.]

AMENDMENTS

This Article was substituted by Protocol No. 1, Art. 1, annexed to the Act of Accession, as amended by the Adaptation Decision, Art. 35. It was subsequently substituted by Protocol No. 1, Art. 1, annexed to the Act of Accession of the Hellenic Republic of May 28, 1979.

ARTICLE 4

[1. The capital of the Bank shall be seven thousand and two hundred million units of account, subscribed by the Member States as follows:

Germany	1,575 million
France	1,575 million
United Kingdom	1,575 million
Italy	1,260 million
Belgium	414·75 million
Netherlands	414·75 million
Denmark	210 million
Greece	112·50 million
Ireland	52·50 million
Luxembourg	10·50 million.]

[The value of the unit of account shall be equal to the sum of the following amounts of the national currencies of the Member States:

German mark	0·828
Pound sterling	0·0885
French franc	1·15
Italian lira	109
Dutch guilder	0·286
Belgian franc	3·66
Luxembourg franc	0·14
Danish krone	0·217
Irish pound	0·00759]

[The Board of Governors, acting unanimously on a proposal from the Board of Directors, may alter the definition of the unit of account.]

The Member States shall be liable only up to the amount of their share of the capital subscribed and not paid up.

2. The admission of a new member shall entail an increase in the subscribed capital corresponding to the capital brought in by the new member.

3. The Board of Governors may, acting unanimously, decide to increase the subscribed capital.

4. The share of a member in the subscribed capital may not be transferred pledged or attached.

AMENDMENTS

The first sub-paragraph of para. (1) was substituted by Protocol No. 1, Art. 2, annexed to the Act of Accession, as amended by the Adaptation Decision, Art. 36. It was subsequently substituted by Protocol No. 1, Art. 2, annexed to the Act. of Accession of the Hellenic Republic of May 28, 1979.

In the second sub-paragraph of para. (1) the words in the first set of square brackets were amended by the decision of the Board of Governors of the European Investment Bank of December 30, 1977 (O.J. 1978, L199/1). The words in the second set of square brackets were added by the Treaty of July 10, 1975, amending certain provisions of the Protocol on the Statute of the European Investment Bank, Art. 1.

ARTICLE 5

[1. The subscribed capital shall be paid up by Member States to the extent of 20 per cent. of the amounts laid down in Article 4 (1).

2. In the event of an increase in the subscribed capital, the Board of Governors, acting unanimously, shall fix the percentage to be paid up and the arrangements for payment.

3. The Board of Directors may require payment of the balance of the subscribed capital, to such extent as may be required for the Bank to meet its obligations towards those who have made loans to it.

Each Member State shall make this payment in proportion to its share of the subscribed capital in the currencies required by the Bank to meet these obligations.]

AMENDMENT

The words in square brackets were substituted by the Act of Accession, Protocol No. 1, Art. 3.

ARTICLE 6

1. The Board of Governors may, acting by a qualified majority on a proposal from the Board of Directors, decide that Member States shall grant the Bank special interest-bearing loans if and to the extent that the Bank requires such loans to finance specific projects and the Board of Directors shows that the Bank is unable to obtain the necessary funds on the capital markets on terms appropriate to the nature and purpose of the projects to be financed.

2. Special loans may not be called for until the beginning of the fourth year after the entry into force of this Treaty. They shall not exceed 400 million units of account in the aggregate or 100 million units of account per annum.

3. The term of special loans shall be related to the term of the loans or guarantees which the Bank proposes to grant by means of the special loans; it shall not exceed twenty years. The Board of Governors may, acting by a qualified majority on a proposal from the Board of Directors, decide upon the prior repayment of special loans.

4. Special loans shall bear interest at 4 per cent. per annum, unless the Board of Governors, taking into account the trend and level of interest rates on the capital markets, decides to fix a different rate.

5. Special loans shall be granted by Member States in proportion to their share in the subscribed capital; payment shall be made in national currency within six months of such loans being called for.

6. Should the Bank go into liquidation, special loans granted by Member States shall be repaid only after the other debts of the Bank have been settled.

ARTICLE 7

[1. Should the value of the currency of a Member State in relation to the unit of account defined in Article 4 be reduced, that State shall adjust the amount of its capital share paid in in its own currency in proportion to the change in value by making a supplementary payment to the Bank.

2. Should the value of the currency of a Member State in relation to the unit of account defined in Article 4 be increased, the Bank shall adjust the amount of the capital share paid in by that State in its own currency in proportion to the change in value by making a repayment to that State.

3. For the purpose of this article, the value of the currency of a Member State in relation to the unit of account, defined in Article 4, shall correspond to the rate for converting the unit of account into this currency and vice versa based on market rates.

4. The Board of Governors, acting unanimously on a proposal from the Board of Directors, may alter the method of converting sums expressed in units of account into national currencies and vice versa.

Furthermore, acting unanimously on a proposal from the Board of Directors, it may define the method for adjusting the capital referred to in paragraphs 1 and 2 of this article; adjustment payments must be made at least once a year.]

AMENDMENTS

This article was amended by the Decision of the Board of Governors of December 30, 1977 and by the Treaty of July 10, 1975 amending certain provisions of the Protocol on the Statute of the European Investment Bank.

It was subsequently substituted by Protocol No. 1, Art. 3, annexed to the Act of Accession of the Hellenic Republic of May 28, 1979.

ARTICLE 8

The Bank shall be directed and managed by a Board of Governors, a Board of Directors and a Management Committee.

ARTICLE 9

1. The Board of Governors shall consist of the Ministers designated by the Member States.

2. The Board of Governors shall lay down general directives for the credit policy of the Bank, with particular reference to the objectives to be pursued as progress is made in the attainment of the common market.

The Board of Governors shall ensure that these directives are implemented.

3. The Board of Governors shall in addition:
   (a) [decide whether to increase the subscribed capital in accordance with Article 4 (3) and Article 5 (2);]
   (b) exercise the powers provided in Article 6 in respect of special loans;
   (c) [exercise the powers provided in Articles 11 and 13 in respect of the appointment and the compulsory retirement of the members of the Board of Directors and of the Management Committee, and those powers provided in the second sub-paragraph of Article 13 (1);]
   (d) authorise the derogation provided for in Article 18 (1);
   (e) approve the annual report of the Board of Directors;
   (f) approve the annual balance sheet and profit and loss account;
   [(g) exercise the powers and functions provided for in Articles 4, 7, 14, 17, 26 and 27;]
   (h) approve the rules of procedure of the Bank.

4. Within the framework of this Treaty and this Statute, the Board of Governors shall be competent to take, acting unanimously, any decisions concerning the suspension of the operations of the Bank and, should the event arise, its liquidation.

AMENDMENTS

In para. (3), sub-paras. (a) and (c) were substituted by Protocol No. 1, Art. 4, annexed to the Act of Accession.

Sub-para. (g) was replaced by the Treaty of July 10, 1975, amending certain provisions of the Protocol on the Statute of the European Investment Bank, Art. 3.

ARTICLE 10

[Save as otherwise provided in this Statute, decisions of the Board of Governors shall be taken by a majority of its members. This majority must represent at least 40 per cent. of the subscribed capital. Voting by the Board of Governors shall be in accordance with the provisions of Article 148 of this Treaty.]

STATUTE OF THE EUROPEAN INVESTMENT BANK

AMENDMENT
This Article was substituted by Protocol No. 1, Art. 5, annexed to the Act of Accession.

ARTICLE 11

1. The Board of Directors shall have sole power to take decisions in respect of granting loans and guarantees and raising loans; it shall fix the interest rates on loans granted and the commission on guarantees; it shall see that the Bank is properly run; it shall ensure that the Bank is managed in accordance with the provisions of this Treaty and of this Statute and with the general directives laid down by the Board of Governors.

At the end of the financial year the Board of Directors shall submit a report to the Board of Governors and shall publish it when approved.

2. [[The Board of Directors shall consist of 19 directors and 11 alternates.

The directors shall be appointed by the Board of Governors for five years as shown below:
3 directors nominated by the Federal Republic of Germany;
3 directors nominated by the French Republic;
3 directors nominated by the Italian Republic;
3 directors nominated by the United Kingdom of Great Britain and Northern Ireland;
1 director nominated by the Kingdom of Belgium;
1 director nominated by the Kingdom of Denmark;
1 director nominated by the Hellenic Republic;
1 director nominated by Ireland;
1 director nominated by the Grand Duchy of Luxembourg;
1 director nominated by the Kingdom of the Netherlands;
1 director nominated by the Commission.

The alternates shall be appointed by the Board of Governors for five years as shown below:
2 alternates nominated by the Federal Republic of Germany;
2 alternates nominated by the French Republic;
2 alternates nominated by the Italian Republic;
2 alternates nominated by the United Kingdom of Great Britain and Northern Ireland;
1 alternate nominated by common accord of the Kingdom of Denmark, the Hellenic Republic and Ireland;
1 alternate nominated by common accord of the Benelux countries;
1 alternate nominated by the Commission.]

The appointments of the directors and the alternates shall be renewable.

Alternates may take part in the meetings of the Board of Directors. Alternates nominated by a State, or by common accord of several States, or by the Commission, may replace directors nominated by that State, by one of those States or by the Commission respectively. Alternates shall have no right of vote except where they replace one director or more than one director or where they have been delegated for this purpose in accordance with Article 12 (1).]

The President of the Management Committee or, in his absence, one of the Vice-Presidents, shall preside over meetings of the Board of Directors but shall not vote.

Members of the Board of Directors shall be chosen from persons whose independence and competence are beyond doubt; they shall be responsible only to the Bank.

3. A director may be compulsorily retired by the Board of Governors only if he no longer fulfils the conditions required for the performance of his duties; the Board must act by a qualified majority.

If the annual report is not approved, the Board of Directors shall resign.

4. Any vacancy arising as a result of death, voluntary resignation, compulsory retirement or collective resignation shall be filled in accordance with paragraph 2. A member shall be replaced for the remainder of his term of office, save where the entire Board of Directors is being replaced.

5. The Board of Governors shall determine the remuneration of members of the Board of Directors. The Board of Governors shall, acting unanimously, lay down what activities are incompatible with the duties of a director or an alternate.

AMENDMENTS
In para. (2) the words in the first set of square brackets were substituted by Protocol No. 1, Art. 4, annexed to the Act of Accession of the Hellenic Republic of May 28, 1979.

The words in the second set of square brackets were substituted by Protocol No. 1, Art. 6, annexed to the Act of Accession, as amended by the Adaptation Decision, Art. 37.

ARTICLE 12

1. [Each director shall have one vote on the Board of Directors. He may delegate his vote in all cases, according to procedures to be laid down in the rules of procedure of the Bank.]

2. Save as otherwise provided in this Statute, decisions of the Board of Directors shall be taken by a simple majority of the members entitled to vote. [A qualified majority shall require thirteen votes in favour.] The rules of procedure of the Bank shall lay down how many members of the Board of Directors constitute the quorum needed for the adoption of decisions.

AMENDMENTS

Para. (1) was substituted by Protocol No. 1, Art. 7, annexed to the Act of Accession.

In para, (2) the words in square brackets were substituted by Protocol No. 1, Art. 8, annexed to the Act of Accession, as amended by the Adaptation Decision, Art. 38. They were subsequently substituted by Protocol No. 1, Art. 5, annexed to the Act of Accession of the Hellenic Republic of May 28, 1979.

ARTICLE 13

1. [[The Management Committee shall consist of a President and five Vice-Presidents appointed for a period of six years by the Board of Governors on a proposal from the Board of Directors. Their appointments shall be renewable.]

The Board of Governors, acting unanimously, may vary the number of members on the Management Committee.]

2. On a proposal from the Board of Directors adopted by a qualified majority, the Board of Governors may, acting in its turn by a qualified majority, compulsorily retire a member of the Management Committee.

3. The Management Committee shall be responsible for the current business of the Bank, under the authority of the President and the supervision of the Board of Directors.

It shall prepare the decisions of the Board of Directors, in particular decisions on the raising of loans and the granting of loans and guarantees; it shall ensure that these decisions are implemented.

4. The Management Committee shall act by a majority when delivering opinions on proposals for raising loans or granting loans and guarantees.

5. The Board of Governors shall determine the remuneration of members of the Management Committee and shall lay down what activities are incompatible with their duties.

6. The President or, if he is prevented, a Vice-President shall represent the Bank in judicial and other matters.

7. The officials and other employees of the Bank shall be under the authority of the President. They shall be engaged and discharged by him. In the selection of staff, account shall be taken not only of personal ability and qualifications but also of an equitable representation of nationals of Member States.

8. The Management Committee and the staff of the Bank shall be responsible only to the Bank and shall be completely independent in the performance of their duties.

AMENDMENTS

Para. (1) was substituted by Protocol No. 1, Art. 9, annexed to the Act of Accession.

Para. (1), first sub-paragraph was substituted by Protocol No. 1, Art. 6, annexed to the Act of Accession of the Hellenic Republic of May 28, 1979.

ARTICLE 14

1. A committee consisting of three members, appointed on the grounds of their competence by the Board of Governors, shall annually verify that the operations of the Bank have been conducted and its books kept in a proper manner.

2. The Committee shall confirm that the balance sheet and profit and loss account are in agreement with the accounts and faithfully reflect the position of the Bank in respect of its assets and liabilities.

ARTICLE 15

The Bank shall deal with each Member State through the authority designated by that State. In the conduct of financial operations the Bank shall have recourse to the bank of issue of the Member State concerned or to other financial institutions approved by that State.

ARTICLE 16

1. The Bank shall co-operate with all international organisations active in fields similar to its own.

2. The Bank shall seek to establish all appropriate contacts in the interests of co-operation with banking and financial institutions in the countries to which its operations extend.

Article 17

At the request of a Member State or of the Commission, or on its own initiative, the Board of Governors shall, in accordance with the same provisions as governed their adoption, interpret or supplement the directives laid down by it under Article 9 of this Statute.

Article 18

1. Within the framework of the task set out in Article 130 of this Treaty, the Bank shall grant loans to its members or to private or public undertakings for investment projects to be carried out in the European territories of Member States, to the extent that funds are not available from other sources on reasonable terms.

However, by way of derogation authorised by the Board of Governors, acting unanimously on a proposal from the Board of Directors, the Bank may grant loans for investment projects to be carried out, in whole or in part, outside the European territories of Member States.

2. As far as possible, loans shall be granted only on condition that other sources of finance are also used.

3. When granting a loan to an undertaking or to a body other than a Member State, the Bank shall make the loan conditional either on a guarantee from the Member State in whose territory the project will be carried out or on other adequate guarantees.

4. The Bank may guarantee loans contracted by public or private undertakings or other bodies for the purpose of carrying out projects provided for in Article 130 of this Treaty.

5. The aggregate amount outstanding at any time of loans and guarantees granted by the Bank shall not exceed 250 per cent. of its subscribed capital.

6. The Bank shall protect itself against exchange risks by including in contracts for loans and guarantees such clauses as it considers appropriate.

Article 19

1. Interest rates on loans to be granted by the Bank and commission on guarantees shall be adjusted to conditions prevailing on the capital market and shall be calculated in such a way that the income therefrom shall enable the Bank to meet its obligations, to cover its expenses and to build up a reserve fund as provided for in Article 24.

2. The Bank shall not grant any reduction in interest rates. Where a reduction in the interest rate appears desirable in view of the nature of the project to be financed, the Member State concerned or some other agency may grant aid towards the payment of interest to the extent that this is compatible with Article 92 of this Treaty.

Article 20

In its loan and guarantee operations, the Bank shall observe the following principles:

1. It shall ensure that its funds are employed as rationally as possible in the interests of the Community.

It may grant loans or guarantees only:
   (a) where, in the case of projects carried out by undertakings in the production sector, interest and amortisation payments are covered out of operating profits or, in other cases, either by a commitment entered into by the State in which the project is carried out or by some other means; and
   (b) where the execution of the project contributes to an increase in economic productivity in general and promotes the attainment of the common market.

2. It shall neither acquire any interest in an undertaking nor assume any responsibility in its management unless this is required to safeguard the rights of the Bank in ensuring recovery of funds lent.

3. It may dispose of its claims on the capital market and may, to this end, require its debtors to issue bonds or other securities.

4. Neither the Bank nor the Member States shall impose conditions requiring funds lent by the Bank to be spent within a specified Member State.

5. The Bank may make its loans conditional on international invitations to tender being arranged.

6. The Bank shall not finance, in whole or in part, any project opposed by the Member State in whose territory it is to be carried out.

ARTICLE 21

1. Applications for loans or guarantees may be made to the Bank either through the Commission or through the Member State in whose territory the project will be carried out. An undertaking may also apply direct to the Bank for a loan or guarantee.

2. Applications made through the Commission shall be submitted for an opinion to the Member State in whose territory the project will be carried out. Applications made through a Member State shall be submitted to the Commission for an opinion. Applications made direct by an undertaking shall be submitted to the Member State concerned and to the Commission.

The Member State concerned and the Commission shall deliver their opinions within two months. If no reply is received within this period, the Bank may assume that there is no objection to the project in question.

3. The Board of Directors shall rule on applications for loans or guarantees submitted to it by the Management Committee.

4. The Management Committee shall examine whether applications for loans or guarantees submitted to it comply with the provisions of this Statute, in particular with Article 20. Where the Management Committee is in favour of granting the loan or guarantee, it shall submit the draft contract to the Board of Directors; the Committee may make its favourable opinion subject to such conditions as it considers essential. Where the Management Committee is against granting the loan or guarantee, it shall submit the relevant documents together with its opinion to the Board of Directors.

5. Where the Management Committee delivers an unfavourable opinion, the Board of Directors may not grant the loan or guarantee concerned unless its decision is unanimous.

6. Where the Commission delivers an unfavourable opinion, the Board of Directors may not grant the loan or guarantee concerned unless its decision is unanimous, the director nominated by the Commission abstaining.

7. Where both the Management Committee and the Commission deliver an unfavourable opinion, the Board of Directors may not grant the loan or guarantee.

ARTICLE 22

1. The Bank shall borrow on the international capital markets the funds necessary for the performance of its tasks.

2. The Bank may borrow on the capital market of a Member State either in accordance with the legal provisions applying to internal issues or, if there are no such provisions in a Member State, after the Bank and the Member State concerned have conferred together and reached agreement on the proposed loan.

The competent authorities in the Member State concerned may refuse to give their assent only if there is reason to fear serious disturbances on the capital market of that State.

ARTICLE 23

1. The Bank may employ any available funds which it does not immediately require to meet its obligations in the following ways:

    (a) it may invest on the money markets;

    (b) it may, subject to the provisions of Article 20 (2), buy and sell securities issued by itself or by those who have borrowed from it;

    (c) it may carry out any other financial operation linked with its objectives.

2. Without prejudice to the provisions of Article 25, the Bank shall not, in managing its investments, engage in any currency arbitrage not directly required to carry out its lending operations or fulfil commitments arising out of loans raised or guarantees granted by it.

3. The Bank shall, in the fields covered by this Article, act in agreement with the competent authorities or with the bank of issue of the Member State concerned.

ARTICLE 24

1. A reserve fund of up to 10 per cent. of the subscribed capital shall be built up progressively. If the state of the liabilities of the Bank should so justify, the Board of Directors may decide to set aside additional reserves. Until such time as the reserve fund has been fully built up, it shall be fed by:

    (a) interest received on loans granted by the Bank out of sums to be paid up by Member States pursuant to Article 5;

    (b) interest received on loans granted by the Bank out of funds derived from repayment of the loans referred to in (a);

to the extent that this income is not required to meet the obligations of the Bank or to cover its expenses.

2. The resources of the reserve fund shall be so invested as to be available at any time to meet the purpose of the fund.

ARTICLE 25

1. The Bank shall at all times be entitled to transfer its assets in the currency of one Member State into the currency of another Member State in order to carry out financial operations corresponding to the task set out in Article 130 of this Treaty, taking into account the provisions of Article 23 of this Statute. The Bank shall, as far as possible, avoid making such transfers if it has cash or liquid assets in the currency required.

2. The Bank may not convert its assets in the currency of a Member State into the currency of a third country without the agreement of the Member State concerned.

3. The Bank may freely dispose of that part of its capital which is paid up in gold or convertible currency and of any currency borrowed on markets outside the Community.

4. The Member States undertake to make available to the debtors of the Bank the currency needed to repay the capital and pay the interest on loans or commission on guarantees granted by the Bank for projects to be carried out in their territory.

ARTICLE 26

If a Member State fails to meet the obligations of membership arising from this Statute, in particular the obligation to pay its share of the subscribed capital, to grant its special loans or to service its borrowings, the granting of loans or guarantees to that Member State or its nationals may be suspended by a decision of the Board of Governors, acting by a qualified majority.

Such decision shall not release either the State or its nationals from their obligations towards the Bank.

ARTICLE 27

1. If the Board of Governors decides to suspend the operations of the Bank, all its activities shall cease forthwith, except those required to ensure the due realisation, protection and preservation of its assets and the settlement of its liabilities.

2. In the event of liquidation, the Board of Governors shall appoint the liquidators and give them instructions for carrying out the liquidation.

ARTICLE 28

1. In each of the Member States, the Bank shall enjoy the most extensive legal capacity accorded to legal persons under their laws; it may, in particular, acquire or dispose of movable or immovable property and may be a party to legal proceedings.
[. . .].

2. The property of the Bank shall be exempt from all forms of requisition or expropriation.

AMENDMENT

The second paragraph of Article 28 (1) was repealed by the Merger Treaty, Art. 28, para. 2. See now *ibid.*, Art. 28, para. 1.

ARTICLE 29

Disputes between the Bank on the one hand, and its creditors, debtors or any other person on the other, shall be decided by the competent national courts, save where jurisdiction has been conferred on the Court of Justice.

The Bank shall have an address for service in each Member State. It may, however, in any contract, specify a particular address for service or provide for arbitration.

The property and assets of the Bank shall not be liable to attachment or to seizure by way of execution except by decision of a court.

DONE at Rome this twenty-fifth day of March in the year one thousand nine hundred and fifty-seven.

P. H. SPAAK	J. Ch. SNOY et d'OPPUERS
ADENAUER	HALLSTEIN
PINEAU	M. FAURE
Antonio SEGNI	Gaetano MARTINO
BECH	Lambert SCHAUS
J. LUNS	J. LINTHORST HOMAN

PROTOCOL ON GOODS ORIGINATING IN AND COMING FROM CERTAIN COUNTRIES AND ENJOYING SPECIAL TREATMENT WHEN IMPORTED INTO A MEMBER STATE

THE HIGH CONTRACTING PARTIES,

DESIRING to define in greater detail the application of this Treaty to certain goods originating in and coming from certain countries and enjoying special treatment when imported into a Member State,

HAVE AGREED upon the following provisions, which shall be annexed to this Treaty:

1. The application of the Treaty establishing the European Economic Community shall not require any alteration in the customs treatment applicable, at the time of the entry into force of this Treaty, to imports:

   (*a*) into the Benelux countries of goods originating in and coming from Surinam or the Netherlands Antilles;

   (*b*) into France of goods originating in and coming from Morocco, Tunisia, the Republic of Vietnam, Cambodia or Laos. This shall also apply to the French Settlements in the Condominium of the New Hebrides;

   (*c*) into Italy of goods originating in and coming from Libya or the Trust Territory of Somaliland currently under Italian administration.

2. Goods imported into a Member state and benefiting from the treatment referred to above shall not be considered to be in free circulation in that State within the meaning of Article 10 of this Treaty when re-exported to another Member State.

3. Before the end of the first year after the entry into force of this Treaty, Member States shall communicate to the Commission and to the other Member States their rules governing the special treatment referred to in this Protocol, together with a list of the goods entitled to such treatment.

They shall also inform the Commission and the other Member States of any changes subsequently made in those lists or in the treatment.

4. The Commission shall ensure that the application of these rules cannot be prejudicial to other Member States; to this end it may take any appropriate measures as regards relations between Member States.

DONE at Rome this twenty-fifth day of March in the year one thousand nine hundred and fifty-seven.

P. H. SPAAK	J. Ch. SNOY et d'OPPUERS
ADENAUER	HALLSTEIN
PINEAU	M. FAURE
Antonio SEGNI	Gaetano MARTINO
BECH	Lambert SCHAUS
J. LUNS	J. LINTHORST HOMAN

IMPLEMENTING CONVENTION ON THE ASSOCIATION OF THE OVERSEAS COUNTRIES AND TERRITORIES WITH THE COMMUNITY

THE HIGH CONTRACTING PARTIES,

DESIRING to enter into the Implementing Convention provided for in Article 136 of this Treaty,

HAVE AGREED upon the following provisions, which shall be annexed to this Treaty:

ARTICLE 1

The Member States shall, under the conditions laid down below, participate in measures which will promote the social and economic development of the countries and territories listed in Annex IV to this Treaty, by supplementing the efforts made by the authorities responsible for those countries and territories.

For this purpose, a Development Fund for the Overseas Countries and Territories is hereby established, into which the Member States shall, over a period of five years, pay the annual contributions set out in Annex A to this Convention.

The Fund shall be administered by the Commission.

Convention on Association of Overseas Countries

Article 2

The authorities responsible for the countries and territories shall, in agreement with the local authorities or with the representatives of the peoples of the countries and territories concerned, submit to the Commission the social or economic projects for which financing by the Community is requested.

Article 3

The Commission shall draw up annually general programmes for allocation to the different classes of project of the funds made available in accordance with Annex B to this Convention.

The general programmes shall contain projects for financing:

(a) certain social institutions, in particular hospitals, teaching or technical research establishments and institutions for vocational guidance and advancement among the peoples concerned;

(b) economic investments which are in the public interest and are directly connected with the implementation of a programme containing specific productive development projects.

Article 4

At the beginning of each financial year the Council shall, acting by a qualified majority after consulting the Commission, determine what funds will be devoted to financing:

(a) the social institutions referred to in Article 3 (a);

(b) the economic investments in the public interest referred to in Article 3 (b).

The decision of the Council shall aim at a rational geographical distribution of the funds made available.

Article 5

1. The Commission shall determine how the funds made available under Article 4 (a) shall be allocated according to the various requests received for the financing of social institutions.

2. The Commission shall draw up proposals for financing the economic investment projects which it is considering under Article 4 (b).

It shall submit these proposals to the Council.

If, within one month, no Member State requests that the Council examine the proposals, they shall be deemed to be approved.

If the Council examines the proposals, it shall act by a qualified majority within two months.

3. Any funds not allocated during any one year shall be carried forward to the following years.

4. The funds allocated shall be made available to the authorities responsible for carrying out the work concerned. The Commission shall ensure that such funds are used for the purposes which have been decided upon, and are expended to the best economic advantage.

Article 6

Within six months of the entry into force of this Treaty, the Council shall, acting by a qualified majority on a proposal from the Commission, lay down rules for the collection and transfer of financial contributions, for budgeting and for the administration of the resources of the Development Fund.

Article 7

The qualified majority referred to in Articles 4, 5 and 6 shall be 67 votes. Member States shall have the following number of votes:

Belgium	11 votes
Germany	33 votes
France	33 votes
Italy	11 votes
Luxembourg	1 vote
Netherlands	11 votes

Article 8

The right of establishment shall, in each country or territory, be progressively extended to nationals, companies or firms of Member States other than the State which has special relations with the country or territory concerned. During the first year in which this Convention is applied, the manner in which this is to be effected shall be so determined by the Council, acting by a qualified majority on a proposal from the Commission, as to ensure the progressive abolition during the transitional period of any discrimination.

PART II—EUROPEAN ECONOMIC COMMUNITY

ARTICLE 9

The customs treatment to be applied to trade between Member States and the countries and territories shall be that provided for in Articles 133 and 134 of this Treaty.

ARTICLE 10

For the duration of this Convention, Member States shall apply to their trade with the countries and territories those provisions of the Chapter of this Treaty relating to the elimination of quantitative restrictions between Member States which they apply to trade with one another during the same period.

ARTICLE 11

1. In each country or territory where import quotas exist, one year after this Convention enters into force, the quotas open to States other than the State with which such country or territory has special relations shall be converted into global quotas open without discrimination to the other Member States. As from the same date, these quotas shall be increased annually in accordance with Article 32 and Article 33 (1), (2), (4), (5), (6) and (7) of this Treaty.

2. Where, in the case of a product which has not been liberalised, the global quota does not amount to 7 per cent. of total imports into a country or territory, a quota equal to 7 per cent. of such imports shall be introduced not later than one year after the entry into force of this Convention, and shall be increased annually in accordance with paragraph 1.

3. Where, in the case of certain products, no quota has been opened for imports into a country or territory, the Commission shall, by means of a decision, determine the manner in which the quotas to be offered to other Member States shall be opened and increased.

ARTICLE 12

Where import quotas established by Member States cover both imports from a State having special relations with a country or territory and imports from the country or territory concerned, the share of imports from the countries and territories shall be the subject of a global quota based on import statistics. Any such quota shall be established during the first year in which this Convention is in force and shall be increased as provided for in Article 10.

ARTICLE 13

The provisions of Article 10 shall not preclude prohibitions or restrictions on imports, exports or goods in transit justified on grounds of public morality; public policy or public security; the protection of health and life of humans, animals or plants; the protection of national treasures possessing artistic, historic or archaeological value; or the protection of industrial and commercial property. Such prohibitions or restrictions shall not, however, constitute a means of arbitrary discrimination or a disguised restriction on trade.

ARTICLE 14

After the date of expiry of this Convention and until provisions covering association for a further period have been adopted, quotas for imports into the countries and territories on the one hand, and into the Member States on the other, of products originating in the countries and territories shall remain at the level set for the fifth year. The arrangements in respect of the right of establishment in force at the end of the fifth year shall also be maintained.

ARTICLE 15

1. Tariff quotas for imports from third countries of raw coffee into Italy and the Benelux countries, and of bananas into the Federal Republic of Germany, shall be introduced in accordance with the Protocols annexed to this Convention.

2. If this Convention expires before the conclusion of a new agreement, the Member States shall, pending such new agreement, enjoy tariff quotas for bananas, cocoa beans and raw coffee at the rates of duty applying at the beginning of the second stage; such quotas shall be equal to the volume of imports from third countries in the course of the latest year for which statistics are available.

Such quotas shall, where appropriate, be increased in proportion to the increase in consumption within the importing countries.

3. Member States enjoying tariff quotas at the rates of duty applied when this Treaty enters into force under the Protocols relating to imports of raw coffee and bananas from third countries may require that, instead of the treatment provided for in paragraph 2, the tariff quotas for these products be maintained at the level reached at the date of expiry of this Convention.

Such quotas shall, where appropriate, be increased as provided in paragraph 2.

4. The Commission shall, at the request of the States concerned, determine the size of the tariff quotas referred to in the preceding paragraphs.

ARTICLE 16

The provisions contained in Articles 1 to 8 of this Convention shall apply to Algeria and the French overseas departments.

ARTICLE 17

Without prejudice to cases in which the provisions of Articles 14 and 15 apply, this Convention is concluded for a period of five years.

DONE at Rome this twenty-fifth day of March in the year one thousand nine hundred and fifty-seven.

P. H. SPAAK	J. Ch. SNOY et d'OPPUERS
ADENAUER	HALLSTEIN
PINEAU	M. FAURE
Antonio SEGNI	Gaetano MARTINO
BECH	Lambert SCHAUS
J. LUNS	J. LINTHORST HOMAN

Annex A referred to in Article 1 of this Convention

Percentages	1st year 10%	2nd year 12·5%	3rd year 16·5%	4th year 22·5%	5th year 38·5%	Total 100%
Countries	IN MILLIONS OF E.P.U. UNITS OF ACCOUNT					
Belgium	7	8·75	11·55	15·75	26·95	10
Germany	20	25	33	45	77	200
France	20	25	33	45	77	200
Italy	4	5	6·60	9	15·40	40
Luxembourg ...	0·125	0·15625	0·20625	0·28125	0·48125	1·25
Netherlands ...	7	8·75	11·55	15·75	26·95	70

Annex B referred to in Article 3 of this Convention

Percentages	1st year 10%	2nd year 12·5%	3rd year 16·5%	4th year 22·5%	5th year 38·5%	Total 100%
Overseas Countries and territories of:	IN MILLIONS OF E.P.U. UNITS OF ACCOUNT					
Belgium	3	3·75	4·95	6·75	11·55	30
France	51·125	63·906	84·356	115·031	196·832	511·25
Italy	0·5	0·625	0·825	1·125	1·925	5
Netherlands ...	3·5	4·375	5·775	7·875	13·475	35

Part III

EUROPEAN ATOMIC ENERGY COMMUNITY

TREATY

ESTABLISHING

THE EUPOPEAN ATOMIC ENERGY COMMUNITY

(ROME, 25 MARCH 1957)

HIS MAJESTY THE KING OF THE BELGIANS, THE PRESIDENT OF THE FEDERAL REPUBLIC OF GERMANY, THE PRESIDENT OF THE FRENCH REPUBLIC, THE PRESIDENT OF THE ITALIAN REPUBLIC, HER ROYAL HIGHNESS THE GRAND DUCHESS OF LUXEMBOURG, HER MAJESTY THE QUEEN OF THE NETHERLANDS,

RECOGNISING that nuclear energy represents and essential resource for the development and invigoration of industry and will permit the advancement of the cause of peace,

CONVINCED that only a joint effort undertaken without delay can offer the prospect of achievements commensurate with the creative capacities of their countries,

RESOLVED to create the conditions necessary for the development of a powerful nuclear industry which will provide extensive energy resources, lead to the modernisation of technical processes and contribute, through its many other applications, to the prosperity of their peoples,

ANXIOUS to create the conditions of safety necessary to eliminate hazards to the life and health of the public,

DESIRING to associate other countries with their work and to co-operate with international organisations concerned with the peaceful development of atomic energy,

HAVE DECIDED TO create a European Atomic Energy Community (EURATOM) and to this end have designated as their Plenipotentiaries:

HIS MAJESTY THE KING OF THE BELGIANS:
   MR. PAUL-HENRI SPAAK, Minister for Foreign Affairs,
   BARON J. CH. SNOY ET D'OPPUERS, Secretary-General of the Ministry of Economic Affairs, Head of the Belgian Delegation to the Intergovernmental Conference;

THE PRESIDENT OF THE FEDERAL REPUBLIC OF GERMANY:
   DR. KONRAD ADENAUER, Federal Chancellor,
   PROFESSOR DR. WALTER HALLSTEIN, State Secretary of the Federal Foreign Office;

THE PRESIDENT OF THE FRENCH REPUBLIC:
   MR. CHRISTIAN PINEAU, Minister for Foreign Affairs,
   MR. MAURICE FAURE, Under-Secretary of State for Foreign Affairs;

THE PRESIDENT OF THE ITALIAN REPUBLIC:
Mr. Antonio Segni, President of the Council of Ministers,
Professor Gaetano Martino, Minister for Foreign Affairs;

HER ROYAL HIGHNESS THE GRAND DUCHESS OF LUXEM-
BOURG:
Mr. Joseph Bech, President of the Government, Minister for Foreign
Affairs,
Mr. Lambert Schaus, Ambassador, Head of the Luxembourg Delegation to
the Intergovernmental Conference;

HER MAJESTY THE QUEEN OF THE NETHERLANDS:
Mr. Joseph Luns, Minister for Foreign Affairs,
Mr. J. Linthorst Homan, Head of the Netherlands Delegation to the
Intergovernmental Conference;

WHO, having exchanged their Full Powers, found in good and due form
HAVE AGREED as follows:

Title One

THE TASKS OF THE COMMUNITY

ARTICLE 1

By this Treaty the High Contracting Parties establish among themselves a
EUROPEAN ATOMIC ENERGY COMMUNITY (EURATOM).
It shall be the task of the Community to contribute to the raising of the
standard of living in the Member States and to the development of relations
with the other countries by creating the conditions necessary for the speedy
establishment and growth of nuclear industries.

ARTICLE 2

In order to perform its task, the Community shall, as provided in this
Treaty:
  (a) promote research and ensure the dissemination of technical infor-
      mation;
  (b) establish uniform safety standards to protect the health of workers
      and of the general public and ensure that they are applied;
  (c) facilitate investment and ensure, particularly by encouraging
      ventures on the part of undertakings, the establishment of the basic
      installations necessary for the development of nuclear energy in the
      Community;
  (d) ensure that all users in the Community receive a regular and equit-
      able supply of ores and nuclear fuels;
  (e) make certain, by appropriate supervision, that nuclear materials
      are not diverted to purposes other than those for which they are
      intended;
  (f) exercise the right of ownership conferred upon it with respect to
      special fissile materials;

(g) ensure wide commercial outlets and access to the best technical facilities by the creation of a common market in specialised materials and equipment, by the free movement of capital for investment in the field of nuclear energy and by freedom of employment for specialists within the Community;

(h) establish with other countries and international organisations such relations as will foster progress in the peaceful uses of nuclear energy.

ARTICLE 3

1. The tasks entrusted to the Community shall be carried out by the following institutions:
—an Assembly,
—a Council,
—a Commission,
—a Court of Justice.
Each institution shall act within the limits of the powers conferred upon it by this Treaty.

2. The Council and the Commission shall be assisted by an Economic and Social Committee acting in an advisory capacity.

[3. The audit shall be carried out by a Court of Auditors acting within the limits of the powers conferred upon it by this Treaty.]

AMENDMENT
Para. (3) was added by the Second Budgetary Treaty of July 22, 1975, Art. 19.

Title Two

PROVISIONS FOR THE ENCOURAGEMENT OF PROGRESS IN THE FIELD OF NUCLEAR ENERGY

CHAPTER I—PROMOTION OF RESEARCH

ARTICLE 4

1. The Commission shall be responsible for promoting and facilitating nuclear research in the Member States and for complementing it by carrying out a Community research and training programme.

2. The activity of the Commission in this respect shall be carried out within the fields listed in Annex 1 to this Treaty.

This list may be amended by the Council, acting by a qualified majority on a proposal from the Commission. The latter shall consult the Scientific and Technical Committee established under Article 134.

ARTICLE 5

For purposes of co-ordinating and complementing research undertaken in Member States, the Commission shall, either by a specific request addressed to a given recipient and conveyed to the Government concerned, or by a general

151

published request, call upon Member States, persons or undertakings to communicate to it their programmes relating to the research which it specifies in the request.

After giving those concerned full opportunity to comment, the Commission may deliver a reasoned opinion on each of the programmes communicated to it. The Commission shall deliver such an opinion if the State, person or undertaking which has communicated the programme so requests.

By such opinions the Commission shall discourage unnecessary duplication and shall direct research towards sectors which are insufficiently explored. The Commission may not publish these programmes without the consent of the State, person or undertaking which has communicated them.

The Commission shall publish at regular intervals a list of those sectors of nuclear research which it considers to be insufficiently explored.

The Commission may bring together representatives of public and private research centres as well as any experts engaged in research in the same or related fields for mutual consultation and exchanges of information.

ARTICLE 6

To encourage the carrying out of research programmes communicated to it the Commission may:

(a) provide financial assistance within the framework of research contracts, without, however, offering subsidies;

(b) supply, either free of charge or against payment, for carrying out such programmes, any source materials or special fissile materials which it has available;

(c) place installations, equipment or expert assistance at the disposal of Member States, persons or undertakings, either free of charge or against payment;

(d) promote joint financing by the Member States, persons or undertakings concerned.

ARTICLE 7

Community research and training programmes shall be determined by the Council, acting unanimously on a proposal from the Commission, which shall consult the Scientific and Technical Committee.

These programmes shall be drawn up for a period of not more than five years.

The funds required for carrying out these programmes shall be included each year in the research and investment budget of the Community.

The Commission shall ensure that these programmes are carried out and shall submit an annual report thereon to the Council.

The Commission shall keep the Economic and Social Committee informed of the broad outlines of Community research and training programmes.

ARTICLE 8

1. After consulting the Scientific and Technical Committee, the Commission shall establish a Joint Nuclear Research Centre.

This Centre shall ensure that the research programmes and other tasks assigned to it by the Commission are carried out.

It shall also ensure that a uniform nuclear terminology and a standard system of measurements are established.

It shall set up a central bureau for nuclear measurements.

2. The activities of the Centre may, for geographical or functional reasons, be carried out in separate establishments.

ARTICLE 9

1. After obtaining the opinion of the Economic and Social Committee the Commission may, within the framework of the Joint Nuclear Research Centre, set up schools for the training of specialists, particularly in the fields of prospecting for minerals, the production of high-purity nuclear materials, the processing of irradiated fuels, nuclear engineering, health and safety and the production and use of radioisotopes.

The Commission shall determine the details of such training.

2. An institution of university status shall be established; the way in which it will function shall be determined by the Council, acting by a qualified majority on a proposal from the Commission.

ARTICLE 10

The Commission may, by contract, entrust the carrying out of certain parts of the Community research programme to Member States, persons or undertakings, or to third countries, international organisations or nationals of third countries.

ARTICLE 11

The Commission shall publish the research programmes referred to in Articles 7, 8 and 10, and also regular progress reports on their implementation.

CHAPTER II—DISSEMINATION OF INFORMATION

SECTION I—INFORMATION OVER WHICH THE COMMUNITY HAS POWER OF DISPOSAL

ARTICLE 12

Member States, persons or undertakings shall have the right, on application to the Commission, to obtain non-exclusive licences under patents, provisionally protected patent rights, utility models or patent applications owned by the Community, where they are able to make effective use of the inventions covered thereby.

Under the same conditions, the Commission shall grant sub-licences under patents, provisionally protected patent rights, utility models or patent applications, where the Community holds contractual licences conferring power to do so.

The Commission shall grant such licences or sub-licences on terms to be agreed with the licensees and shall furnish all the information required for their use. These terms shall relate in particular to suitable remuneration and, where appropriate, to the right of the licensee to grant sub-licences to third parties and to the obligation to treat the information as a trade secret.

Failing agreement on the terms referred to in the third paragraph, the licensees may bring the matter before the Court of Justice so that appropriate terms may be fixed.

Article 13

The Commission shall communicate to Member States, persons and undertakings information acquired by the Community which is not covered by the provisions of Article 12, whether such information is derived from its own research programme or communicated to the Commission with authority to make free use of it.

The Commission may, however, make the disclosure of such information conditional on its being treated as confidential and not passed on to third parties.

The Commission may not disclose information which has been acquired subject to restrictions on its use or dissemination—such as information known as classified information—unless it ensures compliance with these restrictions.

Section II—Other Information

(a) Dissemination by amicable agreement

Article 14

The Commission shall endeavour, by amicable agreement, to secure both the communication of information which is of use to the Community in the attainment of its objectives and the granting of licences under patents, provisionally protected patent rights, utility models or patent applications covering such information.

Article 15

The Commission shall establish a procedure by which Member States, persons and undertakings may use it as an intermediary for exchanging provisional or final results of their research, in so far as these results have not been acquired by the Community under research contracts awarded by the Commission.

This procedure must be such as to ensure the confidential nature of the exchange. The results communicated may, however, be transmitted by the Commission to the Joint Nuclear Research Centre for documentation purposes; this shall not entail any right of use to which the communicating party has not agreed.

(b) Compulsory communication to the Commission

Article 16

1. As soon as an application for a patent or a utility model relating to a specifically nuclear subject is filed with a Member State, that State shall ask the applicant to agree that the contents of the application be communicated to the Commission forthwith.

If the applicant agrees, this communication shall be made within three months of the date of filing the application. If the applicant does not agree, the Member State shall, within the same period, notify the Commission of the existence of the application.

The Commission may require a Member State to communicate the contents of an application of whose existence it has been notified.

The Commission shall make any such request within two months of the date of notification. Any extension of this period shall entail a corresponding extension of the period referred to in the sixth subparagraph of this paragraph.

On receiving such a request from the Commission, the Member State shall again ask the applicant to agree to communication of the contents of the application. If the applicant agrees, communication shall be made forthwith.

If the applicant does not agree, the Member State shall nevertheless be required to make this communication to the Commission within eighteen months of the date on which the application was filed.

2. Member States shall inform the Commission, within eighteen months of the filing date, of the existence of any as yet unpublished application for a patent or utility model which seems to them, prima facie, to deal with a subject which, although not specifically nuclear, is directly connected with and essential to the development of nuclear energy in the Community.

If the Commission so requests, the contents of the application shall be communicated to it within two months.

3. In order that publication may take place as soon as possible, Member States shall reduce to a minimum the time taken to process applications for patents or utility models relating to subjects referred to in paragraphs 1 and 2 concerning which a request has been made by the Commission.

4. The Commission shall treat the above-mentioned communications as confidential. They may only be made for documentation purposes. The Commission may, however, make use of the inventions communicated to it, either with the consent of the applicant or in accordance with Articles 17 to 23.

5. The provisions of this Article shall not apply when an agreement concluded with a third State or an international organisation precludes communication.

(c) Grant of licences by arbitration or under compulsory powers

ARTICLE 17

1. Failing amicable agreement, non-exclusive licences may be granted either by arbitration or under compulsory powers in accordance with Articles 18 to 23:

    (a) to the Community or to Joint Undertakings accorded this right under Article 48 in respect of patents, provisionally protected patent rights or utility models relating to inventions directly connected with nuclear research, where the granting of such licences is necessary for the continuance of their own research or indispensable to the operation of their installations.

        If the Commission so requests, such licences shall include the right to authorise third parties to make use of the invention, where they are carrying out work for or orders placed by the Community or Joint Undertakings;

    (b) to persons or undertakings which have applied to the Commission for them in respect of patents, provisionally protected patent rights or utility models relating to inventions directly connected with and essential to the development of nuclear energy in the Community, provided that all the following conditions are fulfilled:

        (i) At least four years have elapsed since the filing of the patent application, save in the case of an invention relating to a specifically nuclear subject;

        (ii) The requirements arising out of the development of nuclear energy in the Commission's conception of such development, in the territory of a Member State where an invention is protected, are not being met with regard to that invention;

(iii) The proprietor, having been called upon to meet such requirements either himself or through his licensees, has not complied with this request;

(iv) The persons or undertakings applying for licences are in a position to meet such requirements effectively by making use of the invention.

Member States may not, in order to meet such requirements, take any coercive measures provided for in their national legislation which will limit the protection accorded to the invention, save at the prior request of the Commission.

2. A non-exclusive licence may not be granted as provided for in paragraph 1 where the proprietor can establish the existence of legitimate reasons, in particular that he has not had sufficient time at his disposal.

3. The granting of a licence pursuant to paragraph 1 shall confer a right to full compensation, the amount of which shall be agreed between the proprietor of the patent, provisionally protected patent right or utility model and the licensee.

4. The provisions of this Article shall not affect those of the Paris Convention for the Protection of Industrial Property.

ARTICLE 18

An Arbitration Committee is hereby established for the purposes provided for in this Section. The Council shall appoint the members and lay down the rules of procedure of this Committee, acting on a proposal from the Court of Justice.

An appeal, having suspensory effect, may be brought by the parties before the Court of Justice against a decision of the Arbitration Committee within one month of notification thereof. The Court of Justice shall confine its examination to the formal validity of the decision and to the interpretation of the provisions of this Treaty by the Arbitration Committee.

The final decisions of the Arbitration Committee shall have the force of *res judicata* between the parties concerned. They shall be enforceable as provided in Article 164.

ARTICLE 19

Where, failing amicable agreement, the Commission intends to secure the granting of licences in one of the cases provided for in Article 17, it shall give notice of its intention to the proprietor of the patent, provisionally protected patent right, utility model or patent application, and shall specify in such notice the name of the applicant for and the scope of the licence.

ARTICLE 20

The proprietor may, within one month of receipt of the notice referred to in Article 19, propose to the Commission and, where appropriate, to the applicant that they conclude a special agreement to refer the matter to the Arbitration Committee.

Should the Commission or the applicant refuse to enter into such an agreement, the Commission shall not require the Member State or its appropriate authorities to grant the licence or cause it to be granted.

If, when the matter is referred to it under a special agreement, the Arbitration Committee finds that the request from the Commission complies with the provisions of Article 17, it shall give a reasoned decision containing a grant of the licence to the applicant and laying down the terms of the licence and the remuneration therefor, to the extent that the parties have not reached agreement on these points.

ARTICLE 21

If the proprietor does not propose that the matter be referred to the Arbitration Committee, the Commission may call upon the Member State concerned or its appropriate authorities to grant the licence or cause it to be granted.

If, having heard the proprietor's case, the Member State, or its appropriate authorities, considers taht the conditions of Article 17 have not been complied with, it shall notify the Commission of its refusal to grant the licence or to cause it to be granted.

If it refuses to grant the licence or to cause it to be granted, or if, within four months of the date of the request, no information is forthcoming with regard to the granting of the licence, the Commission shall have two months in which to bring the matter before the Court of Justice.

The proprietor must be heard in the proceedings before the Court of Justice.

If the judgment of the Court of Justice establishes that the conditions of Article 17 have been complied with, the Member State concerned, or its appropriate authorities, shall take such measures as enforcement of that judgment may require.

ARTICLE 22

1. If the proprietor of the patent, provisionally protected patent right or utility model and the licensee fail to agree on the amount of compensation, the parties concerned may conclude a special agreement to refer the matter to the Arbitration Committee.

By doing so, the parties waive the right to institute any proceedings other than those provided for in Article 18.

2. If the licensee refuses to conclude a special agreement, the licence he has been granted shall be deemed void.

If the proprietor refuses to conclude a special agreement, the compensation referred to in this Article shall be determined by the appropriate national authorities.

ARTICLE 23

After the lapse of one year, the decisions of the Arbitration Committee or of the appropriate national authorities may, if there are new facts to justify it, be revised with respect to the terms of the licence.

Such revision shall be a matter for the body which gave the decision.

SECTION III—SECURITY PROVISIONS

ARTICLE 24

Information which the Community acquires as a result of carrying out its research programme, and the disclosure of which is liable to harm the defence interests of one or more Member States, shall be subject to a security system in accordance with the following provisions:

1. The Council shall, acting on a proposal from the Commission, adopt security regulations which, account being taken of the provisions of this Article, lay down the various security gradings to be applied and the security measures appropriate to each grading.

2. Where the Commission considers that the disclosure of certain information is liable to harm the defence interests of one or more Member States, it shall provisionally apply to that information the security grading required in that case by the security regulations.

It shall communicate such information forthwith to the Member States, which shall provisionally ensure its security in the same manner.

Member States shall inform the Commission within three months whether they wish to maintain the grading provisionally applied, substitute another or declassify the information.

Upon the expiry of this period, the highest grading of those requested shall be applied. The Commission shall notify the Member States accordingly.

At the request of the Commission or of a Member State, the Council may, acting unanimously, at any time apply another grading or declassify the information. The Council shall obtain the opinion of the Commission before taking any action on a request from a Member State.

3. The provisions of Articles 12 and 13 shall not apply to information subject to a security grading.

Nevertheless, provided that the appropriate security measures are observed,

(a) the information referred to in Articles 12 and 13 may be communicated by the Commission:
  (i) to a Joint Undertaking;
  (ii) to a person or undertaking other than a Joint Undertaking, through the Member State in whose territory that person or undertaking operates;

(b) the information referred to in Article 13 may be communicated by a Member State to a person or to an undertaking other than a Joint Undertaking, operating in the territory of that State, provided that the Commission is notified of this communication;

(c) each Member State has, however, the right to require the Commission to grant a licence under Article 12 to meet the needs of that State or those of a person or undertaking operating in its territory.

ARTICLE 25

1. A Member State notifying the existence or communicating the contents of an application for a patent or utility model relating to a subject specified in Article 16 (1) or (2) shall, where appropriate, draw attention to the need to apply a given security grading for defence reasons, at the same time stating the probable duration of such grading.

The Commission shall pass on to the other Member States all communications received in accordance with the preceding subparagraph. The Commission and the Member States shall take those measures which, under the security regulations, correspond to the grading required by the State of origin.

2. The Commission may also pass on these communications to Joint Undertakings or, through a Member State, to a person or to an undertaking other than a Joint Undertaking operating in the territory of that State.

Inventions which are the subject of applications referred to in paragraph 1 may be used only with the consent of the applicant or in accordance with Articles 17 to 23.

The communications and, where appropriate, the use referred to in this paragraph shall be subject to the measures which, under the security regulations, correspond to the security grading required by the State of origin.

The communications shall in all cases be subject to the consent of the State of origin. Consent to communication and use may be withheld only for defence reasons.

3. At the request of the Commission or of a Member State, the Council may, acting unanimously, at any time apply another grading or declassify the information. The Council shall obtain the opinion of the Commission before taking any action on a request from a Member State.

ARTICLE 26

1. Where information covered by patents, patent applications, provisionally protected patent rights, utility models or applications for utility models has been classified in accordance with Articles 24 and 25, the States which have applied for such classification may not refuse to allow corresponding applications to be filed in the other Member States.

Each Member State shall take the necessary measures to maintain the security of such rights and applications in accordance with the procedure laid down in its own laws and regulations.

2. No applications relating to information classified in accordance with Article 24 may be filed outside the Member States except with the unanimous consent of the latter. Should Member States fail to make known their attitude, their consent shall be deemed to have been obtained on the expiry of six months from the date on which the information was communicated to the Member States by the Commission.

ARTICLE 27

Compensation for any damage suffered by the applicant as a result of classification for defence reasons shall be governed by the provisions of the national laws of the Member States and shall be the responsibility of the State which applied for such classification or which either obtained the upgrading or extension of the classification or caused the filing of applications outside the Community to be prohibited.

Where several Member States have either obtained the upgrading or extension of the classification or caused the filing of applications outside the Community to be prohibited, they shall be jointly responsible for making good any damage arising out of their action.

The Community may not claim any compensation under this Article.

SECTION IV—SPECIAL PROVISIONS

ARTICLE 28

Where, as a result of their communication to the Commission, unpublished applications for patents or utility models, or patents or utility models classified for defence reasons, are improperly used or come to the knowledge of an unauthorised person, the Community shall make good the damage suffered by the party concerned.

Without prejudice to its own rights against the person responsible for the damage, the Community shall, to the extent that it has made good such damage, acquire any rights of action enjoyed by those concerned against third parties. This shall not affect the right of the Community to take action against the person responsible for the damage in accordance with the general provisions in force.

ARTICLE 29

Where an agreement or contract for the exchange of scientific or industrial information in the nuclear field between a Member State, a person or an undertaking on the one hand, and a third State, an international organisation or a national of a third State on the other, requires, on either part, the signature of a State acting in its sovereign capacity, it shall be concluded by the Commission.

Subject to the provisions of Articles 103 and 104, the Commission may, however, on such conditions as it considers appropriate, authorise a Member State, a person or an undertaking to conclude such agreements.

CHAPTER III—HEALTH AND SAFETY

ARTICLE 30

Basic standards shall be laid down within the Community for the protection of the health of workers and the general public against the dangers arising from ionizing radiations.

The expression " basic standards " means:
- (*a*) maximum permissible doses compatible with adequate safety;
- (*b*) maximum permissible levels of exposure and contamination;
- (*c*) the fundamental principles governing the health surveillance of workers.

ARTICLE 31

The basic standards shall be worked out by the Commission after it has obtained the opinion of a group of persons appointed by the Scientific and Technical Committee from among scientific experts, and in particular public health experts, in the Member States. The Commission shall obtain the opinion of the Economic and Social Committee on these basic standards.

After consulting the Assembly the Council shall, on a proposal from the Commission, which shall forward to it the opinions obtained from these Committees, establish the basic standards; the Council shall act by a qualified majority.

ARTICLE 32

At the request of the Commission or of a Member State, the basic standards may be revised or supplemented in accordance with the procedure laid down in Article 31.

The Commission shall examine any request made by a Member State.

ARTICLE 33

Each Member State shall lay down the appropriate provisions, whether by legislation, regulation or administrative action, to ensure compliance with the basic standards which have been established and shall take the necessary measures with regard to teaching, education and vocational training.

The Commission shall make appropriate recommendations for harmonising the provisions applicable in this field in the Member States.

To this end, the Member States shall communicate to the Commission the provisions applicable at the date of entry into force of this Treaty and any subsequent draft provisions of the same kind.

Any recommendations the Commission may wish to issue with regard to such draft provisions shall be made within three months of the date on which such draft provisions are communicated.

ARTICLE 34

Any Member State in whose territories particularly dangerous experiments are to take place shall take additional health and safety measures, on which it shall first obtain the opinion of the Commission.

The assent of the Commission shall be required where the effects of such experiments are liable to affect the territories of other Member States.

ARTICLE 35

Each Member State shall establish the facilities necessary to carry out continuous monitoring of the level of radioactivity in the air, water and soil and to ensure compliance with the basic standards.

The Commission shall have the right of access to such facilities; it may verify their operation and efficiency.

ARTICLE 36

The appropriate authorities shall periodically communicate information on the checks referred to in Article 35 to the Commission so that it is kept informed of the level of radioactivity to which the public is exposed.

ARTICLE 37

Each Member State shall provide the Commission with such general data relating to any plan for the disposal of radioactive waste in whatever form as will make it possible to determine whether the implementation of such plan is liable to result in the radioactive contamination of the water, soil or airspace of another Member State.

The Commission shall deliver its opinion within six months, after consulting the group of experts referred to in Article 31.

ARTICLE 38

The Commission shall make recommendations to the Member States with regard to the level of radioactivity in the air, water and soil.

In cases of urgency, the Commission shall issue a directive requiring the Member State concerned to take, within a period laid down by the Commission, all necessary measures to prevent infringement of the basic standards and to ensure compliance with regulations.

Should the State in question fail to comply with the Commission directive within the period laid down, the Commission or any Member State concerned may forthwith, by way of derogation from Articles 141 and 142, bring the matter before the Court of Justice.

ARTICLE 39

The Commission shall set up within the framework of the Joint Nuclear Research Centre, as soon as the latter has been established, a health and safety documentation and study section.

This section shall in particular have the task of collecting the documentation and information referred to in Articles 33, 36 and 37 and of assisting the Commission in carrying out the tasks assigned to it by this Chapter.

CHAPTER IV—INVESTMENT

Article 40

In order to stimulate action by persons and undertakings and to facilitate co-ordinated development of their investment in the nuclear field, the Commission shall periodically publish illustrative programmes indicating in particular nuclear energy production targets and all the types of investment required for their attainment.

The Commission shall obtain the opinion of the Economic and Social Committee on such programmes before their publication.

Article 41

Persons and undertakings engaged in the industrial activities listed in Annex II to this Treaty shall communicate to the Commission investment projects relating to new installations and also to replacements or conversions which fulfil the criteria as to type and size laid down by the Council on a proposal from the Commission.

The list of industrial activities referred to above may be altered by the Council, acting by a qualified majority on a proposal from the Commission, which shall first obtain the opinion of the Economic and Social Committee.

Article 42

The projects referred to in Article 41 shall be communicated to the Commission and, for information purposes, to the Member State concerned not later than three months before the first contracts are concluded with the suppliers or, if the work is to be carried out by the undertaking with its own resources, three months before the work begins.

The Council may, acting on a proposal from the Commission, alter this time limit.

Article 43

The Commission shall discuss with the persons or undertakings all aspects of investment projects which relate to the objectives of this Treaty.

It shall communicate its views to the Member State concerned.

Article 44

The Commission may, with the consent of the Member States, persons and undertakings concerned, publish any investment projects communicated to it.

CHAPTER V—JOINT UNDERTAKINGS

Article 45

Undertakings which are of fundamental importance to the development of the nuclear industry in the Community may be established as Joint Undertakings within the meaning of this Treaty, in accordance with the following Articles.

ARTICLE 46

1. Every project for establishing a Joint Undertaking, whether originating from the Commission, a Member State or any other quarter, shall be the subject of an inquiry by the Commission.

For this purpose, the Commission shall obtain the views of Member States and of any public or private body which in its opinion can usefully advise it.

2. The Commission shall forward to the Council any project for establishing a Joint Undertaking, together with its reasoned opinion.

If the Commission delivers a favourable opinion on the need for the proposed Joint Undertaking, it shall submit proposals to the Council concerning:

  (*a*) location;
  (*b*) statutes;
  (*c*) the scale of and timetable for financing;
  (*d*) possible participation by the Community in the financing of the Joint Undertaking;
  (*e*) possible participation by a third State, an international organisation or a national of a third State in the financing or management of the Joint Undertaking;
  (*f*) the conferring of any or all of the advantages listed in Annex III to this Treaty.

The Commission shall attach a detailed report on the project as a whole.

ARTICLE 47

The Council may, when the matter has been submitted to it by the Commission, request the latter to supply such further information or to undertake such further inquiries as the Council may consider necessary.

If the Council, acting by a qualified majority, considers that a project forwarded by the Commission with an unfavourable opinion should nevertheless be carried out, the Commission shall submit to the Council the proposals and the detailed report referred to in Article 46.

Where the opinion of the Commission is favourable or in the case referred to in the preceding paragraph, the Council shall act by a qualified majority on each of the proposals from the Commission.

The Council shall, however, act unanimously in respect of:

  (*a*) participation by the Community in the financing of the Joint Undertaking;
  (*b*) participation by a third State, an international organisation or a national of a third State in the financing or management of the Joint Undertaking.

ARTICLE 48

The Council may, acting unanimously on a proposal from the Commission, make applicable to each Joint Undertaking any or all of the advantages listed in Annex III to this Treaty; each Member State shall for its part ensure that these advantages are conferred.

The Council may, in accordance with the same procedure, lay down the conditions governing the conferment of these advantages.

ARTICLE 49

Joint Undertakings shall be established by Council decision.
Each Joint Undertaking shall have legal personality.

In each of the Member States, it shall enjoy the most extensive legal capacity accorded to legal persons under their respective national laws; it may, in particular, acquire or dispose of movable and immovable property and may be a party to legal proceedings.

Save as otherwise provided in this Treaty or in its own statutes, each Joint Undertaking shall be governed by the rules applying to industrial or commercial undertakings; its statutes may make subsidiary reference to the national laws of the Member States.

Save where jurisdiction is conferred upon the Court of Justice by this Treaty, disputes in which Joint Undertakings are concerned shall be determined by the appropriate national courts or tribunals.

ARTICLE 50

The statutes of Joint Undertakings shall be amended, where necessary, in accordance with the special provisions which they contain for this purpose.

Such amendments shall not, however, enter into force until they have been approved by the Council, acting in accordance with the procedure laid down in Article 47 on a proposal from the Commission.

ARTICLE 51

The Commission shall be responsible for carrying out all decisions of the Council relating to the establishment of Joint Undertakings until the bodies responsible for the operation of such Undertakings have been set up.

CHAPTER VI—SUPPLIES

ARTICLE 52

1. The supply of ores, source materials and special fissile materials shall be ensured, in accordance with the provisions of this Chapter, by means of a common supply policy on the principle of equal access to sources of supply.

2. For this purpose and under the conditions laid down in this Chapter:
   - (a) all practices designed to secure a privileged position for certain users shall be prohibited;
   - (b) an Agency is hereby established; it shall have a right of option on ores, source materials and special fissile materials produced in the territories of Member States and an exclusive right to conclude contracts relating to the supply of ores, source materials and special fissile materials coming from inside the Community or from outside.

The Agency may not discriminate in any way between users on grounds of the use which they intend to make of the supplies requested unless such use is unlawful or is found to be contrary to the conditions imposed by suppliers outside the Community on the consignment in question.

SECTION I—THE AGENCY

ARTICLE 53

The Agency shall be under the supervision of the Commission, which shall issue directives to it, possess a right of veto over its decisions and appoint its Director-General and Deputy Director-General.

Any act, whether implied or express, performed by the Agency in the exercise of its right of option or of its exclusive right to conclude supply contracts, may be referred by the parties concerned to the Commission, which shall give a decision thereon within one month.

ARTICLE 54

The Agency shall have legal personality and financial autonomy.

The Council shall lay down the statutes of the Agency, acting by a qualified majority on a proposal from the Commission.

The statutes may be amended in accordance with the same procedure.

The statutes shall determine the Agency's capital and the terms upon which it is to be subscribed. The major part of the capital shall always belong to the Community and to the Member States. The contributions to the capital shall be determined by common accord of the Member States.

The rules for the commercial management of the activities of the Agency shall be laid down in the statutes. The latter may provide for a charge on transactions to defray the operating expenses of the Agency.

ARTICLE 55

The Member States shall communicate or cause to be communicated to the Agency all the information necessary to enable it to exercise its right of option and its exclusive right to conclude supply contracts.

ARTICLE 56

The Member States shall be responsible for ensuring that the Agency may operate freely in their territories.

They may establish one or more bodies having authority to represent, in relations with the Agency, producers and users in the non-European territories under their jurisdiction.

SECTION II—ORES, SOURCE MATERIALS AND SPECIAL FISSILE MATERIALS COMING FROM INSIDE THE COMMUNITY

ARTICLE 57

1. The right of option of the Agency shall cover:
    (a) the acquisition of rights to use and consume materials owned by the Community under the provisions of Chapter VIII;
    (b) the acquisition of the right of ownership in all other cases.
2. The Agency shall exercise its right of option by concluding contracts with producers of ores, source materials and special fissile materials.

Subject to Articles 58, 62 and 63, every producer shall offer to the Agency the ores, source materials or special fissile materials which he produces within the territories of Member States before they are used, transferred or stored.

ARTICLE 58

Where a producer carries out several stages of production from extraction of the ore up to and including production of the metal, he may offer the product to the Agency at whichever stage of production he chooses.

The same shall apply to two or more connected undertakings, where the connection has been duly communicated to the Commission and discussed with it in accordance with the procedures laid down in Articles 43 and 44.

ARTICLE 59

If the Agency does not exercise its right of option on the whole or any part of the output of a producer, the latter

(a) may, either by using his own resources or under contract, process or cause to be processed the ores, source materials or special fissile materials, provided that he offers to the Agency the product of such processing;

(b) shall be authorised by a decision of the Commission to dispose of his available production outside the Community, provided that the terms he offers are not more favourable than those previously offered to the Agency. However, special fissile materials may be exported only through the Agency and in accordance with the provisions of Article 62.

The Commission may not grant such authorisation if the recipients of the supplies fail to satisfy it that the general interests of the Community will be safeguarded or if the terms and conditions of such contracts are contrary to the objectives of this Treaty.

ARTICLE 60

Potential users shall periodically inform the Agency of the supplies they require, specifying the quantities, the physical and chemical nature, the place of origin, the intended use, delivery dates and price terms, which are to form the terms and conditions of the supply contract which they wish to conclude.

Similarly, producers shall inform the Agency of offers which they are able to make, stating all the specifications, and in particular the duration of contracts, required to enable their production programmes to be drawn up. Such contracts shall be of not more than ten years' duration save with the agreement of the Commission.

The Agency shall inform all potential users of the offers and of the volume of applications which it has received and shall call upon them to place their orders by a specified time limit.

When the Agency has received all such orders, it shall make known the terms on which it can meet them.

If the Agency cannot meet in their entirety all the orders received, it shall, subject to the provisions of Articles 68 and 69, share out the supplies proportionately among the orders relating to each offer.

Agency rules, which shall require approval by the Commission, shall determine the manner in which demand is to be balanced against supply.

ARTICLE 61

The Agency shall meet all orders unless prevented from so doing by legal or material obstacles.

When concluding a contract, the Agency may, while complying with the provisions of Article 52, require users to make appropriate advance payments either as security or to assist in meeting the Agency's own long-term commitments to producers where these are essential to carrying out the order.

ARTICLE 62

1. The Agency shall exercise its right of option on special fissile materials produced in the territories of Member States in order

(*a*) to meet demand from users within the Community in accordance with Article 60; or

(*b*) to store such materials itself; or

(*c*) to export such materials with the authorisation of the Commission, which shall comply with the second subparagraph of Article 59 (*b*).

2. Nevertheless, while continuing to be subject to the provisions of Chapter VII, such materials and any fertile wastes shall be left in the possession of the producer, so that he may

(*a*) store them with the authorisation of the Agency; or

(*b*) use them within the limits of his own requirements; or

(*c*) make them available to undertakings in the Community, within the limits of their requirements, where, for carrying out a programme duly communicated to the Commission, these undertakings have with the producer a direct connection which has neither the aim nor the effect of limiting production, technical development or investment or of improperly creating inequalities between users in the Community.

3. The provisions of Article 89 (1) (*a*) shall apply to special fissile materials which are produced in the territories of Member States and on which the Agency has not exercised its right of option.

ARTICLE 63

Ores, source materials and special fissile materials produced by Joint Undertakings shall be allotted to users in accordance with the rules laid down in the statutes or agreements of such Undertakings.

SECTION III—ORES, SOURCE MATERIALS AND SPECIAL FISSILE MATERIALS COMING FROM OUTSIDE THE COMMUNITY

ARTICLE 64

The Agency, acting where appropriate within the framework of agreements concluded between the Community and a third State or an international organisation, shall, subject to the exceptions provided for in this Treaty, have the exclusive right to enter into agreements or contracts whose principal aim is the supply of ores, source materials or special fissile materials coming from outside the Community.

ARTICLE 65

Article 60 shall apply to applications from users and to contracts between users and the Agency relating to the supply of ores, source materials or special fissile materials coming from outside the Community.

The Agency may, however, decide on the geographical origin of supplies provided that conditions which are at least as favourable as those specified in the order are thereby secured for the user.

ARTICLE 66

Should the Commission find, on application by the users concerned, that the Agency is not in a position to deliver within a reasonable period of time all or part of the supplies ordered, or that it can only do so at excessively high prices, the users shall have the right to conclude directly contracts relating to supplies from outside the Community, provided that such contracts meet in essential respects the requirements specified in their orders,

This right shall be granted for a period of one year; it may be extended if the situation which justified its granting continues,

Users who avail themselves of the right provided for in this Article shall communicate to the Commission the direct contracts which they propose to conclude. The Commission may, within one month, object to the conclusion of such contracts if they are contrary to the objectives of this Treaty.

SECTION IV—PRICES

ARTICLE 67

Save where exceptions are provided for in this Treaty, prices shall be determined as a result of balancing supply against demand as provided in Article 60; the national regulations of the Member States shall not contravene such provisions.

ARTICLE 68

Pricing practices designed to secure a privileged position for certain users in violation of the principle of equal access laid down in the provisions of this Chapter shall be prohibited.

If the Agency finds that any such practices are being employed it shall report them to the Commission.

The Commission may, if it accepts the findings, set the prices of the offers in issue at a level compatible with the principle of equal access.

ARTICLE 69

The Council may fix prices, acting unanimously on a proposal from the Commission.

When the Agency lays down, in pursuance of Article 60, the terms on which orders can be met, it may propose to the users who have placed orders that prices be equalised.

SECTION V—PROVISIONS RELATING TO SUPPLY POLICY

ARTICLE 70

Within the limits set by the budget of the Community, the Commission may, on such conditions as it shall determine, give financial support to prospecting programmes in the territories of Member States.

The Commission may make recommendations to the Member States with a view to the development of prospecting for and exploitation of mineral deposits.

The Member States shall submit annually to the commission a report on the development of prospecting and production, on probable reserves and on investment in mining which has been made or is planned in their territories. The reports shall be submitted to the Council, together with an opinion from the Commission which shall state in particular what action has been taken by Member States on recommendations made to them under the preceding paragraph.

If, when the matter has been submitted to it by the Commission, the Council finds by a qualified majority that, although the prospects for extraction appear economically justified on a long-term basis, prospecting activities and the expansion of mining operations continue to be markedly inadequate, the Member State concerned shall, for as long as it has failed to remedy this situation, be deemed to have waived, both for itself and for its nationals, the right of equal access to other sources of supply within the Community.

ARTICLE 71

The Commission shall make all appropriate recommendations to Member States with regard to revenue or mining regulations.

ARTICLE 72

The Agency may, from material available inside or outside the Community, build up the necessary commercial stocks to facilitate supplies to or normal deliveries by the Community.

The Commission may, where necessary, decide to build up emergency stocks. The method of financing such stocks shall be approved by the Council, acting by a qualified majority on a proposal from the Commission.

SECTION VI—SPECIAL PROVISIONS

ARTICLE 73

Where an agreement or contract between a Member State, a person or an undertaking on the one hand, and a third State, an international organisation or a national of a third State on the other, provides *inter alia* for delivery of products which come within the province of the Agency, the prior consent of the Commission shall be required for the conclusion or renewal of that agreement or contract, as far as delivery of the products is concerned.

ARTICLE 74

The Commission may exempt from the provisions of this Chapter the transfer, import or export of small quantities of ores, source materials or special fissile materials such as are normally used in research.

The Agency shall be notified of every transfer, import or export operation effected by virtue of this provision.

ARTICLE 75

The provisions of this Chapter shall not apply to commitments relating to the processing, conversion or shaping of ores, source materials or special fissile materials and entered into

  (a) by several persons or undertakings, where the material is to return to the original person or undertaking after being processed, converted or shaped; or

  (b) by a person or undertaking and an international organisation or a national of a third State, where the material is processed, converted or shaped outside the Community and then returned to the original person or undertaking; or

  (c) by a person or undertaking and an international organisation or a national of a third State, where the material is processed, converted or shaped inside the Community and is then returned either to the original organisation or national or to any other consignee likewise outside the Community designated by such organisation or national.

The persons and undertakings concerned shall, however, notify the Agency of the existence of such commitments and, as soon as the contracts are signed, of the quantities of material involved in the movements. The Commission may prevent the commitments referred to in subparagraph (b) from being undertaken if it considers that the conversion or shaping cannot be carried out efficiently and safely and without the loss of material to the detriment of the Community.

The materials to which such commitments relate shall be subject in the territories of the Member States to the safeguards laid down in Chapter VII. The provisions of Chapter VIII shall not, however, be applicable to special fissile materials covered by the commitments referred to in subparagraph (c).

ARTICLE 76

On the initiative of a Member State or of the Commission, and particularly if unforeseen circumstances create a situation of general shortage, the Council may, acting unanimously on a proposal from the Commission and after consulting the Assembly, amend the provisions of this Chapter. The Commission shall inquire into any request made by a Member State.

Seven years after the entry into force of this Treaty, the Council may confirm these provisions in their entirety. Failing confirmation, new provisions relating to the subject matter of this Chapter shall be adopted in accordance with the procedure laid down in the preceding paragraph.

CHAPTER VII—SAFEGUARDS

ARTICLE 77

In accordance with the provisions of this Chapter, the Commission shall satisfy itself that, in the territories of Member States,

(a) ores, source materials and special fissile materials are not diverted from their intended uses as declared by the users;

(b) the provisions relating to supply and any particular safeguarding obligations assumed by the Community under an agreement concluded with a third State or an international organisation are complied with.

ARTICLE 78

Anyone setting up or operating an installation for the production, separation or other use of source materials or special fissile materials or for the processing of irradiated nuclear fuels shall declare to the Commission the basic technical characteristics of the installations, to the extent that knowledge of these characteristics is necessary for the attainment of the objectives set out in Article 77.

The Commission must approve the techniques to be used for the chemical processing of irradiated materials, to the extent necessary to attain the objectives set out in Article 77.

ARTICLE 79

The Commission shall require that operating records be kept and produced in order to permit accounting for ores, source materials and special fissile materials used or produced. The same requirement shall apply in the case of the transport of source materials and special fissile materials.

Those subject to such requirements shall notify the quthorities of the Member State concerned of any communications they make to the Commission pursuant to Article 78 and to the first paragraph of this Article.

The nature and the extent of the requirements referred to in the first paragraph of this Article shall be defined in a regulation made by the Commission and approved by the Council.

ARTICLE 80

The Commission may require that any excess special fissile materials recovered or obtained as by-products and not actually being used or ready for use shall be deposited with the Agency or in other stores which are or can be supervised by the Commission.

Special fissile materials deposited in this way must be returned forthwith to those concerned at their request.

ARTICLE 81

The Commission may send inspectors into the territories of Member States. Before sending an inspector on his first assignment in the territory of a Member State, the Commission shall consult the State concerned; such consultation shall suffice to cover all future assignments of this inspector.

On presentation of a document establishing their authority, inspectors shall at all times have access to all places and data and to all persons who, by reason of their occupation, deal with materials, equipment or installations subject to the safeguards provided for in this Chapter, to the extent necessary in order to apply such safeguards to ores, source materials and special fissile materials and to ensure compliance with the provisions of Article 77. Should the State concerned so request, inspectors appointed by the Commission shall be accompanied by representatives of the authorities of that State; however, the inspectors shall not thereby be delayed or otherwise impeded in the performance of their duties.

If the carrying out of an inspection is opposed, the Commission shall apply to the President of the Court of Justice for an order to ensure that the inspection be carried out compulsorily. The President of the Court of Justice shall give a decision within three days.

If there is danger in delay, the Commission may itself issue a written order, in the form of a decision, to proceed with the inspection. This order shall be submitted without delay to the President of the Court of Justice for subsequent approval.

After the order or decision has been issued, the authorities of the State concerned shall ensure that the inspectors have access to the places specified in the order or decision.

ARTICLE 82

Inspectors shall be recruited by the Commission.

They shall be responsible for obtaining and verifying the records referred to in Article 79. They shall report any infringement to the Commission.

The Commission may issue a directive calling upon the Member State concerned to take, by a time limit set by the Commission, all measures necessary to bring such infringement to an end; it shall inform the Council thereof.

If the Member State does not comply with the Commission directive by the time limit set, the Commission or any Member State concerned may, in derogation from Articles 141 and 142, refer the matter to the Court of Justice direct.

ARTICLE 83

1. In the event of an infringement on the part of persons or undertakings of the obligations imposed on them by this Chapter, the Commission may impose sanctions on such persons or undertakings.

These sanctions shall be, in order of severity:

(a) a warning;

(b) the withdrawal of special benefits such as financial or technical assistance;

(c) the placing of the undertaking for a period not exceeding four months under the administration of a person or board appointed by common accord of the Commission and the State having jurisdiction over the undertaking;

(d) total or partial withdrawal of source materials or special fissile materials.

2. Decisions taken by the Commission in implementation of paragraph 1 and requiring the surrender of materials shall be enforceable. They may be enforced in the territories of Member States in accordance with Article 164.

By way of derogation from Article 157, appeals brought before the Court of Justice against decisions of the Commission which impose any of the sanctions provided for in paragraph 1 shall have suspensory effect. The Court of Justice may, however, on application by the Commission or by any Member State concerned, order that the decision be enforced forthwith.

There shall be an appropriate legal procedure to ensure the protection of interests that have been prejudiced.

3. The Commission may make any recommendations to Member States concerning laws or regulations which are designed to ensure compliance in their territories with the obligations arising under this Chapter.

4. Member States shall ensure that sanctions are enforced and, where necessary, that the infringements are remedied by those committing them.

ARTICLE 84

In the application of the safeguards, no discrimination shall be made on grounds of the use for which ores, source materials and special fissile materials are intended.

The scope of and procedure for the safeguards and the powers of the bodies responsible for their application shall be confined to the attainment of the objectives set out in this Chapter.

The safeguards may not extend to materials intended to meet defence requirements which are in the course of being specially processed for this purpose or which, after being so processed, are, in accordance with an operational plan, placed or stored in a military establishment.

ARTICLE 85

Where new circumstances so require, the procedures for applying the safeguards laid down in this Chapter may, at the request of a Member State or of the Commission, be adapted by the Council, acting unanimously on a proposal from the Commission and after consulting the Assembly. The Commission shall examine any such request made by a Member State.

CHAPTER VIII—PROPERTY OWNERSHIP

ARTICLE 86

Special fissile materials shall be the property of the Community.

The Community's right of ownership shall extend to all special fissile materials which are produced or imported by a Member State, a person or an undertaking and are subject to the safeguards provided for in Chapter VII.

ARTICLE 87

Member States, persons or undertakings shall have the unlimited right of use and consumption of special fissile materials which have properly come into their possession, subject to the obligations imposed on them by this Treaty, in particular those relating to safeguards, the right of option conferred on the Agency and health and safety.

ARTICLE 88

The Agency shall keep a special account in the name of the Community, called " Special Fissile Materials Financial Account ".

ARTICLE 89

1. In the Special Fissile Materials Financial Account:
    (a) the value of special fissile materials left in the possession of or put at the disposal of a Member State, person or undertaking shall be credited to the Community and debited to that Member State, person or undertaking;
    (b) the value of special fissile materials which are produced or imported by a Member State, person or undertaking and become the property of the Community shall be debited to the Community and credited to that Member State, person or undertaking. A similar entry shall be made when a Member State, person or undertaking restores to the Community special fissile materials previously left in the possession of or put at the disposal of that state, person or undertaking.
2. Variations in value affecting the quantities of special fissile material shall be expressed for accounting purposes in such a way as not to give rise to any loss or gain to the Community. Any loss or gain shall be borne by or accrue to the holder.
3. Balances arising from the transactions referred to above shall become payable forthwith upon the request of the creditor.
4. Where the Agency undertakes transactions for its own account, it shall, for the purposes of this Chapter, be deemed to be an undertaking.

ARTICLE 90

Where new circumstances so require, the provisions of this Chapter relating to the Community's right of ownership may, at the request of a Member State or of the Commission, be adjusted by the Council, acting unanimously on a proposal from the Commission and after consulting the Assembly. The Commission shall examine any such request made by a Member State.

ARTICLE 91

The system of ownership applicable to all objects, materials and assets which are not vested in the Community under this Chapter shall be determined by the law of each Member State.

CHAPTER IX—THE NUCLEAR COMMON MARKET

ARTICLE 92

The provisions of this Chapter shall apply to the goods and products specified in the Lists forming Annex IV to this Treaty.

These Lists may, at the request of the Commission or of a Member State, be amended by the Council, acting on a proposal from the Commission.

ARTICLE 93

Member States shall abolish between themselves, one year after the entry into force of this Treaty, all customs duties on imports and exports or charges having equivalent effect, and all quantitative restrictions on imports and exports, in respect of:

(a) products in Lists A^1 and A^2;

(b) products in List B if subject to a common customs tariff and accompanied by a certificate issued by the Commission stating that they are intended to be used for nuclear purposes.

Non-European territories under the jurisdiction of a Member State may, however, continue to levy import and export duties or charges having equivalent effect where they are of an exclusively fiscal nature. The rates of such duties and charges and the system governing them shall not give rise to any discrimination between that State and the other Member States.

ARTICLE 94

The Member States shall set up a common customs tariff in accordance with the following provisions:

(a) With regard to products specified in List A^1, the common customs tariff shall be fixed at the level of the lowest tariff in force in any Member State on 1 January 1957;

(b) With regard to products specified in List A^2, the Commission shall take all appropriate measures to ensure that negotiations between Member States shall begin within three months of the entry into force of this Treaty. If, on some of these products, no agreement can be reached within one year of the entry into force of this Treaty, the Council shall, acting by a qualified majority on a proposal from the Commission, determine the applicable duties in the common customs tariff;

(c) The common customs tariff on the products specified in Lists A^1 and A^2 shall be applied from the end of the first year following the entry into force of this Treaty.

ARTICLE 95

The Council may, acting unanimously on a proposal from the Commission, decide on the earlier application of the duties in the common customs tariff on products in List B where such a measure would tend to contribute to the development of nuclear energy in the Community.

ARTICLE 96

The Member States shall abolish all restrictions based on nationality affecting the right of nationals of any Member State to take skilled employment in the field of nuclear energy, subject to the limitations resulting from the basic requirements of public policy, public security or public health.

After consulting the Assembly, the Council may, acting by a qualified majority on a proposal from the Commission, which shall first request the opinion of the Economic and Social Committee, issue directives for the application of this Article.

ARTICLE 97

No restrictions based on nationality may be applied to natural or legal persons, whether public or private, under the jurisdiction of a Member State, where they desire to participate in the construction of nuclear installations of a scientific or industrial nature in the Community.

ARTICLE 98

Member States shall take all measures necessary to facilitate the conclusion of insurance contracts covering nuclear risks.

Within two years of the entry into force of this Treaty, the Council, acting by a qualified majority on a proposal from the Commission, which shall first request the opinion of the Economic and Social Committee, shall, after consulting the Assembly, issue directives for the application of this Article.

ARTICLE 99

The Commission may make any recommendations for facilitating movements of capital intended to finance the industrial activities listed in Annex II to this Treaty.

ARTICLE 100

Each Member State undertakes to authorise, in the currency of the Member State in which the creditor or the beneficiary resides, any payments connected with the movement of goods, services or capital, and any transfers of capital and earnings, to the extent that the movement of goods, services, capital and persons between Member States has been liberalised pursuant to this Treaty.

CHAPTER X—EXTERNAL RELATIONS

ARTICLE 101

The Community may, within the limits of its powers and jurisdiction, enter into obligations by concluding agreements or contracts with a third State, an international organisation or a national of a third State.

Such agreements or contracts shall be negotiated by the Commission in accordance with the directives of the Council; they shall be concluded by the Commission with the approval of the Council, which shall act by a qualified majority.

Agreements or contracts whose implementation does not require action by the Council and can be effected within the limits of the relevant budget shall, however, be negotiated and concluded solely by the Commission; the Commission shall keep the Council informed.

ARTICLE 102

Agreements or contracts concluded with a third State, an international organisation or a national of a third State to which, in addition to the Community, one or more Member States are parties, shall not enter into force until the Commission has been notified by all the Member States concerned that those agreements or contracts have become applicable in accordance with the provisions of their respective national laws.

ARTICLE 103

Member States shall communicate to the Commission draft agreements or contracts with a third State, an international organisation or a national of a third State to the extent that such agreements or contracts concern matters within the purview of this Treaty.

If a draft agreement or contract contains clauses which impede the application of this Treaty, the Commission shall, within one month of receipt of such communication, make its comments known to the State concerned.

The State shall not conclude the proposed agreement or contract until it has satisfied the objections of the Commission or complied with a ruling by the Court of Justice, adjudicating urgently upon an application from the State, on the compatibility of the proposed clauses with the provisions of this Treaty. An application may be made to the Court of Justice at any time after the State has received the comments of the Commission.

ARTICLE 104

No person or undertaking concluding or renewing an agreement or contract with a third State, an international organisation or a national of a third State after the entry into force of this Treaty may invoke that agreement or contract in order to evade the obligations imposed by this Treaty.

Each Member State shall take such measures as it considers necessary in order to communicate to the Commission, at the request of the latter, all information relating to agreements or contracts concluded after the entry into force of this Treaty, within the purview thereof, by a person or undertaking with a third State, an international organisation or a national of a third State. The Commission may require such communication only for the purpose of verifying that such agreements or contracts do not contain clauses impeding the implementation of this Treaty.

On application by the Commission, the Court of Justice shall give a ruling on the compatibility of such agreements or contracts with the provisions of this Treaty.

ARTICLE 105

The provisions of this Treaty shall not be invoked so as to prevent the implementation of agreements or contracts concluded before its entry into force by a

Member State, a person or an undertaking with a third State, an international organisation or a national of a third State where such agreements or contracts have been communicated to the Commission not later than thirty days after the entry into force of this Treaty.

Agreements or contracts concluded between the signature and the entry into force of this Treaty by a person or an undertaking with a third State, an international organisation or a national of a third State shall not, however, be invoked as grounds for failure to implement this Treaty if, in the opinion of the Court of Justice, ruling on an application from the Commission, one of the decisive reasons on the part of either of the parties in concluding the agreement or contract was an intention to evade the provisions of this Treaty.

ARTICLE 106

Member States which, before the entry into force of this Treaty, have concluded agreements with third States providing for cooperation in the field of nuclear energy shall be required to undertake jointly with the Commission the necessary negotiations with these third States in order to ensure that the rights and obligations arising out of such agreements shall as far as possible be assumed by the Community.

Any new agreement ensuing from such negotiations shall require the consent of the Member State or States signatory to the agreements referred to above and the approval of the Council, which shall act by a qualified majority.

Title Three

PROVISIONS GOVERNING THE INSTITUTIONS

CHAPTER I—THE INSTITUTIONS OF THE COMMUNITY

SECTION I—THE ASSEMBLY

ARTICLE 107

The Assembly, which shall consist of representatives of the peoples of the States brought together in the Community, shall exercise the advisory and supervisory powers which are conferred upon it by this Treaty.

ARTICLE 108

1. The Assembly shall consist of delegates who shall be designated by the respective Parliaments from among their members in accordance with the procedure laid down by each Member State.

2. [The number of these delegates shall be as follows:

Belgium	14
Denmark	10
Germany	36
France	36
Ireland	10
Italy	36
Luxembourg	6
Netherlands	14
United Kingdom	36.]

3. The Assembly shall draw up proposals for elections by direct universal suffrage in accordance with a uniform procedure in all member States.

The Council shall, acting unanimously, lay down the appropriate provisions, which it shall recommend to Member States for adoption in accordance with their respective constitutional requirements.

AMENDMENT
Para. (2) was substituted by the Act of Accession, Art. 10, as amended by the Adaptation Decision, Art. 4.

ARTICLE 109

[The Assembly shall hold an annual session. It shall meet, without requiring to be convened, on the second Tuesday in March.]

The Assembly may meet in extraordinary session at the request of a majority of its members or at the request of the Council or of the Commission.

AMENDMENT
The first paragraph was repealed and substituted by the merger Treaty, Art. 27.

ARTICLE 110

The Assembly shall elect its President and its officers from among its members.

Members of the Commission may attend all meetings and shall, at their request, be heard on behalf of the Commission.

The Commission shall reply orally or in writing to questions put to it by the Assembly or by its members.

The Council shall be heard by the Assembly in accordance with the conditions laid down by the Council in its rules of procedure.

ARTICLE 111

Save as otherwise provided in this Treaty, the Assembly shall act by an absolute majority of the votes cast.

The rules of procedure shall determine the quorum.

ARTICLE 112

The Assembly shall adopt its rules of procedure, acting by a majority of its members.

The proceedings of the Assembly shall be published in the manner laid down in its rules of procedure.

ARTICLE 113

The Assembly shall discuss in open session the annual general report submitted to it by the Commission.

ARTICLE 114

If a motion of censure on the activities of the Commission is tabled before it, the Assembly shall not vote thereon until at least three days after the motion has been tabled and only by open vote.

If the motion of censure is carried by a two-thirds majority of the votes cast, representing a majority of the members of the Assembly, the members of the Commission shall resign as a body. They shall continue to deal with current business until they are replaced in accordance with Article 127.

SECTION II—THE COUNCIL

ARTICLE 115

The Council shall carry out its duties and exercise its powers of decision in accordance with the provisions of this Treaty.

It shall take all measures within its powers to co-ordinate the actions of the Member States and of the Community.

ARTICLE 116

[*Repealed by the Merger Treaty, Art. 7. See now ibid., Art. 2.*]

ARTICLE 117

[*Repealed by the Merger Treaty, Art. 7. See now ibid., Art. 3.*]

ARTICLE 118

1. Save as otherwise provided in this Treaty, the Council shall act by a majority of its members.

2. [Where the Council is required to act by a qualified majority, the votes of its members shall be weighted as follows:

Belgium	5
Denmark	3
Germany	10
Greece	5
France	10
Ireland	3
Italy	10
Luxembourg	2
Netherlands	5
United Kingdom	10

For their adoption, acts of the Council shall require at least:

—45 votes in favour where this Treaty requires them to be adopted on a proposal from the Commission,

—45 votes in favour, cast by at least six members, in other cases.]

3. Abstentions by members present in person or represented shall not prevent the adoption by the Council of acts which require unanimity.

AMENDMENTS
Para. (2) was substituted by the Act of Accession, Art. 14, as amended by the Adaptation Decision, Art. 8. It was subsequently substituted by the Act of Accession of the Hellenic Republic of May 28, 1979, Art. 14.

ARTICLE 119

Where, in pursuance of this Treaty, the Council acts on a proposal from the Commission, unanimity shall be required for an act constituting an amendment to that proposal.

As long as the Council has not acted, the Commission may alter its original proposal, in particular where the Assembly has been consulted on that proposal.

ARTICLE 120

Where a vote is taken, any member of the Council may also act on behalf of not more than one other member.

ARTICLE 121

[Repealed by the Merger Treaty, Art. 7. See now ibid., Arts. 4 and 5.]

ARTICLE 122

The Council may request the Commission to undertake any studies which the Council considers desirable for the attainment of the common objectives, and to submit to it any appropriate proposals.

ARTICLE 123

[Repealed by the Merger Treaty, Art. 7. See now ibid., Art. 6.]

SECTION III—THE COMMISSION

ARTICLE 124

In order to ensure the development of nuclear energy within the Community, the Commission shall:

—ensure that the provisions of this Treaty and the measures taken by the institutions pursuant thereto are applied;

—formulate recommendations or deliver opinions in the fields covered by this Treaty, if the Treaty expressly so provides or if the Commission considers it necessary;

—have its own power of decision and participate in the shaping of measures taken by the Council and by the Assembly in the manner provided for in this Treaty;

—exercise the powers conferred on it by the Council for the implementation of the rules laid down by the latter.

ARTICLE 125

[Repealed by the Merger Treaty, Art. 19. See now ibid., Art. 18.]

ARTICLE 126

[Repealed by the Merger Treaty, Art. 19. See now ibid., Art. 10.]

ARTICLE 127

[Repealed by the Merger Treaty, Art. 19. See now ibid., Art. 11.]

ARTICLE 128

[Repealed by the Merger Treaty, Art. 19. See now ibid., Art. 12.]

ARTICLE 129

[Repealed by the Merger Treaty, Art. 19. See now ibid., Art. 13.]

ARTICLE 130

[Repealed by the Merger Treaty, Art. 19. See now ibid., Art. 14.]

ARTICLE 131

[Repealed by the Merger Treaty, Art. 19. See now ibid., Arts 15 and 16.]

ARTICLE 132

[*Repealed by the Merger Treaty, Art.* 19. *See now ibid., Art.* 17.]

ARTICLE 133

[*Repealed by the Merger Treaty, Art.* 19. *The article formerly read:*
The Council may, acting unanimously, agree that the Government of a
Member State accredit to the Commission a qualified representative to
undertake permanent liaison duties.]

ARTICLE 134

1. A Scientific and Technical Committee is hereby set up; it shall be attached to the Commission and shall have advisory status.
The Committee must be consulted where this Treaty so provides. The Committee may be consulted in all cases in which the Commission considers this appropriate.
2. [The Committee shall consist of twenty-eight members, appointed by the Council after consultation with the Commission.]
The members of the Committee shall be appointed in their personal capacity for five years. Their appointment shall be renewable. They shall not be bound by any mandatory instructions.
The Scientific and Technical Committee shall each year elect its chairman and officers from among its members.

AMENDMENTS
In para. (2), the first sub-paragraph was substituted by the Act of Accession, Art. 23, as amended by the Adaptation Decision, Art. 12. It was subsequently substituted by the Act of Accession of the Hellenic Republic of May 28, 1979, Art. 19.

ARTICLE 135

The Commission may undertake any consultations and establish any study groups necessary to the performance of its tasks.

SECTION IV—THE COURT OF JUSTICE

ARTICLE 136

The Court of Justice shall ensure that in the interpretation and application of this Treaty the law is observed.

ARTICLE 137

[The Court of Justice shall consist of nine Judges.]
The Court of Justice shall sit in plenary session. It may, however, form chambers, each consisting of three of five Judges, either to undertake certain preparatory inquiries or to adjudicate on particular categories of cases in accordance with rules laid down for these purposes.
[Whenever the Court of Justice hears cases brought before it by a Member State or by one of the institutions of the Community or, to the extent that the chambers of the court do not have the requisite jurisdiction under the Rules of Procedure, has to give preliminary rulings on questions submitted to it pursuant to Article 150, it shall sit in plenary session.]

Should the Court of Justice so request, the Council may, acting unanimously, increase the number of Judges and make the necessary adjustments to the second and third paragraphs of this Article and to the second paragraph of Article 139.

AMENDMENTS
The first paragraph was substituted by the Act of Accession, Art. 17, as amended by the Adaptation Decision, Art. 9.
The third paragraph was replaced by Dec. 74/584, Art. 1 (O.J. 1974, L318/22).

ARTICLE 138

[The Court of Justice shall be assisted by four Advocates-General.]

It shall be the duty of the Advocate-General, acting with complete impartiality and independence, to make, in open court, reasoned submissions on cases brought before the Court of Justice, in order to assist the Court in the performance of the task assigned to it in Article 136.

Should the Court of Justice so request, the Council may, acting unanimously, increase the number of Advocates-General and make the necessary adjustments to the third paragraph of Article 139.

AMENDMENT
The first paragraph was substituted by the Council Decision of January 1, 1973, increasing the number of Advocates-General, Art. 1.

ARTICLE 139

The Judges and Advocates-General shall be chosen from persons whose independence is beyond doubt and who possess the qualifications required for appointment to the highest judicial offices in their respective countries or who are jurisconsults of recognised competence; they shall be appointed by common accord of the Governments of the Member States for a term of six years.

[Every three years there shall be a partial replacement of the Judges. Five and four Judges shall be replaced alternately.]

Every three years there shall be a partial replacement of the Advocates-General. Two Advocates-General shall be replaced on each occasion.]

Retiring Judges and Advocates-General shall be eligible for reappointment.

The Judges shall elect the President of the Court of Justice from among their number for a term of three years. He may be re-elected.

AMENDMENTS
The second and third paragraphs were substituted by the Act of Accession, Art. 19. The second paragraph was subsequently substituted by the Adaptation Decision, Art. 10, and the third paragraph by the Council Decision of January 1, 1973, increasing the number of Advocates-General, Art. 2.

ARTICLE 140

The Court of Justice shall appoint its Registrar and lay down the rules governing his service.

ARTICLE 141

If the Commission considers that a Member State has failed to fulfil an obligation under this Treaty, it shall deliver a reasoned opinion on the matter after giving the State concerned the opportunity to submit its observations.

If the State concerned does not comply with the opinion within the period laid down by the Commission, the latter may bring the matter before the Court of Justice.

ARTICLE 142

A Member State which considers that another Member State has failed to fulfil an obligation under this Treaty may bring the matter before the Court of Justice.

Before a Member State brings an action against another Member State for an alleged infringement of an obligation under this Treaty, it shall bring the matter before the Commission.

The Commission shall deliver a reasoned opinion after each of the States concerned has been given the opportunity to submit its own case and its observations on the other party's case both orally and in writing.

If the Commission has not delivered an opinion within three months of the date on which the matter was brought before it, the absence of such opinion shall not prevent the matter from being brought before the Court of Justice.

ARTICLE 143

If the Court of Justice finds that a Member State has failed to fulfil an obligation under this Treaty, the State shall be required to take the necessary measures to comply with the judgment of the Court of Justice.

ARTICLE 144

The Court of Justice shall have unlimited jurisdiction in:
   (a) proceedings instituted under Article 12 to have the appropriate terms fixed for the granting by the Commission of licences or sub-licences;
   (b) proceedings instituted by persons or undertakings against sanctions imposed on them by the Commission under Article 83.

ARTICLE 145

If the Commission considers that a person or undertaking has committed an infringement of this Treaty to which the provisions of Article 83 do not apply, it shall call upon the Member State having jurisdiction over that person or undertaking to cause sanctions to be imposed in respect of the infringement in accordance with its national law.

If the State concerned does not comply with such a request within the period laid down by the Commission, the latter may bring an action before the Court of Justice to have the infringement of which the person or undertaking is accused established.

ARTICLE 146

The Court of Justice shall review the legality of acts of the Council and the Commission other than recommendations or opinions. It shall for this purpose have jurisdiction in actions brought by a Member State, the Council or the Commission on grounds of lack of competence, infringement of an essential procedural requirement, infringement of this Treaty or of any rule of law relating to its application, or misuse of powers.

Any natural or legal person may, under the same conditions, institute proceedings against a decision addressed to that person or against a decision which, although in the form of a regulation or a decision addressed to another person, is of direct and individual concern to the former.

The proceedings provided for in this Article shall be instituted within two months of the publication of the measure, or of its notification to the plaintiff, or, in the absence thereof, of the day on which it came to the knowledge of the latter, as the case may be.

ARTICLE 147

If the action is well founded, the Court of Justice shall declare the act concerned to be void.

In the case of a regulation, however, the Court of Justice shall, if it considers this necessary, state which of the effects of the regulation which it has declared void shall be considered as definitive.

ARTICLE 148

Should the Council or the Commission, in infringement of this Treaty, fail to act, the Member States and the other institutions of the Community may bring an action before the Court of Justice to have the infringement established.

The action shall be admissible only if the institution concerned has first been called upon to act. If, within two months of being so called upon, the institution concerned has not defined its position, the action may be brought within a further period of two months.

Any natural or legal person may, under the conditions laid down in the preceding paragraphs, complain to the Court of Justice that an institution of the Community has failed to address to that person any act other than a recommendation or an opinion.

ARTICLE 149

The institution whose act has been declared void or whose failure to act has been declared contrary to this Treaty shall be required to take the necessary measures to comply with the judgment of the Court of Justice.

This obligation shall not affect any obligation which may result from the application of the second paragraph of Article 188.

ARTICLE 150

The Court of Justice shall have jurisdiction to give preliminary rulings concerning:

(a) the interpretation of this Treaty;

(b) the validity and interpretation of acts of the institutions of the Community;

(c) the interpretation of the statutes of bodies established by an act of the Council, save where those statutes provide otherwise.

Where such a question is raised before any court or tribunal of a Member State, that court or tribunal may, if it considers that a decision on the question is necessary to enable it to give judgment, request the Court of Justice to give a ruling thereon.

Where any such question is raised in a case pending before a court or tribunal of a Member State, against whose decisions there is no judicial remedy under national law, that court or tribunal shall bring the matter before the Court of Justice.

ARTICLE 151

The Court of Justice shall have jurisdiction in disputes relating to the compensation for damage provided for in the second paragraph of Article 188.

ARTICLE 152

The Court of Justice shall have jurisdiction in any dispute between the Community and its servants within the limits and under the conditions laid down in the Staff Regulations or the Conditions of Employment.

ARTICLE 153

The Court of Justice shall have jurisdiction to give judgment pursuant to any arbitration clause contained in a contract concluded by or on behalf of the Community, whether that contract be governed by public or private law.

ARTICLE 154

The Court of Justice shall have jurisdiction in any dispute between Member States which relates to the subject matter of this Treaty if the dispute is submitted to it under a special agreement between the parties.

ARTICLE 155

Save where jurisdiction is conferred on the Court of Justice by this Treaty, disputes to which the Community is a party shall not on that ground be excluded from the jurisdiction of the courts or tribunals of the Member States.

ARTICLE 156

Notwithstanding the expiry of the period laid down in the third paragraph of Article 146, any party may, in proceedings in which a regulation of the Council or of the Commission is in issue, plead the grounds specified in the first paragraph of Article 146, in order to invoke before the Court of Justice the inapplicability of that regulation.

ARTICLE 157

Save as otherwise provided in this Treaty, actions brought before the Court of Justice shall not have suspensory effect. The Court of Justice may, however, if it considers that circumstances so require, order that application of the contested act be suspended.

ARTICLE 158

The Court of Justice may in any cases before it prescribe any necessary interim measures.

ARTICLE 159

The judgments of the Court of Justice shall be enforceable under the conditions laid down in Article 164.

ARTICLE 160

The Statute of the Court of Justice is laid down in a separate Protocol.

The Court of Justice shall adopt its rules of procedure. These shall require the unanimous approval of the Council.

CHAPTER II—PROVISIONS COMMON TO SEVERAL INSTITUTIONS

ARTICLE 161

In order to carry out their task the Council and the Commission shall, in accordance with the provisions of this Treaty, make regulations, issue directives, take decisions, make recommendations or deliver opinions.

A regulation shall have general application. It shall be binding in its entirety and directly applicable in all Member States.

A directive shall be binding, as to the result to be achieved, upon each Member State to which it is addressed, but shall leave to the national authorities the choice of form and methods.

A decision shall be binding in its entirety upon those to whom it is addressed.

Recommendations and opinions shall have no binding force.

ARTICLE 162

Regulations, directives and decisions of the Council and of the Commission shall state the reasons on which they are based and shall refer to any proposals or opinions which were required to be obtained pursuant to this Treaty.

ARTICLE 163

Regulations shall be published in the Official Journal of the Community. They shall enter into force on the date specified in them or, in the absence thereof, on the twentieth day following their publication.

Directives and decisions shall be notified to those to whom they are addressed and shall take effect upon such notification.

ARTICLE 164

Enforcement shall be governed by the rules of civil procedure in force in the State in the territory of which it is carried out. The order for its enforcement shall be appended to the decision, without other formality than verification of the authenticity of the decision, by the national authority which the Government of each Member State shall designate for this purpose and shall make known to the Commission, to the Court of Justice and to the Arbitration Committee set up by Article 18.

When these formalities have been completed on application by the party concerned, the latter may proceed to enforcement in accordance with the national law, by bringing the matter directly before the competent authority.

Enforcement may be suspended only by a decision of the Court of Justice. However, the courts of the country concerned shall have jurisdiction over complaints that enforcement is being carried out in an irregular manner.

CHAPTER III—THE ECONOMIC AND SOCIAL COMMITTEE

ARTICLE 165

An Economic and Social Committee is hereby established. It shall have advisory status.

The Committee shall consist of representatives of the various categories of economic and social activity.

ARTICLE 166

[The number of members of the Committee shall be as follows:

Belgium	12
Denmark	9
Germany	24
Greece	12
France	24

Ireland	...	...	...	...	...	9
Italy	...	...	...	...	...	24
Luxembourg		...	...	...	...	6
Netherlands		...	...	...	...	12
United Kingdom			...	...	...	24.]

The members of the Committee shall be appointed by the Council, acting unanimously, for four years. Their appointments shall be renewable.

The members of the Committee shall be appointed in their personal capacity and may not be bound by any mandatory instructions.

AMENDMENTS
The first paragraph was substituted by the Act of Accession, Art. 21, as amended by the Adaptation Decision, Art. 11. It was subsequently substituted by the Act of Accession of the Hellenic Republic of May 28, 1979, Art. 17.

ARTICLE 167

1. For the appointment of the members of the Committee, each Member State shall provide the Council with a list containing twice as many candidates as there are seats allotted to its nationals.

The composition of the Committee shall take account of the need to ensure adequate representation of the various categories of economic and social activity.

2. The Council shall consult the Commission. It may obtain the opinion of European bodies which are representative of the various economic and social sectors to which the activities of the Community are of concern.

ARTICLE 168

The Committee shall elect its chairman and officers from among its members for a term of two years.

It shall adopt its rules of procedure and shall submit them to the Council for its approval, which must be unanimous.

The Committee shall be convened by its chairman at the request of the Council or of the Commission.

ARTICLE 169

The Committee may be divided into specialised sections.

These specialised sections shall operate within the general terms of reference of the Committee. They may not be consulted independently of the Committee.

Sub-committees may also be established within the Committee to prepare, on specific questions or in specific fields, draft opinions to be submitted to the Committee for its consideration.

The rules of procedure shall lay down the methods of composition and the terms of reference of the specialised sections and of the sub-committees.

ARTICLE 170

The Committee must be consulted by the Council or by the Commission where this Treaty so provides. The Committee may be consulted by these institutions in all cases in which they consider it appropriate.

The Council or the Commission shall, if it considers it necessary, set the Committee, for the submission of its opinion, a time limit which may not be less than ten days from the date on which the chairman receives notification to this effect. Upon expiry of the time limit, the absence of an opinion shall not prevent further action.

The opinion of the Committee and that of the specialised section, together with a record of the proceedings, shall be forwarded to the Council and to the Commission.

Title Four

FINANCIAL PROVISIONS

ARTICLE 171

1. Estimates shall be drawn up for each financial year of all revenue and expenditure of the Community, other than those of the Agency and the Joint Undertakings, and such revenue and expenditure shall be shown either in the operating budget or in the research and investment budget.

The revenue and expenditure shown in each budget shall be in balance.

2. The revenue and expenditure of the Agency, which shall operate in accordance with commercial principles, shall be budgeted for in a special account.

The manner of estimating, implementing and auditing such revenue and expenditure shall be laid down, with due regard to the statutes of the Agency, in financial regulations made pursuant to Article 183.

3. The estimates of revenue and expenditure, together with the operating accounts and the balance sheets of the Joint Undertakings for each financial year, shall be placed before the Commission, the Council and the Assembly in accordance with the statutes of those Undertakings.

ARTICLE 172

1. The operating budget revenue shall include, irrespective of any other current revenue, financial contributions of Member States on the following scale:

Belgium	7·9
Germany	28
France	28
Italy	28
Luxembourg	0·2
Netherlands	7·9

2. The research and investment budget revenue shall include, irrespective of any other resources, financial contributions of Member States on the following scale:

Belgium	9·9
Germany	30
France	30
Italy	23
Luxembourg	0·2
Netherlands	6·9

3. The scales may be modified by the Council, acting unanimously.

4. Loans for the financing of research or investment shall be raised on terms fixed by the Council in the manner provided for in Article 177 (5).

The Community may borrow on the capital market of a Member State, either in accordance with the legal provisions applying to internal issues, or, if there are no such provisions in a Member State, after the Member State concerned and the Commission have conferred together and have reached agreement upon the proposed loan.

The competent authorities of the Member State concerned may refuse to give their assent only if there is reason to fear serious disturbances on the capital market of that State.

ARTICLE 173

The financial contributions of Member States provided for in Article 172 may be replaced in whole or in part by the proceeds of levies collected by the Community in Member States.

To this end, the Commission shall submit to the Council proposals concerning the assessment of such levies, the method of fixing their rate and the procedure for their collection.

After consulting the Assembly on these proposals the Council may, acting unanimously, lay down the appropriate provisions, which it shall recommend to the Member States for adoption in accordance with their respective constitutional requirements.

ARTICLE 174

1. The expenditure shown in the operating budget shall include in particular:
    (a) administrative expenditure;
    (b) expenditure relating to safeguards and to health and safety.
2. The expenditure shown in the research and investment budget shall include in particular:
    (a) expenditure relating to the implementation of the Community research programme;
    (b) any participation in the capital of the Agency and in its investment expenditure;
    (c) expenditure relating to the equipment of training establishments;
    (d) any participation in Joint Undertakings or in certain joint operations.

ARTICLE 175

The expenditure shown in the operating budget shall be authorised for one financial year, unless the regulations made pursuant to Article 183 provide otherwise.

In accordance with conditions to be laid down pursuant to Article 183, any appropriations, other than those relating to staff expenditure, that are unexpended at the end of the financial year may be carried forward to the next financial year only.

Appropriations to cover expenditure shall be classified under different chapters grouping items of expenditure according to their nature or purpose and subdivided, as far as may be necessary, in accordance with the regulations made pursuant to Article 183.

The expenditure of the Assembly, the Council, the Commission and the Court of Justice shall be set out in separate parts of the budget, without prejudice to special arrangements for certain common items of expenditure.

ARTICLE 176

1. Subject to the limits resulting from programmes or decisions involving expenditure which, in pursuance of this Treaty, require the unanimous approval of the Council, allocations for research and investment expenditure shall include:

    (*a*) commitment appropriations, covering a series of items which constitute a separate unit and form a coherent whole;

    (*b*) payment appropriations which represent the maximum amount payable each year in respect of the commitments entered into under subparagraph (*a*).

2. The schedule of due dates for commitments and payments shall be annexed to the corresponding draft budget proposed by the Commission.

3. Appropriations for research and investment shall be classified under different chapters grouping items of expenditure according to their nature or purpose and subdivided, as far as may be necessary, in accordance with the regulations made pursuant to Article 183.

4. Unused payment authorisations shall be carried forward to the next financial year by decision of the Commission, unless the Council decides otherwise.

ARTICLE 177

[1. The financial year shall run from 1 January to 31 December.

Within the meaning of this Article, " budget " shall include the operating budget and the research and investment budget.

2. Each institution of the Community shall, before 1 July, draw up estimates of its expenditure. The Commission shall consolidate these estimates in a preliminary draft budget. It shall attach thereto an opinion which may contain different estimates.

The preliminary draft budget shall include an estimate of revenue and an estimate of expenditure.

3. The Commission shall place the preliminary draft budget before the Council not later than 1 September of the year preceding that in which the budget is to be implemented.

The Council shall consult the Commission and, where appropriate, the other institutions concerned whenever it intends to depart from the preliminary draft budget.

The Council shall, acting by a qualified majority, establish the draft budget and forward it to the Assembly.

4. The draft budget shall be placed before the Assembly not later than 5 October of the year preceding that in which the budget is to be implemented.

The Assembly shall have the right to amend the draft budget, acting by a majority of its members, and to propose to the Council, acting by an absolute majority of the votes cast, modifications to the draft budget relating to expenditure necessarily resulting from this Treaty or from acts adopted in accordance therewith.

If, within forty-five days of the draft budget being placed before it, the Assembly has given its approval, the budget shall stand as finally adopted. If within this period the Assembly has not amended the draft budget nor proposed any modifications thereto, the budget shall be deemed to be finally adopted.

If within this period the Assembly has adopted amendments or proposed modifications, the draft budget together with the amendments or proposed modifications shall be forwarded to the Council.

5. After discussing the draft budget with the Commission and, where appropriate, with the other institutions concerned, the Council shall act under the following conditions:

    (a) The Council may, acting by a qualified majority, modify any of the amendments adopted by the Assembly;

    (b) With regard to the proposed modifications:

        —where a modification proposed by the Assembly does not have the effect of increasing the total amount of the expenditure of an institution, owing in particular to the fact that the increase in expenditure which it would involve would be expressly compensated by one or more proposed modifications correspondingly reducing expenditure, the Council may, acting by a qualified majority, reject the proposed modification. In the absence of a decision to reject it, the proposed modification shall stand as accepted;

        —where a modification proposed by the Assembly has the effect of increasing the total amount of the expenditure of an institution, the Council may, acting by a qualified majority, accept this proposed modification. In the absence of a decision to accept it, the proposed modification shall stand as rejected;

        —where, in pursuance of one of the two preceding subparagraphs, the Council has rejected a proposed modification, it may, acting by a qualified majority, either retain the amount shown in the draft budget or fix another amount.

The draft budget shall be modified on the basis of the proposed modifications accepted by the Council.

If, within fifteen days of the draft budget being placed before it, the Council had not modified any of the amendments adopted by the Assembly and if the modifications proposed by the latter have been accepted, the budget shall be deemed to be finally adopted. The Council shall inform the Assembly that it has not modified any of the amendments and that the proposed modifications have been accepted.

If within this period the Council has modified one or more of the amendments adopted by the Assembly or if the modifications proposed by the latter have been rejected or modified, the modified draft budget shall again be forwarded to the Assembly. The Council shall inform the Assembly of the results of its deliberations.

6. Within fifteen days of the draft budget being placed before it, the Assembly, which shall have been notified of the action taken on its proposed modifications may, acting by a majority of its members and three fifths of the votes cast, amend or reject the modifications to its amendments made by the Council and shall adopt the budget accordingly. If within this period the Assembly has not acted, the budget shall be deemed to be finally adopted.

7. When the procedure provided for in this Article has been completed, the President of the Assembly shall declare that the budget has been finally adopted.

8. However, the Assembly, acting by a majority of its members and two thirds of the votes cast may, if there are important reasons, reject the draft budget and ask for a new draft to be submitted to it.

9. A maximum rate of increase in relation to the expenditure of the same type to be incurred during the current year shall be fixed annually for the total expenditure other than that necessarily resulting from this Treaty or from acts adopted in accordance therewith.

The Commission shall, after consulting the Economic Policy Committee, declare what this maximum rate is as it results from:

—the trend, in terms of volume, of the gross national product within the Community;

—the average variation in the budgets of the Member States; and

—the trend of the cost of living during the preceding financial year.

The maximum rate shall be communicated, before 1st May, to all the institutions of the Community. The later shall be required to conform to this during the budgetary procedure, subject to the provisions of the fourth and fifth subparagraphs of this paragraph.

If, in respect of expenditure other than that necessarily resulting from this Treaty or from acts adopted in accordance therewith, the actual rate of increase in the draft budget established by the Council is over half the maximum rate, the Assembly may, exercising its right of amendment, further increase the total amount of that expenditure to a limit not exceeding half the maximum rate.

Where the Assembly, the Council or the Commission considers that the activites of the Communities require that the rate determined according to the procedure laid down in this paragraph should be exceeded, another rate may be fixed by agreement between the Council, acting by a qualified majority, and the Assembly, acting by a majority of its members and three fifths of the votes cast.

10. Each institution shall exercise the powers conferred upon it by this Article, with due regard for the provisions of this Treaty and for acts adopted in accordance therewith, in particular those relating to the Communities' own resources and to the balance between revenue and expenditure.]

AMENDMENTS

This Article was substituted by the Budgetary Treaty, Art. 7. It was subsequently replaced by the Second Budgetary Treaty of July 22, 1975, Art. 20.

[ARTICLE 177a

By way of derogation from the provisions of Article 177, the following provisions shall apply to budgets for financial years preceding the financial year 1975:

1. The financial year shall run from 1 January to 31 December.

Within the meaning of this Article, " budget " shall include the operating budget and the research and investment budget.

2. Each institution of the Community shall, before 1 July, draw up estimates of its expenditure. The Commission shall consolidate these estimates in a preliminary draft budget. It shall attach thereto an opinion which may contain different estimates.

The preliminary draft budget shall contain an estimate of revenue and an estimate of expenditure.

3. The Commission shall place the preliminary draft budget before the Council not later than 1 September of the year preceding that in which the budget is to be implemented.

The Council shall consult the Commission and, where appropriate, the other institutions concerned whenever it intends to depart from the preliminary draft budget.

The Council shall, acting by a qualified majority, establish the draft budget and forward it to the Assembly.

4. The draft budget shall be placed before the Assembly not later than 5 October of the year preceding that in which the budget is to be implemented.

The Assembly shall have the right to propose to the Council modifications to the draft budget.

If, within forty-five days of the draft budget being placed before it, the Assembly has given its approval or has not proposed any modifications to the draft budget, the budget shall be deemed to be finally adopted.

If within this period the Assembly has proposed modifications, the draft budget together with the proposed modifications shall be forwarded to the Council.

5. The Council shall, after discussing the draft budget with the Commission and, where appropriate, with the other institutions concerned, adopt the budget, within thirty days of the draft budget being placed before it, under the following conditions.

Where a modification proposed by the Assembly does not have the effect of increasing the total amount of the expenditure of an institution, owing in particular to the fact that the increase in expenditure which it would involve would be expressly compensated by one or more proposed modifications correspondingly reducing expenditure, the Council may, acting by a qualified majority, reject the proposed modification. In the absence of a decision to reject it, the proposed modification shall stand as accepted.

Where a modification proposed by the Assembly has the effect of increasing the total amount of the expenditure of an institution, the Council must act by a qualified majority in accepting the proposed modification.

Where, in pursuance of the second or third subparagraph of this paragraph, the Council has rejected or has not accepted a proposed modification, it may, acting by a qualified majority, either retain the amount shown in the draft budget or fix another amount.

6. When the procedure provided for in this Article has been completed the President of the Council shall declare that the budget has been finally adopted.

7. Each institution shall exercise the powers conferred upon it by this Article, with due regard for the provisions of this Treaty and for acts adopted in accordance therewith, in particular those relating to the Communities' own resources and to the balance between revenue and expenditure.]

AMENDMENT
This Article was added by the Budgetary Treaty, Art. 8.

ARTICLE 178

[If, at the beginning of a financial year, the budget has not yet been voted, a sum equivalent to not more than one twelfth of the budget appropriations for the preceding financial year may be spent each month in respect of any chapter or other subdivision of the budget in accordance with the provisions of the regulations made pursuant to Article 183; this arrangement shall not, however, have the effect of placing at the disposal of the Commission appropriations in excess of one twelfth of those provided for in the draft budget in course of preparation.

The Council may, acting by a qualified majority, provided that the other conditions laid down in the first subparagraph are observed, authorise expenditure in excess of one twelfth.

If the decision relates to expenditure which does not necessarily result from this Treaty or from acts adopted in accordance therewith, the Council shall forward it immediately to the Assembly; within thirty days the Assembly, acting by a majority of its members and three fifths of the votes cast, may adopt a different decision on the expenditure in excess of one twelfth referred to in the first subparagraph. This part of the decision of the Council shall be suspended until the Assembly has taken its decisions. If within this period, the Assembly has not taken a decision which differs from the decision of the Council, the latter shall be deemed to be finally adopted.

The decision referred to in the second and third subparagraphs shall lay down the necessary measures relating to resources to ensure application of this Article.]

AMENDMENT
This Article was replaced by the Second Budgetary Treaty of July 22, 1975, Art. 21.

ARTICLE 179

The Commission shall implement the budgets, in accordance with the provisions of the regulations made pursuant to Article 183, on its own responsibility and within the limits of the appropriations.

The regulations shall lay down detailed rules for each institution concerning its part in effecting its own expenditure.

Within the budgets, the Commission may, subject to the limits and conditions laid down in the regulations made pursuant to Article 183, transfer appropriations from one chapter to another or from one sub-division to another.

[ARTICLE 179a

The Commission shall submit annually to the Council and the Assembly the accounts of the preceding financial year relating to the implementation of the budget. The Commission shall also forward to them a financial statement of the assets and liabilities of the Community.]

AMENDMENT
This article was added by the Second Budgetary Treaty of July 22, 1975, Art. 22.

ARTICLE 180

[1. A Court of Auditors is hereby established.

[2. The Court of Auditors shall consist of ten members.]

3. The members of the Court of Auditors shall be chosen from among persons who belong or have belonged in their respective countries to external audit bodies or who are especially qualified for this office. Their independence must be beyond doubt.

4. The members of the Court of Auditors shall be appointed for a term of six years by the Council, acting unanimously after consulting the Assembly.

However, when the first appointments are made, four members of the Court of Auditors, chosen by lot, shall be appointed for a term of office of four years only.

The members of the Court of Auditors shall be eligible for reappointment.

They shall elect the President of the Court of Auditors from among their number for a term of three years. The President may be re-elected.

5. The members of the Court of Auditors shall, in general interest of the Community, be completely independent in the performance of their duties.

In the performance of these duties, they shall neither seek nor take instructions from any Government, or from any other body. They shall refrain from any action incompatible with their duties.

6. The members of the Court of Auditors may not, during their term of office, engage in any other occupation, whether gainful or not. When entering upon their duties they shall give a solemn undertaking that, both during and after their term of office, they will respect the obligations arising therefrom and in particular their duty to behave with integrity and discretion as regards the acceptance, after they have ceased to hold office, of certain appointments or benefits.

7. Apart from normal replacement, or death, the duties of a member of the Court of Auditors shall end when he resigns, or is compulsorily retired by a ruling of the Court of Justice pursuant to paragraph 8.

The vacancy thus caused shall be filled for the remainder of the member's term of office.

Save in the case of compulsory retirement under the provisions of paragraph 8, members of the Court of Auditors shall remain in office until they have been replaced.

8. A member of the Court of Auditors may be deprived of his office or his right to a pension or other benefits in its stead only if the Court of Justice, at the request of the Court of Auditors finds that he no longer fulfils the requisite conditions or meets the obligations arising from his office.

9. The Council, acting by a qualified majority, shall determine the conditions of employment of the President and the members of the Court of Auditors and in particular their salaries, allowances and pensions. It shall also, by the same majority, determine any payment to be made instead of remuneration.

10. The provisions of the Protocol on the Privileges and Immunities of the European Communities applicable to the Judges of the Court of Justice shall also apply to the members of the Court of Auditors.]

AMENDMENTS
This article was amended by the Budgetary Treaty, Art. 9. It was subsequently replaced by the Second Budgetary Treaty of July 22, 1975, Art. 23.

Para (2) was substituted by the Act of Accession of the Hellenic Republic of May 28, 1979, Art. 18.

[ARTICLE 180a

1. The Court of Auditors shall examine the accounts of all revenue and expenditure of the Community. It shall also examine the accounts of all revenue and expenditure of all bodies set up by the Community insofar as the relevant constituent instrument does not preclude such examination.

2. The Court of Auditors shall examine whether all revenue has been received and all expenditure incurred in a lawful and regular manner and whether the financial management has been sound.

The audit of revenue shall be carried out on the basis both of the amounts established as due and the amounts actually paid to the Communities.

The audit of expenditure shall be carried out on the basis both of commitments undertaken and payments made.

These audits may be carried out before the closure of accounts for the financial year in question.

3. The audit shall be based on records and, if necessary, performed on the spot in the institutions of the Community and in the Member States. In the Member States the audit shall be carried out in liaison with the national audit bodies or, if these do not have the necessary powers, with the competent national departments. These bodies or departments shall inform the Court of Auditors whether they intend to take part in the audit.

The institutions of the Community and the national audit bodies or, if the latter do not have the necessary powers, the competent national departments, shall forward to the Court of Auditors, at its request, any document or information necessary to carry out its task.

4. The Court of Auditors shall draw up an annual report after the close of each financial year. It shall be forwarded to the institutions of the Community and shall be published, together with the replies of these institutions to the observations of the Court of Auditors, in the Official Journal of the European Communities.

The Court of Auditors may also, at any time, submit observations on specific questions and deliver opinions at the request of one of the institutions of the Community.

It shall adopt its annual reports or opinions by a majority of its members.

It shall assist the Assembly and the Council in exercising their powers of control over the implementation of the budget.]

AMENDMENT
   This Article was added by the Second Budgetary Treaty of July 22, 1975, Art. 24.

[ARTICLE 180b

The Assembly, acting on a recommendation from the Council which shall act by a qualified majority, shall give a discharge to the Commission in respect of the implementation of the budget. To this end, the Council and the Assembly in turn shall examine the accounts and the financial statement referred to in Article 179a, and the annual report by the Court of Auditors together with the replies of the institutions under audit to the observations of the Court of Auditors.]

AMENDMENT
   This Article was added by the Second Budgetary Treaty of July 22, 1975, Art. 25.

ARTICLE 181

The budgets and the account provided for in Article 171 (1) and (2) shall be drawn up in the unit of account determined in accordance with the provisions of the financial regulations made pursuant to Article 183.

The financial contributions provided for in Article 172 shall be placed at the disposal of the Community by the Member States in their national currencies.

The available balances of these contributions shall be deposited with the Treasuries of Member States or with bodies designated by them. While on deposit, such funds shall retain the value corresponding to the parity, at the date of deposit, in relation to the unit of account referred to in the first paragraph.

The balances may be invested on terms to be agreed between the Commission and the Member State concerned.

ARTICLE 182

1. The Commission may, provided it notifies the competent authorities of the Member States concerned, transfer into the currency of one of the Member States its holdings of currency of another Member State, to the extent necessary to enable them to be used for purposes which come within the scope of this Treaty. The Commission shall as far as possible avoid making such transfers if it possesses cash or liquid assets in the currencies which it needs.

2. The Commission shall deal with each Member State through the authority designated by the State concerned. In carrying out financial operations the Commission shall employ the services of the bank of issue of the Member State concerned or of any other financial institution approved by that State.

3. As regards expenditure which the Community has to incur in the currencies of third countries, the Commission shall, before the budgets are finally adopted, submit to the Council a programme indicating anticipated revenue and expenditure in the different currencies.

This programme shall be approved by the Council, acting by a qualified majority. It may be modified in the course of the financial year in accordance with the same procedure.

4. Member States shall provide the Commission with the currency of third countries needed for the expenditure shown in the programme provided for in paragraph 3 according to the scales laid down in Article 172. Amounts collected by the Commission in the currency of third countries shall be transferred to Member States in accordance with the same scales.

5. The Commission may freely make use of any amounts in the currency of third countries derived from loans it has raised in such countries.

6. The Council may, acting unanimously on a proposal from the Commission, apply, in whole or in part, to the Agency and to Joint Undertakings the exchange arrangements provided for in the preceding paragraphs, and, where appropriate, adapt these arrangements to their operational requirements.

ARTICLE 183

[The Council, acting unanimously on a proposal from the Commission and after consulting the Assembly and obtaining the opinion of the Court of Auditors, shall:

(a) make financial regulations specifying in particular the procedure to be adopted for establishing and implementing the budget and for presenting and auditing accounts,

(b) determine the methods and procedure whereby the budget revenue provided for under the arrangements relating to the Communities, own resources, shall be made available to the Commission, and determine the measures to be applied, if need be, to meet cash requirements,

(c) lay down rules concerning the responsibility of authorising officers and accounting officers and concerning appropriate arrangements for inspection.]

AMENDMENT
This Article was substituted by the Second Budgetary Treaty of July 22, 1975, Art. 26.

Title Five

GENERAL PROVISIONS

ARTICLE 184

The Community shall have legal personality.

ARTICLE 185

In each of the Member States, the Community shall enjoy the most extensive legal capacity accorded to legal persons under their laws; it may, in particular, acquire or dispose of movable and immovable property and may be a party to legal proceedings. To this end, the Community shall be represented by the Commission.

ARTICLE 186

[*Replealed by the Merger Treaty, Art.* 24 (2). *See now ibid., Art.* 24 (1).]

ARTICLE 187

The Commission may, within the limits and under the conditions laid down by the Council in accordance with the provisions of this Treaty, collect any information and carry out any checks required for the performance of the tasks entrusted to it.

ARTICLE 188

The contractual liability of the Community shall be governed by the law applicable to the contract in question.

In the case of non-contractual liability, the Community shall, in accordance with the general principles common to the laws of the Member States, make good any damage caused by its institutions or by its servants in the performance of their duties.

The personal liability of its servants towards the Community shall be governed by the provisions laid down in the Staff Regulations or in the Conditions of Employment applicable to them.

ARTICLE 189

The seat of the institutions of the Community shall be determined by common accord of the Governments of the Member States.

ARTICLE 190

The rules governing the languages of the institutions of the Community shall, without prejudice to the provisions contained in the rules of procedure of the Court of Justice, be determined by the Council, acting unanimously.

ARTICLE 191

[*Repealed by the Merger Treaty, Art.* 28 (2). *See now ibid., Art.* 28 (1).]

ARTICLE 192

Member States shall take all appropriate measures, whether general or particular, to ensure fulfilment of the obligations arising out of this Treaty or resulting from action taken by the institutions of the Community. They shall facilitate the achievement of the Community's tasks.

They shall abstain from any measure which could jeopardise the attainment of the objectives of this Treaty.

ARTICLE 193

Member States undertake not to submit a dispute concerning the interpretation or application of this Treaty to any method of settlement other than those provided for therein.

ARTICLE 194

1. The members of the institutions of the Community, the members of committees, the officials and other servants of the Community and any other persons who by reason of their duties or their public or private relations with the institutions or installations of the Community or with Joint Undertakings are called upon to acquire or obtain cognizance of any facts, information, knowledge, documents or objects which are subject to a security system in accordance with provisions laid down by a Member State or by an institution of the Community, shall be required, even after such duties or relations have ceased, to keep them secret from any unauthorised person and from the general public.

Each Member State shall treat any infringement of this obligation as an act prejudicial to its rules on secrecy and as one falling, both as to merits and jurisdiction, within the scope of its laws relating to acts prejudicial to the security of the State or to disclosure of professional secrets. Such Member State shall, at the request of any Member State concerned or of the Commission, prosecute anyone within its jurisdiction who commits such an infringement.

2. Each Member State shall communicate to the Commission all provisions regulating within its territories the classification and secrecy of information, knowledge, documents or objects covered by this Treaty.

The Commission shall ensure that these provisions are communicated to the other Member States.

Each Member State shall take all appropriate measures to facilitate the gradual establishment of as uniform and comprehensive a security system as possible. The Commission may, after consulting the Member States concerned, make recommendations for this purpose.

3. The institutions of the Community, their installations and also the Joint Undertakings shall be required to apply the rules of the security system in force in the territory in which each of them is situated.

4. Any authorisation granted either by an institution of the Community or by a Member State to a person carrying out his activities within the field covered by this Treaty to have access to facts, information, documents or objects covered by this Treaty which are subject to a security system, shall be recognised by every other institution and every other Member State.

5. The provisions of this Article shall not prevent application of special provisions resulting from agreements concluded between a Member State and a third State or an international organisation.

ARTICLE 195

The institutions of the Community, the Agency and the Joint Undertakings shall, in applying this Treaty, comply with the conditions of access to ores, source materials and special fissile materials laid down in national rules and regulations made for reasons of public policy or public health.

ARTICLE 196

For the purpose of this Treaty, save as otherwise provided therein:

(a) " person " means any natural person who pursues all or any of his activities in the territories of Member States within the field specified in the relevant Chapter of this Treaty;

(b) " undertaking " means any undertaking or institution which pursues all or any of its activities in the territories of Member States within the field specified in the relevant Chapter of this Treaty, whatever its public or private legal status.

ARTICLE 197

For the purposes of this Treaty:

1. " Special fissile materials " means plutonium-239; uranium-233; uranium enriched in uranium-235 or uranium-233; and any substance containing one or more of the foregoing isotopes and such other fissile materials as may be specified by the Council, acting by a qualified majority on a proposal from the Commission; the expression " special fissil materials " does not, however, include source materials.

2. " Uranium enriched in uranium-235 or uranium-233 " means uranium containing uranium-235 or uranium-233 or both in an amount such that the abundance ratio of the sum of these isotopes to isotope 238 is greater than the ratio of isotope 235 to isotope 238 occurring in nature.

3. " Source materials " means uranium containing the mixture of isotopes occurring in nature; uranium whose content in uranium-235 is less than the normal; thorium; any of the foregoing in the form of metal, alloy, chemical compound or concentrate; any other substance containing one or more of the foregoing in such a concentration as shall be specified by the Council, acting by a qualified majority on a proposal from the Commission.

4. " Ores " means any ore containing, in such average concentration as shall be specified by the Council acting by a qualified majority on a proposal from the Commission, substances from which the source materials defined above may be obtained by the appropriate chemical and physical processing.

ARTICLE 198

Save as otherwise provided, this Treaty shall apply to the European territories of Member States and to non-European territories under their jurisdiction.

It shall also apply to the European territories for whose external relations a Member State is responsible.

[Notwithstanding the previous paragraphs:

(a) This Treaty shall not apply to the Faroe Islands. The Government of the Kingdom of Denmark may, however, give notice, by a declaration deposited by 31 December 1975 at the latest, with the Government of the Italian Republic, which shall transmit a certified copy thereof to each of the Governments of the other Member States, that this Treaty shall apply to those Islands. In that event this Treaty shall apply to those Islands from the first day of the second month following the deposit of the declaration.

(b) This Treaty shall not apply to the Sovereign Base Areas of the United Kingdom of Great Britain and Northern Ireland in Cyprus.

(c) This Treaty shall not apply to those overseas countries and territories having special relations with the United Kingdom of Great Britain and Northern Ireland which are not listed in Annex IV to the Treaty establishing the European Economic Community.

(d) This Treaty shall apply to the Channel Islands and the Isle of Man only to the extent necessary to ensure the implementation of the arrangements for those islands set out in the Treaty concerning the accession of New Member States to the European Economic Community and to the European Atomic Energy Community signed on 22 January 1972.]

AMENDMENT

The third paragraph was added by the Act of Accession, Art. 27, as amended by the Adaptation Decision, Art. 16.

ARTICLE 199

It shall be for the Commission to ensure the maintenance of all appropriate relations with the organs of the United Nations, of its specialised agencies and of the General Agreement on Tariffs and Trade.

The Commission shall also maintain such relations as are appropriate with all international organisations.

ARTICLE 200

The Community shall establish all appropriate forms of co-operation with the Council of Europe.

ARTICLE 201

The Community shall establish close cooperation with the Organisation for European Economic Co-operation, the details to be determined by common accord.

ARTICLE 202

The provisions of this Treaty shall not preclude the existence or completion of regional unions between Belgium and Luxembourg, or between Belgium, Luxembourg and the Netherlands, to the extent that the objectives of these regional unions are not attained by application of this Treaty.

ARTICLE 203

If action by the Community should prove necessary to attain one of the objectives of the Community and this Treaty has not provided the necessary powers, the Council shall, acting unanimously on a proposal from the Commission and after consulting the Assembly, take the appropriate measures.

ARTICLE 204

The Government of any Member State or the Commission may submit to the Council proposals for amendment of this Treaty.

If the Council, after consulting the Assembly and, where appropriate, the Commission, delivers an opinion in favour of calling a conference of representatives of the Governments of the Member States, the conference shall be convened by the President of the Council for the purpose of determining by common accord the amendments to be made to this Treaty.

The amendments shall enter into force after being ratified by all the Member States in accordance with their respective constitutional requirements.

ARTICLE 205

Any European State may apply to become a member of the Community. It shall address its application to the Council, which shall act unanimously after obtaining the opinion of the Commission.

The conditions of admission and the adjustments to this Treaty necessitated thereby shall be the subject of an agreement between the Member States and the applicant State. This agreement shall be submitted for ratification by all the Contracting States in accordance with their respective constitutional requirements.

ARTICLE 206

The Community may conclude with a third State, a union of States or an international organisation agreements establishing an association involving reciprocal rights and obligations, common action and special procedures.

These agreements shall be concluded by the Council, acting unanimously after consulting the Assembly.

Where such agreements call for amendments to this Treaty, these amendments shall first be adopted in accordance with the procedure laid down in Article 204.

ARTICLE 207

The Protocols annexed to this Treaty by common accord of the Member States shall form an integral part thereof.

ARTICLE 208

This Treaty is concluded for an unlimited period.

Title Six

PROVISIONS RELATING TO THE INITIAL PERIOD

SECTION I—SETTING UP OF THE INSTITUTIONS

ARTICLE 209

The Council shall meet within one month of the entry into force of this Treaty.

ARTICLE 210

The Council shall, within three months of its first meeting, take all appropriate measures to constitute the Economic and Social Committee.

ARTICLE 211

The Assembly shall meet within two months of the first meeting of the Council, having been convened by the President of the Council, in order to elect its officers and draw up its rules of procedure. Pending the election of its officers, the oldest member shall take the chair.

ARTICLE 212

The Court of Justice shall take up its duties as soon as its members have been appointed. Its first President shall be appointed for three years in the same manner as its members.

The Court of Justice shall adopt its rules of procedure within three months of taking up its duties.

No matter may be brought before the Court of Justice until its rules of procedure have been published. The time within which an action must be brought shall run only from the date of this publication.

Upon his appointment, the President of the Court of Justice shall exercise the powers conferred upon him by this Treaty.

ARTICLE 213

The Commission shall take up its duties and assume the responsibilities conferred upon it by this Treaty as soon as its members have been appointed.

Upon taking up its duties, the Commission shall undertake the studies and arrange the contacts with Member States, undertakings, workers and consumers needed for making an overall survey of the situation of nuclear industries in the Community. The Commission shall submit a report on this subject to the Assembly within six months.

ARTICLE 214

1. The first financial year shall run from the date when this Treaty enters into force until 31 December following. Should this Treaty, however, enter into force during the second half of the year, the first financial year shall run until 31 December of the following year.

2. Until the budgets for the first financial year have been established, Member States shall make the Community interest-free advances which shall be deducted from their financial contributions to the implementation of these budgets.

3. Until the Staff Regulations of officials and the Conditions of Employment of other servants of the Community provided for in Article 186 have been laid down, each institution shall recruit the staff it needs and to this end conclude contracts of limited duration.

Each institution shall examine together with the Council any question concerning the number, remuneration and distribution of posts.

SECTION II—PROVISIONS FOR THE INITIAL APPLICATION OF THIS TREATY

ARTICLE 215

1. An initial research and training programme, which is set out in Annex V to this Treaty and the cost of which shall not, unless the Council unanimously decides otherwise, exceed 215 million EPU units of account, shall be carried out within five years of the entry into force of this Treaty.

2. A breakdown of the expenditure necessary for the implementation of this programme is set out by way of illustration under main sub-divisions in Annex V.

The Council may, acting by a qualified majority on a proposal from the Commission, modify this programme.

Article 216

The Commission proposals on the way in which the institution of university status referred to in Article 9 is to function shall be submitted to the Council within one year of the entry into force of this Treaty.

Article 217

The security regulations provided for in Article 24 concerning the security gradings applicable to the dissemination of information shall be adopted by the Council within six months of the entry into force of this Treaty.

Article 218

The basic standards shall be determined in accordance with the provisions of Article 31 within one year of the entry into force of this Treaty.

Article 219

Provisions laid down by law, regulation or administrative action to ensure the protection of the health of the general public and of workers in the territories of Member States against the dangers arising from ionising radiations shall, in accordance with Article 33, be communicated to the Commission by these States within three months of the entry into force of this Treaty.

Article 220

The Commission proposals relating to the statutes of the Agency which are provided for in Article 54 shall be submitted to the Council within three months of the entry into force of this Treaty.

Section III—Transitional Provisions

Article 221

The provisions of Articles 14 to 23 and of Articles 25 to 28 shall apply to patents, provisionally protected patent rights and utility models, and also to patent and utility model applications in existence before the entry into force of this Treaty under the following conditions:

(1) When assessing the period of time referred to in Article 17 (2), allowance shall be made, in favour of the owner, for the new situation created by the entry into force of this Treaty.

(2) With regard to the communication of an invention which is not secret, where either or both of the periods of three and eighteen months referred to in Article 16 have expired at the date on which this Treaty enters into force, a further period of six months shall run from that date.

If either or both of those periods remain unexpired at that date, they shall be extended by six months from the date of their normal expiry.

(3) The same provisions shall apply to the communication of a secret invention in accordance with Article 16 and Article 25 (1); in such case, however, the date of entry into force of the security regulations referred to in Article 24 shall be the date taken as the starting point for the new period or for the extension of a current period.

ARTICLE 222

During the period between the date of entry into force of this Treaty and the date fixed by the Commission on which the Agency takes up its duties, agreements and contracts for the supply of ores, source materials or special fissile materials shall be concluded or renewed only with the prior approval of the Commission.

The Commission shall refuse to approve the conclusion or renewal of any agreements and contracts which it considers would prejudice the implementation of this Treaty. It may in particular make its approval dependent upon the insertion in agreements and contracts of clauses permitting the Agency to take part in carrying them out.

ARTICLE 223

By way of derogation from the provisions of Article 60, reactors installed in the territories of a Member State which may go critical before the expiry of a period of seven years from the date of entry into force of this Treaty shall, during a period of not more than ten years from that date, in order to take account of work and studies already initiated, be granted priority which may be exercised in respect both of supplies of ores or source materials coming from the territories of that State and also of supplies of source materials or special fissile materials which are the subject of a bilateral agreement concluded before the entry into force of this Treaty and communicated to the Commission in accordance with Article 105.

The same priority shall be granted during the same period of ten years in respect of supplies for any isotope separation plant, whether or not it constitutes a Joint Undertaking, which comes into operation in the territory of a Member State before the expiry of a period of seven years from the date of entry into force of this Treaty.

The Agency shall conclude the appropriate contracts, after the Commission has ascertained that the conditions for the exercise of the right of priority have been fulfilled.

FINAL PROVISIONS

ARTICLE 224

This Treaty shall be ratified by the High Contracting Parties in accordance with their respective constitutional requirements. The instruments of ratification shall be deposited with the Government of the Italian Republic.

This Treaty shall enter into force on the first day of the month following the deposit of the instrument of ratification by the last signatory State to take this step. If, however, such deposit is made less than fifteen days before the beginning of the following month, this Treaty shall not enter into force until the first day of the second month after the date of such deposit.

ARTICLE 225

This Treaty, drawn up in a single original in the Dutch, French, German and Italian languages, all four texts being equally authentic, shall be deposited in the archives of the Government of the Italian Republic, which shall transmit a certified copy to each of the Governments of the other signatory States.

IN WITNESS WHEREOF, the undersigned Plenipotentiaries have signed this Treaty.

DONE at Rome this twenty-fifth day of March in the year one thousand nine hundred and fifty-seven.

P. H. SPAAK	J. Ch. SNOY et d'OPPUERS
ADENAUER	HALLSTEIN
PINEAU	M. FAURE
Antonio SEGNI	Gaetano MARTINO
BECH	Lambert SCHAUS
J. LUNS	J. LINTHORST HOMAN

Part IV
COMMUNITY TEXTS

Protocols on the Statute of the Court of Justice

PROTOCOL ON THE STATUTE OF THE COURT OF JUSTICE OF THE EUROPEAN COAL AND STEEL COMMUNITY

GENERAL NOTE

The provisions of this Protocol, in so far as they are in conflict with Articles 32 to 32 (c) of the ECSC Treaty, shall be repealed (Convention on Certain Institutions Common to the European Communities, Art. 4 (2) (b)).

THE HIGH CONTRACTING PARTIES,

DESIRING to lay down the Statute of the Court of Justice provided for in Article 45 of this Treaty,

HAVE AGREED as follows:

ARTICLE 1

The Court of Justice established by Article 7 of the Treaty shall be constituted and shall function in accordance with the provisions of this Treaty and of this Statute.

TITLE I—JUDGES

OATH OF OFFICE

ARTICLE 2

Before taking up his duties each Judge shall, in open court, take an oath to perform his duties impartially and conscientiously and to preserve the secrecy of the deliberations of the Court.

PRIVILEGES AND IMMUNITIES

ARTICLE 3

The Judges shall be immune from legal proceedings. After they have ceased to hold office, they shall continue to enjoy immunity in respect of acts performed by them in their official capacity, including words spoken or written.

The Court, sitting in plenary session, may waive the immunity.

Where immunity has been waived and criminal proceedings are instituted against a Judge, he shall be tried, in any of the Member States, only by the court competent to judge the members of the highest national judiciary.

[. . .].

AMENDMENT

The fourth paragraph of this Article was repealed by the Merger Treaty, Art. 28.

DISQUALIFICATIONS

ARTICLE 4

The Judges may not hold any political or administrative office.

They may not engage in any occupation, whether gainful or not, unless exemption is exceptionally granted by the Council, acting by a two-thirds majority.

They may not acquire or retain, directly or indirectly, any interest in any business related to coal and steel during their term of office and for three years after ceasing to hold office.

REMUNERATION

ARTICLE 5

[Repealed by the Merger Treaty, Art. 8 (3) (a). See now ibid., Art. 6.]

TERMINATION OF APPOINTMENT

ARTICLE 6

Apart from normal replacement, the duties of a Judge shall end on his death or resignation.

Where a Judge resigns, his letter of resignation shall be addressed to the President of the Court for transmission to the President of the Council. Upon this notification a vacancy shall arise on the bench.

Save where Article 7 applies, a Judge shall continue to hold office until his successor takes up his duties.

ARTICLE 7

A Judge may be deprived of his office only if, in the unanimous opinion of the other Judges, he no longer fulfils the requisite conditions.

The President of the Council, the President of the High Authority and the President of the Assembly shall be notified thereof by the Registrar.

A vacancy shall arise on the bench upon this notification.

ARTICLE 8

A Judge who is to replace a member of the Court whose term of office has not expired shall be appointed for the remainder of his predecessor's term.

TITLE II—ORGANISATION

ARTICLE 9

The Judges, the Advocates-General and the Registrar shall be required to reside at the place where the Court has its seat.

ARTICLE 10

The Court shall be assisted by two Advocates-General and a Registrar.

ADVOCATES-GENERAL

ARTICLE 11

It shall be the duty of the Advocate-General, acting with complete impartiality and independence, to make, in open court, oral and reasoned submissions on cases brought before the Court, in order to assist the Court in the performance of the task assigned to it in Article 31 of this Treaty.

ARTICLE 12

The Advocates-General shall be appointed for a term of six years in the same manner as the Judges. Every three years there shall be a partial replacement. The Advocate-General whose term of office is to expire at the end of the first three years shall be chosen by lot. The provisions of the third and fourth paragraphs of Article 32 of this Treaty and the provisions of Article 6 of this Statute shall apply to the Advocates-General.

ARTICLE 13

The provisions of Articles 2 to 5 and of Article 8 shall apply to the Advocates-General.

An Advocate-General may be deprived of his office only if he no longer fulfils the requisite conditions. The decision shall be taken by the Council, acting unanimously, after the Court has delivered its opinion.

REGISTRAR

ARTICLE 14

The Court shall appoint its Registrar and lay down the rules governing his service, account being taken of the provisions of Article 15. The Registrar shall take an oath before the Court to perform his duties impartially and conscientiously and to preserve the secrecy of the deliberations of the Court.
[. . .].

AMENDMENT
The second paragraph of this Article was repealed by the Merger Treaty, Art. 28.

ARTICLE 15

[*Repealed by the Merger Treaty, Art. 8 (3) (a). See now ibid., Art. 6.*]

STAFF OF THE COURT

ARTICLE 16

[1. Officials and other servants shall be attached to the Court to enable it to function. They shall be responsible to the Registrar under the authority of the President.
2. On a proposal from the Court, the Council may, acting unanimously, provide for the appointment of Assistant Rapporteurs and lay down the rules governing their service. The Assistant Rapporteurs may be required, under conditions laid down in the rules of procedure, to participate in preparatory inquiries in cases pending before the Court and to co-operate with the Judge who acts as Rapporteur.
The Assistant Rapporteurs shall be chosen from persons whose independence is beyond doubt and who possess the necessary legal qualifications; they shall be appointed by the Council. They shall take an oath before the Court to perform their duties impartially and conscientiously and to preserve the secrecy of the deliberations of the Court.]

AMENDMENT
The words in square brackets were substituted by the Merger Treaty, Art. 8 (3) (b).

FUNCTIONING OF THE COURT

ARTICLE 17

The Court shall remain permanently in session. The duration of the judicial vacations shall be determined by the Court with due regard to the needs of its business.

COMPOSITION OF THE COURT

ARTICLE 18

The Court shall sit in plenary session. It may, however, form two Chambers, each consisting of three Judges, either to undertake certain preparatory inquiries or to adjudicate on particular categories of cases in accordance with rules laid down for these purposes.
[Decisions of the Court shall be valid only when an uneven number of its members is sitting in the deliberations. Decisions of the full Court shall be valid if seven members are sitting. Decisions of the Chambers shall be valid only if three Judges are sitting; in the event of one of the Judges of a Chamber being prevented from attending, a Judge of another Chamber may be called upon to sit in accordance with conditions laid down in the rules of procedure.]
Actions brought by States or by the Council shall in all cases be tried in plenary session.

AMENDMENT
The words in square brackets were substituted by the Act of Accession, Art. 20.

Special Rules

Article 19

No Judge or Advocate-General may take part in the disposal of any case in which he has previously taken part as agent or adviser or has acted for one of the parties, or on which he has been called upon to pronounce as a member of a court or tribunal, of a commission of inquiry or in any other capacity.

If, for some special reason, any Judge or Advocate-General considers that he should not take part in the judgment or examination of a particular case, he shall so inform the President. If, for some special reason, the President considers that any Judge or Advocate-General should not sit or make submissions in a particular case, he shall notify him accordingly.

Any difficulty arising as to the application of this Article shall be settled by decision of the Court.

A party may not apply for a change in the composition of the Court or of one of its Chambers on the grounds of either the nationality of a Judge or the absence from the Court or from the Chamber of a Judge of the nationality of that party.

TITLE III—PROCEDURE

Representation of and Assistance to the Parties

Article 20

The States and the institutions of the Community shall be represented before the Court by an agent appointed for each case; the agent may be assisted by a lawyer entitled to practise before a court of a Member State.

Undertakings and all other natural or legal persons must be assisted by a lawyer entitled to practise before a court of a Member State.

Such agents and lawyers shall, when they appear before the Court, enjoy the rights and immunities necessary to the independent exercise of their duties, under conditions laid down in rules drawn up by the Court and submitted for the approval of the Council [acting unanimously].

As regards such lawyers who appear before it, the Court shall have the powers normally accorded to courts of law, under conditions laid down in those rules.

University teachers being nationals of a Member State whose law accords them a right of audience shall have the same rights before the Court as are accorded by this Article to lawyers entitled to practise before a court of a Member State.

Amendment

In the third paragraph, the words in square brackets were added by the Merger Treaty, Art. 8 (3) (c).

Stages of Procedure

Article 21

The procedure before the Court shall consist of two parts: written and oral.

The written procedure shall consist of the communication to the parties and to the institutions of the Community whose decisions are in dispute of applications, statements of case, defences and observations, and of replies, if any, as well as of all papers and documents in support or of certified copies of them.

Communications shall be made by the Registrar in the order and within the time laid down in the rules of procedure.

The oral procedure shall consist of the reading of the report presented by a Judge acting as Rapporteur, the hearing by the Court of witnesses, experts, agents, and lawyers entitled to practise before a court of a Member State and of the submissions of the Advocate-General.

Applications

Article 22

A case shall be brought before the Court by a written application addressed to the Registrar. The application shall contain the name and address of the party and the description of the signatory, the subject matter of the dispute, the submissions and a brief statement of the grounds on which the application is based.

The application shall be accompanied, where appropriate, by the decision the annulment of which is sought or, in the case of proceedings against an implied decision, by documentary evidence of the date on which the request was lodged. If the documents are not submitted with the application, the Registrar shall ask the party concerned to produce them within a reasonable period, but in that event the rights of the party shall not lapse even if such documents are produced after the time limit for bringing proceedings.

TRANSMISSION OF DOCUMENTS

ARTICLE 23

Where proceedings are instituted against a decision of one of the institutions of the Community, that institution shall transmit to the Court all the documents relating to the case before the Court.

PREPARATORY INQUIRIES

ARTICLE 24

The Court may require the parties, their representatives or agents or the Governments of the Member States to produce all documents and to supply all information which the Court considers desirable. Formal note shall be taken of any refusal.

ARTICLE 25

The Court may at any time entrust any individual, body, authority, committee or other organisation it chooses with the task of holding an inquiry or giving an expert opinion; to this end it may compile a list of individuals or bodies approved as experts.

HEARING TO BE PUBLIC

ARTICLE 26

The hearing in court shall be public, unless the Court decides otherwise for serious reasons.

MINUTES

ARTICLE 27

Minutes shall be made of each hearing and signed by the President and the Registrar.

HEARINGS

ARTICLE 28

The cause list shall be established by the President.

Witnesses may be heard under conditions laid down in the rules of procedure.
They may be heard on oath.

During the hearings the Court may also examine experts, persons entrusted with holding an inquiry, and the parties themselves. The latter, however, may address the court only through their representatives or their lawyers.

Where it is established that a witness or expert has concealed facts or falsified evidence on any matter on which he has testified or been examined by the Court, the Court is empowered to report the misconduct to the Minister of Justice of the State of which the witness or expert is a national, in order that he may be subjected to the relevant penal provisions of the national law.

With respect to defaulting witnesses the Court shall have the powers generally granted to courts and tribunals, under conditions laid down in rules drawn up by the Court and submitted for the approval of the Council [acting unanimously].

AMENDMENT

In the fifth paragraph, the words in square brackets were added by the Merger Treaty, Art. 8 (3) (c).

Secrecy of the Deliberations of the Court

Article 29

The deliberations of the Court shall be and shall remain secret.

Judgments

Article 30

Judgments shall state the reasons on which they are based. They shall contain the names of the Judges who took part in the deliberations.

Article 31

Judgments shall be signed by the President, the Judge acting as Rapporteur and the Registrar. They shall be read in open court.

Costs

Article 32

The Court shall adjudicate upon costs.

Summary Procedure

Article 33

The President of the court may, by way of summary procedure, which may, in so far as necessary, differ from some of the rules contained in this Statute and which shall be laid down in the rules of procedure, adjudicate upon applications to suspend execution, as provided for in the second paragraph of Article 39 of this Treaty, or to prescribe interim measures in pursuance of the last paragraph of Article 39, or to suspend enforcement in accordance with the third paragraph of Article 92.

Should the President be prevented from attending, his place shall be taken by another Judge under conditions laid down in the rules provided for in Article 18 of this Statute.

The ruling of the President or of the Judge replacing him shall be provisional and shall in no way prejudice the decision of the Court on the substance of the case.

Intervention

Article 34

Natural or legal persons establishing an interest in the result of any case submitted to the Court may intervene in that case.

Submissions made in an application to intervene shall be limited to supporting or requesting the rejection of the submissions of one of the parties.

Judgment by Default

Article 35

Where the defending party in proceedings in which the Court has unlimited jurisdiction, after having been duly summoned, fails to file written submissions in defence, judgment shall be given against that party by default. An objection may be lodged against the judgment within one month of it being notified. The objection shall not have the effect of staying enforcement of the judgment by default unless the Court decides otherwise.

Third-Party Proceedings

Article 36

Natural or legal persons and the institutions of the Community may, in cases and under conditions to be determined by the rules of procedure, institute third-party proceedings to contest a judgment rendered without their being heard.

Statute of the Court of Justice of the ECSC

Interpretation

Article 37

If the meaning or scope of a judgment is in doubt, the Court shall construe it on application by any party or any institution of the Community establishing an interest therein.

Revision of a Judgment

Article 38

An application for revision of a judgment may be made to the Court only on discovery of a fact which is of such a nature as to be a decisive factor, and which, when the judgment was given, was unknown to the Court and to the party claiming the revision.

The revision shall be opened by a judgment of the Court expressly recording the existence of a new fact, recognising that it is of such a character as to lay the case open to revision and declaring the application admissible on this ground.

No application for revision may be made after the lapse of ten years from the date of the judgment.

Time Limits

Article 39

The proceedings provided for in Articles 36 and 37 of this Treaty must be instituted within the time limit of one month provided for in the last paragraph of Article 33.

Periods of grace based on considerations of distance shall be laid down in the rules of procedure.

No right shall be prejudiced in consequence of the expiry of a time limit if the party concerned proves the existence of unforeseeable circumstances or of *force majeure*.

Periods of Limitation

Article 40

Proceedings provided for in the first two paragraphs of Article 40 of this Treaty shall be barred after a period of five years from the occurrence of the event giving rise thereto. The period of limitation shall be interrupted if proceedings are instituted before the Court or if prior to such proceedings an application is made by the aggrieved party to the relevant institution of the Community. In the latter event the proceedings must be instituted within the time limit of one month provided for in the last paragraph of Article 33; the provisions of the last paragraph of Article 35 shall apply where appropriate.

Special Rules Relating to Disputes Between Member States

Article 41

Where a dispute between Member States is brought before the Court under Article 89 of this Treaty, the other Member States shall be notified forthwith by the Registrar of the subject matter of the dispute.

Each Member State shall have the right to intervene in the proceedings.

The disputes referred to in this Article must be dealt with in plenary session.

Article 42

If a State intervenes in a case before the Court as provided for in the preceding Article, the interpretation contained in the judgment shall be binding upon that State.

Proceedings by Third Parties

Article 43

Decisions taken by the High Authority under Article 63 (2) of this Treaty must be notified to the purchaser and to the undertakings concerned; if the decision concerns all or a large number of undertakings, publication may be substituted for individual notification.

Appeals may be brought, under Article 36 of this Treaty, by any person on whom a periodic penalty payment has been imposed under the fourth sub-paragraph of Article 66 (5).

Rules of Procedure

Article 44

[The Court of Justice shall adopt its rules of procedure. These shall require the unanimous approval of the Council.] These rules of procedure shall contain all the provisions necessary for applying and, where required, supplementing this Statute.

Amendment

The words in square brackets were substituted by the Merger Treaty, Art. 8 (3) (*d*).

Transitional Provision

Article 45

Immediately after the oath has been taken, the President of the Council shall proceed to choose by lot the Judges and the Advocates-General whose terms of office are to expire at the end of the first three years in accordance with Article 32 of this Treaty.

Done at Paris this eighteenth day of April in the year one thousand nine hundred and and fifty-one.

ADENAUER

Paul VAN ZEELAND
J. MEURICE

SCHUMAN

SFORZA

JOS. BECH

STIKKER

VAN DEN BRINK

PROTOCOL ON THE STATUTE OF THE COURT OF JUSTICE OF THE EUROPEAN ECONOMIC COMMUNITY

THE HIGH CONTRACTING PARTIES TO THE TREATY ESTABLISHING THE EUROPEAN ECONOMIC COMMUNITY,

DESIRING to lay down the Statute of the Court provided for in Article 188 of this Treaty,

HAVE DESIGNATED as their Plenipotentiaries for this purpose:

HIS MAJESTY THE KING OF THE BELGIANS:
Baron J. Ch. SNOY et d'OPPUERS, Secretary-General of the Ministry of Economic Affairs, Head of the Belgian Delegation to the Intergovernmental Conference;

THE PRESIDENT OF THE FEDERAL REPUBLIC OF GERMANY:
Professor Dr. Carl Friedrich OPHÜLS, Ambassador of the Federal Republic of Germany, Head of the German Delegation to the Intergovernmental Conference;

THE PRESIDENT OF THE FRENCH REPUBLIC:
Mr. Robert MARJOLIN, Professor of Law, Deputy Head of the French Delegation to the Intergovernmental Conference;

THE PRESIDENT OF THE ITALIAN REPUBLIC;
Mr. V. BADINI CONFALONIERI, Under-Secretary of State in the Ministry of Foreign Affairs, Head of the Italian Delegation to the Intergovernmental Conference;

HER ROYAL HIGHNESS THE GRAND DUCHESS OF LUXEMBOURG:
Mr. Lambert SCHAUS, Ambassador of the Grand Duchy of Luxembourg, Head of the Luxembourg Delegation to the Intergovernmental Conference;

HER MAJESTY THE QUEEN OF THE NETHERLANDS:
Mr. J. LINTHORST HOMAN, Head of the Netherlands Delegation to the Intergovernmental Conference;

WHO, having exchanged their Full Powers, found in good and due form,

HAVE AGREED upon the following provisions, which shall be annexed to the Treaty establishing the European Economic Community:

ARTICLE 1

The Court established by Article 4 of this Treaty shall be constituted and shall function in accordance with the provisions of this Treaty and of this Statute.

TITLE I—JUDGES AND ADVOCATES-GENERAL

ARTICLE 2

Before taking up his duties each Judge shall, in open court, take an oath to perform his duties impartially and conscientiously and to preserve and secrecy of the deliberations of the Court.

ARTICLE 3

The Judges shall be immune from legal proceedings. After they have ceased to hold office, they shall continue to enjoy immunity in respect of acts performed by them in their official capacity, including words spoken or written.

The Court, sitting in plenary session, may waive the immunity.

Where immunity has been waived and criminal proceedings are instituted against a Judge, he shall be tried, in any of the Member States, only by the Court competent to judge the members of the highest national judiciary.

ARTICLE 4

The Judges may not hold any political or administrative office.

They may not engage in any occupation, whether gainful or not, unless exemption is exceptionally granted by the Council.

When taking up their duties, they shall give a solemn undertaking that, both during and after their term of office, they will respect the obligations arising therefrom, in particular the duty to behave with integrity and discretion as regards the acceptance, after they have ceased to hold office, of certain appointments or benefits.

Any doubt on this point shall be settled by decision of the Court.

ARTICLE 5

Apart from normal replacement, or death, the duties of a Judge shall end when he resigns.

Where a Judge resigns, his letter of resignation shall be addressed to the President of the Court for transmission to the President of the Council. Upon this notification a vacancy shall arise on the bench.

Save where Article 6 applies, a Judge shall continue to hold office until his successor takes up his duties.

ARTICLE 6

A Judge may be deprived of his office or of his right to a pension or other benefits in its stead only if, in the unanimous opinion of the Judges and Advocates-General of the Court, he no longer fulfils the requisite conditions or meets the obligations arising from his office. The Judge concerned shall not take part in any such deliberations.

The Registrar of the Court shall communicate the decision of the Court to the President of the Assembly and to the President of the Commission and shall notify it to the President of the Council.

In the case of a decision depriving a Judge of his office, a vacancy shall arise on the bench upon this latter notification.

ARTICLE 7

A Judge who is to replace a member of the Court whose term of office has not expired shall be appointed for the remainder of his predecessor's term.

ARTICLE 8

The provisions of Articles 2 to 7 shall apply to the Advocates-General.

TITLE II—ORGANISATION

ARTICLE 9

The Registrar shall take an oath before the Court to perform his duties impartially and conscientiously and to preserve the secrecy of the deliberations of the Court.

ARTICLE 10

The Court shall arrange for replacement of the Registrar on occasions when he is prevented from attending the Court.

ARTICLE 11

Officials and other servants shall be attached to the Court to enable it to function. They shall be responsible to the Registrar under the authority of the President.

ARTICLE 12

On a proposal from the Court, the Council may, acting unanimously, provide for the appointment of Assistant Rapporteurs and lay down the rules governing their service. The Assistant Rapporteurs may be required, under conditions laid down in the rules of procedure, to participate in preparatory inquiries in cases pending before the Court and to co-operate with the Judge who acts as Rapporteur.

The Assistant Rapporteurs shall be chosen from persons whose independence is beyond doubt and who possess the necessary legal qualifications; they shall be appointed by the Council. They shall take an oath before the Court to perform their duties impartially and conscientiously and to preserve the secrecy of the deliberations of the Court.

ARTICLE 13

The Judges, the Advocates-General and the Registrar shall be required to reside at the place where the Court has its seat.

ARTICLE 14

The Court shall remain permanently in session. The duration of the judicial vacations shall be determined by the Court with due regard to the needs of its business.

ARTICLE 15

[Decisions of the Court shall be valid only when an uneven number of its members is sitting in the deliberations. Decisions of the full Court shall be valid if seven members are sitting. Decisions of the Chambers shall be valid only if three Judges are sitting; in the event of one of the Judges of a Chamber being prevented from attending, a Judge of another Chamber may be called upon to sit in accordance with conditions laid down in the rules of procedure.]

AMENDMENT
The words in square brackets were substituted by the Act of Accession, Art. 20.

ARTICLE 16

No Judge or Advocate-General may take part in the disposal of any case in which he has previously taken part as agent or adviser or has acted for one of the parties, or on which he has been called upon to pronounce as a member of a court or tribunal, of a commission of inquiry or in any other capacity.

If, for some special reason, any Judge or Advocate-General considers that he should not take part in the judgment or examination of a particular case, he shall so inform the President. If, for some special reason, the President considers that any Judge or Advocate-General should not sit to make submissions in a particular case, he shall notify him accordingly.

Any difficulty arising as to the application of this Article shall be settled by decision of the Court.

A party may not apply for a change in the composition of the Court or of one of its Chambers on the grounds of either the nationality of a Judge or the absence from the Court or from the Chamber of a Judge of the nationality of that party.

TITLE III—PROCEDURE

ARTICLE 17

The States and the institutions of the Community shall be represented before the Court by an agent appointed for each case; the agent may be assisted by an adviser or by a lawyer entitled to practise before a court of a Member State.

Other parties must be represented by a lawyer entitled to practise before a court of a Member State.

Such agents, advisers and lawyers shall, when they appear before the Court, enjoy the rights and immunities necessary to the independent exercise of their duties, under conditions laid down in the rules of procedure.

As regards such advisers and lawyers who appear before it, the Court shall have the powers normally accorded to courts of law, under conditions laid down in the rules of procedure.

University teachers being nationals of a Member State whose law accords them a right of audience shall have the same rights before the Court as are accorded by this Article to lawyers entitled to practise before a court of a Member State.

ARTICLE 18

The procedure before the Court shall consist of two parts: written and oral.

The written procedure shall consist of the communication to the parties and to the institutions of the Community whose decisions are in dispute, of applications, statements of case, defences and observations, and of replies, if any, as well as of all papers and documents in support or of certified copies of them.

Communications shall be made by the Registrar in the order and within the time laid down in the rules of procedure.

The oral procedure shall consist of the reading of the report, presented by a Judge acting as Rapporteur, the hearing by the Court of agents, advisers and lawyers entitled to practise before a court of a Member State and of the submissions of the Advocate-General, as well as the hearing, if any, of witnesses and experts.

ARTICLE 19

A case shall be brought before the Court by a written application addressed to the Registrar. The application shall contain the applicant's name and permanent address and the description of the signatory, the name of the party against whom the application is made, the subject matter of the dispute, the submissions and a brief statement of the grounds on which the application is based.

The application shall be accompanied, where appropriate, by the measure the annulment of which is sought or, in the circumstances referred to in Article 175 of this Treaty, by documentary evidence of the date on which an institution was, in accordance with that Article, requested to act. If the documents are not submitted with the application, the Registrar shall ask the party concerned to produce them within a reasonable period, but in that even the rights of the party shall not lapse even if such documents are produced after the time limit for bringing proceedings.

ARTICLE 20

In the cases governed by Article 177 of this Treaty, the decision of the court or tribunal of a Member State which suspends its proceedings and refers a case to the Court shall be notified to the Court by the court or tribunal concerned. The decision shall then be notified by the Registrar of the Court to the parties, to the Member States and to the Commission, and also to the Council if the act the validity or interpretation of which is in dispute originates from the Council.

Within two months of this notification, the parties, the Member States, the Commission and, where appropriate, the Council, shall be entitled to submit statements of case or written observations to the Court.

ARTICLE 21

The Court may require the parties to produce all documents and to supply all information which the Court considers desirable. Formal note shall be taken of any refusal.

The Court may also require the Member States and institutions not being parties to the case to supply all information which the Court considers necessary for the proceedings.

ARTICLE 22

The Court may at any time entrust any individual, body, authority, committee or other organisation it chooses with the task of giving an expert opinion.

ARTICLE 23

Witnesses may be heard under conditions laid down in the rules of procedure.

ARTICLE 24

With respect to defaulting witnesses the Court shall have the powers generally granted to courts and tribunals and may impose pecuniary penalties under conditions laid down in the rules of procedure.

ARTICLE 25

Witnesses and experts may be heard on oath taken in the form laid down in the rules of procedure or in the manner laid down by the law of the country of the witness or expert.

ARTICLE 26

The Court may order that a witness or expert be heard by the judicial authority of his place of permanent residence.

The order shall be sent for implementation to the competent judicial authority under conditions laid down in the rules of procedure. The documents drawn up in compliance with the letters rogatory shall be returned to the Court under the same conditions.

The Court shall defray the expenses, without prejudice to the right to charge them, where appropriate, to the parties.

Article 27

A Member State shall treat any violation of an oath by a witness or expert in the same manner as if the offence had been committed before one of its courts with jurisdiction in civil proceedings. At the instance of the Court, the Member State concerned shall prosecute the offender before its competent court.

Article 28

The hearing in court shall be public, unless the Court, of its own motion or on application by the parties, decides otherwise for serious reasons.

Article 29

During the hearings the Court may examine the experts, the witnesses and the parties themselves. The latter, however, may address the Court only through their representatives.

Article 30

Minutes shall be made of each hearing and signed by the President and the Registrar.

Article 31

The cause list shall be established by the President.

Article 32

The deliberations of the Court shall be and shall remain secret.

Article 33

Judgments shall state the reasons on which they are based. They shall contain the names of the Judges who took part in the deliberations.

Article 34

Judgments shall be signed by the President and the Registrar. They shall be read in open court.

Article 35

The Court shall adjudicate upon costs.

Article 36

The President of the Court may, by way of summary procedure, which may, in so far as necessary, differ from some of the rules contained in this Statute and which shall be laid down in the rules of procedure, adjudicate upon applications to suspend execution, as provided for in Article 185 of this Treaty, or to prescribe interim measures in pursuance of Article 186, or to suspend enforcement in accordance with the last paragraph of Article 192.

Should the President be prevented from attending, his place shall be taken by another Judge under conditions laid down in the rules of procedure.

The ruling of the President or of the Judge replacing him shall be provisional and shall in no way prejudice the decision of the Court on the substance of the case.

Article 37

Member States and institutions of the Community may intervene in cases before the Court.

The same right shall be open to any other person establishing an interest in the result of any case submitted to the Court, save in cases between Member States, between institutions of the Community or between Member States and institutions of the Community.

Submissions made in an application to intervene shall be limited to supporting the submissions of one of the parties.

Article 38

Where the defending party, after having been duly summoned, fails to file written submissions in defence, judgment shall be given against that party by default. An objection may be lodged against the judgment within one month of it being notified. The objection shall not have the effect of staying enforcement of the judgment by default unless the Court decides otherwise.

ARTICLE 39

Member States, institutions of the Community and any other natural or legal persons may, in cases and under conditions to be determined by the rules of procedure, institute third-party proceedings to contest a judgment rendered without their being heard, where the judgment is prejudicial to their rights.

ARTICLE 40

If the meaning or scope of a judgment is in doubt, the Court shall construe it on application by any party or any institution of the Community establishing an interest therein.

ARTICLE 41

An application for revision of a judgment may be made to the Court only on discovery of a fact which is of such a nature as to be a decisive factor, and which, when the judgment was given, was unknown to the Court and to the party claiming the revision.

The revision shall be opened by a judgment of the Court expressly recording the existence of a new fact, recognising that it is of such a character as to lay the case open to revision and declaring the application admissible on this ground.

No application for revision may be made after the lapse of ten years from the date of the judgment.

ARTICLE 42

Periods of grace based on considerations of distance shall be determined by the rules of procedure.

No right shall be prejudiced in consequence of the expiry of a time limit if the party concerned proves the existence of unforeseeable circumstances or of *force majeure*.

ARTICLE 43

Proceedings against the Community in matters arising from non-contractual liability shall be barred after a period of five years from the occurrence of the event giving rise thereto. The period of limitation shall be interrupted if proceedings are instituted before the Court or if prior to such proceedings an application is made by the aggrieved party to the relevant institution of the Community. In the latter event the proceedings must be instituted within the period of two months provided for in Article 173; the provisions of the second paragraph of Article 175 shall apply where appropriate.

ARTICLE 44

The rules of procedure of the Court provided for in Article 188 of this Treaty shall contain, apart from the provisions contemplated by this Statute, any other provisions necessary for applying and, where required, supplementing it.

ARTICLE 45

The Council may, acting unanimously, make such further adjustments to the provisions of this Statute as may be required by reason of measures taken by the Council in accordance with the last paragraph of Article 165 of this Treaty.

ARTICLE 46

Immediateely after the oath has been taken, the President of the Council shall proceed to choose by lot the Judges and the Advocates-General whose terms of office are to expire at the end of the first three years in accordance with the second and third paragraphs of Article 167 of this Treaty.

IN WITNESS WHEREOF, the undersigned Plenipotentiaries have signed this Protocol.

DONE at Brussels this seventeenth day of April in the year one thousand nine hundred and fifty-seven.

J. Ch. SNOY ET D'OPPUERS

C. F. OPHÜLS

Robert MARJOLIN

Vittorio BADINI CONFALONIERI

Lambert SCHAUS

J. LINTHORST HOMAN

PROTOCOL ON THE STATUTE OF THE COURT OF JUSTICE OF THE EUROPEAN ATOMIC ENERGY COMMUNITY

THE HIGH CONTRACTING PARTIES TO THE TREATY ESTABLISHING THE EUROPEAN ATOMIC ENERGY COMMUNITY,

DESIRING to lay down the Statute of the Court provided for in Article 160 of this Treaty,

HAVE DESIGNATED as their Plenipotentiaries for this purpose:

HIS MAJESTY THE KING OF THE BELGIANS:
BARON J. CH. SNOY ET D'OPPUERS, Secretary-General of the Ministry of Economic Affairs, Head of the Belgian Delegation to the Intergovernmental Conference;

THE PRESIDENT OF THE FEDERAL REPUBLIC OF GERMANY:
PROFESSOR DR. CARL FRIEDRICH OPHÜLS, Ambassador of the Federal Republic of Germany, Head of the German Delegation to the Intergovernmental Conference;

THE PRESIDENT OF THE FRENCH REPUBLIC:
MR. ROBERT MARJOLIN, Professor of Law, Deputy Head of the French Delegation to the Intergovernmental Conference;

THE PRESIDENT OF THE ITALIAN REPUBLIC:
MR. V. BADINI CONFALONIERI, Under-Secretary of State in the Ministry of Foreign Affairs, Head of the Italian Delegation to the Intergovernmental Conference;

HER ROYAL HIGHNESS THE GRAND DUCHESS OF LUXEMBOURG:
MR. LAMBERT SCHAUS, Ambassador of the Grand Duchy of Luxembourg, Head of the Luxembourg Delegation to the Intergovernmental Conference;

HER MAJESTY THE QUEEN OF THE NETHERLANDS:
MR. J. LINTHORST HOMAN, Head of the Netherlands Delegation to the Intergovernmental Conference;

WHO, having exchanged their Full Powers, found in good and due form,

HAVE AGREED upon the following provisions, which shall be annexed to the Treaty establishing the European Atomic Energy Community:

ARTICLE 1

The Court established by Article 3 of this Treaty shall be constituted and shall function in accordance with the provisions of this Treaty and of this Statute.

TITLE I—JUDGES AND ADVOCATES-GENERAL

ARTICLE 2

Before taking up his duties each Judge shall, in open court, take an oath to perform his duties impartially and conscientiously and to preserve the secrecy of the deliberations of the Court.

ARTICLE 3

The Judges shall be immune from legal proceedings. After they have ceased to hold office, they shall continue to enjoy immunity in respect of acts performed by them in their official capacity, including words spoken or written.

The Court, sitting in plenary session, may waive the immunity.

Where immunity has been waived and criminal proceedings are instituted against a Judge, he shall be tried, in any of the Member States, only by the Court competent to judge the members of the highest national judiciary.

Article 4

The Judges may not hold any political or administrative office.

They may not engage in any occupation, whether gainful or not, unless exemption is exceptionally granted by the Council.

When taking up their duties, they shall give a solemn undertaking that, both during and after their term of office, they will respect the obligations arising therefrom, in particular the duty to behave with integrity and discretion as regards the acceptance, after they have ceased to hold office, of certain appointments or benefits.

Any doubt on this point shall be settled by decision of the Court.

Article 5

Apart from normal replacement, or death, the duties of a Judge shall end when he resigns.

Where a Judge resigns, his letter of resignation shall be addressed to the President of the Court for transmission to the President of the Council. Upon this notification a vacancy shall arise on the bench.

Save where Article 6 applies, a Judge shall continue to hold office until his successor takes up his duties.

Article 6

A Judge may be deprived of his office or of his right to a pension or other benefits in its stead only if, in the uanimous opinion of the Judges and Advocates-General of the Court, he no longer fulfils the requisite conditions or meets the obligations arising from his office. The Judge concerned shall not take part in any such deliberations.

The Registrar of the Court shall communicate the decision of the Court to the President of the Assembly and to the President of the Commission and shall notify it to the President of the Council.

In the case of a decision depriving a Judge of his office, a vacancy shall arise on the bench upon this latter notification.

Article 7

A Judge who is to replace a member of the Court whose term of office has not expired shall be appointed for the remainder of his predecessor's term.

Article 8

The provisions of Articles 2 to 7 shall apply to the Advocates-General.

TITLE II—ORGANISATION

Article 9

The Registrar shall take an oath before the Court to perform his duties impartially and conscientiously and to preserve the secrecy of the deliberations of the Court.

Article 10

The Court shall arrange for replacement of the Registrar on occasions when he is prevented from attending the Court.

Article 11

Officials and other servants shall be attached to the Court to enable it to function. They shall be responsible to the Registrar under the authority of the President.

Article 12

On a proposal from the Court, the Council may, acting unanimously, provide for the appointment of Assistant Rapporteurs and lay down the rules governing their service. The Assistant Rapporteurs may be required, under conditions laid down in the rules of procedure, to participate in preparatory inquiries in cases pending before the Court and to co-operate with the Judge who acts as Rapporteur.

The Assistant Rapporteurs shall be chosen from persons whose independence is beyond doubt and who possess the necessary legal qualifications; they shall be appointed by the Council.

They shall take an oath before the Court to perform their duties impartially and conscientiously and to preserve the secrecy of the deliberations of the Court.

ARTICLE 13

The Judges, the Advocates-General and the Registrar shall be required to reside at the place where the Court has its seat.

ARTICLE 14

The Court shall remain permanently in session. The duration of the judicial vacations shall be determined by the Court with due regard to the needs of its business.

ARTICLE 15

[Decisions of the Court shall be valid only when an uneven number of its members is sitting in the deliberations. Decisions of the full Court shall be valid if seven members are sitting. Decisions of the Chambers shall be valid only if three Judges are sitting; in the event of one of the Judges of a Chamber being prevented from attending, a Judge of another Chamber may be called upon to sit in accordance with conditions laid down in the rules of procedure.]

AMENDMENT
The words in square brackets were substituted by the Act of Accession, Art. 20.

ARTICLE 16

No Judge or Advocate-General may take part in the disposal of any case in which he has previously taken part as agent or adviser or has acted for one of the parties, or on which he has been called upon to pronounce as a member of a court or tribunal, of a commission of inquiry or in any other capacity.

If, for some special reason, any Judge or Advocate-General considers that he should not take part in the judgment or exmination of a particular case, he shall so inform the President. If, for some special reason, the President considers that any Judge or Advocate-General should not sit or make submissions in a particular case, he shall notify him accordingly.

Any difficulty arising as to the application of this Article shall be settled by decision of the Court.

A party may not apply for a change in the composition of the Court or of one of its Chambers on the grounds of either the nationality of a Judge or the absence from the Court or from the Chamber of a Judge of the nationality of that party.

TITLE III—PROCEDURE

ARTICLE 17

The States and the institutions of the Community shall be represented before the Court by an agent appointed for each case; the agent may be assisted by an adviser or a lawyer entitled to practise before a court of a Member State.

Other parties must be represented by a lawyer entitled to practise before a court of a Member State.

Such agents, advisers and lawyers shall, when they appear before the Court, enjoy the rights and immunities necessary to the independent exercise of their duties, under conditions laid down in the rules of procedure.

As regards such advisers and lawyers who appear before it, the Court shall have the powers normally accorded to courts of law, under conditions laid down in the rules of procedure.

University teachers being nationals of a Member State whose law accords them a right of audience shall have the same rights before the Court as are accorded by this Article to lawyers entitled to practise before a court of a Member State.

ARTICLE 18

The procedure before the Court shall consist of two parts: written and oral.

The written procedure shall consist of the communication to the parties and to the institutions of the Community whose decisions are in dispute of applications, statements of case, defences and observations, and of replies, if any, as well as of all papers and documents in support or of certified copies of them.

Communications shall be made by the Registrar in the order and within the time laid down in the rules of procedure.

The oral procedure shall consist of the reading of the report presented by a Judge acting as Rapporteur, the hearing by the Court of Agents, advisers and lawyers entitled to practise before a court of a Member State and of the submissions of the Advocate-General, as well as the hearing, if any, of witnesses and experts.

ARTICLE 19

A case shall be brought before the Court by a written application addressed to the Registrar. The application shall contain the applicant's name and permanent address and the description of the signatory, the name of the party against whom the application is made, the subject matter of the dispute, the submissions and a brief statement of the grounds on which the application is based.

The application shall be accompanied, where appropriate, by the measure the annulment of which is sought or, in the circumstances referred to in Article 148 of this Treaty, by documentary evidence of the date on which an institution was, in accordance with that Article, requested to act. If the documents are not submitted with the application, the Registrar shall ask the party concerned to produce them within a reasonable period, but in that event the rights of the party shall not lapse even if such documents are produced after the time limit for bringing proceedings.

ARTICLE 20

A case governed by Article 18 of this Treaty shall be brought before the Court by an appeal addressed to the Registrar. The appeal shall contain the name and permanent address of the appellant and the description of the signatory, a reference to the decision against which the appeal is brought, the names of the respondents, the subject matter of the dispute, the submissions and a brief statement of the grounds on which the appeal is based.

The appeal shall be accompanied by a certified copy of the decision of the Arbitration Committee which is contested.

If the Court rejects the appeal, the decision of the Arbitration Committee shall become final.

If the Court annuls the decision of the Arbitration Committee, the matter may be re-opened, where appropriate, on the initiative of one of the parties in the case, before the Arbitration Committee. The latter shall conform to any decisions on points of law given by the Court.

ARTICLE 21

In the cases governed by Article 150 of this Treaty, the decision of the court or tribunal of a Member State which suspends its proceedings and refers a case to the Court shall be notified to the Court by the court or tribunal concerned. The decision shall then be notified by the Registrar of the Court to the parties, to the Member States and to the Commission, and also the Council if the act the validity or interpretation of which is in dispute originates from the Council.

Within two months of this notification, the parties, the Member States, the Commission and, where appropriate, the Council, shall be entitled to submit statements of case or written observations to the Court.

ARTICLE 22

The Court may require the parties to produce all documents and to supply all information which the Court considers desirable. Formal note shall be taken of any refusal.

The Court may also require the Member States and institutions not being parties to the case to supply all information which the Court considers necessary for the proceedings.

ARTICLE 23

The Court may at any time entrust any individual, body, authority, committee or other organisation it chooses with the task of giving an expert opinion.

ARTICLE 24

Witnesses may be heard under conditions laid down in the rules of procedure.

ARTICLE 25

With respect to defaulting witnesses the Court shall have the powers generally granted to courts and tribunals and may impose pecuniary penalties under conditions laid down in the rules of procedure.

Statute of the Court of Justice of Euratom

Article 26

Witnesses and experts may be heard on oath taken in the form laid down in the rules of procedure or in the manner laid down by the law of the country of the witness or expert.

Article 27

The Court may order that a witness or expert be heard by the judicial authority of his place of permanent residence.

The order shall be sent for implementation to the competent judicial authority under conditions laid down in the rules of procedure. The documents drawn up in compliance with the letters rogatory shall be returned to the Court under the same conditions.

The Court shall defray the expenses, without prejudice to the right to charge them, where appropriate, to the parties.

Article 28

A Member State shall treat any violation of an oath by a witness or expert in the same manner as if the offence had been committed before one of its courts with jurisdiction in civil proceedings. At the instance of the Court, the Member State concerned shall prosecute the offender before its competent court.

Article 29

The hearing in court shall be public, unless the Court, of its own motion or on application by the parties, decides otherwise for serious reasons.

Article 30

During the hearings the Court may examine the experts, the witnesses and the parties themselves. The latter, however, may address the Court only through their representatives.

Article 31

Minutes shall be made of each hearing and signed by the President and the Registrar.

Article 32

The cause list shall be established by the President.

Article 33

The deliberations of the Court shall be and shall remain secret.

Article 34

Judgments shall state the reasons on which they are based. They shall contain the names of the Judges who took part in the deliberations.

Article 35

Judgments shall be signed by the President and the Registrar. They shall be read in open court.

Article 36

The Court shall adjudicate upon costs.

Article 37

The President of the Court may, by way of summary procedure, which may, in so far as necessary, differ from some of the rules contained in this Statute and which shall be laid down in the rules of procedure, adjudicate upon applications to suspend execution, as provided for in Article 157 of this Treaty, or to prescribe interim measures in pursuance of Article 158, or to suspend enforcement in accordance with the last paragraph of Article 164.

Should the President be prevented from attending, his place shall be taken by another Judge under conditions laid down in the rules of procedure.

The ruling of the President or of the Judge replacing him shall be provisional and shall in no way prejudice the decision of the Court on the substance of the case.

PART IV—COMMUNITY TEXTS

ARTICLE 38

Member States and institutions of the Community may intervene in cases before the Court.

The same right shall be open to any other person establishing an interest in the result of any case submitted to the Court, save in cases between Member States, between institutions of the Community or between Member States and institutions of the Community.

Submissions made in an application to intervene shall be limited to supporting the submissions of one of the parties.

ARTICLE 39

Where the defending party, after having been duly summoned, fails to file written submissions in defence, judgment shall be given against that party by default. An objection may be lodged against the judgment within one month of it being notified. The objection shall not have the effect of staying enforcement of the judgment by default unless the Court decides otherwise.

ARTICLE 40

Member States, institutions of the Community and any other natural or legal persons may, in cases and under conditions to be determined by the rules of procedure, institute third-party proceedings to contest a judgment rendered without their being heard, where the judgment is prejudicial to their rights.

ARTICLE 41

If the meaning or scope of a judgment is in doubt, the Court shall construe it on application by any party or any institution of the Community establishing an interest therein.

ARTICLE 42

An application for revision of a judgment may be made to the Court only on discovery of a fact which is of such a nature as to be a decisive factor, and which, when the judgment was given, was unkown to the Court and to the party claiming the revision.

The revision shall be opened by a judgment of the Court expressly recording the existence of a new fact, recognising that it is of such a character as to lay the case open to revision and declaring the application admissible on this ground.

No application for revision may be made after the lapse of ten years from the date of the judgment.

ARTICLE 43

Periods of grace based on considerations of distance shall be determined by the rules of procedure.

No right shall be prejudiced in consequence of the expiry of a time limit if the party concerned proves the existence of unforeseeable circumstances or of *force majeure*.

ARTICLE 44

Proceedings against the Community in matters arising from non-contractual liability shall be barred after a period of five years from the occurrence of the event giving rise thereto. The period of limitation shall be interrupted if proceedings are instituted before the Court or if prior to such proceedings an application is made by the aggrieved party to the relevant institution of the Community. In the latter event the proceedings must be instituted within the period of two months provided for in Article 146; the provisions of the second paragraph of Article 148 shall apply where appropriate.

ARTICLE 45

The ruless of procedure of the Court provided for in Article 160 of this Treaty shall contain, apart from the provisions contemplated by this Statute, any other provisions necessary for applying and, where required, supplementing it.

ARTICLE 46

The Council may, acting unanimously, make such further adjustments to the provisions of this Statute as may be required by reason of measures taken by the Council in accordance with the last paragraph of Article 137 of this Treaty.

ARTICLE 47

Immediately after the oath has been taken, the President of the Council shall proceed to choose by lot the Judges and the Advocates-General whose terms of office are to expire at the end of the first three years in accordance with the second and third paragraphs of Article 139 of this Treaty.

IN WITNESS WHEREOF, the undersigned Plenipotentiaries have signed this Protocol.

DONE at Brussels this seventeenth day of April in the year one thousand nine hundred and fifty-seven.

J. Ch. SNOY ET D'OPPUERS
C. F. OPHÜLS
Robert MARJOLIN
Vittorio BADINI CONFALONIERI
Lambert SCHAUS
J. LINTHORST HOMAN

CONVENTION ON CERTAIN INSTITUTIONS COMMON TO THE EUROPEAN COMMUNITIES

HIS MAJESTY THE KING OF THE BELGIANS, THE PRESIDENT OF THE FEDERAL REPUBLIC OF GERMANY, THE PRESIDENT OF THE FRENCH REPUBLIC, THE PRESIDENT OF THE ITALIAN REPUBLIC, HER ROYAL HIGHNESS THE GRAND DUCHESS OF LUXEMBOURG, HER MAJESTY THE QUEEN OF THE NETHERLANDS.

ANXIOUS to limit the number of institutions responsible for carrying out similar tasks in the European Communities which they have constituted,

HAVE DECIDED to create for these Communities certain single institutions and to this end have designated as their Plenipotentiaries:

HIS MAJESTY THE KING OF THE BELGIANS:
Mr. Paul-Henri SPAAK, Minister for Foreign Affairs;
Baron J. Ch. SNOY et d'OPPUERS, Secretary-General of the Ministry of Economic Affairs, Head of the Belgian Delegation to the Intergovernmental Conference;

THE PRESIDENT OF THE FEDERAL REPUBLIC OF GERMANY:
Dr. Konrad ADENAUER, Federal Chancellor;
Professor Dr. Walter HALLSTEIN, State Secretary of the Federal Foreign Office;

THE PRESIDENT OF THE FRENCH REPUBLIC:
Mr. Christian PINEAU, Minister for Foreign Affairs;
Mr. Maurice FAURE, Under-Secretary of State for Foreign Affairs;

THE PRESIDENT OF THE ITALIAN REPUBLIC:
Mr. Antonio SEGNI, President of the Council of Ministers;
Professor Gaetano MARTINO, Minister for Foreign Affairs;

HER ROYAL HIGHNESS THE GRAND DUCHESS OF LUXEMBOURG:
Mr. Joseph BECH, President of the Government, Minister for Foreign Affairs;
Mr. Lambert SCHAUS, Ambassador, Head of the Luxembourg Delegation to the Intergovernmental Conference;

HER MAJESTY THE QUEEN OF THE NETHERLANDS:
Mr. Joseph LUNS, Minister for Foreign Affairs,
Mr. J. LINTHORST HOMAN, Head of the Netherlands Delegation to the Intergovernmental Conference;

WHO, having exchanged their Full Powers, found in good and due form,
HAVE AGREED as follows:

SECTION I—THE ASSEMBLY

ARTICLE 1

The powers and jurisdiction which the Treaty establishing the European Economic Community and the Treaty establishing the European Atomic Energy Community confer upon the Assembly shall be exercised, in accordance with those Treaties, by a single Assembly composed and designated as provided in Article 138 of the Treaty establishing the European Economic Community and in Article 108 of the Treaty establishing the European Atomic Energy Community.

ARTICLE 2

1. Upon taking up its duties, the single Assembly referred to in Article 1 shall take the place of the Common Assembly provided for in Article 21 of the Treaty establishing the European Coal and Steel Community. It shall exercise the powers and jurisdiction conferred upon the Common Assembly by that Treaty in accordance with the provisions thereof.

2. [*This paragraph amends the ECSC Treaty, Art. 21, and is incorporated therein.*]

SECTION II—THE COURT OF JUSTICE

ARTICLE 3

The jurisdiction which the Treaty establishing the European Economic Community and the Treaty establishing the European Atomic Energy Community confer upon the Court of Justice shall be exercised, in accordance with those Treaties, by a single Court of Justice composed and appointed as provided in Articles 165 to 167 of the Treaty establishing the European Economic Community and in Articles 137 to 139 of the Treaty establishing the European Atomic Energy Community.

ARTICLE 4

1. Upon taking up its duties, the single Court of Justice referred to in Article 3 shall take the place of the Court provided for in Article 32 of the Treaty establishing the European Coal and Steel Community. It shall exercise the jurisdiction conferred upon that Court by that Treaty in accordance with the provisions thereof.

The President of the single Court of Justice referred to in Article 3 shall exercise the powers conferred by the Treaty establishing the European Coal and Steel Community upon the President of the Court provided for in that Treaty.

2. To this end, on the date when the single Court of Justice referred to in Article 3 takes up its duties:

    (a) [*This subparagraph amends the ECSC Treaty, Art.* 32, *and is incorporated therein.*]

    (b) The provisions of the Protocol on the Statute of the Court of Justice annexed to the Treaty establishing the European Coal and Steel Community, in so far as they are in conflict with Articles 32 to 32c of that Treaty, shall be repealed.

SECTION III—THE ECONOMIC AND SOCIAL COMMITTEE

ARTICLE 5

1. The functions which the Treaty establishing the European Economic Community and the Treaty establishing the European Atomic Energy Community confer upon the Economic and Social Committee shall be exercised, in accordance with those Treaties, by a single Economic and Social Committee composed and appointed as provided in Article 194 of the Treaty establishing the European Economic Community and in Article 166 of the Treaty establishing the European Atomic Energy Community.

2. The single Economic and Social Committee referred to in paragraph 1 shall include a section specialising in, and may include subcommittees competent for, the fields or questions dealt with in the Treaty establishing the European Atomic Energy Community.

3. The provisions of Articles 193 and 197 of the Treaty establishing the European Economic Community shall apply to the single Economic and Social Committee referred to in paragraph 1.

SECTION IV—THE FINANCING OF THESE INSTITUTIONS

ARTICLE 6

[*Repealed by the Merger Treaty, Art.* 23. *See now ibid., Art.* 20.]

FINAL PROVISIONS

ARTICLE 7

This Convention shall be ratified by the High Contracting Parties in accordance with their respective constitutional requirements. The instruments of ratification shall be deposited with the Government of the Italian Republic.

This Convention shall enter into force at the same time as the Treaty establishing the European Economic Community and the Treaty establishing the European Atomic Energy Community.

Article 8

This Convention, drawn up in a single original in the Dutch, French, German and Italian languages, all four texts being equally authentic, shall be deposited in the archives of the Government of the Italian Republic, which shall transmit a certified copy to each of the Governments of the other signatory States.

IN WITNESS WHEREOF, the undersigned Plenipotentiaries have signed this Convention.

DONE at Rome this twenty-fifth day of March in the year one thousand nine hundred and fifty-seven.

P. H. Spaak	J. Ch. Snoy et d'Oppuers
Adenauer	Hallstein
Pineau	M. Faure
Antonio Segni	Gaetano Martino
Bech	Lambert Schaus
J. Luns	J. Linthorst Homan

TREATY ESTABLISHING A SINGLE COUNCIL AND A SINGLE COMMISSION OF THE EUROPEAN COMMUNITIES

(BRUSSELS, 8 APRIL 1965)

HIS MAJESTY THE KING OF THE BELGIANS, THE PRESIDENT OF THE FEDERAL REPUBLIC OF GERMANY, THE PRESIDENT OF THE FRENCH REPUBLIC, THE PRESIDENT OF THE ITALIAN REPUBLIC, HIS ROYAL HIGHNESS THE GRAND DUKE OF LUXEMBOURG, HER MAJESTY THE QUEEN OF THE NETHERLANDS,

Having regard to Article 96 of the Treaty establishing the European Coal and Steel Community,

Having regard to Article 236 of the Treaty establishing the European Economic Community,

Having regard to Article 204 of the Treaty establishing the European Atomic Energy Community,

RESOLVED to continue along the road to European unity,

RESOLVED to effect the unification of the three Communities,

MINDFUL of the contribution which the creation of single Community institutions represents for such unification,

HAVE DECIDED to create a single Council and a single Commission of the European Communities and to this end have designated as their Plenipotentiaries:

HIS MAJESTY THE KING OF THE BELGIANS,
   M. Paul-Henri SPAAK, Deputy Prime Minister and Minister for Foreign Affairs;

THE PRESIDENT OF THE FEDERAL REPUBLIC OF GERMANY,
   M. Kurt SCHMÜCKER, Minister for Economic Affairs;

THE PRESIDENT OF THE FRENCH REPUBLIC,
   M. Maurice COUVE de MURVILLE, Minister for Foreign Affairs;

THE PRESIDENT OF THE ITALIAN REPUBLIC,
   M. Amintore FANFANI, Minister for Foreign Affairs;

HIS ROYAL HIGHNESS THE GRAND DUKE OF LUXEMBOURG,
   M. Pierre WERNER, President of the Government, Minister for Foreign Affairs;

HER MAJESTY THE QUEEN OF THE NETHERLANDS,
   M. J. M. A. H. LUNS, Minister for Foreign Affairs;

WHO, having exchanged their Full Powers, found in good and due form, HAVE AGREED as follows:

CHAPTER I—THE COUNCIL OF THE EUROPEAN COMMUNITIES

ARTICLE 1

A Council of the European Communities (hereinafter called the " Council ") is hereby established. This Council shall take the place of the Special Council of Ministers of the European Coal and Steel Community, the Council of the European Economic Community and the Council of the European Atomic Energy Community.

It shall exercise the powers and jurisdiction conferred on those institutions in accordance with the provisions of the Treaties establishing the European Coal and Steel Community, the European Economic Community and the European Atomic Energy Community, and of this Treaty.

ARTICLE 2

The Council shall consist of representatives of the Member States. Each Government shall delegate to it one of its members.

[The office of President shall be held for a term of six months by each member of the Council in turn, in the following order of Member States: Belgium, Denmark, Germany, Greece, France, Ireland, Italy, Luxembourg, Netherlands, United Kingdom.]

AMENDMENTS
The second paragraph was substituted by the Act of Accession, Art. 11, as amended by the Adaptation Decision, Art. 5. It was subsequently substituted by the Act of Accession of the Hellenic Republic of May 28, 1979, Art. 11.

ARTICLE 3

The Council shall meet when convened by its President on his own initiative or at the request of one of its members or of the Commission.

ARTICLE 4

A committee consisting of the Permanent Representatives of the Member States shall be responsible for preparing the work of the Council and for carrying out the tasks assigned to it by the Council.

ARTICLE 5

The Council shall adopt its rules of procedure.

ARTICLE 6

The Council shall, acting by a qualified majority, determine the salaries, allowances and pensions of the President and members of the Commission, and of the President, Judges, Advocates-General and Registrar of the Court of Justice. It shall also, again by a qualified majority, determine any payment to be made instead of remuneration.

ARTICLE 7

[*This Article repeals the ECSC Treaty, Arts.* 27, 28 (1), 28 *and* 30, *the EEC Treaty, Arts.* 146, 147, 151 *and* 154, *and the Euratom Treaty, Arts.* 116, 117, 121 *and* 123.]

ARTICLE 8

1. The conditions governing the exercise of the jurisdiction conferred on the Special Council of Ministers by the Treaty establishing the European Coal and Steel Community and by the Protocol on the Statute of the Court of Justice annexed thereto shall be amended as set out in paragraphs 2 and 3.

2. [*This paragraph amends the ECSC Treaty, Art.* 28, *and is incorporated therein.*]

3. [*This paragraph repeals Arts.* 5 *and* 15 *of the Protocol on the Statute of the Court of Justice annexed to the ECSC Treaty. It also amends ibid., Arts.* 16, 20, 28 *and* 44, *and is incorporated therein.*]

CHAPTER II—THE COMMISSION OF THE EUROPEAN COMMUNITIES

ARTICLE 9

A Commission of the European Communities (hereinafter called the " Commission ") is hereby established. This Commission shall take the place of the High Authority of the European Coal and Steel Community, the Commission of the European Economic Community and the Commission of the European Atomic Energy Community.

It shall exercise the powers and jurisdiction conferred on those institutions in accordance with the provisions of the Treaties establishing the European Coal and Steel Community, the European Economic Community and the European Atomic Energy Community, and of this Treaty.

ARTICLE 10

1. [The Commission shall consist of fourteen members, who shall be chosen on the grounds of their general competence and whose independence is beyond doubt.]

The number of members of the Commission may be altered by the Council, acting unanimously.

Only nationals of Member States may be members of the Commission.

The Commission must include at least one national of each of the Member States, but may not include more than two members having the nationality of the same State.

2. The members of the Commission shall, in the general interest of the Communities, be completely independent in the performance of their duties.

In the performance of these duties, they shall neither seek nor take instructions from any Government or from any other body. They shall refrain from any action incompatible with their duties. Each Member State undertakes to respect this principle and not to seek to influence the members of the Commission in the performance of their tasks.

The members of the Commission may not, during their term of office, engage in any other occupation, whether gainful or not. When entering upon their duties they shall give a solemn undertaking that, both during and after their term of office, they will respect the obligations arising therefrom and in particular their duty to behave with integrity and discretion as regards the acceptance, after they have ceased to hold office, of certain appointments or benefits. In the event of any breach of these obligations, the Court of Justice may, on application by the Council or the Commission, rule that the member concerned be, according to the circumstances, either compulsorily retired in accordance with the provisions of Article 13 or deprived of his right to a pension or other benefits in its stead.

AMENDMENTS
Para. (1) was substituted by the Council Decision of January 1, 1973, altering the number of Members of the Commission. It was subsequently substituted by the Act of Accession of the Hellenic Republic of May 28, 1979, Art. 15.

ARTICLE 11

The members of the Commission shall be appointed by common accord of the Governments of the Member States.

Their term of office shall be four years. It shall be renewable.

ARTICLE 12

Apart from normal replacement, or death, the duties of a member of the Commission shall end when he resigns or is compulsorily retired.

The vacancy thus caused shall be filled for the remainder of the member's term of office. The Council may, acting unanimously, decide that such a vacancy need not be filled.

Save in the case of compulsory retirement under the provisions of Article 13, members of the Commission shall remain in office until they have been replaced.

ARTICLE 13

If any member of the Commission no longer fulfils the conditions required for the performance of his duties or if he has been guilty of serious misconduct, the Court of Justice may, on application by the Council or the Commission, compulsorily retire him.

ARTICLE 14

[The President and the five Vice-Presidents of the Commission shall be appointed from among its members for a term of two years in accordance with the same procedure as that laid down for the appointment of members of the Commission. Their appointments may be renewed.]

Save where the entire Commission is replaced, such appointments shall be made after the Commission has been consulted.

In the event of retirement or death, the President and the Vice-Presidents shall be replaced for the remainder of their term of office in accordance with the preceding provisions.

AMENDMENT
The words in square brackets were substituted by the Act of Accession, Art. 16.

ARTICLE 15

The Council and the Commission shall consult each other and shall settle by common accord their methods of cooperation.

ARTICLE 16

The Commission shall adopt its rules of procedure so as to ensure that both it and its departments operate in accordance with the provisions of the Treaties establishing the European Coal and Steel Community, the European Economic Community and the European Atomic Energy Community, and of this Treaty. It shall ensure that these rules are published.

ARTICLE 17

The Commission shall act by a majority of the number of members provided for in Article 10.

A meeting of the Commission shall be valid only if the number of members laid down in its rules of procedure is present.

ARTICLE 18

The Commission shall publish annually, not later than one month before the opening of the session of the Assembly, a general report on the activities of the Communities.

ARTICLE 19

[This Article repeals the ECSC Treaty, Arts. 9 to 13, 16 (3), 17 and 18 (6), the EEC Treaty, Arts. 156 to 163, and the Euratom Treaty, Arts. 125 to 133.]

CHAPTER III—FINANCIAL PROVISIONS

ARTICLE 20

1. [The administrative expenditure of the European Coal and Steel Community and the revenue relating thereto, the revenue and expenditure of the European Economic Community, and the revenue and expenditure of the European Atomic Energy Community, with the exception of that of the Supply Agency and the Joint Undertakings, shall be shown in the budget of the European Communities in accordance with the appropriate provisions of the Treaties establishing the three Communities. This budget, which shall be in balance as to revenue and expenditure, shall take the place of the administrative budget of the European Coal and Steel Community, the budget of the European Economic Community and the operating budget and research and investment budget of the European Atomic Energy Community.]

2. The portion of the expenditure covered by the levies provided for in Article 49 of the Treaty establishing the European Coal and Steel Community shall be fixed at eighteen million units of account.

As from the financial year beginning 1 January 1967, the Commission shall submit annually to the Council a report on the basis of which the Council shall examine whether there is reason to adjust this figure to changes in the budget of the Communities. The Council shall act by the majority laid down in the first sentence of the fourth paragraph of Article 28 of the Treaty establishing the European Coal and Steel Community. The adjustment shall be made on the basis of an assessment of developments in expenditure arising from the application of the Treaty establishing the European Coal and Steel Community.

3. The portion of the levies assigned to cover expenditure under the budget of the Communities shall be allocated by the Commission for the implementation of that budget in accordance with the timetable provided for in the financial regulations adopted pursuant to Article 209 (b) of the Treaty establishing the European Economic Community and Article 183 (b) of the Treaty establishing the European Atomic Energy Community relating to the

methods and procedure whereby the contributions of the Member States shall be made available.

AMENDMENT
The words in square brackets were substituted by the Budgetary Treaty, Art. 10.

ARTICLE 21

[*This Article amends the ECSC Treaty, Art. 78, and is incorporated therein.*]

ARTICLE 22

[1. The powers and jurisdiction conferred upon the Court of Auditors established by Article 78e of the Treaty establishing the European Coal and Steel Community, by Article 206 of the Treaty establishing the European Economic Community, and by Article 180 of the Treaty establishing the European Atomic Energy Community shall be exercised in accordance with those Treaties by a single Court of Auditors of the European Communities constituted as provided in these articles.

2. Without prejudice to the powers and jurisdiction referred to in paragraph 1, the Court of Auditors of the European Communities shall exercise the powers and jurisdiction conferred, before the entry into force of this Treaty, upon the Audit Board of the European Communities and upon the Auditor of the European Coal and Steel Community under the conditions laid down in the various instruments referring to the Audit Board and to the Auditor. In all these instruments the words " Audit Board " and "Auditor " shall be replaced by the words " Court of Auditors ".]

AMENDMENT
This article was replaced by the Second Budgetary Treaty of July 22, 1975, Art. 27.

ARTICLE 23

[*This Article repeals the Convention on Certain Institutions Common to the European Communities, Art. 6.*]

CHAPTER IV—OFFICIALS AND OTHER SERVANTS OF THE EUROPEAN COMMUNITIES

ARTICLE 24

1. The officials and other servants of the European Coal and Steel Community, the European Economic Community and the European Atomic Energy Community shall, at the date of entry into force of this Treaty, become officials and other servants of the European Communities and form part of the single administration of those Communities.

The Council shall, acting by a qualified majority on a proposal from the Commission and after consulting the other institutions concerned, lay down the Staff Regulations of officials of the European Communities and the Conditions of Employment of other servants of those Communities.

2. [*This paragraph repeals the Convention on the Transitional Provisions annexed to the ECSC Treaty, Art. 7 (3), the EEC Treaty, Art. 212, and the Euratom Treaty, Art. 186.*]

ARTICLE 25

Until the uniform Staff Regulations and Conditions of Employment provided for in Article 24 and the Protocol annexed to this Treaty enter into force, officials and other servants recruited before the date of entry into force of this Treaty shall continue to be governed by the provisions which were until then applicable to them.

Officials and other servants recruited on or after the date of entry into force of this Treaty shall, pending the adoption of the uniform Staff Regulations and Conditions of Employment provided for in Article 24 and of regulations to be made pursuant to Article 13 of the Protocol annexed to this Treaty, be governed by the provisions applicable to officials and other servants of the European Economic Community and of the European Atomic Energy Community.

ARTICLE 26

[*This Article amends the ECSC Treaty, Art. 40, and is incorporated therein.*]

CHAPTER V—GENERAL AND FINAL PROVISIONS

ARTICLE 27

1. [*This paragraph amends the ECSC Treaty, Art. 22 (1), the EEC Treaty, Art. 139 (1), and the Euratom Treaty, Art. 109 (1), and is incorporated therein.*]

2. [*This paragraph amends the ECSC Treaty, Art. 24 (2), and is incorporated therein.*]

ARTICLE 28

The European Communities shall enjoy in the territories of the Member States such privileges and immunities as are necessary for the performance of their tasks, under the conditions laid down in the Protocol annexed to this Treaty. The same shall apply to the European Investment Bank.

[*This paragraph repeals the ECSC Treaty, Art. 76, the EEC Treaty, Art. 218, the Euratom Treaty, Art. 191; the Protocols on Privileges and Immunities annexed to these three Treaties; the Protocol on the Statute of the Court of Justice annexed to the ECSC Treaty, Arts. 3 (4) and 14 (2); the Protocol on the Statute of the European Investment Bank annexed to the EEC Treaty, Art. 28 (1), sub-para. 2.*]

ARTICLE 29

The jurisdiction conferred upon the Council by Articles 5, 6, 10, 12, 13, 24, 34 and 35 of this Treaty and by the Protocol annexed thereto shall be exercised according to the rules laid down in Articles 148, 149 and 150 of the Treaty establishing the European Economic Community and Articles 118, 119 and 120 of the Treaty establishing the European Atomic Energy Community.

ARTICLE 30

The provisions of the Treaties establishing the European Economic Community and the European Atomic Energy Community relating to the jurisdiction shall be applicable to the provisions of this Treaty and of the Protocol annexed thereto, with the exception of those which represent amendments to Articles of the Treaty establishing the European Coal and Steel Community, in respect of which the provisions of the Treaty establishing the European Coal and Steel Community shall remain applicable.

ARTICLE 31

The Council shall take up its duties on the date of entry into force of this Treaty.

On that date the office of President of the Council shall be held by the member of the Council who, in accordance with the rules laid down in the Treaties establishing the European Economic Community and the European Atomic Energy Community, was to take up the office of President of the Council of the European Economic Community and of the European Atomic Energy Community; this will apply for the remainder of his term of office. On expiry of this term, the office of President shall then be held in the order of Member States laid down in Article 2 of this Treaty.

ARTICLE 32

1. Until the date of entry into force of the Treaty establishing a Single European Community, or until three years after the appointment of its members, whichever is the earlier, the Commission shall consist of fourteen members.

During this period, not more than three members may have the nationality of the same State.

2. The President, the Vice-Presidents and the members of the Commission shall be appointed upon the entry into force of this Treaty. The Commission shall take up its duties on the fifth day after the appointment of its members. The term of office of the members of the High Authority and of the Commissions of the European Economic Community and of the European Atomic Energy Community shall end at the same time.

ARTICLE 33

The term of office of the members of the Commission provided for in Article 32 shall expire on the date determined by Article 32 (1). The members of the Commission provided for in Article 10 shall be appointed one month before that date at the latest.

If any or all of these appointments are not made within the required time, the provisions of the third paragraph of Article 12 shall not be applicable to that member who, among the nationals of each State, has least seniority as a member of a Commission or of the High Authority or, where two or more members have the same seniority, to the youngest of them. The provisions of the third paragraph of Article 12 shall remain applicable, however, to all members of the same nationality, where, before the date determined by Article 32 (1), a member of that nationality has ceased to hold office and has not been replaced.

ARTICLE 34

The Council shall, acting unanimously, make financial arrangements for past members of the High Authority and of the Commissions of the European Economic Community and of the European Atomic Energy Community who, having ceased to hold office in pursuance of Article 32, have not been appointed members of the Commission.

ARTICLE 35

1. The first budget of the Communities shall be established and adopted for the financial year beginning 1 January following the entry into force of this Treaty.

2. If this Treaty enters into force before 1 July 1965, the general estimates of the administrative expenditure of the European Coal and Steel Community which expire on 1 July shall be extended until 31 December of the same year; the appropriations made in these estimates shall be proportionately increased, unless the Council, acting by a qualified majority, decides otherwise.

If this Treaty enters into force after 30 June 1965, the Council shall, acting unanimously on a proposal from the Commission, take the appropriate decisions, taking account of the need to ensure that the Communities function smoothly and that the first budget of the Communities is adopted at as early a date as possible.

ARTICLE 36

The chairman and members of the Audit Board of the European Economic Community and of the European Atomic Energy Community shall take up the duties of chairman and members of the Audit Board of the European Communities upon the entry into force of this Treaty and for the remainder of their former term of office.

The auditor who, until the entry into force of this Treaty, is performing his duties pursuant to Article 78 of the Treaty establishing the European Coal and Steel Community shall take up the duties of the auditor provided for in Article 78e of that Treaty for the remainder of his former term of office.

ARTICLE 37

Without prejudice to the application of Article 77 of the Treaty establishing the European Coal and Steel Community, Article 216 of the Treaty establishing the European Economic Community, Article 189 of the Treaty establishing the European Atomic Energy Community and the second paragraph of Article 1 of the Protocol on the Statute of the European Investment Bank, the representatives of the Governments of the Member States shall by common accord lay down the provisions required in order to settle certain problems peculiar to the Grand Duchy of Luxembourg which arise out of the creation of a single Council and a single Commission of the European Communities.

The decision of the representatives of the Governments of the Member States shall enter into force on the same date as this Treaty.

ARTICLE 38

This Treaty shall be ratified by the High Contracting Parties in accordance with their respective constitutional requirements. The instruments of ratification shall be deposited with the Government of the Italian Republic.

The Treaty shall enter into force on the first day of the month following the deposit of the instrument of ratification by the last signatory State to take this step.

ARTICLE 39

This Treaty, drawn up in a single original in the Dutch, French, German and Italian languages, all four texts being equally authentic, shall be deposited in the archives of the Government of the Italian Republic, which shall transmit a certified copy to each of the Governments of the other signatory States.

IN WITNESS WHEREOF, the undersigned Plenipotentiaries have signed this Treaty.

DONE at Brussels this eighth day of April in the year one thousand nine hundred and sixty-five.

Pour Sa Majesté le roi des Belges Voor Zine Majesteit de Koning der Belges.
Paul-Henri SPAAK

Für den Präsidenten der Bundesrepublik Deutschland.
Kurt SCHMÜCKER

Pour le president de la République française.
Maurice COUVE DE MURVILLE

Per il Presidente della Republica italiana.
Amintore FANFANI

Pour Son Altesse royale le grand-duc de Luxembourge.
Pierre WERNER

Voor Hare Majesteit de Koningen der Nederlanden.
J. M. A. H. LUNS

Protocol

PROTOCOL ON THE PRIVILEGES AND IMMUNITIES OF THE EUROPEAN COMMUNITIES

THE HIGH CONTRACTING PARTIES,

CONSIDERING that, in accordance with Article 28 of the Treaty establishing a Single Council and a Single Commission of the European Communities, these Communities and the European Investment Bank shall enjoy in the territories of the Member States such privileges and immunities as are necessary for the performance of their tasks.

HAVE AGREED upon the following provisions, which shall be annexed to this Treaty:

CHAPTER I—PROPERTY, FUNDS, ASSETS AND OPERATIONS OF THE EUROPEAN COMMUNITIES

ARTICLE 1

The premises and buildings of the Communities shall be inviolable. They shall be exempt from search, requisition, confiscation or expropriation. The property and assets of the Communities shall not be the subject of any administrative or legal measure of constraint without the authorisation of the Court of Justice.

ARTICLE 2

The archives of the Communities shall be inviolable.

ARTICLE 3

The Communities, their assets, revenues and other property shall be exempt from all direct taxes.

The Governments of the Member States shall, wherever possible, take the appropriate measures to remit or refund the amount of indirect taxes or sales taxes included in the price of movable or immovable property, where the Communities make, for their official use, substantial purchases the price of which includes taxes of this kind. These provisions shall not be applied, however, so as to have the effect of distorting competition within the Communities.

No exemption shall be granted in respect of taxes and dues which amount merely to charges for public utility services.

ARTICLE 4

The Communities shall be exempt from all customs duties, prohibitions and restrictions on imports and exports in respect of articles intended for their official use; articles so imported shall not be disposed of, whether or not in return for payment, in the territory of the country into which they have been imported, except under conditions approved by the Government of that country.

The Communities shall also be exempt from any customs duties and any prohibitions and restrictions on imports and exports in respect of their publications.

ARTICLE 5

The European Coal and Steel Community may hold currency of any kind and operate accounts in any currency.

CHAPTER II—COMMUNICATIONS AND *LAISSEZ-PASSER*

ARTICLE 6

For their official communications and the transmission of all their documents, the institutions of the Communities shall enjoy in the territory of each Member State the treatment accorded by that State to diplomatic missions.

Official correspondence and other official communications of the institutions of the Communities shall not be subject to censorship.

ARTICLE 7

1. *Laissez-passer* in a form to be prescribed by the Council, which shall be recognised as valid travel documents by the authorities of the Member States, may be issued to members and servants of the institutions of the Communities by the Presidents of these institutions. These *laissez-passer* shall be issued to officials and other servants under conditions laid down in the Staff Regulations of officials and the Conditions of Employment of other servants of the Communities.

The Commission may conclude agreements for these *laissez-passer* to be recognised as valid travel documents within the territory of third countries.

2. The provisions of Article 6 of the Protocol on the Privileges and Immunities of the European Coal and Steel Community shall, however, remain applicable to members and servants of the institutions who are at the date of entry into force of this Treaty in possession of the *laissez-passer* provided for in that Article, until the provisions of paragraph 1 of this Article are applied.

CHAPTER III—MEMBERS OF THE ASSEMBLY

ARTICLE 8

No administrative or other restriction shall be imposed on the free movement of members of the Assembly travelling to or from the place of meeting of the Assembly.

Members of the Assembly shall, in respect of customs and exchange control, be accorded:
- (a) by their own Government, the same facilities as those accorded to senior officials travelling abroad on temporary official missions;
- (b) by the Governments of other Member States, the same facilities as those accorded to representatives of foreign Governments on temporary official missions.

ARTICLE 9

Members of the Assembly shall not be subject to any form of inquiry, detention or legal proceedings in respect of opinions expressed or votes cast by them in the performance of their duties.

ARTICLE 10

During the sessions of the Assembly, its members shall enjoy:
- (a) in the territory of their own State, the immunities accorded to members of their parliament;
- (b) in the territory of any other Member State, immunity from any measure of detention and from legal proceedings.

Immunity shall likewise apply to members while they are travelling to and from the place of meeting of the Assembly.

Immunity cannot be claimed when a member is found in the act of committing an offence and shall not prevent the Assembly from exercising its right to waive the immunity of one of its members.

CHAPTER IV—REPRESENTATIVES OF MEMBER STATES TAKING PART IN THE WORK OF THE INSTITUTIONS OF THE EUROPEAN COMMUNITIES

ARTICLE 11

Representatives of Member States taking part in the work of the institutions of the Communities, their advisers and technical experts shall, in the performance of their duties and during their travel to and from the place of meeting, enjoy the customary privileges, immunities and facilities.

This Article shall also apply to members of the advisory bodies of the Communities.

CHAPTER V—OFFICIALS AND OTHER SERVANTS OF THE EUROPEAN COMMUNITIES

ARTICLE 12

In the territory of each Member State and whatever their nationality, officials and other servants of the Communities shall:

(a) subject to the provisions of the Treaties relating, on the one hand, to the rules on the liability of officials and other servants towards the Communities and, on the other hand, to the jurisdiction of the Court in disputes between the Communities and their officials and other servants, be immune from legal proceedings in respect of acts performed by them in their official capacity, including their words spoken or written. They shall continue to enjoy this immunity after they have ceased to hold office.

(b) together with their spouses and dependent members of their families, not be subject to immigration restrictions or to formalities for the registration of aliens;

(c) in respect of currency or exchange regulations, be accorded the same facilities as are customarily accorded to officials of international organisations;

(d) enjoy the right to import free of duty their furniture and effects at the time of first taking up their post in the country concerned, and the right to re-export free of duty their furniture and effects, on termination of their duties in that country, subject in either case to the conditions considered to be necessary by the Government of the country in which this right is exercised;

(e) have the right to import free of duty a motor car for their personal use, acquired either in the country of their last residence or in the country of which they are nationals on the terms ruling in the home market in that country, and to re-export it free of duty, subject in either case to the conditions considered to be necessary by the Government of the country concerned.

ARTICLE 13

Officials and other servants of the Communities shall be liable to a tax for the benefit of the Communities on salaries, wages and emoluments paid to them by the Communities, in accordance with the conditions and procedure laid down by the Council, acting on a proposal from the Commission.

They shall be exempt from national taxes on salaries, wages and emoluments paid by the Communities.

ARTICLE 14

In the application of income tax, wealth tax and death duties and in the applications of conventions on the avoidance of double taxation concluded between Member States of the Communities, officials and other servants of the Communities who, solely by reason of the performance of their duties in the service of the Communities, establish their residence in the territory of a Member State other than their country of domicile for tax purposes at the time of entering the service of the Communities, shall be considered, both in the country of their actual residence and in the country of domicile for tax purposes, as having maintained their domicile in the latter country provided that it is a member of the Communities. This provision shall also apply to a spouse to the extent that the latter is not separately engaged in a gainful occupation, and to children dependent on and in the care of the persons referred to in this Article.

Movable property belonging to persons referred to in the preceding paragraph and situated in the territory of the country where they are staying shall be exempt from death duties in that country; such property shall, for the assessment of such duty, be considered as being in the country of domicile for tax purposes, subject to the rights of third countries and to the possible application of provisions of international conventions on double taxation.

Any domicile acquired solely by reason of the performance of duties in the service of other international organisations shall not be taken into consideration in applying the provisions of this Article.

ARTICLE 15

The Council shall, acting unanimously on a proposal from the Commission, lay down the scheme of social security benefits for officials and other servants of the Communities.

ARTICLE 16

The Council shall, acting on a proposal from the Commission and after consulting the other institutions concerned, determine the categories of officials and other servants of the Communities to whom the provisions of Article 12, the second paragraph of Article 13, and Article 13 shall apply, in whole or in part.

The names, grades and addresses of officials and other servants included in such categories shall be communicated periodically to the Governments of the Member States.

CHAPTER VI—PRIVILEGES AND IMMUNITIES OF MISSIONS OF THIRD COUNTRIES ACCREDITED TO THE EUROPEAN COMMUNITIES

ARTICLE 17

The Member State in whose territory the Communities have their seat shall accord the customary diplomatic immunities and privileges to missions of third countries accredited to the Communities.

CHAPTER VII—GENERAL PROVISIONS

ARTICLE 18

Privileges, immunities and facilities shall be accorded to officials and other servants of the Communities solely in the interests of the Communities.

Each institution of the Communities shall be required to waive the immunity accorded to an official or other servant wherever that institution considers that the waiver of such immunity is not contrary to the interests of the Communities.

ARTICLE 19

The institutions of the Communities shall, for the purpose of applying this Protocol, cooperate with the responsible authorities of the Member States concerned.

ARTICLE 20

Articles 12 to 15 and Article 18 shall apply to members of the Commission.

ARTICLE 21

Articles 12 to 15 and Article 18 shall apply to the Judges, the Advocates-General, the Registrar and the Assistant Rapporteurs of the Court of Justice, without prejudice to the provisions of Article 3 of the Protocols on the Statute of the Court of Justice concerning immunity from legal proceedings of Judges and Advocates-General.

ARTICLE 22

This Protocol shall also apply to the European Investment Bank, to the members of its organs, to its staff and to the representatives of the Member States taking part in its activities, without prejudice to the provisions of the Protocol on the Statute of the Bank.

The European Investment Bank shall in addition be exempt from any form of taxation or imposition of a like nature on the occasion of any increase in its capital and from the various formalities which may be connected therewith in the State where the Bank has its seat. Similarly, its dissolution or liquidation shall not give rise to any imposition. Finally, the activities of the Bank and of its organs carried on in accordance with its Statute shall not be subject to any turnover tax.

IN WITNESS WHEREOF, the undersigned Plenipotentiaries have signed this Protocol.

DONE at Brussels this eighth day of April in the year one thousand nine hundred and sixty-five.

PAUL-HENRI SPAAK

KURT SCHMÜCKER

MAURICE COUVE DE MURVILLE

AMINTORE FANFANI

PIERRE WERNER

J. M. A. H. LUNS

Final Act

THE PLENIPOTENTIARIES of His Majesty the King of the Belgians, the President of the Federal Republic of Germany, the President of the French Republic, the President of the Italian Republic, His Royal Highness the Grand Duke of Luxembourg, Her Majesty the Queen of the Netherlands, ASSEMBLED at Brussels on 8 April 1965 for the signature of the Treaty establishing a Single Council and a Single Commission of the European Communities,

HAVE ADOPTED the following texts:

The Treaty establishing a Single Council and a Single Commission of the European Communities,

The Protocol on the Privileges and Immunities of the European Communities.

At the time of signature of these texts, the Plenipotentiaries have:

assigned to the Commission of the European Communities the task set out in Annex I; and

taken note of the Declaration by the Government of the Federal Republic of Germany set out in Annex II.

IN WITNESS WHEREOF, the undersigned Plenipotentiaries have signed this Final Act.

DONE at Brussels this eighth day of April in the year one thousand nine hundred and sixty-five.

> PAUL-HENRI SPAAK
>
> KURT SCHMÜCKER
>
> MAURICE COUVE DE MURVILLE
>
> AMINTORE FANFANI
>
> PIERRE WERNER
>
> J. M. A. H. LUNS

DECISION OF THE REPRESENTATIVES OF THE GOVERNMENTS OF THE MEMBER STATES ON THE PROVISIONAL LOCATION OF CERTAIN INSTITUTIONS AND DEPARTMENTS OF THE COMMUNITIES

The Representatives of the Governments of the Member States,

HAVING REGARD TO Article 37 of the Treaty establishing a Single Council and a Single Commission of the European Communities,

CONSIDERING that it is appropriate, at the time of setting up a single Council and a single Commission of the European Communities, in order to settle certain problems peculiar to the Grand Duchy of Luxembourg, to designate Luxembourg as the provisional place of work of certain institutions and departments, without prejudice to the application of Article 77 of the Treaty establishing the European Coal and Steel Community, Article 216 of the Treaty establishing the European Economic Community, Article 189 of the Treaty establishing the European Atomic Energy Community and of the second paragraph of Article 1 of the Protocol on the Statute of the European Investment Bank.

HAVE DECIDED:

ARTICLE 1

Luxembourg, Brussels and Strasbourg shall remain the provisional places of work of the institutions of the Communities.

ARTICLE 2

During the months of April, June and October, the Council shall hold its sessions in Luxembourg.

ARTICLE 3

The Court of Justice shall remain in Luxembourg.

There shall also be located in Luxembourg the judicial and quasi-judicial bodies, including those competent to apply the rules on competition, already existing or yet to be set up pursuant to the Treaties establishing the European Coal and Steel Community, the European Economic Community and the European Atomic Energy Community, or to conventions concluded with the framework of the Communities, whether between Member States or with third countries.

ARTICLE 4

The General Secretariat of the Assembly and its departments shall remain in Luxembourg.

ARTICLE 5

The European Investment Bank shall be located in Luxembourg, where its governing bodies shall meet and all its activities shall be carried on.

This provision relates in particular to the development of its present activities, especially those mentioned in Article 130 of the Treaty establishing the European Economic Community, to the possible extension of those activities to other fields and to such new tasks as may be assigned to the Bank.

An office for liaison between the Commission and the European Investment Bank shall be located in Luxembourg, with the particular task of facilitating the operations of the European Development Fund.

ARTICLE 6

The Monetary Committee shall meet in Luxembourg and in Brussels.

ARTICLE 7

The financial departments of the European Coal and Steel Community shall be located in Luxembourg. These comprise the Directorate-General for Credit and Investments, the department responsible for collecting the levy and the accounts departments attached thereto.

ARTICLE 8

An Official Publications Office of the European Communities with a joint sales office and a medium- long-term translation service attached shall be located in Luxembourg.

ARTICLE 9

Further, the following departments of the Commission shall be located in Luxembourg:
(a) The Statistical Office and the Data-processing Department;
(b) The hygiene and industrial safety departments of the European Economic Community and of the European Coal and Steel Community;
(c) The Directorate-General for the Dissemination of Information, the Directorate for Health Protection and the Directorate for Safeguards of the European Atomic Energy Community;
and the appropriate administrative and technical infrastructure.

ARTICLE 10

The Governments of the Member States are willing to locate in Luxembourg, or to transfer thereto, other Community bodies and departments, particularly those concerned with finance, provided that their proper functioning can be ensured.

To this end, they request the Commission to present to them annually a report on the current situation concerning the location of Community bodies and departments and on the possibility of taking new steps to give effect to this provision account being taken of the need to ensure the proper function of the Communities.

ARTICLE 11

In order to ensure the proper functioning of the European Coal and Steel Community, the Commission is requested to transfer the various departments in a gradual and coordinated manner, transferring last the departments which manage the coal and steel markets.

ARTICLE 12

Subject to the preceding provisions, this Decision shall not affect the provisional places of work of the institutions and departments of the European Communities, as determined by previous decisions of the Governments, nor the regrouping of departments occasioned by the establishing of a single Council and a single Commission.

ARTICLE 13

This Decision shall enter into force on the same date as the Treaty establishing a Single Council and a Single Commission of the European Communities.

DONE at Brussels this eighth day of April in the year one thousand nine hundred and sixty-five.

PAUL-HENRI SPAAK

KURT SCHMÜCKER

MAURICE COUVE DE MURVILLE

AMINTORE FANFANI

PIERRE WERNER

J. M. A. H. LUNS

THE LUXEMBOURG ACCORDS

At the extraordinary Council session of 28 and 29 January 1966 the Six reached agreement and the following statements were issued:

(a) Relations between the Commission and the Council.

Close co-operation between the Council and the Commission is essential for the functioning and development of the Community.

In order to improve and strengthen this co-operation at every level, the Council considers that the following practical methods of co-operation should be applied, these methods to be adopted by joint agreement, on the basis of Article 162 of the EEC Treaty, without compromising the respective competences and powers of the two Institutions.

1. Before adopting any particularly important proposal, it is desirable that the Commission should take up the appropriate contacts with the Governments of the Member States, through the Permanent Representatives, without this procedure compromising the right initiative which the Commission derives from the Treaty.

2. Proposals and any other official acts which the Commission submits to the Council and to the Member States are not to be made public until the recipients have had formal notice of them and are in possession of the texts.

The "Journal Officiel" (official gazette) should be arranged so as to show clearly which acts are of binding force. The methods to be employed for publishing those texts whose publication is required will be adopted in the context of the current work on the re-organisation of the "Journal Officiel."

3. The credentials of Heads of Missions of non-member states accredited to the Community will be submitted jointly to the President of the Council and to the President of the Commission, meeting together for this purpose.

4. The Council and the Commission will inform each other rapidly and fully of any approaches relating to fundamental questions made to either institution by the representatives of non-member states.

5. Within the scope of application of Article 162, the Council and the Commission will consult together on the advisability of, the procedure for, and the nature of any links which the Commission might establish with international organisations pursuant to Article 229 of the Treaty.

6. Co-operation between the Council and the Commission on the Community's information policy, which was the subject of the Council's discussions on 24 September 1963, will be strengthened in such a way that the programme of the Joint Information Service will be drawn up and carried out in accordance with procedures which are to be decided upon at a later date, and which may include the establishment of an *ad hoc* body.

7. Within the framework of the financial regulations relating to the drawing up and execution of the Communities' budgets, the Council and the Commission will decide on means for more effective control over the commitment and expenditure of Community funds.

(b) Majority voting procedure

I. Where, in the case of decisions which may be taken by majority vote on a proposal of the Commission, very important interests of one or more partners are at stake, the Members of the Council will endeavour, within a reasonable time, to reach solutions which can be adopted by all the Members of the Council while respecting their mutual interests and those of the Community, in accordance with Article 2 of the Treaty.

II. With regard to the preceding paragraph, the French delegation considers that where very important interests are at stake the discussion must be continued until unanimous agreement is reached.

III. The six delegations note that there is a divergence of views on what should be done in the event of a failure to reach complete agreement.

IV. The six delegations nevertheless consider that this divergence does not prevent the Community's work being resumed in accordance with the normal procedure.

The members of the Council agreed that decisions on the following should be by common consent:

(*a*) The financial regulation for agriculture;

(*b*) Extensions to the market organisation for fruit and vegetables;

(*c*) The regulation on the organisation of sugar markets;

(*d*) The regulation on the organisation of markets for oils and fats;

(*e*) The fixing of common prices for milk, beef and veal, rice, sugar, olive oil and oil seeds.

Finally the Council drew up the following programme of work:

(1) The draft EEC and Euratom budgets will be approved by written procedure before 15 February 1966.

(2) The EEC Council will meet as soon as possible to settle as a matter of priority the problem of financing the common agricultural policy. Concurrently, discussions will be resumed on the other questions, particularly the trade negotiations in GATT and the problems of adjusting national duties on imports from non-member countries.

(3) The Representatives of the Member States' Governments will meet on the day fixed for the next Council meeting and will begin discussions on the composition of the new single Commission and on the election of the President and Vice-Presidents.

They will also agree on the date—in the first half of 1966—when instruments of ratification of the Treaty on the merger of the institutions are to be deposited, on condition that the required parliamentary ratifications have been obtained and agreement has been reached on the composition and on the presidency and vice-presidency of the Commission.

DECISION OF 21 APRIL 1970 ON THE REPLACEMENT OF FINANCIAL CONTRIBUTIONS FROM MEMBER STATES BY THE COMMUNITIES' OWN RESOURCES

(70/243/ECSC/EEC/EURATOM; J.O. 1970, L94)

THE COUNCIL OF THE EUROPEAN COMMUNITIES,

HAVING REGARD to the Treaty establishing the European Economic Community, and in particular Article 201 thereof;

HAVING REGARD to the Treaty establishing the European Atomic Energy Community, and in particular Article 173 thereof;

HAVING REGARD to the proposal from the Commission;

HAVING REGARD to the Opinion of the European Parliament;

HAVING REGARD to the Opinion of the Economic and Social Committee;

WHEREAS complete replacement of the financial contributions from Member States by the Communities' own resources can only be achieved progressively;

WHEREAS Article 2 (1) of Regulation No. 25 on financing the common agricultural policy stipulates that at the single market stage revenue from agricultural levies shall be allocated to the Community and appropriated to Community expenditure;

WHEREAS Article 201 of the Treaty establishing the European Economic Community refers explicitly, among the Community's own resources which could replace financial contributions from Member States, to revenue accruing from the Common Customs Tariff when the latter has been finally introduced;

REPLACEMENT OF FINANCIAL PROVISIONS

WHEREAS the effects on the budgets of the Member States of the transfer to the Communities of revenue accruing from the Common Customs Tariff should be mitigated; whereas a system should be provided which will make it possible to achieve total transfer progressively and within a definite period of time;

WHEREAS revenue accruing from agricultural levies and customs duties is not sufficient to ensure that the budget of the Communities is in balance; whereas, therefore, it is advisable to allocate to the Communities, in addition, tax revenue, the most appropriate being that accruing from the application of a single rate to the basis for assessing the value added tax, determined in a uniform manner for the Member States;

HAS LAID DOWN THESE PROVISIONS, WHICH IT RECOMMENDS TO THE MEMBER STATES FOR ADOPTION:

ARTICLE 1

The Communities shall be allocated resources of their own in accordance with the following Articles in order to ensure that their budget is in balance.

ARTICLE 2

From 1 January 1971 revenue from:
- (a) levies, premiums, additional or compensatory amounts, additional amounts or factors and other duties established or to be established by the institutions of the Communities in respect of trade with non-member countries within the framework of the common agricultural policy, and also contributions and other duties provided for within the framework of the organisation of the markets in sugar (hereinafter called " agricultural levies ");
- (b) Common Customs Tariff duties and other duties established or to be established by the institutions of the Communities in respect of trade with non-member countries (hereinafter called " customs duties ");

shall, in accordance with Article 3, constitute own resources to be entered in the budget of the Communities.

In addition, revenue accruing from other charges introduced within the framework of a common policy in accordance with the provisions of the Treaty establishing the European Economic Community or the Treaty establishing the European Atomic Energy Community shall constitute own resources to be entered in the budget of the Communities, subject to the procedure laid down in Article 201 of the Treaty establishing the European [Economic Community or in Article 173 of the Treaty establishing the European Atomic] Energy Community having been followed.

CORRECTION

The words in square brackets do not appear in the Official Text but are included in Official Journal: see O.J. 1970 (I), 224.

ARTICLE 3

1. From 1 January 1971 the total revenue from agricultural levies shall be entered in the budget of the Communities.

From the same date, revenue from customs duties shall progressively be entered in the budget of the Communities.

The amount of the customs duties appropriated to the Communities each year by each Member State shall be equal to the difference between a reference amount and the amount of the agricultural levies appropriated to the Communities pursuant to the first subparagraph. Where this difference is negative, there shall be no payment of customs duties by the Member State concerned nor repayment of agricultural levies by the Communities.

The reference amount referred to in the third subparagraph shall be:

—50 per cent. in 1971
—62·5 per cent. in 1972
—75 per cent. in 1973
—87·5 per cent. in 1974
—100 per cent. from 1 January 1975 onwards

of the total amount of the agricultural levies and customs duties collected by each Member State.

251

The Communities shall refund to each Member State 10 per cent. of the amounts paid in accordance with the preceding subparagraphs in order to cover expense incurred in collection.

2. During the period 1 January 1971 to 31 December 1974 the financial contributions from Member States required in order to ensure that the budget of the Communities is in balance shall be apportioned on the following scale:

Belgium	6·8
Germany	32·9
France	32·6
Italy	20·2
Luxembourg	0·2
Netherlands	7·3

3. During the same period, however, the variation from year to year in the share of each Member State in the aggregate of the amounts paid in accordance with paragraphs 1 and 2 may not exceed 1 per cent. upwards of 1·5 per cent. downwards, where these amounts are taken into consideration within the framework of the second subparagraph. For 1971, the financial contributions of each Member State to the combined budgets for 1970 shall be taken as reference for the application of this rule, to the extent that these budgets are taken into consideration within the framework of the second subparagraph.

In the application of the first subparagraph, the following factors shall be taken into consideration for each financial year:

(a) Expenditure relating to payment appropriations decided on for the financial year in question for the research and investment budget of the European Atomic Energy Community, with the exception of expenditure relating to supplementary programmes;

(b) Expenditure relating to appropriations to the European Social Fund;

(c) For the European Agricultural Guidance and Guarantee Fund, expenditure relating to appropriations to the Guarantee Section and to the Guidance Section, with the exception of appropriations entered or re-entered for accounting periods preceding the financial year concerned.

For the reference year 1970 such expenditure shall be:

—for the Guarantee Section, that referred to in Article 8 of Council Regulation (EEC) No. 728/70 of 21 April 1970 laying down additional provisions for financing the common agricultural policy;

—for the Guidance Section, an amount of 285 million units of account apportioned on the basis of the scale laid down in Article 7 of that Regulation;

it being understood that, for calculating the share of Germany, a percentage of 31·5 shall be taken as the reference scale;

(d) Other expenditure relating to the appropriations entered in the Community budget.

Should the application of this paragraph to one or more Member States result in a deficit in the budget of the Communities, the amount of that deficit shall be shared for the year in question between the other Member States within the limits laid down in the first subparagraph and according to the contribution scale fixed in paragraph 2. If necessary, the operation shall be repeated.

4. Financing from the Communities' own resources of the expenditure connected with research programmes of the European Atomic Energy Community shall not exclude entry in the budget of the Communities of expenditure relating to supplementary programmes or the financing of such expenditure by means of financial contributions from Member States determined according to a special scale fixed pursuant to a decision of the Council acting unanimously.

5. By way of derogation from this Article, appropriations entered in a budget preceding that for the financial year 1971 and carried over or re-entered in a later budget shall be financed by financial contributions from Member States according to scales applicable at the time of their first entry.

Appropriations to the Guidance Section which, while being entered for the first time in the 1971 budget, refer to accounting periods of the European Agricultural Guidance and Guarantee Fund preceding 1 January 1971 shall be covered by the scale relating to those periods.

ARTICLE 4

1. From 1 January 1975 the budget of the Communities shall, irrespective of other revenue, be financed entirely from the Communities' own resources.

Such resources shall include those referred to in Article 2 and also those accruing from the value added tax and obtained by applying a rate not exceeding 1 per cent. to an assessment basis which is determined in a uniform manner for Member States according to Community rules. The rate shall be fixed within the framework of the budgetary procedure. If at the beginning of a financial year the budget has not yet been adopted, the rate previously fixed shall remain applicable until the entry into force of a new rate.

During the period 1 January 1975 to 31 December 1977, however, the variation from year to year in the share of each Member State in relation to the preceding year may not exceed 2 per cent. Should this percentage be exceeded, the necessary adjustments shall be made, within that variation limit, by financial compensation between the Member States concerned proportionate to the share borne by each of them in respect of revenue accruing from value added tax or from the financial contributions referred to in paragraphs 2 and 3.

2. By way of derogation from the second subparagraph of paragraph 1, if on 1 January 1975 the rules determining the uniform basis for assessing the value added tax have not yet been applied in all Member States but have been applied in at least three of them, the financial contribution to the budget of the Communities to be made by each Member State not yet applying the uniform basis for assessing the value added tax shall be determined according to the proportion of its gross national product to the sum total of the gross national products of the Member States. The balance of the budget shall be covered by revenue accruing from the value added tax in accordance with the second subparagraph of paragraph 1, collected by the other Member States. This derogation shall cease to be effective as soon as the conditions laid down in paragraph 1 are fulfilled.

3. By way of derogation from the second subparagraph of paragraph 1, if on 1 January 1975 the rules determining the uniform basis for assessing the value added tax have not yet been applied in three or more Member States, the financial contribution of each Member State to the budget of the Communities shall be determined according to the proportion of its gross national product to the sum total of the gross national products of the Member States. This derogation shall cease to be effective as soon as the conditions laid down in paragraphs 1 or 2 are fulfilled.

4. For the purpose of paragraphs 2 and 3, " gross national product " means the gross national product at market prices.

5. From the complete application of the second subparagraph of paragraph 1, any surplus of the Communities' own resources over and above the actual expenditure during a financial year shall be carried over to the following financial year.

6. Financing expenditure connected with research programmes of the European Atomic Energy Community from the Communities' own resources shall not exclude entry in the budget of the Communities of expenditure relating to supplementary programmes nor the financing of such expenditure by means of financial contributions from Member States determined according to a special scale fixed pursuant to a decision of the Council acting unanimously.

ARTICLE 5

The revenue referred to in Article 2, Article 3 (1) and (2) and Article 4 (1) to (5) shall be used without distinction to finance all expenditure entered in the budget of the Communities in accordance with Article 20 of the Treaty establishing a Single Council and a Single Commission of the European Communities.

ARTICLE 6

1. The Community resources referred to in Articles 2, 3 and 4 shall be collected by the Member States in accordance with national provisions imposed by law, regulation or administrative action, which shall, where necessary, be amended for that purpose. Member States shall make these resources available to the Commission.

2. Without prejudice to the auditing of accounts provided for in Article 206 of the Treaty establishing the European Economic Community, or to the inspection arrangements made pursuant to Article 209 (c) of that Treaty, the Council shall, acting unanimously on a proposal from the Commission and after consulting the European Parliament, adopt provisions relating to the supervision of collection, the making available to the Commission, and the payment of the revenue referred to in Articles 2, 3 and 4, and also the procedure for application of Article 3 (3) and Article 4.

ARTICLE 7

Member States shall be notified of this Decision by the Secretary-General of the Council of the European Communities; it shall be published in the *Official Journal of the European Communities*.

Member States shall notify the Secretary-General of the Council of the European Communities without delay of the completion of the procedures for the adoption of this Decision in accordance with their respective constitutional requirements.

This Decision shall enter into force on the first day of the month following receipt of the last of the notifications referred to in the second subparagraph. If, however, the instruments of ratification provided for in Article 12 of the Treaty amending Certain Budgetary Provisions of the

Treaties establishing the European Communities and the Treaty establishing a Single Council and a Single Commission of the European Communities, have not been deposited before that date by all the Member States, this Decision shall enter into force on the first day of the month following the deposit of the last of those instruments of ratification.

Done at Luxembourg, 21 April 1970.

For the Council
The President
P. HARMEL

TREATY AMENDING CERTAIN BUDGETARY PROVISIONS OF THE TREATIES ESTABLISHING THE EUROPEAN COMMUNITIES AND OF THE TREATY ESTABLISHING A SINGLE COUNCIL AND A SINGLE COMMISSION OF THE EUROPEAN COMMUNITIES

(LUXEMBOURG, 22 APRIL 1970)

HIS MAJESTY THE KING OF THE BELGIANS,

THE PRESIDENT OF THE FEDERAL REPUBLIC OF GERMANY,

THE PRESIDENT OF THE FRENCH REPUBLIC,

THE PRESIDENT OF THE ITALIAN REPUBLIC,

HIS ROYAL HIGHNESS THE GRAND DUKE OF LUXEMBOURG,

HER MAJESTY THE QUEEN OF THE NETHERLANDS,

HAVING REGARD to Article 96 of the Treaty establishing the European Coal and Steel Community;

HAVING REGARD to Article 236 of the Treaty establishing the European Economic Community;

HAVING REGARD to Article 204 of the Treaty establishing the European Atomic Energy Community;

CONSIDERING that the Communities will have at their disposal their own resources in order to cover their total expenditure;

CONSIDERING that the replacement of financial contributions of Member States by the Communities' own resources requires a strengthening of the budgetary powers of the Assembly;

RESOLVED to associate the Assembly closely in the supervision of the implementation of the budget of the Communities;

HAVE DECIDED to amend certain budgetary provisions of the Treaties establishing the European Communities and of the Treaty establishing a Single Council and a Single Commission of the European Communities and to this end have designated as their Plenipotentiaries:

HIS MAJESTY THE KING OF THE BELGIANS:
MR. Pierre HARMEL, Minister for Foreign Affairs;

THE PRESIDENT OF THE FEDERAL REPUBLIC OF GERMANY:
MR. Walter SCHEEL, Minister for Foreign Affairs;

THE PRESIDENT OF THE FRENCH REPUBLIC:
Mr. Maurice SCHUMANN, Minister for Foreign Affairs;

THE PRESIDENT OF THE ITALIAN REPUBLIC:
Mr. Aldo MORO, Minister for Foreign Affairs;

HIS ROYAL HIGHNESS THE GRAND DUKE OF LUXEMBOURG:
Mr. Gaston THORN, Minister for Foreign Affairs and for External Trade;

HER MAJESTY THE QUEEN OF THE NETHERLANDS:
Mr. H. J. DE KOSTER, Under-Secretary of State for Foreign Affairs;

WHO, having exchanged their Full Powers, found in good and due form,

HAVE AGREED as follows:

CHAPTER I—PROVISIONS AMENDING THE TREATY ESTABLISHING THE EUROPEAN COAL AND STEEL COMMUNITY

ARTICLE 1

[*This Article amends the ECSC Treaty, Art. 78, and is incorporated therein.*]

ARTICLE 2

[*This Article is incorporated in the ECSC Treaty, following Art. 78.*]

ARTICLE 3

[*This Article amends the ECSC Treaty, Art. 78d, and is incorporated therein.*]

CHAPTER II—PROVISIONS AMENDING THE TREATY ESTABLISHING THE EUROPEAN ECONOMIC COMMUNITY

ARTICLE 4

[*This Article amends the EEC Treaty, Art. 203, and is incorporated therein.*]

ARTICLE 5

[*This Article is incorporated in the EEC Treaty following Art. 203.*]

ARTICLE 6

[*This Article amends the EEC Treaty, Art. 206, and is incorporated therein.*]

CHPATER III—PROVISIONS AMENDING THE TREATY ESTABLISHING THE EUROPEAN ATOMIC ENERGY COMMUNITY

ARTICLE 7

[*This Article amends the Euratom Treaty, Art. 177, and is incorporated therein.*]

ARTICLE 8

[*This Article is incorporated in the Euratom Treaty, following Art.* 177.]

ARTICLE 9

[*This Article amends the Euratom Treaty, Art.* 180, *and is incorporated therein.*]

CHAPTER IV—PROVISIONS AMENDING THE TREATY ESTABLISHING A SINGLE COUNCIL AND A SINGLE COMMISSION OF THE EUROPEAN COMMUNITIES

ARTICLE 10

[*This Article amends the Merger Treaty, Art.* 20 (1), *and is incorporated therein.*]

CHAPTER V—FINAL PROVISIONS

ARTICLE 11

This Treaty shall be ratified by the High Contracting Parties in accordance with their respective constitutional requirements. The instruments of ratification shall be desposited with the Government of the Italian Republic.

ARTICLE 12

This Treaty shall enter into force on the first day of the month following the deposit of the instrument of ratification by the last signatory State to take this step.

If, however, the notification provided for in Article 7 of the Decision of 21 April 1970 on the replacement of financial contributions from Member States by the Communities' own resources has not been given before that date by all the signatory States, this Treaty shall enter into force on the first day of the month after the last notification has been given.

If this Treaty enters into force during the budgetary procedure, the Council shall, after consulting the Commission, lay down the measures required in order to facilitate the application of this Treaty to the remainder of the budgetary procedure.

ARTICLE 13

This Treaty, drawn up in a single original in the Dutch, French, German and Italian languages, all four texts being equally authentic, shall be deposited in the archives of the Government of the Italian Republic, which shall transmit a certified copy to each of the Governments of the other signatory States.

IN WITNESS WHEREOF, the undersigned Plenipotentiaries have signed this Treaty.

DONE at Luxembourg this twenty-second day of April in the year one thousand nine hundred and seventy.

Pierre HARMEL
Walter SCHEEL
Maurice SCHUMANN
Aldo MORO
Gaston THORN
H. J. de KOSTER

TREATY AMENDING CERTAIN FINANCIAL PROVISIONS OF THE TREATIES ESTABLISHING THE EUROPEAN ECONOMIC COMMUNITIES AND OF THE TREATY ESTABLISHING A SINGLE COUNCIL AND A SINGLE COMMISSION OF THE EUROPEAN COMMUNITIES

(BRUSSELS, JULY 22, 1975)

HIS MAJESTY THE KING OF THE BELGIANS,

HER MAJESTY THE QUEEN OF DENMARK,

THE PRESIDENT OF THE FEDERAL REPUBLIC OF GERMANY,

THE PRESIDENT OF THE FRENCH REPUBLIC,

THE PRESIDENT OF IRELAND,

THE PRESIDENT OF THE ITALIAN REPUBLIC,

HIS ROYAL HIGHNESS THE GRAND DUKE OF LUXEMBOURG,

HER MAJESTY THE QUEEN OF THE NETHERLANDS,

HER MAJESTY THE QUEEN OF THE UNITED KINGDOM OF GREAT BRITAIN AND NORTHERN IRELAND,

HAVING REGARD to Article 96 of the Treaty establishing the European Coal and Steel Community,

HAVING REGARD to Article 236 of the Treaty establishing the European Economic Community,

HAVING REGARD to Article 204 of the Treaty establishing the European Atomic Energy Community,

WHEREAS, as of January 1, 1975, the budget of the Communities is financed entirely from the Communities' own resources;

WHEREAS the complete replacement of financial contributions of Member States by the Communities' own resources requires a strengthening of the budgetary powers of the Assembly;

WHEREAS, for the same reasons, the implementation of the budget should be more closely supervised,

HAVE DECIDED to amend certain financial provisions of the Treaties establishing the European Communities and of the Treaty establishing a single Council and a single Commission of the European Communities, and to this end have designated as their Plenipotentiaries:

HIS MAJESTY THE KING OF THE BELGIANS:
R. Van Elslande, Minister for Foreign Affairs and for Co-operation with the Developing Countries:

HER MAJESTY THE QUEEN OF DENMARK:
Niels Ersbøll, Ambassador Extraordinary and Plenipotentiary, Permanent Representative to the European Communities;

THE PRESIDENT OF THE FEDERAL REPUBLIC OF GERMANY:
Hans-Dietrich Genscher, Federal Minister for Foreign Affairs;

THE PRESIDENT OF THE FRENCH REPUBLIC:
Jean-Marie Soutou, Ambassador of France, Permanent Representative to the European Communities;

THE PRESIDENT OF IRELAND:
Garret Fitzgerald, Minister for Foreign Affairs;

THE PRESIDENT OF THE ITALIAN REPUBLIC:
Mariano Rumor, Minister for Foreign Affairs, President-in-Office of the Council of the European Communities;

HIS ROYAL HIGHNESS THE GRAND DUKE OF LUXEMBOURG:
Jean Dondelinger, Ambassador Extraordinary and Plenipotentiary, Permanent Representative to the European Communities;

HER MAJESTY THE QUEEN OF THE NETHERLANDS:
L. J. Brinkhorst, State Secretary for Foreign Affairs;

HER MAJESTY THE QUEEN OF THE UNITED KINGDOM OF GREAT BRITAIN AND NORTHERN IRELAND:
Sir Michael Palliser, k.c.m.g., Ambassador Extraordinary and Plenipotentiary, Permanent Representative to the European Communities:

WHO, having exchanged their Full Powers, found in good and due form,

HAVE AGREED as follows:

CHAPTER I—PROVISIONS AMENDING THE TREATY ESTABLISHING THE EUROPEAN COAL AND STEEL COMMUNITY

Article 1

[*This article amends the ECSC Treaty, Art. 7, and is incorporated therein.*]

Article 2

[*This article amends the ECSC Treaty, Art. 78, and is incorporated therein.*]

Article 3

[*This article amends the ECSC Treaty, Art. 78a, and is incorporated therein.*]

Article 4

[*This article amends the ECSC Treaty, Art. 78b, and is incorporated therein.*]

Article 5

[*This article amends the ECSC Treaty, Art. 78c, and is incorporated therein.*]

Article 6

[*This article amends the ECSC Treaty, Art. 78d, and is incorporated therein.*]

Article 7

[*This article amends the ECSC Treaty, Art. 78e, and is incorporated therein.*]

Article 8

[*This article amends the ECSC Treaty, Art. 78f, and is incorporated therein.*]

Article 9

[*This article is incorporated in the ECSC Treaty following Art. 78f.*]

Article 10

[*This article is incorporated in the ECSC Treaty following Art. 78f.*]

CHAPTER II—PROVISIONS AMENDING THE TREATY ESTABLISHING THE EUROPEAN ECONOMIC COMMUNITY

Article 11

[*This article amends the EEC Treaty, Art. 4, and is incorporated therein.*]

Article 12

[*This article amends the EEC Treaty, Art. 203, and is incorporated therein.*]

Article 13

[*This article amends the EEC Treaty, Art. 204, and is incorporated therein.*]

Article 14

[*This article is incorporated in the EEC Treaty following Art. 205.*]

Article 15

[*This article amends the EEC Treaty, Art. 206, and is incorporated therein.*]

Article 16

[*This article is incorporated in the EEC Treaty following Art. 206.*]

Article 17

[This article is incorporated in the EEC Treaty following Art. 206.]

Article 18

[This article amends the EEC Treaty, Art. 209, and is incorporated therein.]

CHAPTER III—PROVISIONS AMENDING THE TREATY ESTABLISHING THE EUROPEAN ATOMIC ENERGY COMMUNITY

Article 19

[This article amends the Euratom Treaty, Art. 3, and is incorporated therein.]

Article 20

[This article amends the Euratom Treaty, Art. 177, and is incorporated therein.]

Article 21

[This article amends the Euratom Treaty, Art. 178, and is incorporated therein.]

Article 22

[This article is incorporated in the Euratom Treaty following Art. 179.]

Article 23

[This article amends the Euratom Treaty, Art. 180, and is incorporated therein.]

Article 24

[This article is incorporated in the Euratom Treaty following Art. 180.]

Article 25

[This article is incorporated in the Euratom Treaty following Art. 180.]

Article 26

[This article amends the Euratom Treaty, Art. 183, and is incorporated therein.]

CHAPTER IV—PROVISIONS AMENDING THE TREATY ESTABLISHING A SINGLE COUNCIL AND A SINGLE COMMISSION OF THE EUROPEAN COMMUNITIES

Article 27

[This article amends the Merger Treaty, Art. 22, and is incorporated therein.]

261

CHAPTER V—FINAL PROVISIONS

ARTICLE 28

1. The Members of the Court of Auditors shall be appointed upon the entry into force of this Treaty.

2. The terms of office of the members of the Audit Board and that of the auditor shall expire on the day they submit their report on the financial year preceding that in which the members of the Court of Auditors are appointed; their powers of audit shall be confined to operations relating to that Financial year.

ARTICLE 29

This Treaty shall be ratified by the High Contracting Parties in accordance with their respective constitutional requirements. The instruments of ratification shall be deposited with the Government of the Italian Republic.

ARTICLE 30

This Treaty shall enter into force on the first day of the month following the deposit of the instrument of ratification by the last signatory State to take this step.

If this Treaty enters into force during the budgetary procedure, the Council shall, after consulting the Assembly and the Commission, adopt the measures required in order to facilitate the application of this Treaty to the remainder of the budgetary procedure.

ARTICLE 31

This Treaty, drawn up in a single original in the Danish, Dutch, English, French, German, Irish and Italian languages, all seven texts being authentic, shall be deposited in the archives of the Government of the Italian Republic, which shall transmit a certified copy to each of the Governments of the other signatory States.

IN WITNESS WHEREOF, the undersigned Plenipotentiaries have affixed their signatures below this Treaty.

DONE at Brussels on the twenty-second day of July in the year one thousand nine hundred and seventy-five.

> R. VAN ELSLANDE
> Niels ERSBØLL
> Hans-Dietrich GENSCHER
> Jean-Marie SOUTOU
> Garret FITZGERALD
> Mariano RUMOR
> Jean DONDELINGER
> L. J. BRINKHORST
> Sir Michael PALLISER, K.C.M.G.

TREATY AMENDING CERTAIN PROVISIONS OF THE PROTOCOL ON THE STATUTE OF THE EUROPEAN INVESTMENT BANK

(BRUSSELS, JULY 10, 1975)

HER MAJESTY THE KING OF THE BELGIANS,
HER MAJESTY THE QUEEN OF DENMARK,
THE PRESIDENT OF THE FEDERAL REPUBLIC OF GERMANY,
THE PRESIDENT OF THE FRENCH REPUBLIC,
THE PRESIDENT OF IRELAND,
THE PRESIDENT OF THE ITALIAN REPUBLIC,
HIS ROYAL HIGHNESS THE GRAND DUKE OF LUXEMBOURG,
HER MAJESTY THE QUEEN OF THE NETHERLANDS,
HER MAJESTY THE QUEEN OF THE UNITED KINGDOM OF GREAT BRITAIN AND NORTHERN IRELAND,

HAVING REGARD to Article 236 of the Treaty establishing the European Economic Community,

WHEREAS the Protocol on the Statute of the European Investment Bank which is annexed to the Treaty establishing the European Economic Community is an integral part thereof;

WHEREAS the definition of the unit of account and the methods of conversion as between this unit and the currencies of the Member States contained in the present text of the second sub-paragraph of Article 4 (1), and in Article 7 (3) and (4) of the Statute of the Bank are no longer entirely in keeping with the circumstances of international monetary relations;

WHEREAS the future evolution of the international monetary system cannot be foreseen; whereas, consequently, rather than adopting immediately a new definition of the unit of account in the Statute of the Bank, it is desirable, particularly taking into account the position of the unit of account and the methods of conversion to changes, where necessary and on appropriate conditions;

WHEREAS, in order to permit this rapid and flexible adaptation it is appropriate to give the Board of Governors of the Bank powers to alter, if necessary, the definition of the unit of account and the methods of conversion as between the unit of account and the various currencies;

HAVE DECIDED to amend certain provisions of the Protocol on the Statute of the European Investment Bank, hereinafter called " the Protocol," and to this end have designated as their Plenipotentiaries:

HIS MAJESTY THE KING OF THE BELGIANS:
Willy DE CLERCQ, Minister of Finance;
HER MAJESTY THE QUEEN OF DENMARK:
Per HAEKKERUP, Minister for Economic Affairs;
THE PRESIDENT OF THE FEDERAL REPUBLIC OF GERMANY:
Dr Hans APEL, Federal Minister of Finance;
THE PRESIDENT OF THE FRENCH REPUBLIC:
Jean-Pierre FOURCADE, Minister for Economic Affairs and Finance;
THE PRESIDENT OF IRELAND:
Charles MURRAY, Secretary, Department of Finance of Ireland;
THE PRESIDENT OF THE ITALIAN REPUBLIC:
Emilio COLOMBO, Minister of the Treasury;

HIS ROYAL HIGHNESS THE GRAND DUKE OF LUXEMBOURG:
Jean Dondelinger, Ambassador Extraordinary and Plenipotentiary, Permanent Representative to the European Communities;
HER MAJESTY THE QUEEN OF THE NETHERLANDS:
L. J. Brinkhorst, State Secretary for Foreign Affairs;
HER MAJESTY THE QUEEN OF THE UNITED KINGDOM OF
GREAT BRITAIN AND NORTHERN IRELAND:
Sir Michael Palliser, KCMG, Ambassador Extraordinary and Plenipotentiary, Permanent Representative to the European Communities;

WHO, having exchanged their Full Powers, found in good and due form,

HAVE AGREED AS FOLLOWS:

Article 1–3

[*These articles amend the Protocol on the Statue of the European Investment Bank and are incorporated therein.*]

Article 4

This Treaty will be ratified by the High Contracting Parties in accordance with their respective constitutional requirements. The instruments of ratification will be deposited with the Government of the Italian Republic.

Article 5

This Treaty shall enter into force on the first day of the month following the deposit of the instrument of ratification by the last signatory State to take this step.

Article 6

This Treaty, drawn up in a single original in the Danish, Dutch, English, French, German, Irish and Italian languages, all seven texts being authentic, shall be deposited in the archives of the Government of the Italian Republic, which will transmit a certified copy to each of the Governments of the other signatory States.

IN WITNESS WHEREOF, the undersigned Plenipotentiaries have affixed their signatures below this Treaty.

DONE at Brussels on the tenth day of July in the year one thousand nine hundred and seventy-five.

Part V
ACCESSION

COMMISSION OPINION OF 19 JANUARY 1972 ON THE APPLICATIONS FOR ACCESSION TO THE EUROPEAN COMMUNITIES BY THE KINGDOM OF DENMARK, IRELAND, THE KINGDOM OF NORWAY AND THE UNITED KINGDOM OF GREAT BRITAIN AND NORTHERN IRELAND

THE COMMISSION OF THE EUROPEAN COMMUNITIES,

having regard to Article 98 of the Treaty establishing the European Coal and Steel Community, Article 237 of the Treaty establishing the European Economic Community and Article 205 of the Treaty establishing the European Atomic Energy Community;

whereas the Kingdom of Denmark, Ireland, the Kingdom of Norway and the United Kingdom of Great Britain and Northern Ireland have applied to become members of these Communities;

whereas in its Opinions of 29 September 1967 and 1 October 1969 the Commission has already been able to express its views on certain essential aspects of the problems arising in connection with these applications;

whereas the terms for the admission of these States and the adjustments necessitated by their accession have been negotiated in a Conference between the Communities and the applicant States; and whereas singleness of Community representation was ensured with due regard for the institutional dialogue provided for by the Treaties;

whereas, on the completion of these negotiations, it is apparent that the provisions so agreed are fair and proper; and whereas, this being so, the Community's enlargement, while preserving its internal cohesion and dynamism, will enable it to take a fuller part in the development of international relations;

whereas in joining the Communities the applicant States accept without reserve the Treaties and their political objectives, all decisions taken since their entry into force, and the action that has been agreed in respect of the development and reinforcement of the Communities;

whereas it is an essential feature of the legal system set up by the Treaties establishing the Communities that certain of their provisions and certain acts of the Community institutions are directly applicable, that Community law takes precedence over any national provisions conflicting with it, and that procedures exist for ensuring the uniform interpretation of this law, and whereas accession to the Communities entails recognition of the binding force of these rules, observance of which is indispensable to guarantee the effectiveness and unity of Community law,

HEREBY DELIVERS A FAVOURABLE OPINION

on the accession to the European Communities of the Kingdom of Denmark, Ireland, the Kingdom of Norway and the United Kingdom of Great Britain and Northern Ireland.

This Opinion is addressed to the Council.

Brussels, 19 January 1972

> *For the Commission*
> *The President*
> Franco M. MALFATTI

DECISION OF THE COUNCIL OF THE EUROPEAN COMMUNITIES OF 22 JANUARY 1972 CONCERNING THE ACCESSION OF THE KINGDOM OF DENMARK, IRELAND, THE KINGDOM OF NORWAY AND THE UNITED KINGDOM OF GREAT BRITAIN AND NORTHERN IRELAND TO THE EUROPEAN COAL AND STEEL COMMUNITY

THE COUNCIL OF THE EUROPEAN COMMUNITIES,

HAVING REGARD to Article 98 of the Treaty establishing the European Coal and Steel Community,

Part V—Accession

WHEREAS the Kingdom of Denmark, Ireland, the Kingdom of Norway and the United Kingdom of Great Britain and Northern Ireland have applied to accede to the European Coal and Steel Community,

HAVING REGARD to the Opinion of the Commission,

WHEREAS the conditions of accession to be determined by the Council have been negotiated with the aforementioned States,

HAS DECIDED AS FOLLOWS:

Article 1

1. The Kingdom of Denmark, Ireland, the Kingdom of Norway and the United Kingdom of Great Britain and Northern Ireland may become members of the European Coal and Steel Community by acceding, under the conditions laid down in this Decision, to the Treaty establishing that Community, as amended or supplemented.

2. The conditions of accession and the adjustments to the Treaty establishing the European Coal and Steel Community necessitated thereby are set out in the Act annexed to this Decision. The provisions of that Act concerning the European Coal and Steel Community shall form an integral part of this Decision.

3. The provisions concerning the rights and obligations of the Member States and the powers and jurisdiction of the institutions of the Community as set out in the Treaty referred to in paragraph 1 shall apply in respect of this Decision.

Article 2

The instruments of accession of the Kingdom of Denmark, Ireland, the Kingdom of Norway and the United Kingdom of Great Britain and Northern Ireland to the European Coal and Steel Community will be deposited with the Government of the French Republic on 1 January 1973.

Accession will take effect on 1 January 1973, provided that all the instruments of accession have been deposited on that date and that all the instruments of ratification of the Treaty concerning Accession to the European Economic Community and the European Atomic Energy Community have been deposited before that date.

If, however, the States referred to in the first paragraph of this Article have not all deposited their instruments of accession and ratification in due time, accession shall take effect for the other acceding States. In this case, the Council of the European Communities, acting unanimously, shall decide, immediately upon such resulting adjustments as have become indispensable, to Article 3 of this Decision, and Articles 12, 13, 16, 17, 19, 20, 22, 142,155 and 160 of the Act concerning the Conditions of Accession and the Adjustments to the Treaties; acting unanimously, it may also declare that those provisions of the aforementioned Act which refer expressly to a State which has not deposited its instruments of accession and ratification have lapsed, or it may adjust them.

The Government of the French Republic will transmit a certified copy of the instrument of accession of each Acceding State to the Governments of the Member States and of the other acceding States.

Article 3

[This Decision, drawn up in the Danish, Dutch, English, French, German, Irish, Italian and Norwegian languages, the Danish, Dutch, English, French, German, Irish and Italian texts all being equally authentic, shall be communicated to the Member States of the European Coal and Steel Community, the Kingdom of Denmark, Ireland, the Kingdom of Norway and the United Kingdom of Great Britain and Northern Ireland.]

Amendment
This Article was substituted by the Adaptation Decision, Art. 2.

Done at Brussels, 22 January 1972
For the Council

The President

DECISION OF THE COUNCIL OF THE EUROPEAN COMMUNITIES OF 22 JANUARY 1972 ON THE ACCESSION OF THE KINGDOM OF DENMARK, IRELAND, THE KINGDOM OF NORWAY AND THE UNITED KINGDOM OF GREAT BRITAIN AND NORTHERN IRELAND TO THE EUROPEAN ECONOMIC COMMUNITY AND TO THE EUROPEAN ATOMIC ENERGY COMMUNITY

THE COUNCIL OF THE EUROPEAN COMMUNITIES,

having regard to Article 237 of the Treaty establishing the European Economic Community and Article 205 of the Treaty establishing the European Atomic Energy Community;

whereas the Kingdom of Denmark, Ireland, the Kingdom of Norway and the United Kingdom of Great Britain and Northern Ireland have applied to accede to the European Economic Community and to the European Atomic Energy Community;

having obtained the Opinion of the Commission,

HAS DECIDED

to accept these applications for accession; the conditions of admission and the adjustments to the Treaties necessitated thereby are to be the subject of an agreement between the Member States and the Applicant States.

Done at Brussels, 22 January 1972

For the Council
The President
G. THORN

TREATY BETWEEN THE KINGDOM OF BELGIUM, THE FEDERAL REPUBLIC OF GERMANY, THE FRENCH REPUBLIC, THE ITALIAN REPUBLIC, THE GRAND DUCHY OF LUXEMBOURG, THE KINGDOM OF THE NETHERLANDS (MEMBER STATES OF THE EUROPEAN COMMUNITIES), THE KINGDOM OF DENMARK, IRELAND, THE KINGDOM OF NORWAY AND THE UNITED KINGDOM OF GREAT BRITAIN AND NORTHERN IRELAND CONCERNING THE ACCESSION OF THE KINGDOM OF DENMARK, IRELAND, THE KINGDOM OF NORWAY AND THE UNITED KINGDOM OF GREAT BRITAIN AND NORTHERN IRELAND TO THE EUROPEAN ECONOMIC COMMUNITY AND THE EUROPEAN ATOMIC ENERGY COMMUNITY

(Brussels, 22 January 1972)

Treaty between the Kingdom of Belgium, the Federal Republic of Germany, the French Republic, the Italian Republic, the Grand Duchy of Luxembourg, the Kingdom of the Netherlands, Member States of the European Communities, the Kingdom of Denmark, Ireland, the Kingdom of Norway, and the United Kingdom of Great Britain and Northern Ireland concerning the accession of the Kingdom of Denmark, Ireland, the Kingdom of Norway and the United Kingdom of Great Britain and Northern Ireland to the European Economic Community and to the European Atomic Energy Community

HIS MAJESTY THE KING OF THE BELGIANS, HER MAJESTY THE QUEEN OF DENMARK, THE PRESIDENT OF THE FEDERAL REPUBLIC OF GERMANY, THE PRESIDENT OF THE FRENCH REPUBLIC, THE PRESIDENT OF IRELAND, THE PRESIDENT OF THE ITALIAN REPUBLIC, HIS ROYAL HIGHNESS THE GRAND DUKE OF LUXEMBOURG, HER MAJESTY THE QUEEN OF THE NETHERLANDS, HIS MAJESTY THE KING OF NORWAY, HER MAJESTY THE QUEEN OF THE UNITED KINGDOM OF GREAT BRITAIN AND NORTHERN IRELAND

UNITED in their desire to pursue the attainment of the objectives of the Treaty establishing the European Economic Community and the Treaty establishing the European Atomic Energy Community,

DETERMINED in the spirit of those Treaties to construct an ever closer union among the peoples of Europe on the foundations already laid,

CONSIDERING that Article 237 of the Treaty establishing the European Economic Community and Article 205 of the Treaty establishing the European Atomic Energy Community afford European States the opportunity of becoming members of these Communities,

270

CONSIDERING that the Kingdom of Denmark, Ireland, the Kingdom of Norway and the United Kingdom of Great Britain and Northern Ireland have applied to become members of these Communities,

CONSIDERING that the Council of the European Communities, after having obtained the Opinion of the Commission, has declared itself in favour of the admission of these States,

HAVE DECIDED to establish by common agreement the conditions of admission and the adjustments to be made to the Treaties establishing the European Economic Community and the European Atomic Energy Community, and to this end have designated as their Plenipotentiaries:

HIS MAJESTY THE KING OF THE BELGIANS
    Mr. G. Eyskens, Prime Minister:
    Mr. P. Harmel, Minister of Foreign Affairs:
    Mr. J. van der Meulen, Ambassador,
        Permanent Representative to the European Communities:

HER MAJESTY THE QUEEN OF DENMARK
    Mr. J. O. Krag, Prime Minister:
    Mr. I. Nørgaard, Minister of External Economic Affairs:
    Mr. J. Christensen,
        Secretary General for External Economic Affairs,
        Ministry of Foreign Affairs:

THE PRESIDENT OF THE FEDERAL REPUBLIC OF GERMANY
    Mr. W. Scheel, Minister of Foreign Affairs:
    Mr. H.-G. Sachs, Ambassador,
        Permanent Representative to the European Communities:

THE PRESIDENT OF THE FRENCH REPUBLIC
    Mr. M. Schumann, Minister of Foreign Affairs:
    Mr. J.-M. Boegner, Ambassador,
        Permanent Representative to the European Communities:

THE PRESIDENT OF IRELAND
    Mr. J. A. Lynch, Prime Minister:
    Mr. P. J. Hillery, Minister for Foreign Affairs:

THE PRESIDENT OF THE ITALIAN REPUBLIC
    Mr. E. Colombo, Prime Minister:
    Mr. A. Moro, Minister for Foreign Affairs:
    Mr. G. Bombassei Frascani de Vettor, Ambassador,
        Permanent Representative to the European Communities:

HIS ROYAL HIGHNESS THE GRAND DUKE OF LUXEMBOURG
    Mr. G. Thorn, Minister of Foreign Affairs:
    Mr. J. Dondelinger, Ambassador,
        Permanent Representative to the European Communities:

HER MAJESTY THE QUEEN OF THE NETHERLANDS
    Mr. W. K. N. Schmelzer, Minister of Foreign Affairs:
    Mr. T. E. Westerterp, State Secretary,
        Ministry of Foreign Affairs:
    Mr. E. M. J. A. Sassen, Ambassador,
        Permanent Representative to the European Communities:

271

HIS MAJESTY THE KING OF NORWAY
Mr. T. Bratteli, Prime Minister:
Mr. A. Cappelen, Minister of Foreign Affairs:
Mr. S. Chr. Sommerfelt, Ambassador Extraordinary and Plenipotentiary:

HER MAJESTY THE QUEEN OF THE UNITED KINGDOM OF
GREAT BRITAIN AND NORTHERN IRELAND
The Right Honourable Edward Heath, M.B.E., M.P.,
Prime Minister,
First Lord of the Treasûry, Minister for the Civil Service:
The Right Honourable Sir Alec Douglas-Home, K.T., M.P.,
Her Majesty's Principal Secretary of State for Foreign and Com-
monwealth Affairs:
The Right Honourable Geoffrey Rippon, Q.C., M.P.,
Chancellor of the Duchy of Lancaster:

WHO, having exchanged their Full Powers found in good and due form,
HAVE AGREED as follows:

ARTICLE 1

1. The Kingdom of Denmark, Ireland, the Kingdom of Norway and the
United Kingdom of Great Britain and Northern Ireland hereby become members of the European Economic Community and of the European Atomic
Energy Community and Parties to the Treaties establishing these Communities
as amended or supplemented.

2. The conditions of admission and the adjustments to the Treaties
establishing the European Economic Community and the European Atomic
Energy Community necessitated thereby are set out in the Act annexed to this
Treaty. The provisions of that Act concerning the European Economic Community and the European Atomic Energy Community shall form an integral
part of this Treaty.

3. The provisions concerning the rights and obligations of the Member
States and the powers and jurisdiction of the institutions of the Communities as
set out in the Treaties referred to in paragraph 1 shall apply in respect of this
Treaty.

ARTICLE 2

This Treaty will be ratified by the High Contracting Parties in accordance
with their respective constitutional requirements. The instruments of ratification will be deposited with the Government of the Italian Republic by 31
December 1972 at the latest.

This Treaty will enter into force on 1 January 1973, provided that all the instruments of ratification have been deposited before that date and that all the
instruments of accession to the European Coal and Steel Community are
deposited on that date.

If, however, the States referred to in Article 1 (1) have not all deposited their
instruments of ratification and accession in due time, the Treaty shall enter into
force for those States which have deposited their instruments. In this case, the
Council of the European Communities, acting unanimously, shall decide
immediately upon such resulting adjustments as have become indispensable, to
Article 3 of this Treaty, and to Articles 14, 16, 17, 19, 20, 23, 129, 142, 143,
155 and 160 of the Act concerning the Conditions of Accession and the

Adjustments to the Treaties, to the provisions of Annex I to that Act concerning the composition and functioning of various committees, and to Articles 5 and 8 of the Protocol on the Statute of the European Investment Bank; acting unanimously, it may also declare that those provisions of the aforementioned Act which refer expressly to a State which has not deposited its instruments of ratification and accession have lapsed, or it may adjust them.

ARTICLE 3

[This Treaty, drawn up in a single original in the Danish, Dutch, English, French, German, Irish, Italian and Norwegian languages, the Danish, Dutch, English, French, German, Irish and Italian texts all being equally authentic, will be deposited in the archives of the Government of the Italian Republic, which will transmit a certified copy to each of the Governments of the other signatory States.]

AMENDMENT
This Article was substituted by the Adaptation Decision, Art. 1.

IN WITNESS WHEREOF, the undersigned Plenipotentiaries have affixed their signatures below this Treaty.

DONE at Brussels on this twenty-second day of January in the year one thousand nine hundred and seventy-two.

G. EYSKENS	COLOMBO
P. HARMEL	Aldo MORO
J. VAN DER MEULEN	Bombassei de VETTOR
Ivar NØRGAARD	Gaston THORN
Jens CHRISTENSEN	J. DONDELINGER
Jens Otto KRAG	
Walter SCHEEL	N. SCHMELZER
H.-G. SACHS	T. WESTERTERP
	SASSEN
Maurice SCHUMANN	Trygve BRATTELI
J.-M. BOEGNER	Andreas CAPPELEN
	S. Chr. SOMMERFELT
Seán Ó LOINSIGH	Edward HEATH
Pádraig Ó HIRIGHILE	Alec DOUGLAS-HOME
	Geoffrey RIPPON

ACT CONCERNING THE CONDITIONS OF ACCESSION AND THE ADJUSTMENTS TO THE TREATIES

Text of Act

Part One

PRINCIPLES

ARTICLE 1

For the purposes of this Act:
—the expression " original Treaties " means the Treaty establishing the European Coal and Steel Community, the Treaty establishing the European Economic Community and the Treaty establishing the European Atomic Energy Community, as supplemented or amended by treaties or other acts which entered into force before accession; the expressions " ECSC Treaty ", " EEC Treaty " and " Euratom Treaty " mean the relevant original Treaties thus supplemented or amended;
—the expression " original Member States " means the Kingdom of Belgium, the Federal Republic of Germany, the French Republic, the Italian Republic, the Grand Duchy of Luxembourg and the Kingdom of the Netherlands;
—[the expression " new Member States " means the Kingdom of Denmark, Ireland and the United Kingdom of Great Britain and Northern Ireland].

AMENDMENT
The third indent was substituted by the Adaptation Decision, Art. 3.

ARTICLE 2

From the date of accession, the provisions of the original Treaties and the acts adopted by the institutions of the Communities shall be binding on the new Member States and shall apply in those States under the conditions laid down in those Treaties and in this Act.

ARTICLE 3

1. The new Member States accede by this Act to the decisions and agreements adopted by the Representatives of the Governments of the Member States meeting in Council. They undertake to accede from the date of accession to all other agreements concluded by the original Member States relating to the functioning of the Communities or connected with their activities.

2. The new Member States undertake to accede to the conventions provided for in Article 220 of the EEC Treaty, and to the protocols on the interpretation of those conventions by the Court of Justice, signed by the original Member States, and to this end they undertake to enter into negotiations with the original Member States in order to make the necessary adjustments thereto.

274

3. The new Member States are in the same situation as the original Member States in respect of declarations or resolutions of, or other positions taken up by, the Council and in respect of those concerning the European Communities adopted by common agreement of the Member States; they will accordingly observe the principles and guidelines deriving from those declarations, resolutions or other positions and will take such measures as may be necessary to ensure their implementation.

ARTICLE 4

1. The agreements or conventions entered into by any of the Communities with one or more third States, with an international organisation or with a national of a third State, shall, under the conditions laid down in the original Treaties and in this Act, be binding on the new Member States.

2. The new Member States undertake to accede, under the conditions laid down in this Act, to agreements or conventions concluded by the original Member States and any of the Communities, acting jointly, and to agreements concluded by the original Member States which are related to those agreements or conventions. The Community and the original Member States shall assist the new Member States in this respect.

3. The new Member States accede by this Act and under the conditions laid down therein to the internal agreements concluded by the original Member States for the purpose of implementing the agreements or conventions referred to in paragraph 2.

4. The new Member States shall take appropriate measures, where necessary, to adjust their positions in relation to international organisations and international agreements to which one of the Communities or to which other Member States are also parties, to the rights and obligations arising from their accession to the Communities.

ARTICLE 5

Article 234 of the EEC Treaty and Articles 105 and 106 of the Euratom Treaty shall apply, for the new Member States, to agreements or conventions concluded before accession.

ARTICLE 6

The provisions of this Act may not, unless otherwise provided herein, be suspended, amended or repealed other than by means of the procedure laid down in the original Treaties enabling those Treaties to be revised.

ARTICLE 7

Acts adopted by the institutions of the Communities to which the transitional provisions laid down in this Act relate shall retain their status in law; in particular, the procedures for amending those acts shall continue to apply.

ARTICLE 8

Provisions of this Act the purpose or effect of which is to repeal or amend acts adopted by the institutions of the Communities, otherwise than as a transitional measure, shall have the same status in law as the provisions which they repeal or amend and shall be subject to the same rules as those provisions.

ARTICLE 9

1. In order to facilitate the adjustment of the new Member States to the rules in force within the Communities, the application of the original Treaties and acts adopted by the institutions shall, as a transitional measure, be subject to the derogations provided for in this Act.

2. Subject to the dates, time limits and special provisions provided for in this Act, the application of the transitional measures shall terminate at the end of 1977.

Part Two

ADJUSTMENTS TO THE TREATIES

TITLE I—PROVISIONS GOVERNING THE INSTITUTIONS

CHAPTER 1—THE ASSEMBLY

ARTICLE 10

[*This Article amends the Merger Treaty, Art.* 21 (2), *the EEC Treaty, Art.* 138 (2), *and the Euratom Treaty, Art.* 108 (2), *and is incorporated therein.*]

CHAPTER 2—THE COUNCIL

ARTICLE 11

[*This Article amends the Merger Treaty, Art.* 2(2), *and is incorporated therein.*]

ARTICLE 12

[*This Article amends the ECSC Treaty, Art.* 28, *and is incorporated therein.*]

ARTICLE 13

[*This Article amends the ECSC Treaty, Art.* 95 (4), *and is incorporated therein.*]

ARTICLE 14

[*This Article amends the ECSC Treaty, Art.* 148 (2), *and the Euratom Traety, Art.* 118 (2), *and is incorporated therein.*]

CHAPTER 3—THE COMMISSION

ARTICLE 15

[*This Article amends the Merger Treaty, Art.* 10 (1), *subpara.* 1, *and is incorporated therein.*]

ARTICLE 16

[*This Article amends the Merger Treaty, Art.* 14 (1), *and is incorporated therein.*]

276

CHAPTER 4—THE COURT OF JUSTICE

Article 17

[*This Article amends the ECSC Treaty, Art.* 32a (1), *the EEC Treaty, Art.* 165 (1), *and the Euratom Treaty, Art.* 137 (1), *and is incorporated therein.*]

Article 18

[*This Article amends the ECSC Treaty, Art.* 32a (1), *the EEC Treaty Art.* 166 (1), *and the Euratom Treaty, Art.* 138 (1), *and is incorporated therein.*]

Article 19

[*This Article amends the ECSC Treaty, Art.* 32b (2) *and* (3), *the EEC Treaty, Art.* 167 (2) *and* (3), *and the Euratom Treaty, Art.* 139 (2) *and* (3), *and is incorporated therein.*]

Article 20

[*This Article amends the Protocol on the Statute of the Courts of Justice of the ECSC, Art.* 18, *the Protocol on the Statute of the Court of Justice of the EEC, Art.* 15, *and the Protocol on the Statute of the Court of Justice of the Euratom, Art.* 15, *and is incorporated therein.*]

CHAPTER 5—THE ECONOMIC AND SOCIAL COMMITTEE

Article 21

[*This Article amends the EEC Treaty, Art.* 194 (1), *and the Euratom Treaty, Art.* 166 (1), *and is incorporated therein.*]

CHAPTER 6—THE ECSC CONSULTATIVE COMMITTEE

Article 22

[T*his Article amends the ECSC Treaty, Art.* 18 (1), *and is incorporated therein.*]

CHAPTER 7—THE SCIENTIFIC AND TECHNICAL COMMITTEE

Article 23

[*This Article amends the Euratom Treaty, Art.* 134 (1), *subpara.* 1, *and is incorporated therein.*]

TITLE II—OTHER ADJUSTMENTS

Article 24

1. [*This paragraph amends the EEC Treaty, Art.* 131, *and is incorporated therein.*]
2. [*This paragraph amends the EEC Treaty, Annex IV, and is incorporated therein.*]

Article 25

[*This Article amends the ECSC Treaty, Art.* 79 (1), *and is incorporated therein.*]

Article 26

[*This Article amends the EEC Treaty, Art.* 227, *and is incorporated therein.*]

Article 27

[*This Article amends the Euratom Treaty, Art.* 198, *and is incorporated therein.*]

Article 28

Acts of the institutions of the Community relating to the products in Annex II to the EEC Treaty and the products subject, on importation into the Community, to specific rules as a result of the implementation of the common agricultural policy, as well as the acts on the harmonization of legislation of Member States concerning turnover taxes, shall not apply to Gibraltar unless the Council, acting unanimously on a proposal from the Commission, provides otherwise.

Part Three

ADAPTATIONS TO ACTS ADOPTED BY THE INSTITUTIONS

Article 29

The acts listed in Annex I to this Act shall be adapted as specified in that Annex.

Article 30

The adaptations to the acts listed in Annex II to this Act made necessary by accession shall be drawn up in conformity with the guidelines set out in that Annex and in accordance with the procedure and under the conditions laid down in Article 153.

Part Four

TRANSITIONAL MEASURES

TITLE I—FREE MOVEMENT OF GOODS

CHAPTER 1—TARIFF PROVISIONS

Article 31

1. The basic duty to which the successive reductions provided for in Articles 32 and 59 are to be applied shall, for each product, be the duty actually applied on 1 January 1972.

The basic duty used for the moves towards the Common Customs Tariff and the ECSC unified tariff provided for in Articles 39 and 59 shall, for each product, be the duty actually applied by the new Member States on 1 January 1972.

For the purposes of this Act, " ECSC unified tariff" means the customs nomenclature and the existing customs duties for the products in Annex I to the ECSC Treaty, other than coal.

2. If, after 1 January 1972, any tariff reductions deriving from the Agreement Relating Principally to Chemicals supplementary to the Geneva (1967) Protocol to the General Agreement on Tariffs and Trade become applicable, the reduced duties shall replace the basic duties referred to in paragraph 1.

ARTICLE 32

1. Customs duties on imports between the Community as originally constituted and the new Member States and between the new Member States themselves shall be progressively abolished in accordance with the following timetable:
—on 1 April 1973, each duty shall be reduced to 80 per cent. of the basic duty:
—four other reductions of 20 per cent. each shall be made on:
1 January 1974;
1 January 1975;
1 January 1976;
1 July 1977.
2. Notwithstanding paragraph 1:
  (a) customs duties on imports of coal within the meaning of Annex I to the ECSC Treaty shall be abolished between Member States from the date of accession;
  (b) customs duties on imports of products listed in Annex III to this Act shall be abolished on 1 January 1974;
  (c) duty-free entry shall, from the date of accession, apply to imports which benefit from the provisions relating to tax exemptions applicable to persons travelling from one Member State to another.
3. As regards the products listed in Annex IV to this Act which are subject to contractual margins of preference between the United Kingdom and certain other countries enjoying Commonwealth preference, the United Kingdom may defer until 1 July 1973 the first of the tariff reductions referred to in paragraph 1.
4. Paragraph 1 shall not preclude the possibility of opening tariff quotas for certain iron and steel products which are not manufactured or the manufacture of which is inadequate in quantity or quality in the Community as originally constituted.

ARTICLE 33

In no case shall customs duties higher than those applied to third countries enjoying most-favoured-nation treatment be applied within the Community.

In the event of the Common Customs Tariff duties being amended or suspended or the new Member States applying Article 41, the Council, acting by a qualified majority on a proposal from the Commission, may take the necessary measures for the maintenance of Community preference.

Article 34

Any new Member State may suspend in whole or in part the levying of duties on products imported from other Member States. It shall inform the other Member States and the Commission thereof.

Article 35

Any charge having equivalent effect to a customs duty on imports, introduced after 1 January 1972 in trade between the Community as originally constituted and the new Member States or between the new Member States themselves, shall be abolished on 1 January 1973.

Any charge having equivalent effect to a customs duty on imports the rate of which on 31 December 1972 is higher than that actually applied on 1 January 1972 shall be reduced to the latter rate on 1 January 1973.

Article 36

1. Charges having equivalent effect to customs duties on imports shall be progressively abolished between the Community as originally constituted and the new Member States and between the new Member States themselves in accordance with the following timetable:
—by 1 January 1974 at the latest, each charge shall be reduced to 60 per cent. of the rate applied on 1 January 1972;
—the three other reductions of 20 per cent. each shall be made on:
1 January 1975;
1 January 1976;
1 July 1977.
2. Notwithstanding paragraph 1:
   (a) charges having equivalent effect to customs duties on imports of coal within the meaning of Annex I to the ECSC Treaty shall be abolished between Member States from the date of accession;
   (b) charges having equivalent effect to customs duties on imports on the products listed in Annex III to this Act shall be abolished on 1 January 1974.

Article 37

Customs duties on exports and charges having equivalent effect shall be abolished between the Community as originally constituted and the new Member States and between the new Member States themselves by 1 January 1974 at the latest.

Article 38

1. Without prejudice to the following paragraphs, the provisions concerning the progressive abolition of customs duties shall apply to customs duties of a fiscal nature.
2. The new Member States shall retain the right to replace a customs duty of a fiscal nature or the fiscal element of any such duty by an internal tax which is in conformity with Article 95 of the EEC Treaty. If a new Member State avails itself of this right, any element not so replaced by the internal tax shall constitute the basic duty under Article 31. This element shall be abolished in trade within the Community and brought into line with the Common Customs Tariff under the conditions laid down in Articles 32, 39 and 59.

3. Where the Commission finds that in a new Member State there is serious difficulty in replacing a customs duty of a fiscal nature or the fiscal element of any such duty, it shall authorise that State, following a request made before 1 February 1973, to retain the duty or fiscal element, provided the State abolishes it by 1 January 1976 at the latest. The decision of the Commission shall be taken before 1 March 1973.

The protective element, the amount of which shall be fixed by the Commission before 1 March 1973 after consulting the State concerned, shall constitute the basic duty provided for in Article 31. This element shall be abolished in trade within the Community and brought into line with the Common Customs Tariff under the conditions laid down in Articles 32, 39 and 59.

4. The Commission may authorise the United Kingdom to retain customs duties of a fiscal nature or the fiscal element of such duties on tobacco for two additional years if by 1 January 1976 it has not proved possible to convert those duties into internal taxes on manufactured tobacco on a harmonised basis in accordance with Article 99 of the EEC Treaty, either because there are no Community provisions in this field on 1 January 1975 or because the time limit set for the implementation of such Community provisions is later than 1 January 1976.

5. The Council Directive of 4 March 1969 on the harmonisation of provisions laid down by law, regulation or administrative action for deferred payment of customs duties, charges having equivalent effect and agricultural levies shall not apply in the new Member States to the customs duties of a fiscal nature referred to in paragraphs 3 and 4 or to the fiscal element of such duties.

6. The Council Directive of 4 March 1969 on the harmonisation of provisions laid down by law, regulation or administrative action in respect of inward processing shall not apply in the United Kingdom to the customs duties of a fiscal nature referred to in paragraphs 3 and 4 or to the fiscal element of such duties.

ARTICLE 39

1. For the purpose of the progressive introduction of the Common Customs Tariff and of the ECSC unified tariff, the new Member States shall amend their tariffs applicable to third countries as follows:
   (a) in the case of tariff headings in respect of which the basic duties do not differ by more than 15 per cent. in either direction from the duties in the Common Customs Tariff or the ECSC unified tariff, these latter duties shall be applied from 1 January 1974;
   (b) in other cases, each new Member State shall, from the same date, apply a duty reducing by 40 per cent. the difference between the basic duty and the duty in the Common Customs Tariff or the ECSC unified tariff.
      This difference shall be further reduced by 20 per cent. on 1 January 1975 and by 20 per cent. on 1 January 1976.

The new Member States shall apply in full the Common Customs Tariff and the ECSC unified tariff from 1 July 1977.

2. From 1 January 1974, if any duties in the Common Customs Tariff are altered or suspended, the new member States shall simultaneously amend or suspend their tariffs in the proportion resulting from the implementation of paragraph 1.

3. The new Member States shall apply the Common Customs Tariff from 1 January 1974 in respect of the products listed in Annex III to this Act.

4. [The new Member States shall apply the Common Customs Tariff nomenclature from the date of accession. Denmark and the United Kingdom are, however, authorised to defer their application of the nomenclature until 1 January 1974.]

The new Member States may include within this nomenclature existing national subdivisions which are indispensable in order that the progressive alignment of their customs duties with those in the Common Customs Tariff be carried out under the conditions laid down in this Act.

5. With a view to facilitating the progressive introduction of the Common Customs Tariff by the new Member States, the Commission shall determine, if necessary, the provisions whereby new Member States alter their customs duties.

AMENDMENT
In para. (4) the first sub-para. was substituted by the Adaptation Decision, Art. 17.

ARTICLE 40

In respect of the following products in the Common Customs Tariff:

CCT Heading No.	Description of goods (ECSC)
73.01	Pig iron, cast iron and spiegeleisin, in pigs, blocks, lumps and similar forms
73.02	Ferro-alloys: A. Ferro-manganese: I. Containing more than 2 per cent. by weight of carbon (high carbon ferro-manganese)
73.07	Blooms, billets, slabs and sheet bars (including tinplate bars), of iron or steel; pieces roughly shaped by forging, of iron or steel A. Blooms and billets: ex I. Rolled billets

Ireland shall, notwithstanding the provisions of Article 39 apply from 1 January 1975 duties reducing by one third the difference between the rates actually applied on 1 January 1972 and those of the ECSC unified tariff. The difference resulting from the first move towards alignment shall be further reduced by 50 per cent. on 1 January 1976.

Ireland shall apply in full the ECSC unified tariff from 1 July 1977.

ARTICLE 41

In order to bring their tariffs into line with the Common Customs Tariff and the ECSC unified tariff, the new Member States shall remain free to alter their customs duties more rapidly than is provided for in Article 39 (1) and (3). They shall inform the other Member States and the Commission thereof.

CHAPTER 2—ELIMINATION OF QUANTITATIVE RESTRICTIONS

ARTICLE 42

Quantitative restrictions on imports and exports shall, from the date of accession, be abolished between the Community as originally constituted and the new Member States and between the new Member States themselves.

Measures having equivalent effect to such restrictions shall be abolished by 1 January 1975 at the latest.

ARTICLE 43

Notwithstanding Article 42, Member States may, for a period of two years, retain restrictions on exports of waste and scrap metal of iron or steel falling within Common Customs Tariff heading No. 73.03, insofar as these arrangements are not more restrictive than those applied to exports to third countries.

[For Denmark the period shall be three years and for Ireland five years.]

AMENDMENT
The second paragraph was substituted by the Adaptation Decision, Art. 18.

ARTICLE 44

1. The new Member States shall progressively adjust State monopolies of a commercial character within the meaning of Article 37 (1) of the EEC Treaty so as to ensure that by 31 December 1977 no discrimination regarding the conditions under which goods are procured and marketed exists between nationals of Member States.

The original Member States shall have equivalent obligations in relation to the new Member States.

2. From the beginning of 1973 the Commission shall make recommendations as to the manner in which and the time table according to which the adjustment provided for in this Article must be carried out, it being understood that the manner and time table must be the same for the new Member States and the original Member States.

CHAPTER 3—OTHER PROVISIONS

ARTICLE 45

1. The Commission shall, before 1 April 1973 and with due regard for the provisions in force, in particular those relating to Community transit, determine the methods of administrative cooperation designed to ensure that goods fulfilling the requisite conditions benefit from the abolition of customs duties and charges having equivalent effect and quantitative restrictions and measures having equivalent effect.

2. The Commission shall, before the expiry of that time limit, lay down the provisions applicable to trade within the Community in goods obtained in the Community in the manufacture of which have been incorporated:

—products on which the customs duties or charges having equivalent effect which were applicable to them in the Community as originally constituted or in a new Member State have not been levied, or which have benefited from a total or partial drawback of such duties or charges;

—agricultural products which do not fulfil the conditions required for admission to free movement in the Community as originally constituted or in a new Member State.

In adopting these provisions, the Commission shall take into account the rules laid down in this Act for the elimination of customs duties between the Community as originally constituted and the new Member States and between the new Member States themselves, and for the progressive introduction by the new Member States of the Common Customs Tariff and the provisions relating to the common agricultural policy.

ARTICLE 46

1. Save as otherwise provided in this Act, the provisions in force with regard to customs legislation for trade with third countries shall apply under the same conditions to trade within the Community, for such time as customs duties are levied in that trade.

For the purpose of establishing the customs value in respect of that trade, the customs territory to be taken into consideration shall be that defined by the provisions existing in the Community and in the new Member States on 31 December 1972.

2. [The new Member States apply the Common Customs Tariff nomenclature in trade within the Community from the date of accession. Denmark and the United Kingdom are, however, authorised to defer their application of this nomenclature until 1 January 1974.]

The new Member States may include within this nomenclature existing national subdivisions which are indispensable in order that the progressive elimination of their customs duties within the Community be carried out under the conditions laid down in this Act.

AMENDMENT
In para, (2) the first sub-para. was substituted by the Adaptation Decision, Art. 19.

ARTICLE 47

1. Where the compensatory amounts referred to in Article 55 (1) (*a*) are levied in trade between the Community as originally constituted and the new Member States and between the New Member States themselves on imports of primary products considered as having been used in the manufacture of goods covered by Regulation No. 170/67/EEC on the common system of trade for ovalbumin and lactalbumin and Regulation (EEC) No. 1059/69 determining the system of trade applicable to certain goods processed from agricultural products, a compensatory amount, calculated on the basis of the said amounts and in accordance with the rules laid down by the above Regulations for calculating either the charge or the variable component applicable to the goods under consideration, shall be applied on importation of those goods.

When these same goods are imported from third countries into the new Member States, the charge laid down by Regulation No. 170/67/EEC and the variable component laid down by Regulation (EEC) No. 1059/69 shall be reduced or increased as the case may be, by the compensatory amount under the same conditions as those laid down in Article 55 (1) (*b*).

2. Article 61 (2) shall apply for the determination of the customs duty constituting the fixed component of the charge applicable in the new Member States to goods covered by Regulation (EEC) No. 1059/69.

Each fixed component applied in trade between the Community as originally constituted and the new Member States and between the new Member States themselves shall be abolished in accordance with Article 32 (1).

Each fixed component applied by the new Member States to imports from third countries shall be brought into line with the Common Customs Tariff in accordance with Article 39.

3. The new Member States shall, for the goods covered by Regulations No. 170/67/EEC and (EEC) No. 1059/69, apply in full the Common Customs Tariff Nomenclature by 1 February 1973 at the latest.

4. The new Member States shall abolish customs duties and charges having equivalent effect, other than those provided for in paragraphs 1 and 2, on 1 February 1973.

On the same date, the new Member States shall abolish the measures having equivalent effect to quantitative restrictions in trade between themselves and with the Community as originally constituted.

5. The Council shall, acting by a qualified majority on a proposal from the Commission, adopt provisions to implement this Article, taking account, in particular, of the special situations which may result from the implementation for the same goods of the first sub-paragraph of paragraph 1 and of Article 97.

ARTICLE 48

1. The provisions of this Title shall not prevent Ireland from applying to products originating in the United Kingdom arrangements enabling customs duties and protective elements contained in customs duties of a fiscal nature to be eliminated more rapidly, in accordance with the Anglo-Irish Free Trade Area Agreement, signed on 14 December 1965, and related Agreements.

2. The provisions adopted pursuant to Article 45 (2) shall apply from 1 January 1974 in the context of the customs arrangements in force between Ireland and the United Kingdom.

ARTICLE 49

1. Protocols Nos. 8 to 15 annexed to this Act shall not preclude any alteration to or suspension of duties decided under Article 28 of EEC Treaty.

2. The protocols annexed to the Agreement on the determination of part of the Common Customs Tariff in respect of the products in List G annexed to the EEC Treaty are hereby revoked with the exception of Protocol No. XVII.

TITLE II—AGRICULTURE

CHAPTER 1—GENERAL PROVISIONS

ARTICLE 50

Save as otherwise provided in this Title, the rules provided for in this Act shall apply to agricultural products.

ARTICLE 51

1. This Article shall apply to prices in respect of which Chapters 2 and 3 refer to this Article.

2. Before the first move towards price alignment referred to in Article 52, the prices to be applied in each new Member State shall be fixed in accordance with the rules provided for in the common organisation of the market in the sector in question at a level which allows producers in that sector to obtain returns equivalent to those obtained under the previous national system.

3. [In respect of the United Kingdom, those prices shall, however, be fixed at a level such that the application of the Community rules results in a level of market prices comparable with the level recorded in the Member State concerned during a representative period preceding the implementation of the Community rules.]

AMENDMENT
Para. (3) was substituted by the Adaptation Decision, Art. 20.

ARTICLE 52

1. If the application of the provisions of this Title results in a price level different from that of the common prices, the prices in respect of which Chapters 2 and 3 refer to this Article shall be aligned with the level of the common prices in six stages.

2. Subject to paragraph 4, the moves towards alignment shall be carried out each year at the beginning of the marketing year according to the following provisions:

(a) when the price of a product in a new Member State is lower than the common price, the price in that Member State shall, at the time of each move towards alignment, be increased successively by a sixth, a fifth, a quarter, a third and a half of the difference between the price level in that new Member State and the common price level which are applicable before each move towards alignment; the price resulting from this calculation shall be increased proportionately to any rise in the common price for the following marketing year;

(b) when the price of a product in a new Member State is higher than the common price, the difference between the price level applicable before each move towards alignment in the new Member State and the common price level applicable for the next marketing year shall be reduced successively by a sixth, a fifth, a quarter, a third and a half.

3. In the interest of the smooth functioning of the process of integration, the Council, acting in accordance with the procedure laid down in Article 43 (2) of the EEC Treaty, may decide that, notwithstanding paragraph 2, the price of one or more products in one or more of the new Member States shall for one marketing year depart from the prices resulting from the application of paragraph 2.

This departure may not exceed 10 per cent. of the amount of the price move to be made.

In that event, the price level for the following marketing year shall be that which would have resulted from applying paragraph 2 if the departure had not been decided upon. A further departure from this price level may, however, be decided upon for that marketing year in accordance with the conditions in the preceding subparagraphs.

4. The common prices shall be applied in the new Member States by 1 January 1978 at the latest.

ARTICLE 53

If the difference between the price level of a product in a new Member State and the common price level is found to be minimal, the Council, acting in accordance with the procedure laid down in Article 43 (2) of the EEC Treaty, may decide that the common price shall be applied in that new Member State in respect of the product concerned.

ARTICLE 54

1. For such time as there is a difference in the United Kingdom between prices obtained under the national system of guaranteed prices and market prices resulting from the application of the mechanisms of the common agricultural policy and the provisions of this Title, that Member State is authorised to retain production subsidies.

2. The United Kingdom shall, for each of the products to which paragraph 1 applies, endeavour to abolish these subsidies as soon as possible during the period referred to in Article 9 (2).

3. These subsidies may not have the effect of raising the returns of producers above the level which would have resulted from the application to these returns of the rules for the alignment of prices laid down in Article 52.

4. The Council, acting in accordance with the procedure laid down in Article 43 (2) of the EEC Treaty, shall adopt the rules necessary for the application of this Article with a view to ensuring the proper functioning of the common agricultural policy and in particular of the common organisation of the market.

ARTICLE 55

1. The differences in price levels shall be compensated as follows:
    (a) in trade between the new Member States themselves and with the Community as originally constituted, compensatory amounts shall be levied by the importing State or granted by the exporting State;
    (b) in trade between the new Member States and third countries, levies or other import charges applied under the common agricultural policy and export refunds shall be reduced or increased, as the case may be, by the compensatory amounts applicable in trade with the Community as originally constituted. Customs duties may not, however, be reduced by the compensatory amount.

2. For products in respect of which prices are fixed in accordance with Articles 51 and 52, the compensatory amounts applicable in trade between the Community as originally constituted and the new Member States, and between those States and third countries, shall be equal to the difference between the prices fixed for the new Member State concerned and the common prices.

For the other products, the compensatory amounts shall be determined in the cases provided for in Chapters 2 and 3 and in accordance with the rules which they lay down.

3. The compensatory amounts applicable in trade between the new Member States shall be determined by direct reference to the compensatory amounts fixed for each of those States in accordance with paragraph 2.

4. No compensatory amount shall, however, be fixed if the application of paragraphs 2 and 3 results in a minimal amount.

5. For products in respect of which the duty in the Common Customs Tariff is bound under the General Agreement on Tariffs and Trade, the binding shall be taken into account.

6. The compensatory amount levied or granted by a Member State in accordance with paragraph 1 (a) may not exceed the total amount levied by that same Member State on imports from third countries.

The Council, acting by a qualified majority on a proposal from the Commission, may derogate from this rule, in particular in order to avoid deflections of trade and distortions of competition.

ARTICLE 56

If the world market price for a product is higher than the price used in calculating the import charge introduced under the common agricultural policy, less the compensatory amount deducted from the import charge in accordance with Article 55, or if the refund on exports to third countries is less than the compensatory amount, or if no refund is applicable, appropriate measures may be taken with a view to ensuring the proper functioning of the common organisation of the market.

ARTICLE 57

In fixing the level of the various elements of the price and intervention system, except for the prices referred to in Articles 51 and 70, account shall be taken for the new Member States, to the extent necessary for the proper functioning of the Community rules, of the difference in prices expressed by the compensatory amount.

ARTICLE 58

The compensatory amounts granted shall be financed by the Community from the Guarantee Section of the European Agricultural Guidance and Guarantee Fund.

ARTICLE 59

The following provisions shall apply to products the importation of which from third countries into the Community as originally constituted is subject to customs duties:

1. Customs duties on imports shall be progressively abolished between the Community as originally constituted and the new Member States and between the new Member States themselves in five stages. The first reduction, which shall reduce the customs duties to 80 per cent. of the basic duty, and the four other reductions of 20 per cent. each, shall be made in accordance with the following timetable:

    (a) for products covered by the common organisation of the market in beef and veal: at the start of each marketing year, the first reduction taking place in 1973.

    (b) for products covered by Regulation No. 23 on the progressive establishment of a common organisation of the market in fruit and vegetables, by Regulation (EEC) No. 234/68 on the establishment of a common organisation of the market in live trees and other plants, bulbs, roots and the like, cut flowers and ornamental foliage, and by Regulation (EEC) No. 865/68 on the establishment of a common organisation of the market in products processed from fruit and vegetables: on 1 January each year, the first reduction taking place on 1 January 1974;

    (c) for other agricultural products: in accordance with the timetable laid down in Article 32 (1), the first reduction, however, taking place on 1 July 1973.

2. For the purpose of the progressive introduction of the Common Customs Tariff, each new Member State shall reduce the difference between the basic duty and the duty in the Common Customs Tariff by successive amounts of 20 per cent. These moves towards alignment shall be made on the dates laid down in paragraph 1 for the products in question. For the products referred to in paragraph 1 (c), the moves towards alignment shall follow the timetable laid down in Article 39 (1).

However, in the case of tariff headings in respect of which the basic duties do not differ by more than 15 per cent. in either direction from the duties in the Common Customs Tariff, the latter duties shall be applied from the date of the first move towards alignment for each category of products in question.

3. In respect of the second, third and fourth reductions or moves towards alignment, the Council, acting by a qualified majority on a proposal from the Commission, may decide that, in respect of one or more of the new Member States, the duties applicable to one or more of the products referred to in paragraph 1 (*b*) shall, for one year, depart from the duties resulting from the application of paragraph 1 or, as the case may be, paragraph 2.

This departure may not exceed 10 per cent. of the amount of the modification to be made under paragraph 1 or 2.

In that event, the duties to be applied for the following year shall be those which would have resulted from applying paragraph 1 or, as the case may be, paragraph 2, if the departure had not been decided upon. However, for that year, a further departure from those duties may be decided upon in accordance with the conditions set out in the above sub-paragraphs.

On 1 January 1978 the customs duties on these products shall be abolished and the new Member States shall apply in full the Common Customs Tariff.

4. In respect of products covered by a common organisation of the market, the new Member States may, in accordance with the procedure laid down in Article 26 of Regulation No. 120/67/EEC on the common organisation of the market in cereals or, as the case may be, laid down in the corresponding Articles of the other Regulations on the establishment of a common organisation of agricultural markets, be authorised to abolish the customs duties referred to in paragraph 1, or to align duties as provided for in paragraph 2, or both, at a more rapid rate than that laid down in the preceding paragraphs or to suspend in whole or in part the customs duties on products imported from other Member States.

In respect of other products, no authorisation shall be required for the introduction of the measures referred to in the preceding subparagraph.

The customs duties resulting from an accelerated alignment shall not be less than the customs duties on imports of the same products from other Member States.

Each new Member State shall inform the other Member States and the Commission of the measures taken.

ARTICLE 60

1. In respect of products covered, on the date of accession, by a common organisation of the market, the system applicable in the Community as originally constituted in respect of customs duties and charges having equivalent effect and quantitative restrictions and measures having equivalent effect shall, subject to Articles 55 and 59, apply in the new Member States from 1 February 1973.

2. In respect of products not covered, on the date of accession, by a common organisation of the market, the provisions of Title I concerning the progressive abolition of charges having equivalent effect to customs duties and of quantitative restrictions and measures having equivalent effect shall not apply to those charges, restrictions and measures if they form part of a national market organisation on the date of accession.

This provision shall apply only to the extent necessary to ensure the maintenance of the national organisation until the common organisation of the market for these products is implemented.

3. The new Member States shall apply the Common Customs Tariff nomenclature by 1 February 1973 at the latest, in respect of agricultural products covered by a common organisation of the market.

To the extent that no difficulties arise in the application of the Community rules and, in particular, in the functioning of the common organisation of markets and of the transitional mechanisms provided for in this Title, the Council, acting by a qualified majority on a proposal from the Commission, may authorise a new Member State to include within this nomenclature such existing national subdivisions as would be indispensable for carrying out the progressive moves towards alignment with the Common Customs Tariff or the elimination of the duties in the Community under the conditions laid down in this Act.

ARTICLE 61

1. The component for protection of the processing industry which is used in calculating the charge on imports from third countries of products covered by the common organisation of the markets in cereals, rice and products processed from fruit and vegetables shall be levied on imports from the new Member States into the Community as originally constituted.

2. For imports into the new Member States, the amount of that component shall be determined by separating out, from the total protection applied on 1 January 1972, the component or components designed to ensure the protection of the processing industry.

Such component or components shall be levied on imports from other Member States; they shall replace, as regards the charge on imports from third countries, the Community protective component.

3. Article 59 shall apply to the component referred to in paragraphs 1 and 2. The reductions or alignments in question shall, however, in respect of cereal and rice products be made at the beginning of the marketing year fixed for the basic product concerned.

ARTICLE 62

1. The Council, acting by a qualified majority on a proposal from the Commission, shall adopt the provisions necessary for implementing this title.

2. The Council, acting unanimously on a proposal from the Commission after consulting the Assembly, may make the necessary adaptations to the provisions of Chapters 2, 3 and 4 of this Title, if made necessary as a result of a change in Community rules.

ARTICLE 63

1. If transitional measures are necessary to facilitate the passage from the existing arrangements in the new Member States to those resulting from the application of the common organisation of the markets as provided for in this Title, particularly if for certain products the implementation to the new arrangements on the scheduled date meets with appreciable difficulties, such measures shall be adopted in accordance with the procedure provided for in Article 26 of Regulation No. 120/67/EEC or, as the case may be, in the corresponding Articles of the other Regulations on the common organisation of agricultural markets. Such measures may be taken during the period up to 31 January 1974, but their application may not extend beyond that date.

2. The Council may, acting unanimously on a proposal from the Commission after consulting the Assembly, extend the time limit in paragraph 1 up to 31 January 1975.

ARTICLE 64

The provisions of this Title shall not affect the degree of freedom of trade in agricultural products which results from the Anglo-Irish Free Trade Area Agreement, signed on 14 December 1965, and related Agreements.

CHAPTER 2—PROVISIONS RELATING TO CERTAIN COMMON ORGANISATIONS OF MARKETS

SECTION 1—FRUIT AND VEGETABLES

ARTICLE 65

1. A compensatory amount shall be fixed for fruit and vegetables in respect of which:
   (a) the new Member State concerned applied, during 1971, quantitative restrictions or measures having equivalent effect,
   (b) a common basic price is fixed, and
   (c) the producer price in that new Member State appreciably exceeds the basic price applicable in the Community as originally constituted during the period preceding the application of the Community system to the new Member States.

2. The producer price referred to in paragraph 1 (c) shall be calculated by applying to the national data of the new Member State concerned the principles set out in Article 4 (2) of Regulation No. 159/66/EEC laying down additional provisions in respect of the common organisation of the market in fruit and vegetables.

3. The compensatory amount shall apply only during the period for which the basic price is in force.

ARTICLE 66

1. Until the first move towards alignment, the compensatory amount applicable in trade between a new Member State in which the conditions referred to in Article 65 (1) are fulfilled and the Community as originally constituted, another new Member State, with the exception of those referred to in the following subparagraph, or third countries, shall be equal to the difference between the prices referred to in Article 65 (1) (c).

In trade between two new Member States in which the conditions referred to in Article 65 (1) are fulfilled, the compensatory amount shall be equal to the difference between their respective producer prices. The compensatory amount shall not be applied if this difference is insignificant.

The differences referred to in the above subparagraphs shall be adjusted, to the extent necessary, by the incidence of customs duties.

2. Where subsequent compensatory amounts are fixed, the compensatory amount shall be reduced by one fifth of the original amount on 1 January every year, beginning on 1 January 1974.

Article 52 (3) shall apply by analogy. The compensatory amount shall be abolished on 1 January 1978.

ARTICLE 67

For the purpose of determining entry prices, the price quotations recorded in the new Member States shall be reduced by:

(a) the compensatory amount, if any;

(b) the duties applicable to imports into those Member States from third countries instead of the duties of the Common Customs Tariff.

ARTICLE 68

The provisions relating to the common quality standards shall apply to the marketing of home produce in the United Kingdom only from:

(a) 1 February 1974, in respect of artichokes, asparagus, Brussels sprouts, ribbed celery, witloof chicory, garlic and onions;

(b) 1 February 1975, in respect of beans, roundheaded cabbages, carrots, lettuces, curled-leaved endives and broad-leaved (Batavian) endives, shelling peas, spinach and strawberries.

SECTION 2—WINE

ARTICLE 69

Until 31 December 1975, Ireland and the United Kingdom are authorised to retain the use of composite names including the word wine for the designation of certain beverages in respect of which the use of such names is incompatible with Community rules. This derogation shall not, however apply to products exported to the Member States of the Community as originally constituted.

SECTION 3—OILSEEDS

ARTICLE 70

1. Article 52 shall apply to the derived intervention prices for oilseeds.

2. The intervention prices applicable in the new Member States until the first move towards alignment shall be fixed in accordance with the rules provided for within the common organisation of the market, account being taken of the normal relationship which should exist between the income to be obtained from oilseeds and that obtained from the production of the products which compete in crop rotation with oilseeds.

ARTICLE 71

The amount of aid in respect of oilseeds harvested in a new Member State shall be adjusted by the compensatory amount applicable in that State, increased by the incidence of the customs duties applied therein.

ARTICLE 72

In trade in oilseeds, the compensatory amount shall be applied only to refunds granted on exports to third countries of oilseeds harvested in a new Member State.

SECTION 4—CEREALS

ARTICLE 73

Articles 51 and 52 shall apply to the derived intervention prices for cereals.

ARTICLE 74

The compensatory amounts applicable in trade between the Community as originally constituted and the new Member States and between those States and third countries shall be fixed as follows:

1. The compensatory amount applicable until the first move towards alignment in the case of cereals for which no derived intervention price is fixed
for the new Member States shall be derived from the compensatory
amount applicable in the case of a competing cereal for which a derived
intervention price is fixed, account being taken of the relationship existing
between the threshold prices of the cereals in question. However, if the
relationship between the threshold prices differs appreciably from that
between the prices recorded on the market of the new Member State concerned, the latter relationship may be taken into consideration.

The subsequent compensatory amounts shall be fixed on the basis of
those referred to in the first sub-paragraph and according to the rules in
Article 52 for the alignment of prices.

2. The compensatory amount for the products specified in Article 1 (c) and
(d) of Regulation No. 120/67/EEC shall be derived from the compensatory amount for the cereals to which they relate with the help of the
coefficients or rules used in determining the levy, or the variable component of the levy, on those products.

SECTION 5—PIGMEAT

ARTICLE 75

1. The compensatory amount per kilogramme of pig carcase shall be
calculated on the basis of the compensatory amounts applicable to the quantity
of feed grain required for the production in the Community of one kilogramme
of pigmeat.

2. The compensatory amount for the products, other than pig carcases,
specified in Article 1 (1) of Regulation No. 121/67/EEC on the common
organisation of the market in pigmeat shall be derived from the compensatory
amount referred to in paragraph 1 with the help of the coefficients used in
calculating the levy.

ARTICLE 76

1. Until 31 December 1975, products which do not correspond to the provisions of point 23 of Annex I to Directive No. 64/433/EEC, on health protection questions in intra-Community trade in fresh meat, may be brought in by
intervention agencies in Denmark, Ireland and the United Kingdom.

2. Until 31 October 1974, the United Kingdom is authorised not to apply
the Community scale of classification for pig carcases.

SECTION 6—EGGS

ARTICLE 77

1. The compensatory amount per kilogramme of eggs in shell shall be
calculated on the basis of the compensatory amounts applicable to the quantity
of feed grain required for the production in the Community of one kilogramme
of eggs in shell.

2. The compensatory amount per hatching egg shall be calculated on the
basis of the compensatory amounts applicable to the quantity of feed grain
required for the production in the Community of one hatching egg.

3. The compensatory amount for the products specified in Article 1 (1) (b)
of Regulation No. 122/67/EEC on the common organisation of the market in

eggs shall be derived from the compensatory amount for eggs in shell with the help of the coefficients used in calculating the levy.

ARTICLE 78

With regard to egg-marketing standards, Ireland and the United Kingdom may retain on their markets a system of grading in four and five weight-categories respectively, on condition that the marketing of eggs which comply with Community standards shall not be subject to restrictions because of different systems of grading.

SECTION 7—POULTRY MEAT

ARTICLE 79

1. The compensatory amount per kilogramme of slaughtered poultry shall be calculated on the basis of the compensatory amounts applicable to the quantity of feed grain differentiated according to species of poultry, which is required for the production in the Community of one kilogramme of slaughtered poultry.

2. The compensatory amount applicable per chick shall be calculated on the basis of the compensatory amounts applicable to the quantity of feed grain required for the production in the Community of one chick.

3. The compensatory amount for the products specified in Article 1 (2) (d) of Regulation No. 123/67/EEC on the common organisation of the market in poultry meat shall be derived from the compensatory amount for slaughtered poultry with the help of the coefficients used in calculating the levy.

SECTION 8—RICE

ARTICLE 80

The compensatory amounts applicable in trade between the Community as originally constituted and the new Member States and between those States and third countries shall be fixed as follows:

1. The compensatory amount applicable until the first move towards alignment for round-grained husked rice, long-grained husked rice and broken rice shall be established on the basis of the difference between the threshold price and the market prices recorded on the market of the new Member State concerned during a reference period.

   The subsequent compensatory amounts shall be fixed on the basis of those provided for in the first subparagraph and according to the rules in Article 52 for the alignment of prices.

2. The compensatory amount for paddy rice, semi-milled rice, wholly-milled rice and the products specified in Article 1 (1) (c) of Regulation No. 359/67/EEC on the common organisation of the market in rice shall, for each of those products, be derived from the compensatory amount for the product referred to in paragraph 1 to which it relates with the help of the coefficients used in determining the levy or the variable component of the levy.

SECTION 9—SUGAR

ARTICLE 81

Articles 51 and 52 shall apply to the derived intervention price for white sugar, the intervention price for raw sugar and to the minimum price for beet.

ARTICLE 82

The compensatory amounts applicable in trade between the Community as originally constituted and the new Member States and between those States and third countries shall:

(a) in the case of the products, other than fresh beet, in Article 1 (1) (b) of Regulation No. 1009/67/EEC on the common organisation of the market in sugar, be derived from the compensatory amount for the primary product in question, in accordance with the rules in force for calculating the levy;

(b) in the case of the products in Article 1 (1) (d) of Regulation No. 1009/67/EEC, be derived from the compensatory amount for the primary product in question, in accordance with the rules in force for calculating:

—the levy, in respect of the compensatory amount applicable to imports,

—the refund, in respect of the compensatory amount applicable to exports.

ARTICLE 83

The amount referred to in Article 25 (3) of Regulation No. 1009/67/EEC shall, in the new Member States, be adjusted by the compensatory amount calculated in accordance with Article 55 (2)

SECTION 10—LIVE TREES AND OTHER PLANTS, BULBS, ROOTS AND THE LIKE, CUT FLOWERS AND ORNAMENTAL FOLIAGE

ARTICLE 84

The provisions relating to common quality standards shall be applicable to the marketing of home produce in the United Kingdom only from 1 February 1974 and, in respect of cut flowers only, from 1 February 1975.

SECTION 11—MILK AND MILK PRODUCTS

ARTICLE 85

Articles 51 and 52 shall apply to the intervention prices for butter and skim milk powder.

ARTICLE 86

In trade between the Community as originally constituted and the new Member States, and between those States and third countries, compensatory amounts shall be fixed as follows:

1. For pilot products other than those referred to in Article 85, the compensatory amount applicable until the first move towards alignment shall be determined on the basis of the difference between the representative market price level of the new Member State concerned and the representative market price level of the Community as originally constituted over a representative period preceding the introduction of the Community rules in the new Member State in question.

In fixing the compensatory amounts applicable from the first move towards alignment, account shall be taken of the amount fixed in accordance with the first subparagraph or paragraph 3 and of the rules for alignment of prices in Article 52.

2. For products other than pilot products, the compensatory amounts shall be derived from the compensatory amount for the pilot product of the group to which the product concerned belongs, in accordance with the rules in force for calculating the levy.

3. If the first subparagraph of paragraph 1 and paragraph 2 cannot be applied or if their application results in compensatory amounts leading to abnormal price relationships, the compensatory amount shall be calculated on the basis of the compensatory amounts applicable for butter and skim milk powder.

ARTICLE 87

1. If a system providing for a different valuation of milk according to its use existed in a new Member State before accession, and if the application of Article 86 leads to difficulties on the market, the compensatory amount applicable until the first move towards alignment for one or more products falling within Common Customs Tariff heading No. 04.01 shall be fixed on the basis of the difference between market prices.

When subsequent compensatory amounts are fixed, the compensatory amount shall be reduced annually at the beginning of the marketing year by one-sixth of the original amount and shall be abolished on 1 January 1978.

2. Appropriate measures shall be adopted to avoid distortions of competition which might result from the application of paragraph 1, either in respect of the products in question or in respect of other milk products, and to take account of possible changes in the common price.

ARTICLE 88

1. Ireland is authorised to grant a subsidy on the direct consumption of butter to the extent necessary to allow, during the transitional period, the price paid by the consumer to be progressively adjusted to the price level obtaining in the Community as originally constituted.

In the event of Ireland making use of the authorisation referred to in the first subparagraph, it shall grant a subsidy of the same amount on the consumption of butter imported from the other Member States.

2. This subsidy shall be abolished in six stages coinciding with the stages for aligning the price of butter.

ARTICLE 89

1. Until 31 December 1975 in the United Kingdom and until 31 December 1977 in Ireland, the supply to consumers as whole milk of milk with a fat content of less than 3.5 per cent. is authorised.

Milk sold as whole milk pursuant to the first subparagraph must not, however, have been subjected to any skimming. Furthermore, the provisions in respect of whole milk shall apply to such milk.

2. Denmark is authorised to maintain until 31 December 1977 the exclusive milk supply licences which existed in certain areas at the date of accession. Licences which expire before 1 January 1978 may not be renewed.

SECTION 12—BEEF AND VEAL

ARTICLE 90

Articles 51 and 52 shall apply to the guide prices for adult bovine animals and calves.

ARTICLE 91

1. The compensatory amount for calves and adult bovine animals calculated in accordance with Article 55 shall be corrected to the extent necessary, by the incidence of customs duties.

If the incidence of the customs duty applicable to trade between the Community as originally constituted and the new Member States and between the new Member States themselves is higher than the compensatory amount calculated in accordance with Article 55, the customs duty shall be suspended at a level such that its incidence corresponds to the compensatory amount.

2. If the third subparagraph of Article 10 (1) of Regulation (EEC) No. 805/68 on the common organisation of the market in beef and veal, or if Article 11 (1) of that Regulation, is applied, the appropriate measures shall be adopted in order to maintain Community preference and avoid deflections of trade.

3. The compensatory amount for the products referred to in the Annex to Regulation (EEC) No. 805/68 shall be fixed taking account of the provisions laid down in the preceding paragraphs and with the help of the rules laid down for fixing the levies applicable to those products.

ARTICLE 92

In respect of the products specified in Article 1 (*b*) and (*c*) of Regulation (EEC) No. 805/68, the refund on exports to third countries by the new Member States shall be corrected by the incidence of the difference between the customs duties on the products listed in the Annex to the said Regulation to imports from third countries into the Community as originally constituted on the one hand and into the new Member States on the other.

ARTICLE 93

For such time as the United Kingdom, pursuant to Article 54 retains production subsidies for slaughter cattle, Ireland is authorised, in order to avoid distortion of the Irish cattle market, to retain the measures relating to the export of beef and veal which it applied before accession, in correlation with the system of subsidies applied in the United Kingdom.

SECTION 13—PRODUCTS PROCESSED FROM FRUIT AND VEGETABLES

ARTICLE 94

Compensatory amounts shall be determined on the basis of the compensatory amounts fixed for sugar, glucose, or glucose syrup, as the case may be, and in accordance with the rules applicable for calculating:
—the levy in, respect of the compensatory amount applicable to imports;
—the refund, in respect of the compensatory amount applicable to exports.

SECTION 14—FLAX

ARTICLE 95

1. The amount of aid for flax shall, for the new Member States, be fixed on the basis of the difference between the income to be obtained by flax producers and the return resulting from the foreseeable market price for this product.

2. The income to be received by flax producers shall be established taking into account the price of competing products in the crop rotation in the new Member State in question and the relationship in the Community as originally constituted between the income resulting from flax production and that resulting from the production of competing products.

SECTION 15—SEEDS

ARTICLE 96

When an aid is granted for seed production, the amount of the aid may be fixed, in respect of the new Member States, at a level different from that fixed for the Community as originally constituted if the income of producers in a new Member State was previously appreciably different from the income of producers in the Community as originally constituted.

In that event, the amount of aid in respect of the new Member State must take account of the income previously received by seed producers and of the need to avoid any distortion of production patterns, and the need to align that amount gradually with the Community amount.

SECTION 16—AGRICULTURAL PRODUCTS EXPORTED IN THE FORM OF GOODS NOT COVERED BY ANNEX II TO THE EEC TREATY

ARTICLE 97

Compensatory amounts shall be determined on the basis of the compensatory amounts fixed for the basic products and in accordance with the rules applicable for the calculation of the refunds provided for in Regulation (EEC) No. 204/69, establishing the general rules concerning the granting of export refunds and the rules for fixing the amounts thereof, with respect to certain agricultural products exported in the form of goods not covered by Annex II to the Treaty.

CHAPTER 3—PROVISIONS RELATING TO FISHERIES

SECTION 1—COMMON ORGANISATION OF THE MARKET

ARTICLE 98

Articles 51 and 52 shall apply to the guide price for fisheries products. The moves towards price alignment shall be made at the beginning of the fishing year, and for the first time on 1 February 1973.

ARTICLE 99

The compensatory amounts shall be corrected, to the extent necessary, by the incidence of the customs duties.

SECTION 2—FISHING RIGHTS

ARTICLE 100

1. Notwithstanding the provisions of Article 2 Regulation (EEC) No. 2141/70 on the establishment of a common structural policy for the fishing industry, the Member States of the Community are authorised, until 31 December 1982, to restrict fishing in waters under their sovereignty or jurisdic-

tion, situated within a limit of six nautical miles, calculated from the base lines of the coastal Member State, to vessels which fish traditionally in those waters and which operate from ports in that geographical coastal area; however, vessels from other regions of Denmark may continue to fish in the waters of Greenland until 31 December 1977 at the latest.

Member States may not, insofar as they avail themselves of this derogation, adopt provisions dealing with conditions for fishing in those waters which are less restrictive than those applied in practice at the time of accession.

2. The provisions laid down in the preceding paragraph and in Article 101 shall not prejudice the special fishing rights which each of the original Member States and the new Member States might have enjoyed on 31 January 1971 in regard to one or more other Member States; the Member States may exercise these rights for such time as derogations continue to apply in the areas concerned. As regards the waters of Greenland, however, the special rights shall expire on the dates laid down for these rights.

3. If a Member State extends its fishing limits in certain areas to twelve nautical miles, the existing fishing activities within twelve nautical miles must be so pursued that there is no retrograde change by comparison with the situation on 31 January 1971.

4. In order to permit a satisfactory overall balance of fishing operations to be established within the Community during the period referred to in the first paragraph, the Member States need not make full use of the opportunities presented by the provisions of the first subparagraph of paragraph 1 in certain areas of the maritime waters under their sovereignty or jurisdiction.

The Member States shall inform the Commission of the measures which they adopt for this purpose; on a report from the Commission, the Council shall examine the situation and, in the light thereof, shall, where necessary, address recommendations to the Member States.

ARTICLE 101

[The limit of six nautical miles referred to in Article 100 shall be extended to twelve nautical miles for the following areas:
1. *Denmark*
    —the Faroe Islands
    —Greenland
    —the west coast, from Thyborøn to Blaavandshuk.
2. *France*
    The coasts of the départements of Manche, Ille-et-Vilaine, Côtes du Nord, Finistère and Morbihan.
3. *Ireland*
    —the north and west coasts, from Lough Foyle to Cork Harbour in the south-west
    —the east coast, from Carlingford Lough to Carnsore Point, for crustaceans and molluscs (shellfish).
4. *United Kingdom*
    —The Shetlands and the Orkneys
    —The north and east of Scotland, from Cape Wrath to Berwick
    —The north-east of England, from the river Coquet to Flamborough Head
    —The south-west from Lyme Regis to Hartland Point (including twelve nautical miles around Lundy Island)
    —County Down.]

AMENDMENT
This Article was substituted by the Adaptation Decision, Art. 21.

ARTICLE 102

From the sixth year after Accession at the latest, the Council, acting on a proposal from the Commission, shall determine conditions for fishing with a view to ensuring protection of the fishing grounds and conservation of the biological resources of the sea.

ARTICLE 103

Before 31 December 1982, the Commission shall present a report to the Council on the economic and social development of the coastal areas of the Member States and the state of stocks. On the basis of that report, and of the objectives of the common fisheries policy, the Council, acting on a proposal from the Commission, shall examine the provisions which could follow the derogations in force until 31 December 1982.

CHAPTER 4—OTHER PROVISIONS

SECTION 1—VETERINARY MEASURES

ARTICLE 104

Directive No. 64/432/EEC on veterinary health inspection questions in intra-Community trade in bovine animals and swine shall be applied account being taken of the following provisions:

1. Until 31 December 1977, the new Member States are authorised to retain, in compliance with the general rules of the EEC Treaty, their national rules on imports of bovine animals and swine for breeding, store and slaughter with the exception, in the case of Denmark, of slaughter cattle.

Adjustments will be sought, within the framework of those national rules, to ensure the progressive development of trade; to this end, those rules will be examined by the Standing Veterinary Committee.

2. Until 31 December 1977, the Member States into which cattle are imported shall grant to the Member States from which cattle are exported the derogation provided for in Article 7 (1) (A) (a) of the Directive.

3. Until 31 December 1977, the New Member States are authorised to retain the methods applied in their territory for declaring a herd of cattle officially free of tuberculosis or brucellosis within the meaning of Article 2 of the Directive, subject to the application of the provisions of the Directive relating to the presence of animals vaccinated against brucellosis. The provisions relating to the tests laid down for animals traded within the Community shall continue to apply, subject to paragraphs 4 and 6.

4. Until 31 December 1977, exports of cattle from Ireland to the United Kingdom may be carried out:

(a) by way of derogation from the provisions of the Directive relating to brucellosis; however, the provisions relating to the test laid down for animals traded within the Community shall continue to apply to exports of uncastrated cattle;

(b) by way of derogation from the provisions of the Directive relating to tuberculosis, provided that, at the time of export a declaration is made certifying that the exported animal comes from a herd declared officially free of tuberculosis according to the methods in force in Ireland;

(c) by way of derogation from the provisions of the Directive relating to the obligation to separate store and breeding cattle on the one hand and slaughter cattle on the other.

5. Until 31 December 1975, Denmark is authorised to use "alttuberculin" by way of derogation from the provisions in Annex B to the Directive.

6. Until the implementation of the Community provisions concerning trade within the Member States, in respect of the matters governed by the Directive, Ireland and the United Kingdom are authorised to retain their national rules governing trade between Ireland and Northern Ireland.

The Member States concerned may take appropriate measures in order to limit this derogation exclusively to the trade referred to above.

ARTICLE 105

Directive No. 64/433/EEC on health protection questions in intra-Community trade in fresh meat shall apply, account being taken of the following provisions:

[Until 31 December 1977, Ireland and the United Kingdom in respect of Northern Ireland, are authorised to retain for the import of fresh meat their national rules relating to protection against foot-and-mouth disease, while complying with the general provisions of the EEC Treaty.]

AMENDMENT
The second paragraph was substituted by the Adaptation Decision, Art. 22.

ARTICLE 106

Before the expiry of the time limits referred to in Articles 104 and 105, a review of the situation in the Community as a whole and in its various parts will be carried out in the light of developments in the veterinary field.

By 1 July 1976 at the latest, the Commission shall submit a report to the Council and, in so far as is necessary, appropriate proposals taking account of these developments.

SECTION 2—MISCELLANEOUS PROVISIONS

ARTICLE 107

The acts listed in Annex V to this Act shall apply in respect of the new Member States under the conditions laid down in that Annex.

TITLE III—EXTERNAL RELATIONS

CHAPTER 1—AGREEMENTS OF THE COMMUNITIES WITH CERTAIN THIRD COUNTRIES

ARTICLE 108

1. From the date of accession, the new Member States shall apply the provisions of the agreements referred to in paragraph 3, taking into account the transitional measures and adjustments which may appear necessary and which will be the subject of protocols to be concluded with the co-contracting third countries and annexed to those agreements.

2. These transitional measures, which will take into account the corresponding measures adopted within the Community and which may not extend beyond the period of validity thereof, shall be designed to ensure the progressive application by the Community of a single system for its relations with the co-contracting third countries as well as the identity of the rights and obligations of the Member States.

3. Paragraphs 1 and 2 shall apply to the agreements concluded with Greece, Turkey, Tunisia, Morocco, Israel, Spain and Malta.

Paragraphs 1 and 2 shall also apply to agreements which the Community concludes with other third countries in the Mediterranean region before the entry into force of this Act.

CHAPTER 2—RELATIONS WITH THE ASSOCIATED AFRICAN AND MALAGASY STATES AND WITH CERTAIN DEVELOPING COMMONWEALTH COUNTRIES

ARTICLE 109

1. The arrangements resulting from the Convention of Association between the European Economic Community and the African and Malagasy States associated with that Community, signed on 29 July 1969, and from the Agreement establishing an Association between the European Economic Community and the United Republic of Tanzania, the Republic of Uganda and the Republic of Kenya, signed on 24 September 1969, shall not apply in relations between the new Member States and the States associated with the Community under the above acts.

The new Member States need not accede to the Agreement on products within the competence of the European Coal and Steel Community, signed on 29 July 1969.

2. Subject to the provisions of Articles 110 and 111, products originating in the Associated States referred to in paragraph 1 shall, on importation into the new Member States, be subject to the arrangements applied to those products before accession.

3. Subject to the provisions of Articles 110 and 111, products originating in the independent Commonwealth countries listed in Annex VI to this Act shall, on importation into the Community, be subject to the arrangements applied to those products before accession.

ARTICLE 110

For those products listed in Annex II to the EEC Treaty which are subject to a common organisation of the market and for those products subject on importation into the Community to specific rules as a result of the implementation of the common agricultural policy, which originate in the Associated States referred to in Article 109 (1) or in the independent Commonwealth countries referred to in Article 109 (3), the new Member States shall apply on importation the Community rules under the conditions laid down in this Act and subject to the following provisions:

    (a) where the Community rules provide for the levying of customs duties on imports from third countries, the new Member States shall, subject to the provisions of Article 111, apply the tariff arrangements which they applied before accession;

(*b*) as regards protective components other than customs duties, the Council shall, acting by a qualified majority on a proposal from the Commission, determine, should it prove necessary, adaptations to Community rules designed to ensure that those products are imported under conditions similar to those existing before accession.

ARTICLE 111

Where alignment with the Common Customs Tariff leads to the reduction of a customs duty in a new Member State, the reduced customs duty shall apply to imports covered by Articles 109 and 110.

ARTICLE 112

1. Products imported into the United Kingdom before the dates determined under Article 115 which originate in the independent Commonwealth countries referred to in Article 109 (3) shall not, when they are re-exported to another new Member State or to the Community as originally constituted, be considered to be in free circulation within the meaning of Article 10 of the EEC Treaty.

2. Products imported into the Community as originally constituted during that same period which originated in the Associated States referred to in Article 109 (1) shall not, when re-exported to another Member State, be considered to be in free circulation in the Community as originally constituted, within the meaning of Article 10 of the EEC Treaty.

3. Where there is no risk of deflection of trade, and in particular in the event of minimal disparities in the import arrangements, the Commission may derogate from paragraphs 1 and 2.

ARTICLE 113

1. From accession, the new Member States shall communicate to the original Member States and the Commission the provisions concerning the arrangements which they apply to imports of products originating in or coming from the independent Commonwealth countries referred to in Article 109 (3) or the Associated States referred to in Article 109 (1).

2. From accession, the Commission shall communicate to the new Member States the internal or conventional provisions concerning arrangements applicable to imports into the Community as originally constituted of products originating in or coming from the independent Commonwealth countries referred to in Article 109 (3) or the Associated States referred to in Article 109 (1).

ARTICLE 114

When the Council takes decisions and when the Committee of the European Development Fund gives opinions within the framework of the Internal Agreement on measures to be taken and procedures to be followed for the implementation of the Convention of Association between the European Economic Community and the African and Malagasy States associated with that Community, signed on 29 July 1969, of the Internal Agreement on the financing and administration of Community aid, signed on 29 July 1969, and of the Internal Agreement on measures to be taken and procedures to be followed for the implementation of the Agreement establishing an Association between the

European Economic Community and the United Republic of Tanzania, the Republic of Uganda and the Republic of Kenya, signed on 24 September 1969, only the votes of the original Member States shall be counted, as the case may be, either in accordance with the weighted voting in force before accession for calculating a qualified majority or in accordance with Article 13 (3) of the above-mentioned Internal Agreement on the financing and administration of Community aid.

ARTICLE 115

1. Articles 109 to 114 shall apply until 31 January 1975.

2. However, imports originating in any independent Commonwealth country referred to in Article 109 (3) which has before that date established its relations with the Community on a basis other than association shall be subject in the new Member States from the date of entry into force of its agreement with the Community and in respect of matters not covered by that agreement to the third country arrangements applicable to those imports taking into account the transitional provisions of this Act.

3. The Council may, acting unanimously after consulting the Commission, decide to defer the date laid down in paragraph 1 in the event of implementation of the transitional provisions laid down in the second paragraph of Article 62 of the Convention of Association between the European Economic Community and the African and Malagasy States associated with that Community, signed on 29 July 1969, or in the second paragraph of Article 36 of the Agreement establishing an Association between the European Economic Community and the United Republic of Tanzania, the Republic of Uganda and the Republic of Kenya, signed on 24 September 1969, for the period during which such transitional provisions are being implemented.

CHAPTER 3—RELATIONS WITH PAPUA-NEW GUINEA

ARTICLE 116

1. Articles 109 (3) and 110 to 113 apply until 31 December 1977 to products originating in or coming from Papua-New Guinea imported into the United Kingdom.

2. These arrangements may be reviewed, in particular if that territory becomes independent before 1 January 1978. The Council shall, acting by a qualified majority on a proposal from the Commission, adopt, if the need arises, such provisions as are appropriate and may prove necessary.

TITLE IV—ASSOCIATION OF OVERSEAS COUNTRIES AND TERRITORIES

ARTICLE 117

1. [The association of the non-European territories maintaining special relations with the United Kingdom and of the Anglo-French Condominium of the New Hebrides, listed in Article 24 (2), shall take effect on 1 February 1975 at the earliest upon a decision of the Council taken under Article 136 of the EEC Treaty.]

2. The new Member States need not accede to the Agreement on trade with overseas countries and territories in products within the province of the European Coal and Steel Community, signed on 14 December 1970.

AMENDMENT
Para. (1) was substituted by the Adaptation Decision, Art. 23.

ARTICLE 118

The provisions of the third part of Protocol No. 22 on relations between the European Economic Community and the Associated African and Malagasy States and the independent developing Commonwealth countries situated in Africa, the Indian Ocean, the Pacific Ocean and the Caribbean shall apply both to the overseas countries and territories referred to in Article 117 and to the non-European countries and territories maintaining special relations with the original Member States.

ARTICLE 119

1. The arrangements resulting from the Council Decision of 29 September 1970 on the association of the overseas countries and territories with the European Economic Community shall not apply in relations between those countries and territories and the new Member States.

2. Products originating in the countries and territories associated with the Community shall, on importation into the new Member States, be subject to the arrangements applied to those products before accession.

[Products originating in the non-European territories maintaining special relations with the United Kingdom and in the Anglo-French Condominium of the New Hebrides, listed in Article 24 (2), shall, on importation into the Community, be subject to the arrangements applied to those products before accession.]

Articles 110 to 114 shall apply.

3. This Article shall apply until 31 January 1975. If Article 115 (3) is applied, this date may be deferred in accordance with the procedure and under the conditions laid down in that Article.

AMENDMENT
In para. (2), the second sub-paragraph was substituted by the Adaptation Decision, Art. 24.

TITLE V—CAPITAL MOVEMENTS

ARTICLE 120

1. The new Member States may, under the conditions and within the time limits in Articles 121 to 126, defer the liberalisation of capital movements provided for in the First Council Directive of 11 May 1960 for the implementation of Article 67 of the EEC Treaty and in the Second Council Directive of 18 December 1962 adding to and amending the First Directive for the implementation of Article 67 of the EEC Treaty.

2. Appropriate consultations shall take place in due course between the new Member States and the Commission about procedures for applying measures of liberalisation or relaxation, the implementation of which may be deferred under the following provisions.

ARTICLE 121

1. Denmark may:
  (a) for a period of two years after accession, defer the liberalisation of purchases by non-residents of bonds denominated in Danish kroner and dealt in on the stock exchange in Denmark, including physical transfers of the securities in question;

(*b*) for a period of five years after accession, defer the liberalisation of purchases by persons resident in Denmark of foreign securities dealt in on the stock exchange and of repurchases from abroad of Danish securities dealt in on the stock exchange, denominated entirely or partly in foreign currency, including physical transfers of the securities in question.

2. From the date of accession, Denmark will proceed to a progressive liberalisation of the operations referred to in paragraph 1 (*a*).

ARTICLE 122

1. Ireland may:
    (*a*) for a period of two years after accession, defer the liberalisation of direct investments in Member States by persons resident in Ireland and the liberalisation of the liquidation of direct investments in Member States by persons resident in Ireland;
    (*b*) for a period of thirty months after accession, defer the liberalisation of the following capital movements of a personal nature:
        —transfers of capital belonging to persons resident in Ireland who are emigrating, other than transfers connected with freedom of movement for workers which shall be liberalised from the date of accession;
        —gifts and endowments, dowries, succession duties, and real estate investments other than those connected with freedom of movement for workers which shall be liberalised from the date of accession;
    (*c*) for a period of five years after accession, defer the liberalisation of the operations set out in List B annexed to the Directives referred to in Article 120 and carried out by persons resident in Ireland.

2. Recognising that it is desirable to proceed, from the date of accession, to a substantial relaxation in the rules concerning the operations referred to in paragraph 1 (*a*), Ireland will endeavour to take appropriate measures to this end.

ARTICLE 123

[This Article has lapsed by virtue of the Adaptation Decision, Art. 25.]

ARTICLE 124

1. The United Kingdom may:
    (*a*) for a period of two years after accession, defer the liberalisation of direct investments in Member States by persons resident in the United Kingdom and the liberalisation of the liquidation of direct investments in Member States by persons resident in the United Kingdom;
    (*b*) for a period of thirty months after accession, defer the liberalisation of the following capital movements of a personal nature:
        —transfers of capital belonging to persons resident in the United Kingdom who are emigrating, other than transfers connected with freedon of movement for workers which shall be liberalised from the date of accession;
        —gifts and endowments, dowries, succession duties, and real estate investments other than those connected with freedom of movement for workers which shall be liberalised from the date of accession;

(c) for a period of five years after accession, defer the liberalisation of the operations set out in List B annexed to the Directives referred to in Article 120, and carried out by persons resident in the United Kingdom.

2. From the date of accession, the United Kingdom will proceed to a substantial relaxation in the rules concerning the operations referred to in paragraph 1 (a).

ARTICLE 125

The new Member States will, circumstances permitting, carry out the liberalisation of capital movements referred to in Articles 121 to 124 before the expiry of the time limits laid down in those Articles.

ARTICLE 126

For the purpose of implementing the provisions of this Title, the Commission may consult the Monetary Committee and submit appropriate proposals to the Council.

TITLE VI—FINANCIAL PROVISIONS

ARTICLE 127

The Decision of 21 April 1970 on the replacement of financial contributions from Member States by the Communities' own resources, hereinafter referred to as the " Decision of 21 April 1970 ", shall be applied, account being taken of the following provisions.

ARTICLE 128

The revenue referred to in Article 2 of the Decision of 21 April 1970 shall also include:

(a) among those designated as agricultural levies, the revenue from any compensatory amount levied on imports under Articles 47 and 55, and from the fixed components applied in trade between the Community as oringinally constituted and the new Member States and between the new Member States themselves under Article 61;

(b) among those designated as customs duties, the customs duties levied by the new Member States in trade with non-member States, and also customs duties levied in trade between the Community as originally constituted and the new Member States and between the new Member States themselves.

ARTICLE 129

1. [The financial contributions from Member States referred to in Article 3 (2) of the Decision of 21 April 1970 shall be apportioned as follows:

—for the new Member States:

Denmark	... ...	2·46%
Ireland	... ...	0·61%
United Kingdom	... ...	19·32%

—and for the original Member States, in accordance with the scale laid down in Article 3 (2) of the Decision of 21 April 1970, after the financial contributions of the new Member States specified above have been deducted.]

2. For 1973, the basis for calculating the variations referred to in Article 3 (3) of the Decision of 21 April 1970 shall be:
—for the new Member States, the percentages referred to in paragraph 1;
—for the original Member States, their relative share for the preceding year, account being taken of the percentages for the new Member States specified above.

AMENDMENT
Para. (1) was substituted by the Adaptation Decision, Art. 26.

ARTICLE 130

The Communities' own resources and also the financial contributions and, where appropriate, the contributions referred to in Article 4 (2), (3) and (4) of the Decision of 21 April 1970 shall be due from the new Member States to the following extent only:

—45·0 per cent. in 1973
—56·0 per cent. in 1974
—67·5 per cent. in 1975
—79·5 per cent. in 1976
—92·0 per cent. in 1977.

ARTICLE 131

1. From 1 January 1978, the Communities' own resources and, where appropriate, the financial contributions referred to in Article 4 (2), (3) and (4) of the Decision of 21 April 1970, shall be due from the new Member States, in full, subject to the following provisions:

(a) The increase in the relative share to be paid by each new Member State under the head of the Communities' own resources and of the financial contributions for 1978 in comparison with the relative share due for 1977, shall not exceed two fifths of the difference between the relative share due under the head of the Communities' own resources and of the financial contributions for 1977 and the relative share which each new Member State would have had to pay under the same head for the same year, if this relative share had been calculated in accordance with the arrangements laid down for the original Member States from 1978 by the Decision of 21 April 1970.

(b) For 1979, the increase in the relative share of each new Member State in comparison with 1978 shall not exceed that for 1978 in comparison with 1977.

2. The Commission shall carry out the calculations necessary for the application of this Article.

ARTICLE 132

Until 31 December 1979, that part of the Communities' budget which is not covered as a result of applying Articles 130 and 131 shall be incorporated into the amount apportioned for the original Member States in accordance with Article 129. The total amount thus determined shall be apportioned among the original Member States in accordance with the Decision of 21 April 1970.

TITLE VII—OTHER PROVISIONS

ARTICLE 133

The acts listed in Annex VII to this Act shall apply in respect of the new Member States under the conditions laid down in that Annex.

ARTICLE 134

1. During the five years following accession, the Commission will examine, with the Governments concerned, whether existing measures arising from provisions laid down by law, regulation or administrative action in force in the new Member States, which had they been introduced after accession would have fallen within the scope of Article 67 of the ECSC Treaty, could, by comparison with the measures in force in the original Member States, give rise to serious distortions in conditions of competition in the coal and steel industries whether within the common market or the export markets. The Commission may, after consulting the Council, propose to the Governments concerned any action which it considers appropriate to correct such measures or to offset their effects.

2. Until 31 December 1977, the prices charged by undertakings for sales of steel on the Irish market, reduced to their equivalent at the point chosen for their price list, may not be below the prices shown in the price list in question for comparable transactions, save when authorisation has been given by the Commission, in agreement with the Government of Ireland, without prejudice to the last subparagraph of Article 60 (2) (*b*) of the ECSC Treaty.

3. [If Decision No. 1/64 of the High Authority of 15 January 1964 prohibiting alignment on quotations for steel products and pig iron from state-trading countries or territories is extended after accession, that prohibition shall not apply until 31 December 1975 to products for the Danish market.]

AMENDMENT
  Para. (3) was substituted by the Adaptation Decision, Art. 27.

ARTICLE 135

1. If, before 31 December 1977, difficulties arise which are serious and liable to persist in any sector of the economy or which could bring about serious deterioration in the economic situation of a given area, a new Member State may apply for authorisation to take protective measures in order to rectify the situation and adjust the sector concerned to the economy of the common market.

2. On application by the State concerned, the Commission shall, by emergency procedure, determine without delay the protective measures which it considers necessary, specifying the circumstances and the manner in which they are to be put into effect.

3. The measures authorised under paragraph 2 may involve derogations from the rules of the EEC Treaty and of this Act to such an extent and for such periods as are strictly necessary in order to attain the objective referred to in paragraph 1. Priority shall be given to such measures as will least disturb the functioning of the common market.

4. In the same circumstances and according to the same procedure, any original Member State may apply for authorisation to take protective measures in regard to one or more new Member States.

ARTICLE 136

1. If, before 31 December 1977, the Commission, on application by a Member State or by any other interested party, finds that dumping is being practised between the Community as originally constituted and the new Member States or between the new Member States themselves, it shall address recommendations to the person or persons with whom such practices originate for the purpose of putting an end to them.

Should the practices continue, the Commission shall authorise the injured Member State or States to take protective measures, the conditions and details of which the Commission shall determine.

2. For the application of this Article to the products listed in Annex II to the EEC Treaty, the Commission shall evaluate all relevant factors, in particular the level of prices at which these products are imported into the market in question from elsewhere, account being taken of the provisions of the EEC Treaty relating to agriculture, in particular Article 39.

ARTICLE 137

1. Notwithstanding Article 136, Ireland may, until 31 December 1977, take the necessary measures in cases of extreme urgency. It shall forthwith notify such measures to the Commission, which may decide to abolish or modify them.

2. This provision shall not apply to the products in Annex II to the EEC Treaty.

ARTICLE 138

Notwithstanding the second paragraph of Article 95 of the EEC Treaty, Denmark may retain until 30 June 1974 the special excise duties on table wines imported in bottles or other similar containers.

Part Five

PROVISIONS RELATING TO THE IMPLEMENTATION OF THIS ACT

TITLE I—SETTING UP OF THE INSTITUTIONS

ARTICLE 139

1. The Parliaments of the new Member States shall, upon accession, designate their delegates to the Assembly.

2. The Assembly shall meet at the latest one month after accession. It shall make such adaptations to its rules of procedure as are made necessary by accession.

ARTICLE 140

1. Upon accession, the office of President of the Council shall be held by the member of the Council who would have held that office in accordance with the original text of Article 2 of the Treaty establishing a Single Council and a Single Commission of the European Communities. On expiry of his term of

office, the office of President shall then be held in the order of Member States laid down in the Article referred to above as amended by Article 11.

2. The Council shall make such adaptations to its rules of procedure as are made necessary by accession.

ARTICLE 141

1. The President, the Vice-Presidents and the members of the Commission shall be appointed upon accession. The Commission shall take up its duties on the fifth day after its members have been appointed. The terms of office of the members in office at the time of accession shall terminate at the same time.

2. The Commission shall make such adaptations to its rules of procedure as are made necessary by accession.

ARTICLE 142

1. [Upon accession, new judges shall be appointed to the Court of Justice in order to bring the number of judges up to nine as provided for in Article 17 of this Act.

2. The term of office of one of the judges appointed in accordance with paragraph 1 shall expire on 6 October 1976. That judge shall be chosen by lot. The term of office of the other judge shall expire on 6 October 1979.]

3. Upon accession, a third Advocate-General shall be appointed. His term of office shall expire on 6 October 1979.

4. The Court shall make such adaptations to its rules of procedure as are made necessary by accession. The rules of procedure as adapted shall require the unanimous approval of the Council.

5. In order to give judgment in cases pending before the Court on 1 January 1973 in respect of which oral proceedings have started before that date, the full Court and the Chambers shall be composed as before accession and shall apply the rules of procedure in force on 31 December 1972.

AMENDMENT
Paras. (1) and (2) were substituted by the Adaptation Decision, Art. 28.

ARTICLE 143

[Upon accession, the Economic and Social Committee shall be enlarged by the appointment of forty-two members representing the various categories of economic and social activity in the new Member States. The terms of office of the members thus appointed shall expire at the same time as those of the members in office at the time of accession.]

AMENDMENT
This Article was substituted by the Adaptation Decision, Art. 29.

ARTICLE 144

Upon accession, the Consultative Committee of the European Coal and Steel Community shall be enlarged by the appointment of additional members. The terms of office of the members thus appointed shall expire at the same time as those of the members in office at the time of accession.

ARTICLE 145

Upon accession, the members of the Scientific and Technical Committee shall be appointed in accordance with the procedure laid down in Article 134 of the Euratom Treaty. The Committee shall take up its duties on the fifth day after its members have been appointed. The terms of office of the members in office at the time of accession shall expire at that time.

ARTICLE 146

Upon accession, the Monetary Committee shall be enlarged by the appointment of members representing the new Member States. Their terms of office shall expire at the same time as those of the members in office at the time of accession.

ARTICLE 147

Adaptations to the Rules of the Committees established by the original Treaties and to their rules of procedure necessitated by accession, shall be made as soon as possible after accession.

ARTICLE 148

1. The terms of office of the new members of the Committees listed in Annex VIII shall expire at the same time as those of the members in office at the time of accession.

2. Upon accession, the membership of the Committees listed in Annex IX shall be completely renewed.

TITLE II—APPLICABILITY OF THE ACTS OF THE INSTITUTIONS

ARTICLE 149

From accession, the new Member States shall be considered as being addressees of and as having received notification of directives and decisions within the meaning of Article 189 of the EEC Treaty and of Article 161 of the Euratom Treaty, and of recommendations and decisions within the meaning of Article 14 of the ECSC Treaty, provided that those directives, recommendations and decisions have been notified to all the original Member States.

ARTICLE 150

The application in each new Member State of the acts listed in Annex X to this Act shall be deferred until the dates specified in that list.

ARTICLE 151

1. The following shall be deferred until 1 February 1973:
   (a) the application to the new Member States of the Community rules established for production of and trade in agricultural products and for trade in certain goods processed from agricultural products which are the subject of special arrangements;
   (b) the application to the Community as originally constituted of the amendments made to these rules by this Act, including those arising from Article 153.

2. Paragraph 1 shall not apply to the adaptations referred to in Part II, point A, of Annex I, referred to in Article 29 of this Act.

3. Until 31 January 1973, the arrangements applicable to trade between, on the one hand, a new Member State and, on the other hand, the Community as originally constituted, the other new Member States or third countries, shall be those applied before accession.

ARTICLE 152

The new Member States shall put into effect the measures necessary for them to comply from the date of accession with the provisions of directives and decisions within the meaning of Article 189 of the EEC Treaty and of Article 161 of the Euratom Treaty, and with recommendations and decisions within the meaning of Article 14 of the ECSC Treaty, unless a time limit is provided for in the list in Annex XI or in any other provisions of this Act.

ARTICLE 153

1. Adaptations to the acts of the institutions of the Communities not included in this Act or its Annexes, made by the institutions before accession in accordance with the procedure in paragraph 2 to bring those acts into line with the provisions of this Act, in particular those of Part Four, shall enter into force on accession.

2. The Council, acting by a qualified majority on a proposal from the Commission, or the Commission, according to which of these two institutions adopted the original act, shall to this end draw up the necessary texts.

ARTICLE 154

Notwithstanding Article 3 (3), the principles concerning the general arrangements for regional aid, elaborated within the framework of the application of Articles 92 to 94 of the EEC Treaty and contained in the communication of the Commission of 23 June 1971 and also in the resolution of the Representatives of the Governments of the Member States, meeting in Council, of 20 October 1971, shall apply to the new Member States on 1 July 1973 at the latest.

These texts will be supplemented to take account of the new situation of the Community after accession, so that all the Member States are in the same situation in regard to them.

ARTICLE 155

[The texts of the acts of the institutions of the Communities adopted before accession and drawn up by the Council or the Commission in the Danish and English languages shall, from the date of accession, be authentic under the same conditions as the texts drawn up in the four original languages. They shall be published in the *Official Journal of the European Communities* if the texts in the original languages were so published.]

AMENDMENT
This Article was substituted by the Adaptation Decision, Art. 30.

ARTICLE 156

Agreements, decisions and concerted practices in existence at the time of accession which come within the scope of Article 65 of the ECSC Treaty by reason of accession must be notified to the Commission within three months of accession. Only agreements and decisions which have been notified shall remain provisionally in force until a decision has been taken by the Commission.

ARTICLE 157

Provisions laid down by law, regulation or administrative action designed to ensure the protection of the health of the workers and the general public in the territories of the new Member States against the dangers arising from ionizing radiations shall, in accordance with Article 33 of the Euratom Treaty, be communicated by those States to the Commission within three months of accession.

TITLE III—FINAL PROVISIONS

ARTICLE 158

Annexes I to XI, Protocols Nos. 1 to 30 and the Exchange of Letters on Monetary Questions, which are attached to this Act shall form an integral part thereof.

ARTICLE 159

[The Government of the French Republic shall transmit a certified copy of the Treaty establishing the European Coal and Steel Community and the Treaties amending that Treaty to the Governments of the Kingdom of Denmark, Ireland and the United Kingdom of Great Britain and Northern Ireland.]

AMENDMENT
  This Article was substituted by the Adaptation Decision, Art. 31.

ARTICLE 160

[The Government of the Italian Republic shall transmit a certified copy of the Treaty establishing the European Economic Community, the Treaty establishing the European Atomic Energy Community and the Treaties amending or supplementing them, in the Dutch, French, German and Italian languages to the Governments of the Kingdom of Denmark, Ireland and the United Kingdom of Great Britain and Northern Ireland.

The texts of the Treaty establishing the European Economic Community and the Treaty establishing the European Atomic Energy Community, and the Treaties amending or supplementing them, drawn up in the Danish, English, Irish and Norwegian languages, shall be annexed to this Act. The texts drawn up in the Danish, English and Irish languages shall be authentic under the same conditions as the original texts of the Treaties referred to above.]

AMENDMENT
  This Article was substituted by the Adaptation Decision, Art. 32.

ARTICLE 161

A certified copy of the international agreements deposited in the archives of the Secretariat of the Council of the European Communities shall be transmitted to the Governments of the new Member States by the Secretary-General.

ANNEX VI—LIST OF THE COUNTRIES REFERRED TO IN ARTICLE 109 OF THE ACT OF ACCESSION AND IN PROTOCOL No. 22

Barbados
Botswana
Fiji
The Gambia
Ghana
Guyana
Jamaica
Kenya
Lesotho
Malawi
Mauritius
Nigeria
Sierra Leone
Swaziland
Tanzania
Tonga
Trinidad and Tobago
Uganda
Western Samoa
Zambia

Protocols

PROTOCOL NO. 1 ON THE STATUTE OF THE EUROPEAN INVESTMENT BANK

Part 1

ADJUSTMENTS TO THE STATUTE OF THE EUROPEAN INVESTMENT BANK

ARTICLE 1

[*This Article amends the Protocol on the Statute of the European Investment Bank, Art. 3, and is incorporated therein.*]

ARTICLE 2

[*This Article amends the Protocol on the Statute of the European Investment Bank, Art. 4 (1), and is incorporated therein.*]

ARTICLE 3

[*This Article amends the Protocol on the Statute of the European Investment Bank, Art. 5, and is incorporated therein.*]

ARTICLE 4

[*This Article amends the Protocol on the Statute of the European Investment Bank, Art. 9 (3) (a) and (c), and is incorporated therein.*]

ARTICLE 5

[*This Article amends the Protocol on the Statute of the European Investment Bank, Art. 10, and is incorporated therein.*]

ARTICLE 6

[*This Article amends the Protocol on the Statute of the European Investment Bank, Art. 11 (2), and is incorporated therein.*]

ARTICLE 7

[*This Article amends the Protocol on the Statute of the European Investment Bank, Art. 12 (1), and is incorporated therein.*]

ARTICLE 8

[*This Article amends the Protocol on the Statute of the European Investment Bank, Art. 12 (2), and is incorporated therein.*]

ARTICLE 9

[*This Article amends the Protocol on the Statute of the European Investment Bank, Art. 13 (1), and is incorporated therein.*]

Part II

OTHER PROVISIONS

ARTICLE 10

1. The new Member States shall, not later than two months from the date of accession, make the payments laid down in paragraph 1 of the amended Article 5 of the Statute of the Bank set out in Article 3 of this Protocol. These payments shall be made in their respective national

currencies. One-fifth of the payment shall be in cash and four-fifths in the form of non-interest-bearing government notes, maturing in four equal instalments, nine months, twenty-three months and thirty months respectively from the date of accession. Part or all of the government notes may be redeemed before their due date by agreement between the Bank and the new Member State concerned. The cash payments and the proceeds of the government notes when repaid, shall be freely convertible.

2. Article 7 of the Statute of the Bank shall apply to all payments made by the new Member States in their respective national currencies under this Article. Any necessary adjustments relating to outstanding government notes shall be made at the date of maturity or advance redemption of these notes.

ARTICLE 11

1. [The new Member States shall contribute towards the statutory reserve and those provisions equivalent to reserves, as at 31 December of the year prior to accession, as stated in the Bank's approved balance sheet, the amounts corresponding to the following percentages of these reserves:

United Kingdom	...	...	...	...	...	30%
Denmark	...	...	...	...	...	4%
Ireland	...	...	...	...	...	1%]

2. The amounts of the payments under this Article shall be calculated in units of account after the Bank's annual balance sheet for the year prior to accession has been approved.

3. These amounts shall be paid in five equal instalments not later than two months, nine months, sixteen months, twenty-three months and thirty months after accession. Each of these five instalments shall be paid in the freely convertible national currency of each new Member State.

AMENDMENT
Para. (1) was substituted by the Adaptation Decision, Art. 39.

ARTICLE 12

1. [Upon accession, the Board of Governors shall increase the Board of Directors by appointing:

3 directors nominated by the United Kingdom of Great Britain and Northern Ireland;
1 director nominated by the Kingdom of Denmark;
1 director nominated by Ireland;
1 director nomainted by the Grand Duchy of Luxembourg;
2 alternatives nominated by the United Kingdom of Great Britain and Northern Ireland.]

2. The terms of office of the directors and alternates thus appointed shall expire at the end of the annual meeting of the Board of Governors during which the annual report for the 1977 financial year is examined.

3. At the end of the annual meeting during which the annual report for the 1972 financial year is examined, the Board of Governors shall appoint for a term of office of five years:

3 directors nominated by the Federal Republic of Germany;
3 directors nominated by the French Republic;
3 directors nominated by the Italian Republic;
1 director nominated by the Kingdom of Belgium;
1 director nominated by the Kingdom of the Netherlands;
1 director nominated by the Commission;
2 alternates nominated by the Federal Republic of Germany;
2 alternates nominated by the French Republic;
2 alternates nominated by the Italian Republic;
1 alternate nominated by common accord of the Benelux countries;
1 alternate nominated by the Commission.

AMENDMENT
Para. (1) was substituted by the Adaptation Decision, Art. 40.

ARTICLE 13

Upon accession, the membership of the Management Committee shall be increased by the appointment of an additional Vice-President. His term of office shall expire at the same time as those of the members of the Management Committee who hold office on the date of accession.

PROTOCOL NO. 3 ON THE CHANNEL ISLANDS AND THE ISLE OF MAN

ARTICLE 1

1. The Community rules on customs matters and quantitative restrictions, in particular those of the Act of Accession, shall apply to the Channel Islands and the Isle of Man under the same conditions as they apply to the United Kingdom. In particular customs duties and charges having equivalent effect between those territories and the Community as originally constituted and between those territories and the new Member States shall be progressively reduced in accordance with the timetable laid down in Articles 32 and 36 of the Act of Accession. The Common Customs Tariff and the ECSC unified tariff shall be progressively applied in accordance with the timetable laid down in Articles 39 and 59 of the Act of Accession, and account being taken of Articles 109, 110 and 119 of the Act.

2. In respect of agricultural products and products processed therefrom which are the subject of a special trade regime, the levies and other import measures laid down in Community rules and applicable by the United Kingdom shall be applied to third countries.

Such provisions of Community rules, in particular those of the Act of Accession, as are necessary to allow free movement and observance of normal conditions of competition in trade in these products shall also be applicable.

The Council, acting by a qualified majority on a proposal from the Commission, shall determine the conditions under which the provisions referred to in the preceding subparagraphs shall be applicable to these territories.

ARTICLE 2

The rights enjoyed by Channel Islanders or Manxmen in the United Kingdom shall not be affected by the Act of Accession. However, such persons shall not benefit from Community provisions relating to the free movement of persons and services.

ARTICLE 3

The provisions of the Euratom Treaty applicable to persons or undertakings within the meaning of Article 196 of that Treaty shall apply to those persons or undertakings when they are established in the aforementioned territories.

ARTICLE 4

The authorities of these territories shall apply the same treatment to all natural and legal persons of the Community.

ARTICLE 5

If, during the application of the arrangements defined in this Protocol, difficulties appear on either side in relations between the Community and these territories, the Commission shall without delay propose to the Council such safeguard measures as it believes necessary, specifying their terms and conditions of application.

The Council shall act by a qualified majority within one month.

ARTICLE 6

In this Protocol, Channel Islander or Manxman shall mean any citizen of the United Kingdom and Colonies who holds that citizenship by virtue of the fact that he, a parent or grandparent was born, adopted, naturalised or registered in the island in question; but such a person shall not for this purpose be regarded as a Channel Islander or Manxman if he, a parent or a grandparent was born, adopted, naturalised or registered in the United Kingdom. Nor shall he be so regarded if he has at any time been ordinarily resident in the United Kingdom for five years.

The administrative arrangements necessary to identify these persons will be notfied to the Commission.

318

PROTOCOL NO. 4 ON GREENLAND

Article 1

Denmark may retain its national provisions whereby a six month period of residence in Greenland is required to obtain a licence for engaging in certain commercial activities in that territory.

The Council may, acting in accordance with the procedure laid down in Article 57 of the EEC Treaty, decide upon a liberalisation of this system.

Article 2

The institutions of the Community will seek, within the framework of the common organisation of the market in fishery products, adequate solutions to the specific problems of Greenland.

PROTOCOL NO. 17 ON THE IMPORT OF SUGAR BY THE UNITED KINGDOM FROM THE EXPORTING COUNTRIES AND TERRITORIES REFERRED TO IN THE COMMONWEALTH SUGAR AGREEMENT

1. Until 28 February 1975, the United Kingdom is authorised to import from the exporting countries and territories referred to in the Commonwealth Sugar Agreement, on the following terms, quantities of sugar within the negotiated price quotas under that Agreement.

2. The following shall be charged at the time of importation:

   (a) a special levy equal to the difference between the c.i.f. equivalent of the agreed purchase price and the price at which the sugar is marketed in the United Kingdom. Article 55 (1) (b) of the Act of Accession shall not apply;

   (b) a charge based on the difference between the world c.i.f. price of raw sugar and the c.i.f. equivalent of the agreed purchase price; this charge will be used to finance the costs involved in the re-selling of the sugar by the United Kingdom Sugar Board.

   However, if the world c.i.f. price of raw sugar exceeds the c.i.f. equivalent of the agreed purchase price, the Board shall pay the difference to the importer.

3. The price at which the sugar in question is marketed in the United Kingdom shall be fixed at a level such as to allow the quantities in question effectively to be marketed without prejudicing the marketing of Community sugar.

4. Notwithstanding the provisions of Article 15 (1) of Regulation (EEC) No. 766/68 laying down general rules for the grant of export refunds for sugar, the export refund applicable in the United Kingdom may be granted for white sugar produced from raw sugar imported under the terms of this Protocol.

5. The Council shall, acting by a qualified majority on a proposal from the Commission, adopt the measures necessary for implementing the provisions of this Protocol in such a way as to ensure the proper functioning of the common organisation of the market in sugar and in particular to ensure that, in the application of the provisions laid down in paragraph 2, the price at which the sugar is marketed in the United Kingdom is respected.

PROTOCOL NO. 22 ON RELATIONS BETWEEN THE EUROPEAN ECONOMIC COMMUNITY AND THE ASSOCIATED AFRICAN AND MALAGASY STATES AND ALSO THE INDEPENDENT DEVELOPING COMMONWEALTH COUNTRIES SITUATED IN AFRICA, THE INDIAN OCEAN, THE PACIFIC OCEAN AND THE CARIBBEAN

I

1. The European Economic Community shall offer the independent Commonwealth countries listed in Annex VI to the Act of Accession the possibility of ordering their relations with the Community in the spirit of the Declaration of Intent adopted by the Council at its meeting held on 1/2 April 1963, according to one of the following formulae at their choice:

—participation in the Convention of Association which, upon the expiry of the Convention of Association signed on 29 July 1969, will govern relations between the Community and the Associated African and Malagasy States which signed the latter Convention;

—the conclusion of one or more special conventions of association on the basis of Article 238 of the EEC Treaty comprising reciprocal rights and obligations, particularly in the field of trade;

—the conclusion of trade agreements with a view to facilitating and developing trade between the Community and those countries.

2. For practical reasons, the Community desires that the independent Commonwealth countries to which its offer is addressed, should take up a position with respect to this offer as soon as possible after accession.

The Community proposes to the independent Commonwealth countries listed in Annex VI to the Act of Accession that the negotiations envisaged for the conclusion of agreements based on one of the formulae contained in the offer should begin as from 1 August 1973.

The Community accordingly invites the independent Commonwealth countries which choose to negotiate within the framework of the first formula to participate side by side with the Associated African and Malagasy States in negotiating the new Convention to follow the Convention signed on 29 July 1969.

3. In the event of Botswana, Lesotho or Swaziland choosing one of the first two formulae contained in the offer:

—appropriate solutions must be found for the specific problems arising from the special circumstances of these countries, which are in a customs union with a third country;

—the Community must, in the territory of those States, enjoy tariff treatment not less favourable than that applied by those States to the most-favoured third country;

—the provisions of the system applied, and particularly the rules of origin must be such as to avoid any risk of trade deflection to the detriment of the Community resulting from the participation of those States in a customs union with a third country.

II

1. As regards the association arrangements to be made on the expiry of the Convention of Association signed on 29 July 1969, the Community is ready to pursue its policy of association both with regard to the Associated African and Malagasy States and with regard to the independent developing Commonwealth countries which become parties to the same association.

2. The accession of the new Member States to the Community and the possible extension of the policy of association should not be the source of any weakening in the Community's relations with the Associated African and Malagasy States which are parties of the Convention of Association signed on 29 July 1969.

The Community's relations with the Associated African and Malagasy States ensure for those States a range of advantages and are based on structures which give the Association its distinctive character in the fields of trade relations, financial and technical cooperation and joint institutions.

3. The Community's objective in its policy of association shall remain the safe-guarding of what has been achieved and of the fundamental principles referred to above.

4. The provisions of this association, which will be defined during the negotiations referred to in the third subparagraph in Part I (2) of this Protocol, must similarly take account of the special economic conditions common to the independent developing Commonwealth countries situated in Africa, the Indian Ocean, the Pacific Ocean and the Caribbean, and the Associated African and Malagasy States, the experience acquired within the framework of association, the wishes of the Associated States and the consequences for those States of the introduction of the generalised preference scheme.

320

III

The Community will have as its firm purpose the safeguarding of the interests of all the countries referred to in this Protocol whose economies depend to a considerable extent on the export of primary products, and particularly of sugar.

The question of sugar will be settled within this framework, bearing in mind with regard to exports of sugar the importance of this product for the economies of several of these countries and of the Commonwealth countries in particular.

PROTOCOL NO. 24 ON THE PARTICIPATION OF THE NEW MEMBER STATES IN THE FUNDS OF THE EUROPEAN COAL AND STEEL COMMUNITY

[The contributions of the new Member States to the funds of the European Coal and Steel Community shall be fixed as follows:

United Kingdom	57,000,000 ua
Denmark	635,500 ua
Ireland	77,500 ua

Payment of these contributions shall take place in three equal annual instalments beginning on accession.

Each instalment shall be paid in the freely convertible national currency of each new Member State.]

AMENDMENT

This Protocol was substituted by the Adaptation Decision, Art. 45.

PROTOCOL NO. 30 ON IRELAND

THE HIGH CONTRACTING PARTIES,

desiring to settle certain special problems of concern to Ireland, and

having agreed the following provisions,

recall that the fundamental objectives of the European Economic Community include the steady improvement of the living standards and working conditions of the peoples of the Member States and the harmonious development of their economies by reducing the differences existing between the various regions and the backwardness of the less-favoured regions;

take note of the fact that the Irish Government has embarked upon the implementation of a policy of industrialization and economic development designed to align the standards of living in Ireland with those of the other European nations and to eliminate underemployment while progressively evening out regional differences in levels of development;

recognize it to be in their common interest that the objectives of this policy be so attained;

agree to recommend to this end that the Community institutions implement all the means and procedures laid down by the EEC Treaty, particularly by making adequate use of the Community resources intended for the realization of the Community's above-mentioned objectives;

recognize in particular that, in the application of Articles 92 and 93 of the EEC Treaty, it will be necessary to take into account the objectives of economic expansion and the raising of the standard of living of the population.

EXCHANGE OF LETTERS ON MONETARY QUESTIONS

Brussels, 22 January 1972

Your Excellency,

1. At the Ministerial Meeting of the Conference on 7 June 1971, it was agreed that the declaration on monetary questions which I made at the Meeting should form the subject of an exchange of letters annexed to the Act concerning the Conditions of Accession and the Adjustments to the Treaties. I therefore now have the honour to confirm that at that Meeting I made the following declaration:

" (a) We are prepared to envisage an orderly and gradual run-down of official sterling balances after our accession.

(b) We shall be ready to discuss after our entry into the Communities what measures might be appropriate to achieve a progressive alignment of the external characteristics and practices in relation to sterling with those of other currencies in the Community in the context of progress towards economic and monetary union in the enlarged Community, and we are confident that official sterling[1] can be handled in a way which will enable us to take our full part in that progress.

(c) In the meantime we shall manage our policies with a view to stabilising the official sterling balances in a way which would be consistent with these longer term objectives.

(d) I hope that the Community will regard this statement as disposing satisfactorily of the question of sterling and associated matters, leaving only the arrangements for U.K. compliance with the Directives relating to capital movements under the Treaty of Rome to be settled in the course of the negotiations."

2. At the same meeting on 7 June, the above declaration was agreed by the Community delegation.

3. I understand that the delegations of the Kingdom of Denmark, Ireland and the Kingdom of Norway have also signified their agreement to the above-mentioned declaration as confirmed by the present letter.

4. I would be grateful if you would kindly acknowledge receipt of this letter and confirm the agreement of the Governments of the Member States of the Community and of the Government of the Kingdom of Denmark, Ireland and the Kingdom of Norway to the above-mentioned declaration.

Please accept, Your Excellency, the assurance of my highest consideration.

GEOFFREY RIPPON
Chancellor of the Duchy of Lancaster.

Monsieur G. Thorn,
Ministre des Affaires Etrangères du
Grand-Duché du Luxembourg.

Brussels, 22 January 1972

Your Excellency,

You were good enough to make the following communication to me in your letter to today's date:

" 1. At the Ministerial Meeting of the Conference on 7 June 1971, it was agreed that the declaration on monetary questions which I made at the Meeting should form the subject of an exchange of letters annexed to the Act concerning the Conditions of Accession and the Adjustments to the Treaties. I therefore now have the honour to confirm that at that Meeting I made the following declaration:

' (a) We are prepared to envisage an orderly and gradual run-down of official sterling balances after our accession.

(b) We shall be ready to discuss after our entry into the Communities what measures might be appropriate to achieve a progressive alignment of the external characteristics and practices in relation to sterling with those of other currencies in the Community in the context of progress towards economic and monetary union in the enlarged Community, and we are confident that official sterling[1] can be handled in a way which will enable us to take our full part in that progress.

(c) In the meantime we shall manage our policies with a view to stabilising the official sterling balances in a way which would be consistent with these longer term objectives.

(d) I hope that the Community will regard this statement as disposing satisfactorily of the question of sterling and associated matters, leaving only the arrangements for U.K. compliance with the Directives relating to capital movements under the Treaty of Rome to be settled in the course of the negotiations '.

2. At the same meeting on 7 June, the above declaration was agreed by the Community delegation.

3. I understand that the delegations of the Kingdom of Denmark, Ireland and the Kingdom of Norway have also signified their agreement to the above-mentioned declaration as confirmed by the present letter.

---

[1] " Official sterling " means " official sterling balances."

4. I would be grateful if you would kindly acknowledge receipt of this letter and confirm the agreement of the Governments of the Member States of the Community and of the Governments of the Kingdom of Denmark, Ireland and the Kingdom of Norway to the above-mentioned declaration ".

I have the honour to acknowledge receipt of this communication and to confirm the agreement of the Governments of the Member States of the Community and the Governments of the Kingdom of Denmark, Ireland and the Kingdom of Norway to the declaration contained in paragraph 1 of your letter.

Please accept, Your Excellency, the assurance of my highest consideration.

GASTON THORN
*Ministère des Affaires Etrangères du
Grand-Duché du Luxembourg.*

P. HARMEL
Ministre des Affaires Estrangères
du Royaume de Belgique
Minister van Buitenlandse Zaken
van het Koninkrijk België

IVAR NØRGAARD
Kongeriget Danmarks
Udenrigsøkonomiminister

WALTER SCHEEL
Bundesminister des Auswärtigen
der Bundesrepublik Deutschland

MAURICE SCHUMANN
Ministre des Affaires Etrangères
de la République Française

PÁDRAIG O HIRIGHILE
Aire Gnóthaí Eachtracha
na hÉireann

ALDO MORO
Ministro per gli Affari Esteri
della Repubblica Italiana

N. SCHMELZER
Minister van Buitenlandse Zaken
van het Koninkrijk der Nederlanden

ANDREAS CAPPELEN
Kongeriket Norges Utenriksminister

The Right Honourable Geoffrey Rippon, Q.C., M.P.,
Chancellor of the Duchy of Lancaster

FINAL ACT

Text of Final Act

The Plenipotentiaries of HIS MAJESTY THE KING OF THE BELGIANS, HER MAJESTY THE QUEEN OF DENMARK, THE PRESIDENT OF THE FEDERAL REPUBLIC OF GERMANY, THE PRESIDENT OF THE FRENCH REPUBLIC, THE PRESIDENT OF IRELAND, THE PRESIDENT OF THE ITALIAN REPUBLIC, HIS ROYAL HIGHNESS THE GRAND DUKE OF LUXEMBOURG, HER MAJESTY THE QUEEN OF THE NETHERLANDS, HIS MAJESTY THE KING OF NORWAY, HER MAJESTY THE QUEEN OF THE UNITED KINGDOM OF GREAT BRITAIN AND NORTHERN IRELAND AND THE COUNCIL OF THE EUROPEAN COMMUNITIES represented by its President,

Assembled at Brussels on the twenty-second day of January one thousand nine hundred and seventy-two on the occasion of the signature of the Treaty relating to the accession of the Kingdom of Denmark, Ireland, the Kingdom of Norway and the United Kingdom of Great Britain and Northern Ireland to the European Economic Community and the European Atomic Energy Community,

Have placed on record the fact that the following texts have been drawn up and adopted within the Conference between the European Communities and the States which have applied for accession to those Communities:

    I. the Treaty concerning the accession of the Kingdom of Denmark, Ireland, the Kingdom of Norway and the United Kingdom of Great Britain and Northern Ireland to the European Economic Community and to the European Atomic Energy Community;

   II. the Act concerning the Conditions of Accession and the Adjustments to the Treaties;

  III. the texts listed below which are annexed to the Act concerning the Conditions of Accession and the Adjustments to the Treaties:

A.	ANNEX I	List referred to in Article 29 of the Act of Accession,
	ANNEX II	List referred to in Article 30 of the Act of Accession,
	ANNEX III	List of products referred to in Articles 32, 36 and 39 of the Act of Accession (Euratom),
	ANNEX IV	List of products referred to in Article 32 of the Act of Accession (Commonwealth products which are subject to contractual margins of preference in the United Kingdom),
	ANNEX V	List referred to in Article 107 of the Act of Accession,
	ANNEX VI	List of countries referred to in Article 109 of the Act of Accession and in Protocol No. 22,
	ANNEX VII	List referred to in Article 133 of the Act of Accession,
	ANNEX VIII	List referred to in Article 148 (1) of the Act of Accession,
	ANNEX IX	List referred to in Article 148 (2) of the Act of Accession,
	ANNEX X	List referred to in Article 150 of the Act of Accession,
	ANNEX XI	List referred to in Article 152 of the Act of Accession.

B.	PROTOCOL No. 1	on the Statute of the European Investment Bank,
	PROTOCOL No. 2	on the Faroe Islands,
	PROTOCOL No. 3	on the Channel Islands and the Isle of Man,
	PROTOCOL No. 4	on Greenland,
	PROTOCOL No. 5	on Svalbard (Spitzbergen),
	PROTOCOL No. 6	on certain quantitative restrictions relating to Ireland
	PROTOCOL No. 7	on imports of motor vehicles and the motor vehicle assembly industry in Ireland,
	PROTOCOL No. 8	on phosphorus (CCT subheading No. 28.04 C IV),
	PROTOCOL No. 9	on aluminium oxide and hydroxide (alumina) (CCT subheading No. 28.20 A),
	PROTOCOL No. 10	on tanning extracts of wattle (mimosa) (CCT subheading No. 32.01 A) and tanning extracts of chestnut (CCT subheading No. 32.01 C),
	PROTOCOL No. 11	on plywood (CCT heading No. 44.15),
	PROTOCOL No. 12	on wood pulp (CCT subheading No. 47.01 A II),
	PROTOCOL No. 13	on newsprint (CCT subheading No. 48.01 A),
	PROTOCOL No. 14	on unwrought lead (CCT subheading No. 78.01 A),
	PROTOCOL No. 15	on unwrought zinc (CCT subheading No. 79.01 A),
	PROTOCOL No. 16	on markets and trade in agricultural products,

PROTOCOL No. 17   on the import of sugar by the United Kingdom from the exporting countries and territories referred to in the Commonwealth Sugar Agreement,

PROTOCOL No. 18   on the import of New Zealand butter and cheese into the United Kingdom,

PROTOCOL No. 19   on spirituous beverages obtained from cereals,

PROTOCOL No. 20   on Norwegian agriculture,

PROTOCOL No. 21   on the fisheries regime for Norway,

PROTOCOL No. 22   on relations between the European Economic Community and the Associated African and Malagasy States and also the independent developing Commonwealth countries situated in Africa, the Indian Ocean, the Pacific Ocean and the Caribbean,

PROTOCOL No. 23   on the application by the new Member States of the generalised tariff preference scheme applied by the European Economic Community,

PROTOCOL No. 24   on the participation of the new Member States in the funds of the European Coal and Steel Community,

PROTOCOL No. 25   on the exchange of information with Denmark in the field of nuclear energy,

PROTOCOL No. 26   on the exchange of information with Ireland in the field of nuclear energy.

PROTOCOL No. 27   on the exchange of information with Norway in the field of nuclear energy,

PROTOCOL No. 28   on the exchange of information with the United Kingdom in the field of nuclear energy,

PROTOCOL No. 29   on the Agreement with the International Atomic Energy Agency,

PROTOCOL No. 30   on Ireland;

C. Exchange of Letters on Monetary Questions;

D. The texts of the Treaty establishing the European Economic Community and of the Treaty establishing the European Atomic Energy Community, together with the Treaties amending or supplementing them, in the Danish, English, Irish and Norwegian languages.

The Plenipotentiaries have taken note of the Decision of the Council of the European Communities of 22 January 1972 concerning the accession of the Kingdom of Denmark, Ireland, the Kingdom of Norway and the United Kingdom of Great Britain and Northern Ireland to the European Coal and Steel Community.

Furthermore, the Plenipotentiaries and the Council have adopted the Declarations listed below and annexed to this Final Act:

1. Joint Declaration on the Court of Justice,
2. Joint Declaration on the Sovereign Base Areas of the United Kingdom of Great Britain and Northern Ireland in Cyprus,
3. Joint Declaration on the fisheries sector,
4. Joint Declaration of Intent on the development of trade relations with Ceylon, India, Malaysia, Pakistan and Singapore,
5. Joint Declaration on the free movement of workers.

The Plenipotentiaries and the Council have also taken note of the following Declaration to this Final Act:

Declaration by the Government of the Federal Republic of Germany on the application to Berlin of the Decision concerning Accession to the European Coal and Steel Community and of the Treaty of Accession to the European Economic Community and to the European Atomic Energy Community.

The Plenipotentiaries and the Council have also taken note of the arrangement regarding the procedure for adopting certain decisions and other measures to be taken during the period preceding accession which has been reached within the Conference between the European Communities and the States which have applied for accession to those Communities and which is annexed to this Final Act.

Finally, the following declarations have been made and are annexed to this Final Act:

1. Declaration by the Government of the United Kingdom of Great Britain and Northern Ireland on the definition of the term " nationals ",
2. Declarations on the economic and industrial development of Ireland,

3. Declarations on liquid milk, pigmeat and eggs,
4. Declaration on the system for fixed Community farm prices,
5. Declarations on hill farming.

In witness whereof, the undersigned Plenipotentiaries have signed this Final Act.

Done at Brussels this twenty-second day of January in the year one thousand nine hundred and seventy-two.

G. EYSKENS
P. HARMEL
J. VAN DER MEULEN

Jens Otto KRAG
Ivar NØRGAARD
Jens CHRISTENSEN

Walter SCHEEL
H. G. SACHS

Maurice SCHUMANN
J.-M. BOEGNER

Sean O LOINSIGH
Padraig O HIRIGHILE

COLOMBO
Aldo MORO
BOMBASSEI DE VETTOR

Gaston THORN
J. DONDELINGER

N. SCHMELZER
T. WESTERTERP
SASSEN

Trygve BRATTELI
Andreas CAPPELEN
S. Chr. SOMMERFELT

Edward HEATH
Alec DOUGLAS-HOME
Geoffrey RIPPON

Declarations

JOINT DECLARATION ON THE COURT OF JUSTICE

Such additional measures as may prove necessary following the accession of the new Member States should be taken by the Council which, at the request of the Court, may increase the number of Advocates-General to four and adjust the provisions of the third paragraph of Article 32 of the ECSC Treaty, the third paragraph of Article 165 of the EEC Treaty and the third paragraph of Article 137 of the Euratom Treaty accordingly.

JOINT DECLARATION ON THE SOVEREIGN BASE AREAS OF THE UNITED KINGDOM OF GREAT BRITAIN AND NORTHERN IRELAND IN CYPRUS

The arrangements applicable to relations between the European Economic Community and the Sovereign Base Areas of the United Kingdom of Great Britain and Northern Ireland in Cyprus will be defined within the context of any agreement between that Community and the Republic of Cyprus.

JOINT DECLARATION ON THE FISHERIES SECTOR

1. The institutions of the European Economic Community will examine the problems of the fish meal and fish oils sector with a view to adopting measures which might prove necessary in that sector in respect to the raw material used. These measures should meet the need for protection and rational use of the sea's biological resources while avoiding the creation or retention of insufficiently profitable production units.

2. The application of common marketing standards for certain fresh or chilled fish must not have the effect of excluding any marketing method and, conversely, no marketing method should hinder the application of the said standards; it is in this spirit that the problems which could arise may be settled when the time comes by the institutions of the European Economic Community.

3. The European Economic Community is aware of the importance of Norwegian exports of fish products to third countries, which are subject like other Community exports to Regulation (EEC) No. 2142/70.

4. It is understood that the Norwegian law on " marketing of fish coming from processing industries " of 18 December 1970 will be the subject, as soon as possible, of a detailed study with a view to examining the conditions under which it might be applied, having regard to the provisions of Community law.

JOINT DECLARATION OF INTENT ON THE DEVELOPMENT OF TRADE RELATIONS WITH CEYLON, INDIA, MALAYSIA, PAKISTAN AND SINGAPORE

Inspired by the will to extend and strengthen the trade relations with the developing independent Commonwealth countries in Asia (Ceylon, India, Malaysia, Pakistan and Singapore), the European Economic Community is ready, from the date of accession, to examine with these countries such problems as may arise in the field of trade with a view to seeking appropriate solutions, taking into account the effect of the generalised tariff preference scheme and the situation of the other developing countries in the same geographical area.

The question of exports of sugar from India to the Community after the expiry of the Commonwealth Sugar Agreement on 31 December 1974 must be settled by the Community in the light of this Declaration of Intent, taking account of the provisions which may be adopted as regards imports of sugar from the independent Commonwealth countries listed in Protocol No. 22 on relations between the European Economic Community and the Associated African and Malagasy States and also the independent Commonwealth countries in Africa, the Indian Ocean, the Pacific Ocean and the Caribbean.

JOINT DECLARATION ON THE FREE MOVEMENT OF WORKERS

The enlargement of the Community could give rise to certain difficulties for the social situation in one or more Member States as regards the application of the provisions relating to the free movement of workers.

The Member States declare that they reserve the right, should difficulties of that nature arise, to bring the matter before the institutions of the Community in order to obtain a solution to this problem in accordance with the·provisions of the Treaties establishing the European Communities and the provisions adopted in application thereof.

DECLARATION BY THE GOVERNMENT OF THE FEDERAL REPUBLIC OF GERMANY ON THE APPLICATION TO BERLIN OF THE DECISION CONCERNING ACCESSION TO THE EUROPEAN COAL AND STEEL COMMUNITY AND OF THE TREATY OF ACCESSION TO THE EUROPEAN ECONOMIC COMMUNITY AND TO THE EUROPEAN ATOMIC ENERGY COMMUNITY

The Government of the Federal Republic of Germany reserve the right to declare, when the accession of the Kingdom of Denmark, Ireland, the Kingdom of Norway and the United Kingdom of Great Britain and Northern Ireland to the European Coal and Steel Community takes effect and upon depositing its instrument of ratification of the Treaty concerning the accession of the above-mentioned countries to the European Economic Community and to the European Atomic Energy Community, that the Decision of the Council of 22 January 1972 concerning accession to the European Coal and Steel community and the Treaty referred to above shall equally apply to Land Berlin.

DECLARATION BY THE GOVERNMENT OF THE UNITED KINGDOM OF GREAT BRITAIN AND NORTHERN IRELAND ON THE DEFINITION OF THE TERM " NATIONALS "

At the time of signature of the Treaty of Accession, the Government of the United Kingdom of Great Britain and Northern Ireland make the following Declaration:

" As to the United Kingdom of Great Britain and Northern Ireland, the terms ' nationals ', ' nationals of Member States ' or ' nationals of Member States and overseas countries and territories ' wherever used in the Treaty establishing the European Economic Community, the Treaty establishing the European Atomic Energy Community or the Treaty establishing the European Coal and Steel Community or in any of the Community acts deriving from those Treaties, are to be understood to refer to:

(a) persons who are citizens of the United Kingdom and Colonies or British subject not possessing that citizenship or the citizenship of any other Commonwealth country or territory, who, in either case, have the right of abode in the United Kingdom, and are therefore exempt from United Kingdom immigration control;

(b) persons who are citizens of the United Kingdom and Colonies by birth or by registration or naturalization in Gibraltar, or whose father was so born, registered or naturalized."

DECLARATIONS ON THE ECONOMIC AND INDUSTRIAL DEVELOPMENT OF IRELAND

At the 6th Ministerial Meeting in the negotiations between the Community and Ireland, held on 19 October 1971, Mr. A. Moro, Minister for Foreign Affairs of the Italian Republic, made, on behalf of the Community delegation, the declaration appearing under I hereinafter.

Mr. P. J. Hillery, Minister for Foreign Affairs of Ireland, replied, on behalf of the Irish delegation, with the declaration appearing under II hereinafter.

Declaration on Ireland

I. *Declaration made by Mr. A. MORO, Minister of Foreign Affairs of the Italian Republic on behalf of the Community delegation*

I.

1. The Irish delegation has stressed that the Irish Government is faced with serious economic and social imbalances of a regional and structural nature. This delegation has stated that these imbalances should be remedied in order to achieve a degree of harmonisation consistent with the objectives of the Community and particularly with the realisation of economic and monetary union. The Irish delegation has asked the Community to undertake to employ its means to support the Irish Government's programmes aimed at eliminating these imbalances and to take full account of Ireland's special problems in this field in the development of a major Community regional policy at a later date.

2. The Irish delegation has submitted documents to the Community delegation indicating the general direction and the instruments of the Irish regional programmes. The Irish delegation has also explained how the Irish exporting industries are supported by tax relief. In this respect it is also a question of measures the aim of which is to do away with economic and social imbalances by the development of industry.

II.

1. The Community delegation emphasises in this connection that—as follows from the Preamble to the Treaty of Rome—the essential objectives of the Community consist in the constant improvement of the living and working conditions of the peoples of the Member States, and the harmonious development of the economies of these States by reducing the differences existing between the various regions and the backwardness of the less-favoured regions.

2. The common policies and the various instruments created by the Community in the economic and social sectors are a positive realisation of the abovementioned objectives and are furthermore likely to develop. The European Social Fund has been directed along new lines. The European Investment Bank is constantly expanding the field of its activities. At the present time, the institutions of the Community are engaged in discussions to decide the Community instruments, which it is possible to introduce, and according to what procedures, in order to achieve the objectives of the regional policy.

The aids granted by the States, including those granted by way of tax exemptions, are subject to the rules laid down in Articles 92 to 94 of the EEC Treaty. With regard to State aids for regional purposes it should be stressed that, under the terms of Article 92 (3) (*a*) " aid to promote the economic development of areas where the standard of living is abnormally low or where there is serious under-employment " may be considered to be compatible with the common market. Experience shows that this provision is flexible enough for the Community authorities to be able to take into consideration the special requirements of the under-developed regions.

Tax exemptions—in common with all other aids existing in Ireland at the time of accession—will be studied by the Commission in the normal framework of the permanent examination of existing aids. If this examination were to reveal that it would not be possible to retain any particular aid in its existing form, it will fall to the Commission under the rules of the Treaty to establish the appropriate time limits and transitional procedures.

3. Having regard to the abovementioned special problems with which Ireland is confronted, the Community delegation proposes to annex to the Act of Accession a protocol on the economic and industrial development of Ireland.

II. *Declaration made by Mr. P. J. HILLERY, Minister for Foreign Affairs of Ireland, on behalf of the Irish delegation*

I am pleased to record the Irish delegation's acceptance of the proposed Protocol concerning Ireland which has been the subject of discussions between our two delegations and the background to which has been so clearly set out in your introductory statement. The text adopted will enable the Irish Government to proceed with their plans for economic and social development in the knowledge that the Community, through its institutions and agencies, will be ready to co-operate with us in the pursuit of the objectives which we have set ourselves.

I have on a number of occasions in the course of the negotiations, drawn attention to the problems posed by differences in the level of economic development in an entity such as the enlarged Community. I have endeavoured also to explain to you the difficulties which a country such as Ireland, situated on the periphery of the enlarged Community, must overcome in order to approximate its level of economic development to that of the other Member States. I am fully aware of the Community's will and purpose to achieve the aims set out in the EEC Treaty of ensuring the constant improvement of the living and working conditions of the peoples of the Member States and the harmonious development of their economies. The Protocol on which we have reached agreement today is a convincing demonstration of the Community's determination to give real content to these fundamental aims. This Protocol will be an instrument of practical value in enabling my country to play a full part within the enlarged Community in achieving these aims. Its effectiveness for this purpose will be greatly enhanced by the development of a comprehensive Community regional policy. In this connection may I say that I am heartened by the efforts being made to deal with this important issue as part of the evolution of the Community.

In Irish circumstances, the effectiveness of development measures, whether at the national or Community level, must be judged by progress in the reduction of unemployment and emigration and the raising of living standards. This is essentially a matter of providing for our growing work force the necessary job opportunities without which a substantial proportion of our most valuable economic resources will remain unused or be lost through emigration and the pace of economic development will be retarded.

My Government will be gratified that our discussions today have shown that Ireland's accession to the Community will enable them to maintain the drive towards the realisation of their aims as recited in the Protocol. I have particularly in mind here the continuing growth of industry which is central to our general aim of economic expansion. It is of vital importance to us that progress in this area be maintained through the application of effective measures of industrial promotion. I understand that, like any other incentive scheme, our industrial incentives will come up for examination under Community rules after accession. I note with satisfaction that you recognise the necessity for an incentive policy in Ireland but that questions may arise about the particular forms our scheme of incentives has taken while we have been outside the Community.

I would like to draw your attention to the fact that the question would arise in this connection of the commitments which we had previously entered into. We shall, of course, have to honour these commitments but we shall be ready to discuss in all its aspects the change-over to whatever new incentive system is devised and we shall collaborate in solving these problems in an appropriate way.

I am fully satisfied from what you have said about the flexible nature of the relevant Treaty provisions that in the examination of our incentives the Community institutions will take full account of our special problems. I am also satisfied in the light of the identity of aims of both the Irish government and the Community that if adjustments of these incentives is called for, the Irish government will be able to maintain the growth of Irish industry, and achieve a continuous improvement in the level of employment and living standards.

Finally, may I say in conclusion that I appreciate the sympathy and understanding which the Community has shown in its approach to and examination of the questions of our regional problems and industrial incentives which are of the greatest importance to my country. The agreement which we have reached augurs well for our future co-operation within the enlarged Community in pursuit of the fundamental aims of the Treaty. I see in this future co-operation the means by which we in Ireland can best achieve our national economic objectives.

PROCEDURE FOR THE ADOPTION OF CERTAIN DECISIONS AND OTHER MEASURES TO BE TAKEN DURING THE PERIOD PRECEDING ACCESSION

I.

INFORMATION AND CONSULTATION PROCEDURE FOR THE ADOPTION OF CERTAIN DECISIONS

1. In order to ensure that the Kingdom of Denmark, Ireland, the Kingdom of Norway and the United Kingdom of Great Britain and Northern Ireland, hereinafter referred to as the " acceding States " are kept adequately informed, and proposal or communication from the Commission of the European Communities which might lead to decisions by the Council of these Communities shall be brought to the knowledge of the acceding States after being transmitted to the Council.

2. Consultations shall take place pursuant to a reasoned request by an acceding State, which shall set out expressly therein its interests as a future member of the Communities and its observations.

3. Administrative decisions shall not, as a general rule, give rise to consultations.

4. Consultations shall take place within an Interim Committee composed of representatives of the Communities and of the acceding States.

5. On the Community side, the members of the Interim Committee shall be the members of the Committee of Permanent Representatives or persons designated by them for this purpose, who shall, as a general rule, be their deputies. The Commission shall be invited to be represented in this work.

6. The Interim Committee shall be assisted by a Secretariat which shall be that of the Conference, continued for this purpose.

7. Consultations shall normally take place as soon as the preparatory work carried out at Community level with a view to the adoption of decisions by the Council has produced common guidelines enabling such consultations to be usefully arranged.

8. If serious difficulties remain after consultations, the matter may be raised at Ministerial level at the request of an acceding State.

9. The procedure laid down in the above paragraphs shall also apply to any decision to be taken by the acceding States which might affect the commitments resulting from their position as future members of the Communities.

II.

The Kingdom of Denmark, Ireland, the Kingdom of Norway and the United Kingdom of Great Britain and Northern Ireland shall take the necessary measures to ensure that their accession to the agreements or conventions referred to in Articles 3 (2) and 4 (2) of the Act concerning the Conditions of Accession and the Adjustments to the Treaties coincides so far as possible, and under the conditions laid down in that Act, with the entry into force of the Treaty of Accession.

In so far as the agreements or conventions between the Member States, referred to in the second sentence of Article 3 (1) and in Article 3 (2), exist only in draft, have not yet been signed, and probably cannot be signed in the period before accession, the acceding States will be invited to be associated, after the signature of the Treaty of Accession and in accordance with appropriate procedures, in the preparation of those drafts in a positive spirit and in such manner as to facilitate their conclusion.

III.

With regard to the negotiation of the agreements envisaged with the EFTA States which have not applied for membership of the European Communities, and the negotiation of certain adjustments to the preferential agreements concluded under the Treaties establishing the European Communities, the representatives of the acceding States shall be associated with the work as observers, side by side with the representatives of the original Member States.

Certain non-preferential agreements concluded by the Community which remain in force after 1 January 1973 may be the subject of adaptations or adjustments in order to take account of the enlargement of the Community. These adaptations or adjustments will be negotiated by the Community in association with the representatives of the acceding States in accordance with the procedure under the preceding paragraph.

IV.

With regard to the Treaty on the Non-Proliferation of Nuclear Weapons, the Kingdom of Denmark, Ireland and the Kingdom of Norway shall coordinate their positions with that of the European Atomic Energy Community when negotiating a verification agreement with the International Atomic Energy Agency. With regard to the control agreements which they might conclude with the Agency, they shall ask for the inclusion in these agreements of a clause allowing them to replace these agreements as soon as possible after accession by the verification agreement which the Community may conclude with the Agency.

In the period preceding accession the United Kingdom and the Community shall enter into consultations occasioned by the fact that the control and inspection system applicable under the agreement between several Member States and the European Atomic Energy Community on the one hand and the International Atomic Energy Agency on the other hand will be accepted by the United Kingdom.

V.

The consultations between the acceding States and the Commission provided for in Article 120 (2) of the Act concerning the Conditions of Accession and the Adjustments to the Treaties shall take place before accession.

VI.

The acceding States undertake that the granting of the licences referred to in Article 2 of Protocols Nos. 25 to 28 on the exchange of information in the field of nuclear energy shall not be deliberately accelerated before accession with a view to reducing the scope of the commitments contained in those Protocols.

331

VII.

The institutions of the Community shall, in due course, draw up the texts referred to in Article 153 of the Act concerning the Conditions of Accession and the Adjustments to the Treaties.

VIII.

The Community shall adopt the necessary provisions to ensure that the measures provided for in Protocol No. 19 on spirituous beverages obtained from cereals shall enter into force on accession.

COUNCIL DECISION OF THE EUROPEAN COMMUNITIES OF 1 JANUARY 1973 ADJUSTING THE INSTRUMENTS CONCERNING THE ACCESSION OF NEW MEMBER STATES TO THE EUROPEAN COMMUNITIES

(O.J. 1973, L2/1)

THE COUNCIL OF THE EUROPEAN COMMUNITIES,

Having regard to the Treaty between the Kingdom of Belgium, the Federal Republic of Germany, the French Republic, the Italian Republic, the Grand Duchy of Luxembourg, the Kingdom of the Netherlands (Member States of the European Communities), the Kingdom of Denmark, Ireland, the Kingdom of Norway and the United Kingdom of Great Britain and Northern Ireland concerning the accession of the Kingdom of Denmark, Ireland, the Kingdom of Norway and the United Kingdom of Great Britain and Northern Ireland to the European Economic Community and to the European Atomic Energy Community, and in particular Article 2 thereof;

Having regard to the Decision of the European Communities of 22 January 1972 concerning the accession of the Kingdom of Denmark, Ireland, the Kingdom of Norway and the United Kingdom of Great Britain and Northern Ireland to the European Coal and Steel Community and in particular Article 2 thereof;

Whereas the Kingdom of Norway has not deposited its instruments of accession and ratification in due time and has therefore not become a member of the European Communities;

Whereas adjustments to certain provisions listed in the Article 2 referred to above have therefore become indispensable;

Whereas it is further necessary to adjust those provisions of the Act concerning the Conditions of Accession and the Adjustments to the Treaties which refer expressly to Norway or to declare that those provisions have lapsed;

HAS DECIDED:

ARTICLES 1–47

[*These articles and the Annex to this Decision amend certain articles of the Community Treaties and have been incorporated therein.*]

ARTICLE 48

This Decision, drawn up in the Danish, Dutch, English, French, German, Irish and Italian languages, all seven texts being equally authentic, shall enter into force on 1 January 1973.

Done at Brussels, 1 January 1973.

For the Council
The President
P. HARMEL.

COMMISSION OPINION OF MAY 23, 1979, ON THE APPLICATION FOR ACCESSION TO THE EUROPEAN COMMUNITIES BY THE HELLENIC REPUBLIC

THE COMMISSION OF THE EUROPEAN COMMUNITIES,

HAVING REGARD to Article 98 of the Treaty establishing the European Coal and Steel Community, Article 237 of the Treaty establishing the European Economic Community and Article 205 of the Treaty establishing the European Atomic Energy Community,

WHEREAS the Hellenic Republic has applied to become a member of these Communities;

WHEREAS in its opinion of January 29, 1976 the Commission has already been able to express its views on certain essential aspects of the problems arising in connection with this application;

WHEREAS the terms for the admission of the Hellenic Republic and the adjustments to the Treaties necessitated by its accession have been negotiated in a Conference between the Communities and the applicant State; whereas singleness of Community representation was ensured with due regard for the institutional dialogue provided for by the Treaties;

WHEREAS, on the completion of these negotiations, it is apparent that the provisions so agreed are fair and proper; whereas, this being so, the Community's enlargement, while preserving its internal cohesion and dynamism, will enable it to take a fuller part in the development of international relations;

WHEREAS in joining the Communities the applicant State accepts without reserve the Treaties and their political objectives, all decisions taken since their entry into force, and the action that has been agreed in respect of the development and reinforcement of the Communities;

WHEREAS it is an essential feature of the legal system set up by the Treaties establishing the Communities that certain of their provisions and certain acts of the Community institutions are directly applicable, that Community law takes precedence over any national provisions conflicting with it, and that procedures exist for ensuring the uniform interpretation of this law; whereas accession to the Communities entails recognition of the binding force of these rules, observance of which is indispensable to guarantee the effectiveness and unity of Community law;

WHEREAS the principles of pluralist democracy and respect for human rights form part of the common heritage of the peoples of the States brought together in the European Communities and are therefore essential elements of membership of the said Communities;

WHEREAS enlargement of the Communities through the accession of the Hellenic Republic will help to preserve and strengthen peace and liberty in Europe,

HEREBY DELIVERS A FAVOURABLE OPINION:

on the accession to the European Communities of the Hellenic Republic.

This opinion is addressed to the Council.

Done at Brussels, May 23, 1979.

DECISION OF THE COUNCIL OF THE EUROPEAN COMMUNITIES OF MAY 24, 1979, ON THE ACCESSION OF THE HELLENIC REPUBLIC TO THE EUROPEAN COAL AND STEEL COMMUNITY

THE COUNCIL OF THE EUROPEAN COMMUNITIES,

HAVING REGARD to Article 98 of the Treaty establishing the European Coal and Steel Community,

HAVING REGARD to the opnion of the Commission,

WHEREAS the Hellenic Republic has applied to accede to the European Coal and Steel Community;

WHEREAS the conditions of accession to be determined by the Council have been negotiated with the Hellenic Republic,

HAS DECIDED AS FOLLOWS:

Article 1

1. The Hellenic Republic may become a member of the European Coal and Steel Community by acceding, under the conditions laid down in this Decision, to the Treaty establishing that Community, as amended or supplemented.

2. The conditions of accession and the adjustments to the Treaty establishing the European Coal and Steel Community necessitated thereby are set out in the Act annexed to this Decision. The provisions of that Act concerning the European Coal and Steel Community shall form an integral part of this Decision.

3. The provisions concerning the rights and obligations of the Member States and the powers and jurisdiction of the institutions of the Communities as set out in the Treaty referred to in paragraph (1) shall apply in respect of this Decision.

Article 2

The instrument of accession of the Hellenic Republic to the European Coal and Steel Community will be deposited with the Government of the French Republic on January 1, 1981.

Accession will take effect on January 1, 1981, provided that the Hellenic Republic has deposited its instrument of accession on that date and that all the signatory States to the Treaty concerning accession of the Hellenic Republic to the European Economic Community and the European Atomic Energy Community have deposited their instruments of ratification before that date.

The Government of the French Republic will transmit a certified copy of the instrument of accession of the Hellenic Republic to the Governments of the Member States.

Article 3

This Decision, drawn up in the Danish, Dutch, English, French, German, Greek, Irish and Italian languages, each of these languages being equally authentic, shall be communicated to the Member States of the European Coal and Steel Community and the Hellenic Republic.

DECISION OF THE COUNCIL OF THE EUROPEAN COMMUNITIES OF MAY 24, 1979, ON THE ADMISSION OF THE HELLENIC REPUBLIC TO THE EUROPEAN ECONOMIC COMMUNITY AND TO THE EUROPEAN ATOMIC ENERGY COMMUNITY

THE COUNCIL OF THE EUROPEAN COMMUNITIES,

HAVING REGARD to Article 237 of the Treaty establishing the European Economic Community and Article 205 of the Treaty establishing the European Atomic Energy Community,

WHEREAS the Hellenic Republic has applied to become a member of the European Economic Community and of the European Atomic Energy Community,

HAVING obtained the opinion of the Commission,

HAS DECIDED:
to accept this application for admission; the conditions of admission and the adjustments to the Treaties necessitated thereby are to be the subject of an agreement between the Member States and the Hellenic Republic.

Done at Brussels, May 24, 1979.

TREATY BETWEEN THE KINGDOM OF BELGIUM, THE KINGDOM OF DENMARK, THE FEDERAL REPUBLIC OF GERMANY, THE FRENCH REPUBLIC, IRELAND, THE ITALIAN REPUBLIC, THE GRAND DUCHY OF LUXEMBOURG, THE KINGDOM OF THE NETHERLANDS, THE UNITED KINGDOM OF GREAT BRITAIN AND NORTHERN IRELAND (MEMBER STATES OF THE EUROPEAN COMMUNITIES) AND THE HELLENIC REPUBLIC CONCERNING THE ACCESSION OF THE HELLENIC REPUBLIC TO THE EUROPEAN ECONOMIC COMMUNITY AND TO THE EUROPEAN ATOMIC ENERGY COMMUNITY

(ATHENS, MAY 28, 1979)

HIS MAJESTY THE KING OF THE BELGIANS, HER MAJESTY THE QUEEN OF DENMARK, THE PRESIDENT OF THE FEDERAL REPUBLIC OF GERMANY, THE PRESIDENT OF THE HELLENIC REPUBLIC, THE PRESIDENT OF THE FRENCH REPUBLIC, THE PRESIDENT OF IRELAND, THE PRESIDENT OF THE ITALIAN REPUBLIC, HIS ROYAL HIGHNESS THE GRAND DUKE OF LUXEMBOURG, HER MAJESTY THE QUEEN OF THE NETHERLANDS, HER MAJESTY THE QUEEN OF THE UNITED KINGDOM OF GREAT BRITAIN AND NORTHERN IRELAND,

UNITED in their desire to pursue the attainment of the objectives of the Treaty establishing the European Economic Community and the Treaty establishing the European Atomic Energy Community,

DETERMINED in the spirit of those Treaties to construct an ever closer union among the peoples of Europe on the foundation already laid,

CONSIDERING that Article 237 of the Treaty establishing the European Economic Community and Article 205 of the Treaty establishing the European Atomic Energy Community afford European States the opportunity of becoming members of these Communities,

CONSIDERING that the Hellenic Republic has applied to become a member of these Communities,

CONSIDERING that the Council of the European Communities, after having obtained the opinion of the Commission, has declared itself in favour of the admission of this State,

HAVE DECIDED to establish by common agreement the conditions of admission and the adjustment to be made to the Treaties establishing the European Economic Community and the European Atomic Energy Community, and to this end have designated as their plenipotentiaries:

HIS MAJESTY THE KING OF THE BELGIANS,
Mr. Wilfried Martens, Prime Minister;
Mr. Henri Simonet, Minister of Foreign Affairs;
Mr. Joseph van der Meulen, Ambassador, Permanent Representative to the European Communities;

HER MAJESTY THE QUEEN OF DENMARK,
Mr. Niels Anker Kofoed, Minister for Agriculture;
Mr. Gunnar Riberholdt, Ambassador, Permanent Representative to the European Communities;

THE PRESIDENT OF THE FEDERAL REPUBLIC OF GERMANY,
Mr. Hans-Dietrich Genscher, Federal Minister of Foreign Affairs;
Mr. Helmut Sigrist, Ambassador, Permanent Representative to the European Communities;

THE PRESIDENT OF THE HELLENIC REPUBLIC,
Mr. Constantinos Karamanlis, Prime Minister;
Mr. Georgios Rallis, Minister of Foreign Affairs;
Mr. Georgios Contogeorgis, Minister without Portfolio, responsible for relations with the European Communities;

THE PRESIDENT OF THE FRENCH REPUBLIC,
Mr. Jean François-Poncet, Minister of Foreign Affairs;
Mr. Pierre Bernard-Reymond, State Secretary for Foreign Affairs;
Mr. Luc de La Barre de Nanteuil, Ambassador, Permanent Representative to the European Communities;

THE PRESIDENT OF IRELAND,
Mr. John Lynch, Prime Minister;
Mr. Michael O'Kennedy, Minister of Foreign Affairs;
Mr. Brendan Dillon, Ambassador, Permanent Representative to the European Communities;

THE PRESIDENT OF THE ITALIAN REPUBLIC,
Mr. Giulio Andreotti, President of the Council of Ministers;
Mr. Adolfo Battaglia, Under-Secretary of State for Foreign Affairs;
Mr. Eugenio Plaja, Ambassador, Permanent Representative to the European Communities;

HIS ROYAL HIGHNESS THE GRAND DUKE OF LUXEMBOURG,
Mr. Gaston Thorn, President of the Government, Minister of Foreign Affairs;
Mr. Jean Dondelinger, Ambassador, Permanent Representative to the European Communities;

HER MAJESTY THE QUEEN OF THE NETHERLANDS,
Mr. Ch. A. van der Klaauw, Minister of Foreign Affairs;
Mr. J. H. Lubbers, Ambassador, Permanent Representative to the European Communities;

HER MAJESTY THE QUEEN OF THE UNITED KINGDOM OF GREAT BRITAIN AND NORTHERN IRELAND,
The Right Honourable Lord Carrington, Secretary of State for Foreign and Commonwealth Affairs;
Sir Donald Maitland, Ambassador, Permanent Representative to the European Communities;

WHO, having exchanged their Full Powers found in good and due form,

HAVE AGREED AS FOLLOWS:

ARTICLE 1

1. The Hellenic Republic hereby becomes a member of the European Economic Community and of the European Atomic Energy Community and Party to the Treaties establishing these Communities as amended or supplemented.

2. The conditions of admission and the adjustments to the Treaties establishing the European Economic Community and the European Atomic Energy Community necessitated thereby are set out in the Act annexed to this Treaty. The provisions of that Act concerning the European Economic Community and the European Atomic Energy Community shall form an integral part of this Treaty.

3. The provisions concerning the rights and obligations of the Member States and the powers and jurisdiction of the institutions of the Communities as set out in the Treaties referred to in paragraph (1) shall apply in respect of this Treaty.

ARTICLE 2

This Treaty will be ratified by the High Contracting Parties in accordance with their respective constitutional requirements. The instruments of ratification will be deposited with the Government of the Italian Republic by December 31, 1980 at the latest.

This Treaty will enter into force on January 1, 1981, provided that all the instruments of ratification have been deposited before that date and that the instrument of accession of the Hellenic Republic to the European Coal and Steel Community is deposited on that date.

ARTICLE 3

This Treaty, drawn up in a single original in the Danish, Dutch, English, French, German, Greek, Irish and Italian languages, the texts in each of these languages being equally authentic, will be deposited in the archives of the Government of the Italian Republic, which will transmit a certified copy to each of the Governments of the other signatory States.

IN WITNESS WHEREOF the undersigned Plenipotentiaries have signed this Treaty.

DONE at Athens on the twenty-eighth day of May in the year one thousand nine hundred and seventy-nine.

ACT CONCERNING THE CONDITIONS OF ACCESSION OF THE HELLENIC REPUBLIC AND THE ADJUSTMENTS TO THE TREATIES

Part One

PRINCIPLES

ARTICLE 1

For the purposes of this Act:
—the expression "original Treaties" means the Treaty establishing the European Coal and Steel Community, the Treaty establishing the European Economic Community and the Treaty establishing the European Atomic Energy Community, as supplemented or amended by treaties or other acts which entered into force before accession of the Hellenic Republic; the expression "ECSC Treaty", "EEC Treaty" and "Euratom Treaty" mean the relevant original Treaties thus supplemented or amended.
—the expression "present Member States" means the Kingdom of Belgium, the Kingdom of Denmark, the Federal Republic of Germany, the French Republic, Ireland, the Italian Republic, the Grand Duchy of Luxembourg, the Kingdom of the Netherlands and the United Kingdom of Great Britain and Northern Ireland.

ARTICLE 2

From the date of accession, the provisions of the original Treaties and the acts adopted by the institutions of the Communities shall be binding on the Hellenic Republic and shall apply in that State under the conditions laid down in those Treaties and in this Act.

ARTICLE 3

1. The Hellenic Republic accedes by this Act to the Decisions and Agreements adopted by the representatives of the Governments of the Member States meeting in Council. It undertakes to accede from the date of accession to all other Agreements concluded by the present Member States relating to the functioning of the Communities or connected with their activities.

2. The Hellenic Republic undertakes to accede to the Conventions provided for in Article 220 of the EEC Treaty and to the Protocols on the interpretation of those Conventions by the Court of Justice, signed by the Member States of the Community as originally or at present constituted, and to this end it undertakes to enter into negotiations with the present Member States in order to make the necessary adjustments thereto.

3. The Hellenic Republic is in the same situation as the present Member States in respect of declarations or resolutions of, or other positions taken up by, the Council and in respect of those concerning the European Communities adopted by common agreement of the Member States; it will accordingly observe the principles and guidelines deriving from those declarations, resolu-

338

tions or other positions and will take such measures as may be necessary to ensure their implementation.

ARTICLE 4

1. The Agreements or Conventions entered into by any of the Communities with one or more third States, with an international organisation or with a national of a third State, shall, under the conditions laid down in the original Treaties and in this Act, be binding on the Hellenic Republic.

2. The Hellenic Republic undertakes to accede, under the conditions laid down in this Act, to Agreements or Conventions concluded by the present Member States and any of the Communities, acting jointly, and to Agreements concluded by the present Member States which are related to those Agreements or Conventions. The Community and the present Member States shall assist the Hellenic Republic in this respect.

3. The Hellenic Republic accedes by this Act and under the conditions laid down therein to the Internal Agreements concluded by the present Member States for the purpose of implementing the Agreements or Conventions referred to in paragraph (2).

4. The Hellenic Republic shall take appropriate measures, where necessary, to adjust its position in relation to international orgnisations and International Agreements to which one of the Communities or to which other Member States are also parties, to the rights and obligations arising from its accession to the Communities.

ARTICLE 5

Article 234 of the EEC Treaty and Articles 105 and 106 of the Euratom Treaty shall apply, for the Hellenic Republic to Agreements or Conventions concluded before its accession.

ARTICLE 6

The provisions of this Act may not, unless otherwise provided herein, be suspended, amended or repealed other than by means of the procedure laid down in the original Treaties enabling those Treaties to be revised.

ARTICLE 7

Acts adopted by the institutions of the Communities to which the transitional provisions laid down in this Act relate shall retain their status in law; in particular, the procedures for amending those acts shall continue to apply.

ARTICLE 8

Provisions of this Act the purpose or effect of which is to repeal or amend acts adopted by the institutions of the Communities; otherwise than as a transitional measure, shall have the same status in law as the provisions which they repeal or amend and shall be subject to the same rules as those provisions.

ARTICLE 9

1. The application of the original Treaties and acts adopted by the institutions shall, as a transitional measure, be subject to the derogations provided for in this Act.

2. Subject to special provisions in this Act laying down different dates or shorter or longer time limits, the application of the transitional measures shall terminate at the end of 1985.

Part Two

ADJUSTMENTS TO THE TREATIES

TITLE I—PROVISIONS COVERING THE INSTITUTIONS

CHAPTER 1—THE ASSEMBLY

ARTICLE 10

[This article amends the Act concerning the election of the representatives of the Assembly by direct universal suffrage, Art. 2, annexed to Dec. 76/787, and is incorporated therein.]

CHAPTER 2—THE COUNCIL

ARTICLE 11

[This article amends the Merger Treaty, Art. 2 and is incorporated therein.]

ARTICLE 12

[This article amends the ECSC Treaty, Art. 28 and is incorporated theren.]

ARTICLE 13

[This article amends the ECSC Treaty, Art. 95 and is incorporated therein.]

ARTICLE 14

[This article amends the EEC Treaty, Art. 148 (2) and the Euratom Treaty, Art. 188 (2) and is incorporated therein.]

CHAPTER 3—THE COMMISSION

ARTICLE 15

[This article amends the Merger Treaty, Art. 10 (1) and is incorporated therein.]

CHAPTER 4—THE COURT OF JUSTICE

ARTICLE 16

Upon the accession of the Hellenic Republic, the Council of the European Communities, acting unanimously, shall decide on the adjustments to be made to the first paragraph of Article 32 of the ECSC Treaty, the first paragraph of Article 165 of the EEC Treaty and the first paragraph of Article 137 of the Euratom Treaty in order to increase by one the number of judges constituting the Court of Justice. It shall also decide on the necessary consequential adjustments to be made to the second paragraph of Article 32b of the ECSC Treaty, the second paragraph of Article 167 of the EEC Treaty, the second paragraph of Article 139 of the Euratom Treaty and to the second paragraph of Article 18 of the Protocol on the Statute of the Court of Justice of the European Coal and Steel Community, Article 15 of the Protocol on the Statute of the Court of Justice of the European Economic Community and Article 15 of the Protocol on the Statute of the Court of Justice of the European Atomic Energy Community.

CHAPTER 5—THE ECONOMIC AND SOCIAL COMMITTEE

ARTICLE 17

[*This article amends the EEC Treaty, Art.* 194 *and the Euratom Treaty, Art.* 166 *and is incorporated therein.*]

CHAPTER 6—THE COURT OF AUDITORS

ARTICLE 18

[*This article amends the ECSC Treaty, Art.* 78e (2), *the EEC Treaty, Art.* 206 (2) *and the Euratom Treaty, Art.* 180 (2) *and is incorporated therein.*]

CHAPTER 7—THE SCIENTIFIC AND TECHNICAL COMMITTEE

ARTICLE 19

[*This article amends the Euratom Treaty, Art.* 134 (2) *and is incorporated therein.*]

TITLE II—OTHER ADJUSTMENTS

ARTICLE 20

[*This article amends the EEC Treaty, Art.* 227 (1) *and is incorporated therein.*]

Part Three

ADAPTATIONS TO ACTS ADOPTED BY THE INSTITUTIONS

ARTICLE 21

The acts listed in Annex 1 to this Act shall be adapted as specified in that Annex.

ARTICLE 22

The adaptations to the acts listed in Annex II to this Act made necessary by accession shall be drawn up in conformity with the guidelines set out in that Annex and in accordance with the procedure and under the conditions laid down in Article 146.

Part Four

TRANSITIONAL MEASURES

TITLE I—PROVISIONS GOVERNING THE INSTITUTIONS

ARTICLE 23

1. During 1981 the Hellenic Republic shall hold an election by direct universal suffrage of 24 representatives to the Assembly, of the people of Greece, in accordance with the provisions of the Act of September 20, 1976 concerning the election of representatives of the Assembly by direct universal suffrage.

The term of office of these representatives shall end at the same time as that of the representatives elected in the present Member States.

2. From accession and until the election referred to in paragraph (1) the 24 representatives, of the Assembly, of the people of Greece shall be appointed by the Hellenic Parliament within itself in accordance with the procedure laid down by the Hellenic Republic.

TITLE II—FREE MOVEMENT OF GOODS

CHAPTER 1—TARIFF PROVISIONS

ARTICLE 24

1. The basic duty to which the successive reductions provided for in Articles 25 and 64 are to be applied shall, for each product, be the duty actually applied on July 1, 1980.

The basic duty used for the moves towards alignment on the Common Customs Tariff and the ECSC unified tariff provided for in Articles 31, 32 and 64 shall, for each product, be the duty actually applied by the Hellenic Republic on July 1, 1980.

2. The Community as at present constituted and the Hellenic Republic shall inform each other of their respective basic duties.

ARTICLE 25

1. Customs duties on imports between the Community as at present constituted and the Hellenic Republic shall be progressively abolished in accordance with the following timetable:
—on January 1, 1981 each duty shall be reduced to 90 per cent of the basic duty.
—on January 1, 1982 each duty shall be reduced to 80 per cent of the basic duty,
—the four other reductions of 20 per cent each shall be made on:
—January 1, 1983,
—January 1, 1984,
—January 1, 1985,
—January 1, 1986.

2. Nothwithstanding paragraph (1):
  (*a*) duty-free entry shall, from the date of accession, apply to imports which benefit from the provisions relating to tax exemptions applicable to persons travelling from one Member State to another;
  (*b*) duty-free entry shall, from the date of accession, apply to imports of goods sent in small consignments, not of a commercial nature, which benefit from the provisions relating to tax exemptions applicable between Member States.

Article 26

In no case shall customs duties higher than those applied to third countries enjoying most-favoured-nation treatment be applied within the Community.

In the event of the Common Customs Tariff duties being amended or suspended or the Hellenic Republic applying Article 34, the Council, acting by a qualified majority on a proposal from the Commission, may take the necessary measures for the maintenance of Community preference.

Article 27

The Hellenic Republic may suspend in whole or in part the levying of duties on products imported from the Community as at present constituted. It shall inform the other Member States and the Commission thereof.

The Council, acting by a qualified majority on a proposal from the Commission, may suspend in whole or in part the levying of duties on products imported from Greece.

Article 28

Any charge having equivalent effect to a customs duty on imports introduced as from January 1, 1979 in trade between the Community as at present constituted and Greece shall be abolished on January 1, 1981.

Article 29

Charges having equivalent effect to customs duties on imports shall be progressively abolished between the Community as at present constituted and Greece in accordance with the following timetable:
  —on January 1, 1981, each charge shall be reduced to 90 per cent of the rate applied on December 31, 1980,
  —on January 1, 1982, each charge shall be reduced to 80 per cent of the rate applied on December 31, 1980,
  —the four other reductions of 20 per cent each shall be made on:
  —January 1, 1983,
  —January 1, 1984
  —January 1, 1985,
  —January 1, 1986.

Article 30

Customs duties on exports and charges having equivalent effect shall be abolished between the Community as at present constituted and Greece on January 1, 1981.

Article 31

For the purpose of the progressive introduction of the Common Customs

Tariff, the Hellenic Republic shall amend its tariff applicable to third countries as follows:

—from January 1, 1981 the Hellenic Republic shall apply a duty reducing by 10 per cent the difference between the basic duty and the duty in the Common Customs Tariff,

—from January 1, 1982:

(a) in the case of tariff headings in respect of which the basic duties do not differ by more than 15 per cent in either direction from the duties in the Common Customs Tariff, these latter duties shall be applied;

(b) in other cases, the Hellenic Republic shall apply a duty reducing again by 10 per cent the difference between the basic duty and the duty in the Common Customs Tariff.

This difference shall be further reduced by 20 per cent on January 1, 1983, by 20 per cent on January 1, 1984 and by 20 per cent on January 1, 1985.

The Hellenic Republic shall apply in full the Common Customs Tariff from January 1, 1986.

ARTICLE 32

1. For the purpose of the progressive introduction of the ECSC unified tariff, the Hellenic Republic shall amend its tariff applicable to third countries as follows:

(a) in the case of tariff headings in respect of which the basic duties do not differ by more than 15 per cent in either direction from the duties in the ECSC unified tariff, these latter duties shall be applied from January 1, 1982;

(b) in other cases, the Hellenic Republic shall, from the same date, apply a duty reducing by 20 per cent the difference between the basic duty and the duty in the ECSC unified tariff.

This difference shall be further reduced by 20 per cent on January 1, 1983, by 20 per cent on January 1, 1984 and by 20 per cent on January 1, 1985.

The Hellenic Republic shall apply in full the ECSC unified tariff from January 1, 1986.

2. In respect of lignite, whether or not agglomerated, falling within heading No 27.02 of the Common Customs Tariff, the Hellenic Republic shall introduce in accordance with the same timetable of progressivity as that laid down in paragraph (1) the provisions in the Common Customs Tariff for these products and shall apply a duty of 5 per cent by January 1, 1986 at the latest.

ARTICLE 33

1. Where duties in the customs tariff of the Hellenic Republic differ in nature from the corresponding duties in the Common Customs Tariff or the ECSC unified tariff, the progressive alignment of the former on the latter shall be effected by adding the components of the Greek basic duty to those of the Common Customs Tariff or the ECSC unified tariff, the Greek basic duty being reduced to zero progressively, in accordance with the timetable set out in Articles 31, 32 and 64, and the duty in the Common Customs Tariff or the ECSC unified tariff increasing from zero to reach the full amount progressively in accordance with the same timetable.

2. From January 1, 1981, if any duties in the Common Customs Tariff or the ECSC unified tariff are altered or suspended, the Hellenic Republic shall simultaneously amend or suspend its tariff in the proportion resulting from the implementation of Articles 31, 32 and 64.

3. The Hellenic Republic shall apply the Common Customs Tariff and the ECSC unified tariff nomenclature from January 1, 1981.

The Hellenic Republic may include within these nomenclatures national subdivisions existing at the time of accession which are indispensable in order that the progressive alignment of its customs duties with those in the Common Customs Tariff and the ECSC unified tariff be carried out under the conditions laid down in this Act.

4. With a view to facilitating the progressive introduction of the Common Customs Tariff and the ECSC unified tariff by the Hellenic Republic, the Commission shall determine, if necessary, the implementing provisions whereby the Hellenic Republic alters its customs duties.

ARTICLE 34

In order to bring its tariff into line with the Common Customs Tariff and the ECSC unified tariff, the Hellenic Republic shall remain free to alter its customs duties more rapidly than is provided for in Articles 31, 32 and 64. It shall inform the other Member States and the Commission thereof.

CHAPTER 2—ELIMINATION OF QUANTITATIVE RESTRICTIONS AND MEASURES HAVING EQUIVALENT EFFECT

ARTICLE 35

Quantitative restrictions on imports and exports and any measures having equivalent effect shall, from the date of accession, be abolished between the Community as at present constituted and Greece.

ARTICLE 36

1. Notwithstanding Article 35, the Hellenic Republic may retain quantitative restrictions until December 31, 1985 on products listed in Annex III to this Act coming from the present Member States.

2. The restrictions referred to in paragraph (1) shall take the form of quotas. The quotas for 1981 are listed in Annex III.

3. The minimum rate of progressive increase for such quotas shall be 25 per cent at the beginning of each year for quotas expressed in units of account, and 20 per cent at the beginning of each year for quotas expressed in terms of volume. Such increase shall be added to each quota and the next increase calculated on the basis of the total thus obtained.

Where a quota is expressed in terms of both volume and value, the quota relating to the volume shall be raised by at least 20 per cent a year and the quota relating to the value by at least 25 per cent a year, the succeeding quotas to be calculated each year on the basis of the preceding quota plus the increase.

However, with regard to motor coaches and buses and other vehicles falling within subheading ex 87.02 A I of the Common Customs Tariff, the volume quota shall be raised by 15 per cent a year and the quota relating to the value by 20 per cent a year.

4. Where the Commission records by a decision that imports into Greece of a product listed in Annex III have for two consecutive years been less than 90 per cent of the quota, the Hellenic Republic shall liberalise imports of that product from the present Member States.

5. Quotas for fertilisers falling within heading Nos 31.02, 31.03 and sub-headings 31.05 A I, II and IV of the Common Customs Tariff shall also constitute transitional measures required in order to abolish exclusive import rights. Such quotas shall be accessible to all importers in Greece and products imported under the said quotas may not be made subject in Greece to exclusive marketing rights.

ARTICLE 37

Nothwithstanding Article 35, the present Member States and the Hellenic Republic may, in trade between the present Member States and Greece, retain restrictions on imports of waste and scrap metal of iron or steel falling within heading No 73.03 of the Common Customs Tariff for a period of two years from January 1, 1981, in so far as these arrangements are not more restrictive than those applied to exports to third countries.

ARTICLE 38

Nothwithstanding Article 35, import deposits and cash payments in force in Greece on December 31, 1980 with regard to imports from the present Member States shall be progressively eliminated over a period of three years from January 1, 1981.

The rate of import deposits and cash payments shall be reduced in accordance with the following timetable:
—January 1, 1981: 25 per cent
—January 1, 1982: 25 per cent,
—January 1, 1983: 25 per cent,
—January 1, 1984: 25 per cent.

ARTICLE 39

1. Notwithstanding Article 35, the 8 per cent general preference applied in Greece to public contracts shall be progressively eliminated by the Hellenic Republic in accordance with the same timetable as that established in Article 25 for the abolition of customs duties on imports between Greece and the Community as at present constituted.

2. Notwithstanding Article 35, the Hellenic Republic may, for two years from January 1, 1981, postpone opening its lists of approved suppliers to Community suppliers.

ARTICLE 40

1. Without prejudice to the provisions of paragraph (2) of this article, the Hellenic Republic shall, from January 1, 1981 progressively adjust State monopolies of a commercial character within the meaning of Article 37 (1) of the EEC Treaty so as to ensure that by December 31, 1985 no discrimination regarding the conditions under which goods are procured and marketed exists between nationals of the Member States.

The present Member States shall have equivalent obligations in relation to the Hellenic Republic.

The Commission shall make recommendations as to the manner in which and the timetable according to which the adjustment provided for in the first subparagraph above must be carried out, it being understood that the manner and timetable must be the same for the Hellenic Republic and the present Member States.

2. The Hellenic Republic shall, from January 1, 1981, abolish all exclusive export rights. It shall also abolish, on the same date exclusive rights on imports of copper sulphate falling within subheading ex 28.38 A II of the Common Customs Tariff, saccharin falling within subheading ex 29.26 A I of the Common Customs Tariff and flimsy paper falling within heading No ex 48.18 of the Common Customs Tariff.

CHAPTER 3—OTHER PROVISIONS

ARTICLE 41

1. The Commission shall, with due regard for the provisions in force, in particular those relating to Community transit, determine the methods of administrative co-operation designed to ensure that goods fulfilling the requisite conditions benefit, from January 1, 1981, from the abolition of customs duties and charges having equivalent effect and quantitative restrictions and measures having equivalent effect.

2. The Commission shall lay down the provisions applicable from January 1, 1981 to trade within the Community in goods obtained in the Community in the manufacture of which have been incorporated:
— products on which the customs duties or charges having equivalent effect which were applicable to them in the Community as at present constituted or in Greece have not been levied, or which have benefited from a total or partial drawback of such duties or charges,
— agricultural products which do not fulfil the conditions required for admission to free movement in the Community as at present constituted or in Greece.

In adopting these provisions, the Commission shall take into account the rules laid down in this Act for the elmination of customs duties between the Community as at present constituted and Greece, and for the progressive introduction by the Hellenic Republic of the Common Customs Tariff and the provisions relating to the common agricultural policy.

ARTICLE 42

1. Save as otherwise provided in this Act, the provisions in force with regard to customs legislation for trade with third countries shall apply under the same conditions to trade within the Community, for such time as customs duties are levied in that trade.

For the purpose of establishing the customs value in respect of trade within the Community, and trade with third countries, until January 1, 1986 the customs territory to be taken into consideration shall be that defined by the provisions existing in the Community and in the Hellenic Republic on December 31, 1980.

2. The Hellenic Republic shall apply the Common Customs Tariff and ECSC unified nomenclatures in trade within the Community from January 1, 1981.

The Hellenic Republic may include within these nomenclatures national subdivisions existing at the time of accession which are indispensable in order that the progressive elimination of its customs duties within the Community be carried out under the conditions laid down in this Act.

ARTICLE 43

1. Where the compensatory amounts referred to in Article 61 are applied in trade between the Community as at present constituted and Greece on one or more of the basic products considered as having been used in the manufacture of goods covered by Regulation 1059/69 determining the system of trade applicable to certain goods processed from agricultural products, Regulation 2730/75 on glucose and lactose and Regulation 2783/75 on the common system of trade for ovalbumin and lactalbumin, the following transitional measures shall be applied:

—a compensatory amount calculated on the basis of the compensatory amounts referred to in Article 61 and in accordance with the rules laid down by Regulation 1059/69 for calculating the variable component applicable to the goods covered by this Regulation shall be applied on importation of those goods into the Community from Greece.

—when the goods covered by Regulation 1059/69 are imported from third countries into Greece the variable component laid down by this Regulation shall be increased or reduced as the case may be by the compensatory amount referred to in the first indent.

—a compensatory amount determined on the basis of the compensatory amounts fixed for the basic products and in accordance with the rules applicable for the calculation of the refunds provided for in Regulation 2682/72 laying down the general rules for granting export refunds on certain agricultural products exported in the form of goods not covered by Annex II to the Treaty and the criteria for fixing the amount of such refunds shall for the goods covered by this Regulation with the exception of albumins be applied on exportation of those goods from the Community into Greece,

—on importation into Greece from third countries and from the Community and into the Community from Greece of products covered by Regulations 2730/75 and 2783/75 there shall be applied a compensatory amount calculated on the basis of the compensatory amounts referred to in Article 61 and in accordance with the rules laid down by the above Regulations for the calculation of the import charge.

—where products covered by Regulations 2682/72 and 2730/75 are exported from Greece to third countries they shall be subject to the compensatory amounts referred to in the third or fourth indent respectively.

2. If, during the application of compensatory amounts, there should be deflections in trade in the products covered by Regulations 2783/75 and 2730/75 the Commission may take appropriate corrective measures.

3. The customs duty constituting the fixed component of the charge applicable on importation into Greece from third countries to goods covered by Regulation 1059/69 shall be determined by excluding from the total protection applied by the Hellenic Republic on the date of accession the agricultural protection to be introduced taking into consideration the transitional measures mentioned in paragraph (1).

Each fixed component determined in accordance with the first subparagraph applied by the Hellenic Republic to imports from third countries

348

shall be aligned upon the Common Customs Tariff in accordance with the timetable laid down in Article 31. However, if the fixed component to be applied by the Hellenic Republic upon accession is lower than the fixed component in the Common Customs Tariff, the Hellenic Republic may align upon the latter immediately upon accession. Moreover the fixed components determined in accordance with the first subparagraph shall take account, as far as possible, of any particular difficulties which the Hellenic Republic foresees for specific products.

4. The Hellenic Republic shall, for the goods covered by Regulations 1059/69, 2682/72 and 2730/75, apply in full the Common Customs Tariff nomenclature upon accession.

5. The Hellenic Republic shall upon accession abolish any customs duties or charges having equivalent effect other than those provided for in paragraphs (1), (2) and (3) for products covered by Regulation 1059/69 and any export aid or aid having equivalent effect to export aid for products covered by Regulations 2682/72 and 2730/75.

On imports from the Community the Hellenic Republic shall upon accession abolish any quantitative restrictions as well as all measures having equivalent effect to quantitative restrictions for products covered by Regulations 1059/69, 2730/75 and 2783/75.

6. The Council shall, acting by a qualified majority on a proposal from the Commission, adopt provisions to implement this Article.

TITLE III—FREE MOVEMENT OF PERSONS, SERVICES AND CAPITAL

CHAPTER 1— WORKERS

ARTICLE 44

The provisions of Article 48 of the EEC Treaty shall only apply in relation to the freedom of movement of workers between the present Member States and Greece subject to the transitional provisions laid down in Articles 45, 46 and 47 of this Act.

ARTICLE 45

1. Articles 1 to 6 and 13 to 23 of Regulation 1612/68 on the freedom of movement of workers within the Community shall only apply in the present Member States with regard to Hellenic nationals and in Greece with regard to nationals of the present Member States as from January 1, 1988.

The present Member States and the Hellenic Republic may maintain in force until January 1, 1988, with regard to Hellenic nationals and to nationals of the present Member States respectively, national provisions submitting to prior authorisation immigration undertaken with a view to pursuing an activity as an employed person and/or the taking up and pursuit of paid employment.

2. Article 11 of Regulation 1612/68 shall only apply in the present Member States with regard to Hellenic nationals and in Greece with regard to nationals of the present Member States as from January 1, 1986.

However the members of workers' families within the meaning of Article 10 of Regulation 1612/68 shall have the right to be employed in the territory of the Member State where they have settled with the worker, if they are resident for at least three years in this territory. This period of residence shall be reduced to 18 months as from January 1, 1984.

The rules of this paragraph shall not prejudice more favourable national provisions.

ARTICLE 46

In so far as certain provisions of Directive 68/360 on the abolition of restrictions on movement and residence within the Community for workers of Member States and their families, may not be dissociated from those of Regulation 1612/68 whose application is deferred pursuant to Article 45, the present Member States and the Hellenic Republic may derogate from these provisions, in so far as is necessary for the application of the provisions for derogation which are laid down in Article 45 in connection with the said Regulation.

ARTICLE 47

The present Member States and the Hellenic Republic shall take, with the assistance of the Commission, the necessary measures so that the application of the Commission Decision of December 8, 1972 on the uniform system established pursuant to Article 15 of Council Regulation 1612/68, known as "Sedoc" and the Commission Decision of December 14, 1972 on the "Community plan" for the collection and circulation of information provided for in Article 14 (3) of Council Regulation 1612/68 may be extended to Greece on January 1, 1988 at the latest.

ARTICLE 48

Until December 31, 1983, the provisions of Articles 73 (1) and (3), 74 (1) and 75 (1) of Regulation 1408/71 on the application of social security schemes to employed persons and their families moving within the Community, and Articles 86 and 88 of Regulation 574/72 fixing the procedure for implementing Regulation 1408/71 shall not apply to Greek workers employed in a Member State other than Greece, whose family members are resident in Greece.

The provisions of Articles 73 (2), 74 (2) and 75 (2) of Regulation 1408/71, and Articles 87, 89 and 98 of Regulation 574/72 shall apply by analogy to these workers.

However, the legislative provisions of a Member State laying down that family benefits shall be payable to a worker irrespective of the country where members of his family reside shall not be prejudiced.

CHAPTER 2—CAPITAL MOVEMENTS AND INVISIBLE TRANSACTIONS

SECTION 1—CAPITAL MOVEMENTS

ARTICLE 49

1. The Hellenic Republic may, under the conditions and within the time limits set out in Articles 50 to 53, defer the liberalisation of capital movements provided for in the First Council Directive of May 11, 1960 for the implementation of Article 67 of the EEC Treaty and in the Second Council Directive of December 18, 1962 adding to and amending the First Directive for the implementation of Article 67 of the EEC Treaty.

2. Appropriate consultations shall take place in due course between the Hellenic authorities and the Commission about procedures for applying measures of liberalisation or relaxation, the implementation of which may be deferred under the following provisions.

ARTICLE 50

1. The Hellenic Republic may defer:
   (a) until December 31, 1985 the liberalisation of direct investments in the present Member States made by persons resident in Greece;
   (b) until December 31, 1983 the liberalisation of the transfer of the proceeds of the liquidation of direct investments in Greece made before June 12, 1975 by persons resident in the Community. During the period of application of this temporary derogation, the general or special facilities relating to the free transfer of the proceeds of the liquidation of these investments and existing by virtue of Hellenic arrangements or of agreements governing relations between the Hellenic Republic and any present Member State shall be maintained and applied in a non-discriminatory manner.
2. Recognising that it is desirable to proceed, from January 1, 1981, to a substantial relaxation in the rules concerning the operations referred to in paragraph (1) (a), the Hellenic Republic will endeavour to take appropriate measures to this end.

ARTICLE 51

1. The Hellenic Republic may defer until December 31, 1985:
   (a) the liberlisation of real estate investments, in a present Member State, by persons resident in Greece who do not fall within the category of those who emigrate in the context of freedom of movement for workers and self-employed persons;
   (b) the liberalisation of real estate investment, in a present Member State, by self-employed persons resident in Greece who emigrate, other than investments connected with their establishment.
2. The repatriation of the proceeds from the liquidation of real estate investments situated in Greece and acquired before accession by persons resident in the present Member States shall be the subject of a gradual liberalisation through the inclusion of the operations in question in the liberalisation system introduced for the funds blocked in Greece as defined in Article 52.

ARTICLE 52

Funds blocked in Greece belonging to persons resident in the present Member States shall be progressively released by equal annual instalments starting from accession until December 31, 1985, in six stages, the first of which shall begin on January 1, 1981.

Capital on deposit in each blocked fund on January 1, 1981 or which may be paid into blocked funds between this date and December 31, 1985 shall be released, at the beginning of each stage, successively by one-sixth, one-fifth, a quarter, a third and a half of the amount on deposit at the beginning of each of these stages.

On January 1, 1986 blocked funds belonging to persons resident in the present Member States shall be abolished.

ARTICLE 53

The Hellenic Republic may defer until December 31, 1985 the liberalisation of the operations set out in List B annexed to the Directives referred to in Article 49, and carried out by persons resident in Greece.

However, operations in securities issued by the Communities and by the European Investment Bank carried out by persons resident in Greece shall be the subject of progressive liberalisation over this period as follows:

(a) for 1981 these operations may be limited to 20 million European units of account;·

(b) this ceiling shall then be raised, at the beginning of each year by 20 per cent in relation to that fixed for 1981.

SECTION 2—INVISIBLE TRANSACTIONS

ARTICLE 54

1. The Hellenic Republic may, until December 31, 1985 and under the conditions set out in paragraph (2), maintain restrictions on transfers relating to tourism.

2. On January 1, 1981, the annual tourist allowance per person may not be less than 400 European units of account.

From January 1, 1982, this allowance shall be increased each year by at least 20 per cent in relation to the annual amount fixed for 1981.

SECTION 3—GENERAL PROVISIONS

ARTICLE 55

The Hellenic Republic will, circumstances permitting, carry out the liberalisation of capital movements and invisible transactions referred to in Articles 50 to 54 before the expiry of the time limits laid down in those articles.

ARTICLE 56

For the purpose of implementing the provisions of this Chapter, the Commission may consult the Monetary Committees and submit appropriate proposals to the Council.

TITLE IV—AGRICULTURE

CHAPTER 1—GENERAL PROVISIONS

ARTICLE 57

Save as otherwise provided in this Title, the rules provided for in this Act shall apply to agricultural products.

ARTICLE 58

1. This article shall apply to prices in respect of which, in Chapter 2, reference is made to this article.

2. Before the first move towards price alignment referred to in Article 59, the prices to be applied in Greece shall be fixed, in accordance with the rules

provided for in the common organisation of the market in the sector in question, at a level which allows producers in that sector to obtain market prices equivalent to those obtained, for a representative period to be determined for each product, under the previous national system.

However, in the absence of price data in respect of certain products on the Greek market, the price to be applied in that Member State shall be calculated on the basis of the prices obtaining in the Community as at present constituted of similar products or groups of similar products, or products with which they are in competition.

ARTICLE 59

1. If the application of the provisions of this Title results in a price level different from that of the common prices, the prices in respect of which, in Chapter 2, reference is made to this article shall, subject to paragraph (4), be aligned with the level of the common prices each year at the beginning of the marketing year in accordance with the provisions of paragraphs (2) and (3).

2. As regards:

—tomatoes and peaches falling within Regulation 1035/72 on the common organisation of the market in fruit and vegetables,

and

—products processed from tomatoes or peaches, falling within Regulation 516/77 on the common organisation of the market in products processed from fruit and vegetables, alignment shall be carried out in seven stages as follows:

(a) when the price of a product in Greece is lower than the common price, the price in that Member State shall, at the time of the first six moves towards alignment, be increased successively, by a seventh, a sixth, a fifth, a quarter, a third and a half of the difference between the price level in that Member State and the common price level which are applicable before each move towards alignment; the price resulting from this calculation shall be increased proportionately to any rise in the common price for the next marketing year; the common price shall be applied at the time of the seventh move towards alignment;

(b) when the price of a product in Greece is higher than the common price, the difference between the price level applicable before each move towards alignment in the Member State and the common price level applicable for the next marketing year shall be reduced successively, at the time of the first six moves towards alignment by a seventh, a sixth, a fifth, a quarter, a third and a half, the common price shall be applied at the time of the seventh move towards alignment.

3. As regards other products, the moves towards alignment shall be carried out in five stages as follows:

(a) when the price of a product in Greece is lower than the common price, the price applicable in that Member State shall, at the time of the first four moves towards alignment, be increased successively by a fifth, a quarter, a third and a half of the difference between the price level in that Member State and the common price level which are applicable before each move towards alignment; the price resulting from this calculation shall be increased proportionately to any rise in the common price for the next marketing year; the common price shall be applied at the time of the fifth move towards alignment;

(b) when the price of a product in Greece is higher than the common price, the difference between the price level applicable before each move towards alignment in the Member State and the common price level applicable for the next marketing year shall be reduced successively at the time of the first four moves towards alignment by a fifth, a quarter, a third and a half; the common price shall be applied at the time of the fifth move towards alignment.

4. In the interest of the smooth functioning of the process of integration, the Council, acting in accordance with the procedure laid down in Article 43 (2) of the EEC Treaty, may decide that, notwithstanding paragraphs (2) and (3), the price of one or more products in Greece shall for one marketing year depart from the prices resulting from the application of paragraphs (2) or (3).

This departure may not exceed 10 per cent of the amount of the price move to be made.

In that event, the price level for the following marketing year shall be that which would have resulted from applying paragraph (2) or (3) if the departure had not been decided upon. A further departure from this price level may, however, be decided upon for that marketing year in accordance with the conditions in the first and second subparagraphs.

The derogation laid down in the first sub-paragraph shall not apply to the last move towards alignment referred to in paragraph (2) or (3).

ARTICLE 60

The Council, acting in accordance with the procedure laid down in Article 43 (2) of the EEC Treaty may decide that the common price shall be applied to Greece for a specified product:

(a) if it is found that the difference between the price level for the product in question in this Member State and the common price level is minimal;

(b) if the price in Greece or the price on the world market for the product in question is higher than the common price.

ARTICLE 61

The differences in price levels in respect of which, in Chapter 2, reference is made to this article shall be compensated as follows:

1. For products in respect of which prices are fixed in accordance with Articles 58 and 59, the compensatory amounts applicable in trade between the Community as at present constituted and Greece, and between Greece and third countries, shall be equal to the difference between the prices fixed for Greece and the common prices.

2. No compensatory amount shall, however, be fixed if the application of paragraph (1) results in a minimal amount.

3. (a) In trade between Greece and the Community as at present constituted, compensatory amounts shall be levied by the importing State or granted by the exporting State.

(b) In trade between Greece and third countries, levies or other import charges applied under the common agricultural policy, and export refunds, shall be reduced or increased, as the case may be, by the compensatory amounts applicable in trade with the Community as at present constituted. Customs duties may not, however, be reduced by the compensatory amount.

4. For products in respect of which the duty in the Common Customs Tariff is bound under the General Agreement on tariffs and trade, the binding shall be taken into account.

5. The compensatory amount levied or granted by a Member State in accordance with paragraph (1) may not exceed the total amount levied by the same Member State on imports from third countries, benefiting from the most-favoured-nation clause.

The Council, acting by a qualified majority on a proposal from the Commission, may derogate from this rule, in particular in order to avoid deflections of trade and distortions of competition.

6. The Council, acting by a qualified majority on a proposal from the Commission, may derogate, in so far as is necessary for the proper functioning of the common agricultural policy, from the first sub-paragraph of Article 42 (1) for products to which compensatory amounts apply.

ARTICLE 62

If the world market price for a product is higher than the price used in calculating the import charge introduced under the common agricultural policy, less the compensatory amount deducted from the import charge in accordance with Article 61, or if the refund on exports to third countries is less than the compensatory amount, or if no refund is applicable, appropriate measures may be taken with a view to ensuring the proper functioning of the common organisation of the market.

ARTICLE 63

The compensatory amounts granted shall be financed by the Community from the Guarantee Section of the European Agricultural Guidance and Guarantee Fund.

ARTICLE 64

The following provisions shall apply to products the importation of which from third countries into the Community as at present constituted is subject to customs duties:

1. Customs duties on imports shall be progressively abolished between the Community as at present constituted and Greece on the date and following the timetable laid down in Article 25.

However, for products falling within Regulation 805/68 on the common organisation of the market in beef and veal, customs duties on imports shall be progressively abolished in five stages by 20 per cent at the beginning of each of the five marketing years following accession.

If, for products referred to in paragraph (2) (b) the duties in the Common Customs Tariff are less than the basic duties, the latter shall, for the application of this paragraph, be replaced by the duties in the Common Customs Tariff.

2. (a) For the purpose of the progressive introduction of the Common Customs Tariff, the Hellenic Republic shall reduce the difference between the basic duty and the duty in the Common Customs Tariff under the conditions, on the dates and following the timetable laid down in Article 31.

(*b*) Notwithstanding point (*a*), the duty in the Common Customs Tariff shall be applied by the Hellenic Republic in its entirety as from January 1, 1981 for the following products:

—products falling within Regulation 805/68,

—products falling within Regulation 1035/72 and for which, for the whole or part of the marketing year, a reference price is fixed,

—products falling within Regulation 100/76 on the common organisation of the market in fishery products and for which a reference price is fixed,

—products falling within Regulation 337/79 on the common organisation of the market in wine and for which a reference price is fixed.

3. For the purpose of paragraphs (1) and (2) the basic duty shall be as defined in Article 24.

As regards products falling within Regulation 136/66 on the establishment of a common organisation of the market in oils and fats the basic duties shall be fixed as follows:

CCT heading No.	Description	Rate of basic duty to be considered as the rate actually applied by the Hellenic Republic on July 1, 1980.	
		vis-à-vis third countries	*vis-à-vis the Community as at present constituted*
12.01	Oil seed and oleaginous fruit, whole or broken:		
	ex B. Other, except linseed and castor seed	40%	36%
12.02	Flours or meals of oil seeds or oleaginous fruit, non-defatted (excluding mustard flour):		
	ex B. Other, except linseed and castor seed		
15.07	Fixed vegetable oils, fluid or solid, crude, refined or purified:		
	ex D. Other oils except		
	—Linseed oil		
	—Coconut (copra) oil and palm oil, for technical or industrial uses other than the manufacture of foodstuffs for human consumption	130%	104%
15.12	Animal or vegetable oils and fats, wholly or partly hydrogenated, or solidified or hardened by any other process, whether or not refined, but not further prepared:		
	A. In immediate packings of a net capacity of 1 kg or less		
	B. Other		

4. In respect of products covered by a common organisation of the market it may be decided in accordance with the procedure laid down in Article 38 of Regulation 136/66 or, as the case may be, in corresponding articles of other Regulations on the common organisation of agricultural markets that:

(a) the Hellenic Republic shall be authorised:

—to abolish customs duties referred to in paragraph (1) or more towards the alignment referred to in paragraph (2) at a more rapid rate than laid down there,

—to suspend in whole or in part the customs duties on products imported from the present Member States,

—to suspend in whole or in part the customs duties on products imported from third countries:

(b) the Community as at present constituted shall:

—abolish the customs duties referred to in paragraph (1) at a more rapid rate than laid down there,

—suspend in whole or in part the customs duties on products imported from Greece.

In respect of other products, not authorisation shall be required for the Hellenic Republic to apply the measures referred to in the first and second indents of point (a) of the first sub-paragraph. The Hellenic Republic shall inform the other Member States and the Commission of measures taken.

The customs duties resulting from an accelerated alignment may not be less than the customs duties on importers of the same products from other Member States.

ARTICLE 65

1. In respect of products covered, on the date of accession, by a common organisation of the market, the system applicable in the Community as at present constituted in respect of customs duties and charges having equivalent effect and quantitative restrictions and measures having equivalent effect shall, subject to Articles 61, 64 and 115, apply in Greece as from January 1, 1981.

2. In respect of products not covered, on the date of accession, by a common organisation of the market, the provisions of Title II concerning the progressive abolition of charges having equivalent effect to customs duties and of quantitative restrictions and measures having equivalent effect shall not apply to those charges, restrictions and measures if they form part of a national market organisation on the date of accession.

This provision shall only apply until the common organisation of the market for these products is implemented and not later than December 31, 1985 and to the extent strictly necessary to ensure the maintenance of the national organisation.

3. The Hellenic Republic shall apply the Common Customs Tariff nomenclature as from January 1, 1981, in respect of products falling within Annex II to the EEC Treaty.

To the extend that no difficulties arise in the application of the Community rules and, in particular, in the functioning of the common organisation of markets and of the transitional mechanisms provided for in this Title, the Council, acting by a qualified majority on a proposal from the Commission, may authorise the Hellenic Republic to include within this nomenclature such existing national subdivisions as would be indispensable for carrying out the progressive moves towards alignment with the Common Customs Tariff or the elimination of the duties in the Community under the conditions laid down in this Act.

ARTICLE 66

1. The component for protection of the processing industry which is used in calculating the charge on imports from third countries of products covered by the common organisation of the markets in cereals and rice shall be levied on imports from Greece into the Community as at present constituted.

2. For imports into Greece, the amount of that component shall be determined by separating out, from the total protection applied on January 1, 1979, the component or components designed to ensure the protection of the processing industry.

Such component or components shall be levied on imports from other Member States; they shall replace, as regards the charge on imports from third countries, the Community protective component.

3. Article 64 shall apply to the component referred to in paragraphs (1) and (2), which shall be considered as the basic component. The reductions or alignments in question shall, however, be made in five stages by 20 per cent at the beginning of the five marketing years following accession fixed for the basic product concerned.

ARTICLE 67

In fixing the level of the various amounts laid down within the common agricultural policy, except for the prices referred to in Article 58, account shall be taken for Greece, to the extent necessary for the proper functioning of the common agricultural policy, of the compensatory amount applied, or in absence thereof, of the difference in prices recorded and, where appropriate, of the incidence of customs duties.

ARTICLE 68

1. The provisions of this article shall apply to aids, premiums or other analogous amounts instituted under the common agricultural policy for which, in Chapter 2, reference is made to this article.

2. For the purposes of introducing Community aid in Greece, the following provisions shall apply:

    (a) the level of Community aid to be granted for a specific product in Greece as from January 1, 1981 shall be equal to an amount defined on the basis of aids granted by Greece, for a representative period to be determined, under the previous national system. However, this amount may not exceed the amount of aid granted on the date of accession in the Community as at present constituted. If no analogous aid was granted under the previous national system, and subject to the following provisions, no Community aid shall be granted to Greece on the date of accession;

    (b) thereafter, either Community aid shall be introduced in Greece, or the level of Community aid in Greece shall, where there is a difference, be aligned with aid granted in the Community as at present constituted in accordance with the following timetable:

      —at the beginning of each of the four marketing years—or in the absence of a period of application of the aid, following accession, successively by a fifth, a quarter, a third and a half;

        —either of the amount of Community aid applicable for the next marketing year or period,

        —or of the difference between the level of aid in Greece and the

level of aid applicable in the Community as at present constituted for the next marketing year or period,
—the level of Community aid shall be applied in its entirety in
Greece at the beginning of the fifth marketing year or the period
of application of the aid following accession.

ARTICLE 69

1. Without prejudice to the provisions of Article 68, the Hellenic Republic
shall be authorised to maintain national aids on a transitional basis and in a
degressive manner until December 31, 1985. However, a derogation may be
made to the principle of degressivity for Greek national aids that are to be
assessed by taking into consideration the scope of the socio-structural
Directives referred to in Annex IV.

2. The Council, acting by a qualified majority on a proposal from the Commission, shall adopt as from accession, the necessary measures for the implementation of the provisions of this article. These measures shall include in
particular the list and the exact wording of the aids referred to in paragraph (1),
the amount of the aids and the timetable of their abolition, and detailed rules
necessary to ensure the proper functioning of the common agricultural policy;
these detailed rules must, in addition, ensure that the means of production,
whether they originate from Greece or from the present Member States, enjoy
equal access to the Greek market.

ARTICLE 70

1. Until the entry into force of the supplementary provisions to be adopted
by the Community, and:
—at the latest until the beginning of the first marketing year following accession for products referred to in paragraph (2) (a),
—at the latest until December 31, 1985 for products referred to in
paragraph (2) (b).
the Hellenic Republic shall be authorised to maintain for these products
amongst the measures in force under the previous national system in its
territory for a representative period to be determined those measures which are
strictly necessary in order to maintain the income of the Greek producer at the
level obtained under the previous national system.

2. The products referred to in paragrah (1) are as follows:
   (a) dried figs falling within subheading 08.03 B of the Common
       Customs Tariff,
       dried grapes falling within subheading 08.04 B of the Common
       Customs Tariff;
   (b) olives for uses other than the production of oil falling within sub-
       headings 07.01 N I, ex 07.02 A, 07.03 A I, ex 07.04 B, ex 20.01 B,
       ex 20.02 F of the Common Customs Tariff.

3. The Council, acting by a qualified majority on a proposal from the Commission, shall establish as from accession the measures referred to in paragraph
(1) that the Hellenic Republic shall be authorised to maintain.

ARTICLE 71

Any stock of products in free circulation in Greek territory on January 1,
1981 and which in quantity exceeds what may be considered representative of
a normal carry-over stock must be eliminated by and at the expense of the
Hellenic Republic under Community procedures to be specified and within
time limits to be determined.

ARTICLE 72

1. The Council, acting by a qualified majority on a proposal from the Commission, shall adopt the provisions necessary for implementing this Title.

2. The Council, acting unanimously on a proposal from the Commission after consulting the Assembly, may make the adaptations to the provisions appearing in this Title, which may prove to be necessary as a result of a modification in Community rules.

ARTICLE 73

1. If transitional measures are necessary to facilitate the passage from the existing arrangements in Greece to those resulting from the application of the common organisation of the markets as provided for in this Title, particularly if for certain products the implementation of the new arrangements on the scheduled date meets with appreciable difficulties, such measures shall be adopted in accordance with the procedure provided for in Article 38 of Regulation 136/66 or, as the case may be, in the corresponding articles of the other Regulations on the common organisation of agricultural markets. Such measures may be taken during the period up to December 31, 1982, but their application may not extend beyond that date.

2. The Council may, acting unanimously on a proposal from the Commission after consulting the Assembly, extend the period referred to in paragraph (1).

CHAPTER 2—PROVISIONS RELATING TO CERTAIN COMMON ORGANISATIONS OF MARKETS

SECTION I—FRUIT AND VEGETABLES

ARTICLE 74

For fruit and vegetables, Article 59 shall apply to basic prices.

The basic price shall be fixed in Greece, at the time of accession, taking into account the difference between the average producer prices in Greece and in the Community as at present constituted, recorded over a reference period to be determined.

ARTICLE 75

1. A compensatory mechanism shall be introduced on importation, into the Community as at present constituted, for fruit and vegetables coming from Greece for which an institutional price is fixed.

2. This mechanism shall be governed by the following rules:

    (a) A comparison shall be drawn between the offer price of the Greek product, as calculated in (b) and a Community offer price calculated annually on the one hand, on the basis of the arithmetical average of producer prices of each Member State of the Community as at present constituted increased by the transport and packaging costs borne by the products from the areas of production up to the representative centres of Community consumption and, on the other hand, taking into account the trend of production costs. The abovementioned producer prices shall correspond to an average of the price quotations recorded over the three years prior to the date of fixing the abovementioned Community offer price. The annual Community price may not exceed the level of the reference price applied *vis-à-vis* third countries. This Community offer price shall be reduced by 3 per cent at the time of the first move towards price alignment referred to in Article 59, by 6 per cent at the time of the second move, 9 per cent at the time of the third move, by 12 per cent at the time of the fourth move, by 15 per cent at the time of the fifth move and, as regards peaches and tomatoes, by 18 per cent at the time of the sixth move, and by 21 per cent at the time of the seventh move.

(*b*) The offer price of the Greek product shall be calculated, each market day, on the basis of the representative price quotations recorded or reduced to the importer-wholesaler stage in the Community as at present constituted. The price for products coming from Greece shall be equal to the lowest representative price quotation or the average of the lowest representative price quotations recorded for at least 30 per cent of the quantities of the products in question marketed throughout the representative markets for which price quotations are available. This or these price quotations shall be reduced by any corrective amount that may be introduced in accordance with the provisions laid down hereinafter in (*c*).

(*c*) If the Greek price, thus calculated, shall be less than the Community price, as indicated in (*a*), a corrective amount equal to the difference between these two prices shall be levied on importation into the Community as at present constituted by the importing Member State. If the daily offer price of the Community produce calculated from the markets of the centres of consumption is at a lower level than that of the Community price as defined in (*a*), the corrective amount may however, not exceed the difference between, on the one hand, the arithmetical average of these two prices and, on the other hand, the price of the Greek product.

(*d*) The corrective amount shall be levied until records taken show that the price of the Greek product is equal to or greater than either, the Community price as defined in (*a*) or, where appropriate, the arithmetical average of Community prices referred to in (*c*).

3. The compensatory mechanism provided for in this article shall remain in force:

(*a*) until December 31, 1987 for the products referred to in Article 59 (2);

(*b*) until December 31, 1985 for the products referred to in Article 59 (3).

4. If the Greek market is disturbed by the fact of imports from the present Member States, appropriate measures, which may provide for a compensatory mechanism similar to that provided for in the preceding paragraphs, may be decided in respect of imports into Greece of fruit and vegetables from the Community as at present constituted for which an institutional price is fixed.

ARTICLE 76

Article 68 shall apply to the financial compensation referred to in Article 6 of Regulation 2511/69 laying down special measures for improving the production and marketing of Community citrus fruit.

This financial compensation shall be considered as an aid which is not granted in Greece under the previous national system.

361

Article 77

The minimum price and the financial compensation applicable in Greece, laid down in Articles 2 and 3 of Regulation 2601/69 laying down special measures to encourage the processing of certain varieties of oranges and to Articles 1 and 2 of Regulation 1035/77 laying down special measures to encourage the marketing of products processed from lemons, shall be fixed as follows:

1. Until the first move towards price alignment referred to in Article 59, the minimum price applicable shall be established on the basis of prices paid in Greece to producers of citrus for processing, recorded during a representative period to be determined, under the previous national system. The financial compensation shall be that of the Community as at present constituted, less, where appropriate, the difference between, on the one hand, the common minimum price and, on the other hand, the minimum price applicable in Greece.

2. For fixing subsequent prices, the minimum price applicable in Greece shall be aligned on the common minimum price in accordance with the provisions laid down in Article 59. The financial compensation applicable in Greece at the time of each stage of alignment shall be that of the Community as at present constituted less, where appropriate, the difference between, on the one hand, the common minimum price, and, on the other hand, the minimum price applicable in Greece.

3. However, if the minimum price resulting from the application of paragraph (1) or (2) shall be greater than the common minimum price, the latter price may be definitively adopted for Greece.

Article 78

Until December 31, 1987, the Hellenic Republic shall be authorised to lay down for all the producers of fruit and vegetables the obligation of marketing through local markets all their fruit and vegetable production, which is subject to common quality standards.

Section 2—Oils and Fats

Article 79

1. For olive oil, Articles 58, 59 and 61 shall apply at intervention prices.

However, the compensatory amount which results from the application of Article 61 shall be corrected, where appropriate, by the incidence of the difference between Community aids to consumption applicable in the Community as at present constituted and in Greece.

2. For oil seeds, target prices and guide prices shall be fixed on the basis of the difference existing between the price of competing products in crop rotation in Greece and in the Community as at present constituted, during a reference period to be determined. If the prices of these competing products are close, the common price shall be applicable in Greece as from accession. If the contrary holds true, Article 59 shall apply to the target or guide prices fixed for these products. However the target or guide prices to be applied in Greece may not exceed the common target or guide prices.

Article 80

Notwithstanding Article 67, at the time of fixing the level of the various amounts laid down for oil seeds other than the prices referred to in Article 79

(2) account shall be taken, for Greece, to the extent necessary for the proper functioning of the common organisation of the market for these products, of the difference arising from the application of Article 79 (2).

ARTICLE 81

1. Article 68 shall apply to aid for olive oil. However the first move towards alignment concerning production aid for this product shall occur on January 1, 1981.

To this end, the level of Community production aid to be adopted for the calculation of the level of aid applicable in Greece shall be that fixed for the marketing year obtaining on the date of accession.

The second stage of alignment shall occur at the beginning of the second marketing year following accession, the only possible movement at the beginning of the first marketing year being that resulting, where appropriate, from the modification of Community aid applicable in the Community as at present constituted.

2. The amount of aid of colza, rape, sunflower and castor seeds harvested in Greece shall be adjusted by the difference existing, where appropriate, between the target for guide price applicable in Greece and in the Community as at present constituted.

Without prejudice to the application of the first sub-paragraph, the amount of aid for colza, rape, sunflower and castor seeds processed in Greece shall be reduced by the incidence of the customs duties applied by the Hellenic Republic to the import of these products from third countries.

3. The amount of aid for soya beans and linseed harvested in Greece shall be adjusted by the difference existing, where apprproiate, between guide prices applicable in Greece and in the Community as at present constituted and reduced by the incidence of customs duties applied by the Hellenic Republic to the import of these products from third countries.

ARTICLE 82

The Hellenic Republic may apply until December 31, 1983 and in accordance with detailed rules to be defined the system of import control of oil seeds and vegetable oils and fats that it applies on January 1, 1979.

SECTION 3—MILK AND MILK PRODUCTS

ARTICLE 83

Articles 58, 59 and 61 shall apply to the intervention prices for butter and skimmed-milk powder.

ARTICLE 84

The compensatory amount for milk products other than butter and skimmed-milk powder shall be fixed with the help of coefficients to be determined.

SECTION 4—BEEF AND VEAL

ARTICLE 85

Articles 58, 59 and 61 shall apply to the prices for adult bovine animals in Greece and in the Community as at present constituted.

ARTICLE 86

The compensatory amount for products referred to in the Annex to Regulation 805/68 shall be fixed with the help of coefficients to be determined.

SECTION 5—TOBACCO

ARTICLE 87

1. Article 58 shall apply to the intervention price fixed for each variety or group of varieties.

2. The norm price corresponding to the intervention price referred to in paragraph (1) shall be fixed in Greece for the first harvest following accession at a level that shall reflect the relation existing between the norm price and the intervention price, in accordance with the second sub-paragraph of Article 2 (2) of Regulation 727/70 on the common organisation of the market in raw tobacoo.

3. For the four following harvests this norm price shall be:
   (a) fixed in accordance with the criteria laid down in the first sub-paragraph of Article 2 (2) of Regulation 727/70 taking, however, into account the aids that the Hellenic Republic is authorised to maintain for tobacco pursuant to Article 69;
   (b) increased in four stages, the first increase occurring for the second harvest following accession by the incidence of the reduction in national aids that the Hellenic Republic is authorised to maintain in a degressive fashion for tobacco pursuant to Article 69.

ARTICLE 88

Notwithstanding Article 71, any stock of tobacco existing in Greece coming from harvests prior to accession must be entirely eliminated by and at the expense of the Hellenic Republic under Community procedures to be specified and in accordance with time limits to be determined.

SECTION 6—FLAX AND HEMP

ARTICLE 89

Article 68 shall apply to aid for fibre flax and hemp.

SECTION 7—HOPS

ARTICLE 90

Article 68 shall apply to aid for hops.

SECTION 8—SEEDS

ARTICLE 91

Article 68 shall apply to aid for seeds.

SECTION 9—SILK WORMS

ARTICLE 92

Article 68 shall apply to aid for silk worms.

SECTION 10—SUGAR

ARTICLE 93

Articles 58, 59 and 61 shall apply to the intervention price for white sugar and the minimum price for beet.

ARTICLE 94

Compensatory amounts for products, other than fresh beet, in Article 1 (1) (b) and for products in Article 1 (1) (d) of Regulation 3330/74 on the common organisation of the market in sugar shall be derived from the compensatory amount for the primary product in question, with the help of coefficients to be determined.

ARTICLE 95

The amount referred to in Article 26 (3) of Regulation 3330/74 applicable in Greece shall be adjusted by the compensatory amount.

SECTION 11—CEREALS

ARTICLE 96

For cereals, Articles 58, 59 and 61 shall apply to the intervention price and, for common wheat, to the reference price.

ARTICLE 97

The compensatory amounts shall be fixed as follows:
1. The compensatory amount applicable until the first move towards alignment in the case of cereals for which no intervention price is fixed shall be derived from the compensatory amount applicable in the case of a competing cereal for which an intervention price is fixed, account being taken of:
   —the price relationship on the Greek market,
      or
   —the relationship existing between the threshold prices of the cereals in question.
   The subsequent compensatory amounts shall be fixed on the basis of those referred to in the first sub-paragraph and according to the rules in Article 59 for price alignment.
   However, in the case referred to in the first indent of the first sub-paragraph the relationship adopted must be aligned on the relationship existing between the threshold prices in accordance with the rules laid down in Article 59.
2. The compensatory amount for the products referred to in Article 1 (c) and (d) of Regulation 2727/75 on the common organisation of the market in cereals shall be derived from the compensatory amount for cereals to which they relate with the help of coefficients to be determined.
3. Without prejudice to the application of paragraph (2), where products processed from common wheat and durum wheat are concerned, the compensatory amount shall be fixed at a level which also takes into account any national aid that the Hellenic Republic would maintain pursuant to Article 69 for wheat used for the bread grain milling industry.

PART V—ACCESSION

ARTICLE 98

Article 68 shall apply to aid to durum wheat referred to in Article 10 of Regulation 2727/75.

SECTION 12—PIGMEAT

ARTICLE 99

1. For pigmeat, Articles 58, 59 and 61 shall apply to the price of this product in Greece and in the Community as at present constituted.

2. However, in order to avoid any risk of disturbance in trade between the Community as at present constituted and Greece, the compensatory amount may be calculated on the basis of the compensatory amounts for feed grain. To this end, the compensatory amount per kilogram of pig carcase shall be calculated on the basis of the compensatory amounts applicable to the quantity of grain required for the production in the Community of one kilogram of pigmeat.

Without prejudice to the application of the first sub-paragraph, the compensatory amount may be fixed at a level that also takes into account the national aid that the Hellenic Republic maintains pursuant to Article 69 for grain used in pig farming.

3. For products, other than pig carcases, referred to in Article 1 (1) of Regulation 2759/75 on the common organisation of the market in pigmeat, the compensatory amount shall be derived from the compensatory amount applied in accordance with paragraph (1) or (2) with the help of coefficients to be determined.

SECTION 13—EGGS

ARTICLE 100

1. For eggs, Articles 58, 59 and 61 shall apply to the price of these products in Greece and in the Community as at present constituted.

2. However, in order to avoid any risk of disturbance in trade between the Community as at present constituted and Greece, the compensatory amount may be calculated on the basis of compensatory amounts for feed grain. To this end:

(a) for eggs in shell, the compensatory amount per kilogram of eggs in shell shall be calculated on the basis of the compensatory amounts applicable to the quantity of feed grain required for the production in the Community of one kilogram of eggs in shell;

(b) for hatching eggs, the compensatory amount per hatching egg shall be calculated on the basis of the compensatory amounts applicable to the quantity of feed grain required for the production in the Community of one hatching egg.

Without prejudice to the application of the first sub-paragraph the compensatory amount may be fixed at a level that also takes into account the national aid that the Hellenic Republic maintains pursuant to Article 69 for grain used in poultry farming.

3. For the products referred to in Article 1 (1) (b) of Regulation 2771/75 on the common organisation of the market in eggs, the compensatory amount shall be derived from the compensatory amount applied in accordance with paragraph (1) or (2) with the help of coefficients to be determined.

SECTION 14—POULTRYMEAT

ARTICLE 101

1. For poultrymeat, Articles 58, 59 and 61 shall apply to the price of these products in Greece and in the Community as at present constituted.

2. However, in order to avoid any risk of disturbance in trade between the Community as at present constituted and Greece, the compensatory amount may be calculated on the basis of compensatory amounts for feed grain. To this end:

    (a) for slaughtered poultry, the compensatory amount per kilogram of slaughtered poultry shall be calculated on the basis of the compensatory amounts applicable to the quantity of feed grain required for the production in the Community of one kilogram of slaughtered poultry, differentiated by species;

    (b) for chicks, the compensatory amount applicable per chick shall be calculated on the basis of the compensatory amounts applicable to the quantity of feed grain required for the production in the Community of one chick.

Without prejudice to the application of the first sub-paragraph the compensatory amount may be fixed at a level that also takes into account the national aid that the Hellenic Republic maintains pursuant to Article 69 for grain used in poultry farming.

3. For the products referred to in Article 1 (2) (d) of Regulation 2777/75 on the common organisation of the market in poultrymeat, the compensatory amount shall be derived from the compensatory amount applied in accordance with paragraph (1) or (2) with the help of coefficients to be determined.

SECTION 15—RICE

ARTICLE 102

1. For rice, Articles 58, 59 and 61 shall apply to the intervention price of paddy rice.

2. The compensatory amount for husked rice shall be the compensatory amount for paddy rice, converted by means of the conversion rate referred to in Article 1 of Regulation 467/67.

3. For wholly milled rice, the compensatory amount shall be the compensatory amount for husked rice, converted by means of the conversion rate referred to in Article 1 of Regulation 467/67.

4. For semi-milled rice, the compensatory amount shall be the compensatory amount for wholly milled rice, converted by means of the conversion rate referred to in Article 1 of Regulation 467/67.

5. For the products referred to in Article 1 (1) (c) of Regulation 1418/76 on the common organisation of the market in rice, the compensatory amount shall be derived from the compensatory amount applicable to products to which they are related, with the help of coefficients to be determined.

6. The compensatory amount for broken rice shall be fixed at a level that takes into account the difference existing between the supply price in Greece and the threshold price.

SECTION 16—PRODUCTS PROCESSED FROM FRUIT AND VEGETABLES

ARTICLE 103

For products benefiting from the system of aid laid down in Article 3A of Regulation 516/77 on the common organisation of the market in products processed from fruit and vegetables, the following provisions shall apply in Greece:

1. Until the first move towards alignment of prices referred to in Article 59 the minimum price referred to in Article 3A (3) of Regulation 516/77 shall be established on the basis of prices paid in Greece to producers for a product for processing, recorded over a representative period to be determined, under the previous national system.

2. If the minimum price referred to in paragraph (1) differs from the common price, the price in Greece shall be modified at the beginning of each marketing year following accession, in accordance with the detailed rules laid down in Article 59.

3. The amount of Community aid granted in Greece shall be fixed in such a fashion as to compensate the difference between the level of prices of products of third countries, determined under Article 3A (3) of Regulation 516/77 and the level of prices of Greek products established taking into account the minimum price referred to in paragraph (2), and the processing costs obtaining in Greece, without taking into consideration undertakings which have higher costs. This aid may not however exceed aid granted in the Community as at present constituted.

4. Community aid shall be applied in its entirety in Greece as from the beginning of the seventh marketing year following accession for tomato concentrates, peeled tomatoes, tomato juice and tinned peaches, and as from the beginning of the fifth marketing year following accession for prunes derived from dried plums ("prunes d'Ente").

5. However, if the minimum price resulting from the application of paragraph (1) or (2) is greater than the common minimum price, the latter price may be definitively adopted for Greece.

SECTION 17—DRIED FODDER

ARTICLE 104

1. The guide price referred to in Article 4 of Regulation 1117/78 on the common organisation of the market in dried fodder, applicable in Greece on January 1, 1981, shall be fixed at a level equivalent to the world market price increased by any aid granted in Greece, during a reference period to be determined, under the previous national system, excepting aids maintained pursuant to Article 69, and customs duties applied on July 1, 1980 by Greece towards third countries. However the guide price, thus determined, may not exceed the common guide price.

2. Article 59 shall apply to the guide price calculated in accordance with the provisions of paragraph (1) if it is less than the common guide price.

3. Supplementary aid applicable in Greece shall be reduced by an amount equal to:

—the difference, if any, existing between the guide price applied in Greece and the common guide price,

and

—the incidence of customs duties applied by Greece to the import of these products from third countries,

this amount being multiplied by the percentage referred to in Article 5 (2) of Regulation 1117/78.

4. Article 68 shall apply to the flat rate aid referred to in Article 3 of Regulation 1117/78.

SECTION 18—PEAS AND FIELD BEANS

ARTICLE 105

1. For peas and field beans, the activating price applicable in Greece on January 1, 1981 shall be fixed on the basis of the difference existing between the prices of competing products in crop rotation in Greece and in the Community as at present constituted during a reference period to be determined.

If the prices of these competing products are similar, the common price shall be applicable in Greece as from accession. If the contrary holds true, Article 59 shall apply to the activating price for these products. However, the activating price to be applied in Greece may not exceed the common activating price.

2. The amount of the aid referred to in Article 2 (1) of Regulation 1119/78 laying down special measures for peas and field beans used in the feeding of animals, for peas and field beans harvested in Greece, shall be reduced by an amount equal to the difference, if any, existing between the activating price applied in Greece and the common activating price.

Without prejudice to the application of the first sub-paragraph, the amount of the aid in question for a product processed in Greece shall be reduced by the incidence of the customs duties applied in Greece to the import of soya oil cakes from third countries.

The amounts resulting from the application of the first and second sub-paragraphs shall be multiplied by the percentage referred to in Article 2 (1) of Regulation 1119/78.

ARTICLE 106

Notwithstanding Article 67 at the time of fixing the level of the different amounts laid down for peas and field beans, other than the prices referred to in Article 105 (1), account shall be taken, for Greece, to the extent necessary for the proper functioning of the common organisation of the market for these products of the difference in prices arising from the application of Article 105 (1).

SECTION 19—WINE

ARTICLE 107

1. Articles 58 and 59 shall apply to guide prices for table wines. Article 61 shall apply to the same products subject to paragraph (3).

2. The compensatory amount for the other products for which a reference price is fixed, shall be determined, to the extent necessary for the proper functioning of the common organisation of the market, on the basis of the compensatory amount fixed for table wines. However, for liqueur wines, the compensatory amount applicable on January 1, 1981 shall be equal to the amount of the countervailing charge to be applied *vis-à-vis* third countries on this date. This compensatory amount shall be eliminated in accordance with the timetable laid down in Article 59.

3. No compensatory amount shall apply to the import into Greece from third countries for goods subject to reference prices.

ARTICLE 108

Notwithstanding Article 67, the activating price referred to in Article 3 of Regulation 337/79 on the common organisation of the market in wine, applicable in Greece, shall not be adjusted by the compensatory amount. However, this amount shall be added to the average price fixed for each representative Greek market.

ARTICLE 109

For such time as the Hellenic Republic shall apply Article 70 to dried grapes, the volume of alcohol from dried grapes which may be added to certain wines in Greece pursuant to Regulation 351/79 concerning the addition of alcohol to products in the wine sector shall be limited to an annual volume not exceeding the annual average in volume of this alcohol used for this purpose in Greece during 1978, 1979 and 1980.

CHAPTER 3—PROVISIONS RELATING TO FISHERIES

ARTICLE 110

1. Notwithstanding Article 2 (1) of Regulation 101/76 laying down a common structural policy for the fishing industry, and Article 100 of the Act of Accession 1972, the Italian Republic and the Hellenic Republic shall be authorised, until December 31, 1985, to restrict, as between each other, fishing in waters under their sovereignty or jurisdiction, situated within the areas indicated in Article 111, to vessels which traditionally fish from ports in the geographical coastal area in these waters.

2. The provisions of paragraph (1) and of Article 111 shall not prejudice the special fishing rights which the Hellenic Republic and the Italian Republic may enjoy, as between each other, on January 1, 1981.

ARTICLE 111

The demarcation of areas referred to in Article 110 (1) shall be made as follows:

1. *Greece*
   Waters situated inside a limit of six nautical miles calculated from the base lines.

2. *Italy*
   Waters situated inside a limit of six nautical miles calculated from the base lines. This limit shall be extended to 12 nautical miles for the following areas:
   (a) Adriatic Sea, from the south of the mouth of the Po di Goro;
   (b) Ionian Sea;
   (c) Sicilian Sea and Straits of Sicily, including the islands;
   (d) waters of Sardinia.

CHAPTER 4—OTHER PROVISIONS

SECTION 1—VETERINARY MEASURES

ARTICLE 112

1. The Hellenic Republic shall not send to the territory of other Member States, from those of its regions specified in accordance with the procedure of the Standing Veterinary Committee on the basis of guarantees offered, any bovine animal or swine, nor fresh meat from bovine animals, swine, goats, sheep or lambs, until, in the said regions, a period of 12 months has elapsed since the appearance of the last source of exotic virus foot-and-mouth disease or since the last vaccination against this disease.

2. Before December 31, 1985 an examination of the situation shall be carried out concerning exotic virus foot and mouth disease.

At the latest by July 1, 1984 the Commission shall present to the Council a report with proposals with a view to adopting appropriate Community provisions in this field.

SECTION 2—MEASURES CONCERNING SEED AND SEEDLING LEGISLATION

ARTICLE 113

1. Until December 31, 1985 the Hellenic Republic may apply its own admission rules to varieties of agricultural or horticultural species or to basic material of forestry species, as well as rules of certification and control of its production of seeds and agricultural, horticultural and forestry seedlings.

2. The Hellenic Republic:

  (a) shall take all the necessary measures to comply progressively and at the latest before the expiry of the time limit referred to in paragraph (1) to Community provisions concerning the admission of varieties, basic materials, and the marketing of seeds, and agricultural, horticultural and forestry seedlings;

  (b) may restrict, wholly or partically, before the expiry of the time limit referred to in paragraph (1), the marketing of seeds and agricultural and horticultural seedlings to seeds and seedlings of the varieties admitted into its territory; this provision shall also apply to basic materials in respect of reproductive forestry materials;

  (c) shall only export to the territory of present Member States seeds and seedings that comply with Community provisions.

3. In accordance with the procedure of the Standing Committee on Seeds and Propagating Material for Agriculture, Horticulture and Forestry it may be decided, before December 31, 1985, to liberalise progressively trade in seeds and seedlings of certain species between Greece and the Community as at present constituted as soon as it appears that the necessary conditions for such liberalisation are met.

SECTION 3—MISCELLANEOUS PROVISIONS

ARTICLE 114

The acts listed in Annex IV to this Act shall apply in respect of Greece under the conditions laid down in that Annex.

TITLE V—EXTERNAL RELATIONS

CHAPTER 1—COMMON COMMERCIAL POLICY

ARTICLE 115

1. Until December 31, 1985 the Hellenic Republic may maintain quantitative restrictions in the form of global quotas for the products and amounts listed in Annex V as temporary derogations from the common liberalisation lists contained in Regulations 109/70, 1439/74 and 2532/78. These products shall be fully liberalised on January 1, 1986 and the quotas shall be progressively increased until that date. The procedures for the increase in the quotas shall be identical to those laid down in Article 36.

If imports made in two consecutive years are less than 90 per cent of the annual quota opened, the Hellenic Republic shall abolish the quantitative restrictions in force, if the product in question is at that time liberalised *vis-à-vis* the present Member States.

2. Until December 31, 1985 the Hellenic Republic shall not liberalise *vis-à-vis* third countries, products not yet liberalised *vis-à-vis* the Community as at present constituted, or give third countries any other advantage over the Community as at present constituted as regards the quotas set for these products. The Hellenic Republic shall not liberalise with regard to State-trading countries referred to in Regulations 109/70 and 2532/78 products not yet liberalised with regard to the Community as at present constituted or countries to which Regulation 1439/74 applies or give such countries any other advantage over the Community as at present constituted or countries to which Regulation 1439/74 applies as regards the quotas fixed for these products.

3. Until December 31, 1985 the Hellenic Republic shall maintain quantitative restrictions, in the form of quotas, *vis-à-vis* all third countries for the products listed in Annex VI which are not liberalised by the Community as at present constituted and which the Hellenic Republic has not yet liberalised *vis-à-vis* the former. The quotas for 1981 for countries to which Regulation 1439/74 applies other than those referred to in Article 120 and with regard to State-trading countries referred to in Regulations 109/70 and 2532/78 shall be the amounts shown in that Annex.

Any alteration of these quotas shall only be made in accordance with Community procedures.

ARTICLE 116

The Hellenic Republic shall abolish *vis-à-vis* third countries its system, as it exists at the time of accession, of import deposits and cash payments in accordance with the same timetable and under the same conditions as those laid down in Article 38 as regards the present Member States.

ARTICLE 117

1. On January 1, 1981 the Hellenic Republic shall apply the Community system of generalised preferences for products other than those listed in Annex II of the EEC Treaty; however, as regards the products listed in Annex VII, the Hellenic Republic shall progressively align until December 31, 1985 on the rates of the system of generalised preferences. The timetable of alignment for these products shall be the same as those laid down in Article 31.

2. In the case of products listed in Annex II to the EEC Treaty, the preferential rates provided for or calculated shall be applied to the duties actually levied by the Hellenic Republic in respect of third countries as laid down in Article 64.

In no case should Greek imports from third countries benefit from rates of duty more favourable than those applied to products from the Community as at present constituted.

CHAPTER 2—AGREEMENTS OF THE COMMUNITIES WITH CERTAIN THIRD COUNTRIES

ARTICLE 118

1. As from January 1, 1981 the Hellenic Republic shall apply the provisions of the Agreements referred to in Article 120.

The transitional measures and adjustments shall be the subject of Protocols concluded with the co-contracting third countries and annexed to those Agreements.

2. These transitional measures, which shall take into account the corresponding measures adopted within the Community and which may not extend beyond the period of validity thereof, shall be designed to ensure the application by the Community of a single system for its relations with the co-contracting third countries as well as the identity of the rights and obligations of the Member States.

3. These transitional measures applicable to the countries listed in Article 120 shall not, in any field, involve the Hellenic Republic granting them more favourable treatment than will apply to the Community as at present constituted.

In particular, all products subject to transitional measures in respect of quantitative restrictions applicable to the Community as at present constituted shall be subject to such measures *vis-à-vis* all the countries listed in Article 120, and for an identical period of time.

4. These transitional measures applicable to the countries listed in Article 120 shall not result in the Hellenic Republic giving less favourable treatment to these countries than to other third countries. In particular, transitional measures in respect of quantitative restrictions cannot be envisaged for the countries listed in Article 120 in respect of products which will be free of such restrictions when imported into Greece from other third countries.

ARTICLE 119

If the Protocols referred to in Article 118 (1) are not, for reasons outside the control of the Community or the Hellenic Republic, concluded on January 1, 1981 the Community shall take the necessary measures to deal with this situation after accession.

In any case, most-favoured-nation-treatment shall be applied as from January 1, 1981 by the Hellenic Republic to the countries listed in Article 120.

ARTICLE 120

Articles 118 and 119 shall apply to the Agreements concluded with Algeria, Austria, Cyprus, Egypt, Finland, Iceland, Israel, Jordan, Lebanon, Malta, Morocoo, Norway, Portugal, Spain, Sweden, Switzerland, Syria, Tunisia and Turkey.

Articles 118 and 119 shall also apply to Agreements which the Community concludes with other third countries in the Mediterranean region before the entry into force of this Act.

CHAPTER 3—RELATIONS WITH THE AFRICAN, CARIBBEAN AND PACIFIC STATES

ARTICLE 121

The arrangements resulting from the ACP-EEC Convention of Lomé and the Agreement on products within the province of the European Coal and Steel Community, signed on February 28, 1975, shall not apply in relations between the Hellenic Republic and the African, Caribbean and Pacific States, with the exception of Protocol 3 on sugar.

ARTICLE 122

The provisions of Articles 118 and 119 shall apply to any new Agreement that the Community concludes with the African, Caribbean and Pacific countries before the entry into force of this Act.

CHAPTER 4—TEXTILES

ARTICLE 123

1. As from January 1, 1981 the Hellenic Republic shall apply the Arrangement of December 20, 1973 regarding international trade in textiles as well as the bilateral Agreements concluded by the Community under this Arrangement. Protocols of adjustment of these Agreements shall be negotiated by the Community with third countries, that are parties to the Agreements, in order to provide for voluntary restraint on exports to Greece in the case of products and origins for which there are limitations on exports to the Community.

2. Should these Protocols not have been concluded by January 1, 1981, the Community shall take measures designed to deal with this situation concerning the necessary transitional adjustments to ensure that the Agreements are implemented by the Community.

TITLE VI—FINANCIAL PROVISIONS

ARTICLE 124

The Decision of April 21, 1970 on the replacement of financial contributions from Member States by the Communities' own resources, hereinafter referred to as "the Decision of 21 April 1970", shall be applied, in accordance with the provisions referred to in Articles 125, 126 and 127.

ARTICLE 125

The revenue designated as "agricultural levies", referred to in Article 2 (a) of the Decision of April 21, 1970, shall also include the revenue from any compensatory amount levied on imports under Articles 43, 61 and 75 and from the fixed components applied in trade between the Community as at present constituted and Greece and in trade between Greece and third countries under Article 66.

ARTICLE 126

The revenue designated as "customs duties", referred to in Article 2 (b) of the Decision of April 21, 1970, shall include, until December 31, 1985, customs duties calculated as if the Hellenic Republic applied as from accession the rates in trade with third countries determined by the Common Customs Tariff and the reduced rates determined by any tariff preference applied by the Community.

The Hellenic administration shall make a monthly calculation of these customs duties on the basis of customs declarations of a single month, which shall be made available to the Commission by, at the latest, the 20th of the second month following that of the declarations.

As from January 1, 1986 the total amount of customs duties levied shall be due in its entirety.

ARTICLE 127

The amount of duties established under own resources accruing from value added tax or from financial contributions based upon the gross national product pursuant to Article 4 (1) to (5) of the Decision of April 21, 1970 shall be due in its entirety as from January 1, 1981.

However, the Community shall refund to the Hellenic Republic, during the month following its availability to the Commission, a proportion of the amount referred to in the preceding paragraph in accordance with the following procedure:
—70 per cent in 1981,
—50 per cent in 1982,
—30 per cent in 1983,
—20 per cent in 1984,
—10 per cent in 1985.

TITLE VII—OTHER PROVISIONS

ARTICLE 128

The acts listed in Annex VIII to this Act shall apply in respect of the Hellenic Republic under the conditions laid down in that Annex.

ARTICLE 129

Until December 31, 1985 iron and steel undertakings in Greece are authorised to apply the system of multiple basing points.

2. Until December 31, 1985 the prices charged by undertakings in the present Member States for sales of iron and steel products on the Greek market, reduced to their equivalent at the point chosen for their price list, may not be below the prices shown in the price list in question for comparable transactions, save when authorisation has been given by the Commission, in agreement with the Hellenic Government, without prejudice to the last subparagraph of Article 60 (2) (b) of the ECSC Treaty. Undertakings in the present Member States shall retain the right to align their delivered prices in Greece on those charged there by third countries for the same products.

The first sub-paragraph shall only concern alignment on price lists of producers in the present Member States and Greece for products actually produced in Greece on January 1, 1981. A list of such products will be published by the Commission on that date.

ARTICLE 130

1. If, before December 31, 1985, difficulties arise which are serious and liable to persist in any sector of the economy or which could bring about serious deterioration in the economic situation of a given area, the Hellenic Republic may apply for authorisation to take protective measures in order to rectify the situation and adjust the sector concerned to the economy of the common market.

In the same circumstances, any present Member State may apply for authorisation to take protective measures with regard to the Hellenic Republic.

The provision shall apply until December 31, 1987 for products or sectors in respect of which this Act allows transitional derogations of equivalent duration.

2. On application by the State concerned, the Commission shall, by emergency procedures, determine the protective measures which it considers necessary specifying the circumstances and the manner in which they are to be put into effect.

In the event of serious economic difficulties, the Commission shall act within five working days. The measures thus decided on shall be applicable forthwith.

In the agricultural sector, where trade between the Community as at present constituted and Greece causes or threatens to cause serious disturbances on the market of a Member State, the Commission shall act upon a request by a Member State for the application of appropriate measures within 24 hours of receiving such request. The measures thus decided on shall be applicable forthwith and shall take account of the interests of all parties concerned and, in particular, transport problems.

3. The measures authorised under paragraph (2) may involve derogations from the rules of the EEC Treaty and of this Act to such an extent and for such periods as are strictly necessary in order to attain the objectives referred to in paragraph (1). Priority shall be given to such measures as will least disturb the functioning of the common market.

ARTICLE 131

1. If before the expiry of the period of application of the transitional measures laid down under this Act for each case the Commission, on application by a Member State or by any other interested party, finds that dumping is being practised between the Community as at present constituted and Greece, it shall address recommendations to the person or persons with whom such practices originate for the purpose of putting an end to them.

Should the practices continue, the Commission shall authorise the injured Member State or States to take protective measures, the conditions and details of which the Commission shall determine.

2. For the application of this article, to the products listed in Annex II to the EEC Treaty, the Commission shall evaluate all relevant factors, in particular the level of prices at which these products are imported into the market in question from elsewhere, account being taken of the provisions of the EEC Treaty relating to agriculture and in particular Article 39 thereof.

Part Five

PROVISIONS RELATING TO THE IMPLEMENTATION OF THIS ACT

TITLE I—SETTING UP OF THE INSTITUTIONS

ARTICLE 132

The Assembly shall meet at the latest one month after accession of the Hellenic Republic. It shall make such adaptations to its rules of procedure as are made necessary by this accession.

ARTICLE 133

1. Upon accession of the Hellenic Republic the office of President of the Council shall be held by the member of the Council who would have held that office in accordance with Article 2 of the Treaty establishing a single Council and a single Commission of the European Communities in its original version. On expiry of this term of office, the office of President shall then be held in the order of Member States laid down in the article referred to above, as amended by Article 11.

2. The Council shall make such adaptations to its rules of procedure as are made necessary by the accession of the Hellenic Republic.

ARTICLE 134

1. The President, the Vice-Presidents and the members of the Commission shall be appointed upon accession of the Hellenic Republic. The Commission shall take up its duties on the fifth day after its members have been appointed. The terms of office of the members in office at the time of accession shall terminate at the same time.

2. The Commission shall make such adaptations to its rules of procedure as are made necessary by the accession of the Hellenic Republic.

ARTICLE 135

1. Upon accession of the Hellenic Republic one new judge shall be appointed to the Court of Justice.

2. The term of office of this judge shall expire on October 6, 1985.

3. The Court shall make such adaptations to its rules of procedure as are made necessary by the accession of the Hellenic Republic. The rules of procedure as adapted shall require the unanimous approval of the Council.

4. In order to give judgment in cases pending before the Court on January 1, 1981 in respect of which oral proceedings have started before that date, the full Court and the Chambers shall be composed as before the accession of the Hellenic Republic and shall apply the rules of procedure in force on December 31, 1980.

ARTICLE 136

Upon accession of the Hellenic Republic, the Economic and Social Committee shall be enlarged by the appointment of 12 members representing the various categories of economic and social activity in Greece. The terms of office of the members thus appointed shall expire at the same time as those of the members in office at the time of accession.

ARTICLE 137

Upon accession of the Hellenic Republic, the Court of Auditors shall be enlarged by the appointment of one additional member. The term of office of the member thus appointed shall expire at the same time as those of the members in office at the time of accession.

ARTICLE 138

Upon accession of the Hellenic Republic, the Consultative Committee of the European Coal and Steel Community shall be enlarged by the appointment of three additional members. The terms of office of the members thus appointed shall expire at the same time as those of the members in office at the time of accession.

Article 139

Upon accession of the Hellenic Republic, the Scientific and Technical Committee shall be enlarged by the appointment of one additional member. The term of office of the member thus appointed shall expire at the same time as those of the members in office at the time of accession.

Article 140

Upon accession of the Hellenic Republic, the Monetary Committee shall be enlarged by the appointment of members representing this new Member State. Their terms of office shall expire at the same time as those of the members in office at the time of accession.

Article 141

Adaptations to the Rules of the Committees established by the original Treaties and to their rules of procedure, necessitated by accession of the Hellenic Republic, shall be made as soon as possible after this accession.

Article 142

1. The terms of office of the new members of the Committees listed in Annex IX shall expire at the same time as those of the members in office at the time of accession.

2. Upon accession, the membership of the Committees listed in Annex X shall be completely renewed.

TITLE II—APPLICABILITY OF THE ACTS OF THE INSTITUTIONS

Article 143

From its accession the Hellenic Republic shall be considered as being an addressee of and as having received notification of directives and decisions within the meaning of Article 189 of the EEC Treaty and of Article 161 of the Euratom Treaty, and of recommendations and decisions within the meaning of Article 14 of the ECSC Treaty, provided that those directives, recommendations and decisions have been notified to all the present Member States.

Article 144

The application in Greece of the acts listed in Annex XI to this Act shall be deferred until the dates specified in that list.

Article 145

The Hellenic Republic shall put into effect the measures necessary for it to comply from the date of accession with the provisions of directives and decisions within the meaning of Article 189 of the EEC Treaty and of Article 161 of the Euratom Treaty, and with recommendations and decisions within the meaning of Article 14 of the ECSC Treaty, unless a time limit is provided for in the list in Annex XII or in any other provisions of this Act.

ARTICLE 146

1. Adaptations to the acts of the institutions of the Communities not included in this Act or its Annexes, made by the institutions before the accession of the Hellenic Republic in accordance with the procedures in paragraph (2) to bring those acts into line with the provisions of this Act, in particular those of Part Four, shall enter into force as from the said accession.

2. The Council, acting by a qualified majority on a proposal from the Commission, or the Commission, according to which of these two institutions adopted the original act, shall to this end draw up the necessary texts.

ARTICLE 147

The texts of the acts of the institutions of the Communities adopted before the accession of the Hellenic Republic and drawn up by the Council or the Commission in the Greek language shall, from the date of the said accession, be authentic under the same conditions as the texts drawn up in the present six languages. They shall be published in the *Official Journal of the European Communities* if the texts in the present languages were so published.

ARTICLE 148

Agreements, decisions and concerted practices in existence at the time of the accession of the Hellenic Republic which come within the scope of Article 65 of the ECSC Treaty by reason of this accession must be notified to the Commission within three months of accession. Only agreements and decisions which have been notified shall remain provisionally in force until a decision has been taken by the Commission.

ARTICLE 149

Provisions laid down by law, regulation or administrative action designed to ensure the protection of the health of the workers and the general public in the territory of the Hellenic Republic against the dangers arising from ionising radiations shall, in accordance with Article 33 of the Euratom Treaty, be communicated by that State to the Commission within three months of accession.

TITLE III—FINAL PROVISIONS

ARTICLE 150

Annexes I to XII and Protocols 1 to 7, which are annexed to this Act, shall form an integral part thereof.

ARTICLE 151

The Government of the French Republic shall transmit a certified copy of the Treaty establishing the European Coal and Steel Community and the Treaties amending that Treaty to the Government of the Hellenic Republic.

ARTICLE 152

The Government of the Italian Republic shall transmit a certified copy of the Treaty establishing the European Economic Community, the Treaty establishing the European Atomic Energy Community and the Treaties amending or supplementing them, including the Treaty concerning the accession of the Kingdom of Denmark, Ireland and the United Kingdom of Great Britain and Northern Ireland to the European Economic Community and the European Atomic Energy Community, in the Danish, Dutch, English, French, German, Irish and Italian languages to the Government of the Hellenic Republic.

The texts of these Treaties, drawn up in the Greek language, shall be annexed to this Act. These texts shall be authentic under the same conditions as the texts of the Treaties referred to in the first paragraph, drawn up in the present languages.

ARTICLE 153

A certified copy of the international agreements deposited in the archives of the General Secretariat of the Council of the European Communities shall be transmitted to the Hellenic Republic by the Secretary-General.

Protocols

PROTOCOL NO. 1 ON THE STATUTE OF THE EUROPEAN INVESTMENT BANK

Part One

ADJUSTMENTS TO THE STATUTE OF THE EUROPEAN INVESTMENT BANK

ARTICLE 1

[*This article amends the Protocol on the Statute of the European Investment Bank, Art. 3, and is incorporated therein.*]

ARTICLE 2

[*This article amends the Protocol on the Statute of the European Investment Bank, Art. 4, and is incorporated therein.*]

ARTICLE 3

[*This article amends the Protocol on the Statute of the European Investment Bank, Art. 7, and is incorporated therein.*]

ARTICLE 4

[*This article amends the Protocol on the Statute of the European Investment Bank, Art. 11, and is incorporated therein.*]

ARTICLE 5

[*This article amends the Protocol on the Statute of the European Investment Bank, Art. 12, and is incorporated therein.*]

ARTICLE 6

[*This article amends the Protocol on the Statute of the European Investment Bank, Art. 13, and is incorporated therein.*]

Part Two

OTHER PROVISIONS

ARTICLE 7

1. The Hellenic Republic shall pay the sum of 8,840,000 units of account as its contribution to the subscribed capital paid in by the Member States as at December 31, 1979, payment of this sum to be made in five equal six-monthly instalments falling due on April 30 and October 31. The first instalment shall be payable on whichever of these two dates next follows the date of accession, provided that there is an interval of at least two months between this date and the due date for this instalment.

2. From the day of its accession, the Hellenic Republic shall contribute to the increase in the Bank's capital decided on June 19, 1978, by making payments towards this increase in proportion to its contribution to the subscribed capital and in accordance with the timetable laid down by the Board of Governors. If the Member States have already made one or more such payments before the accession of the Hellenic Republic, the sum of such payment(s) corresponding to the share of the capital to be subscribed by the Hellenic Republic shall be added in five equal instalments to the payments to be made by the Hellenic Republic in accordance with the first paragraph of this Article.

ARTICLE 8

The Hellenic Republic shall, at the dates indicated in Article 7(1), contribute towards the statutory reserve, the supplementary reserve and those provisions equivalent to reserves, and to the amount still to be appropriated to the reserves and provisions corresponding to the balance of the profit and loss account as at December 31 of the year prior to accession, as stated in units of account in the Bank's approved balance sheet, an amount corresponding to 1.56 per cent of these reserves and provisions.

ARTICLE 9

The payments laid down in Articles 7 and 8 of this Protocol shall be made by the Hellenic Republic in its freely convertible national currency. The amounts payable shall be calculated on the basis of the rate of conversion between the unit of account and the drachma applicable on the last working day of the month preceding the relevant due dates for payment.

ARTICLE 10

1. Upon accession, the Board of Governors shall increase the Board of Directors by appointing one director nominated by the Hellenic Republic together with one alternate nominated by common accord of the Kingdom of Denmark, the Hellenic Republic and Ireland.

2. The terms of office of the director and alternate thus appointed shall expire at the end of the annual meeting of the Board of Governors during which the annual report for the 1982 financial year is examined.

ARTICLE 11

The Board of Governors, acting on a proposal from the Board of Directors shall appoint the fifth Vice-President referred to in Article 6 of this Protocol at the latest at its annual meeting during which the annual report for the 1981 financial year is examined.

PROTOCOL NO. 5 ON THE PARTICIPATION OF THE HELLENIC REPUBLIC IN THE FUNDS OF THE EUROPEAN COAL AND STEEL COMMUNITY

The contribution of the Hellenic Republic to the funds of the European Coal and Steel Community shall be fixed at 3 million European units of account.

This contribution shall be paid in three interest-free equal annual instalments starting from January 1, 1981.

Each instalment shall be paid in the freely convertible national currency of the Hellenic Republic.

PROTOCOL NO. 6 ON THE EXCHANGE OF INFORMATION WITH THE HELLENIC REPUBLIC IN THE FIELD OF NUCLEAR ENERGY

ARTICLE 1

1. From the date of accession, such information as has been communicated to Member States, persons and undertakings, in accordance with Article 13 of the Euratom Treaty, shall be placed at the disposal of the Hellenic Republic which shall give it limited distribution within its territory under the conditions laid down in that Article.

2. From the date of accession, the Hellenic Republic shall place at the disposal of the European Atomic Energy Community information obtained in the nuclear field in Greece which is given limited distribution, insofar as strictly commercial applications are not involved. The Commission shall communicate this information to Community undertakings under the conditions laid down in the abovementioned Article.

3. This information shall mainly concern:
—studies on the application of radioisotopes in the following fields: medicine, agriculture, entomology, environmental protection,
—the application of nuclear technology to archeometry,
—the development of electronic medical apparatus,
—the development of methods of radioactive ore prospecting.

ARTICLE 2

1. In those sectors in which the Hellenic Republic places information at the disposal of the Community, the competent authorities shall grant upon request licences on commercial terms to Member States, persons and undertakings of the Community where they possess exclusive rights to patents filed in Member States of the Community and insofar as they have no obligation or commitment in respect of third parties to grant or offer to grant an exclusive or partially exclusive licence to the rights in these patents.

2. Where an exclusive or partially exclusive licence has been granted, the Hellenic Republic shall encourage and facilitate the granting of sub-licences on commercial terms to Member States, persons and undertakings of the Community by the holders of such licences.

Such exclusive or partially exclusive licences shall be granted on a normal commercial basis.

Final Act

The Plenipotentiaries of His Majesty The King of the Belgians, Her Majesty The Queen of Denmark, The President of the Federal Republic of Germany, The President of the Hellenic Republic, The President of the French Republic, The President of Ireland, The President of the Italian Republic, His Royal Highness The Grand Duke of Luxembourg, Her Majesty The Queen of the Netherlands, Her Majesty The Queen of the United Kingdom of Great Britain and Northern Ireland, and The Council of the European Communities represented by its President, Assembled at Athens on the twenty-eighth day of May one thousand nine hundred and seventy-nine on the occasion of the signature of the Treaty relating to the accession of the Hellenic Republic to the European Economic Community and the European Atomic Energy Community,

have placed on record the fact that the following texts have been drawn up and adopted within the Conference between the European Communities and the Hellenic Republic:
- I. the Treaty concerning the accession of the Hellenic Republic to the European Economic Community and to the European Atomic Energy Community;
- II. the Act concerning the Conditions of Accession of the Hellenic Republic and the Adjustments to the Treaties;
- III. the texts listed below which are annexed to the Act concerning the Conditions of Accession of the Hellenic Republic and the Adjustments to the Treaties;
  - A. Annex   I List referred to in Article 21 of the Act of Accession,
    - Annex   II List referred to in Article 22 of the Act of Accession,
    - Annex   III List of products referred to in Article 36(1) and (2) of the Act of Accession (Euratom),
    - Annex   IV List of products referred to in Article 114 of the Act of Accession,
    - Annex   V List referred to in Article 115(1) of the Act of Accession,
    - Annex   VI List referred to in Article 115(3) of the Act of Accession,
    - Annex VII List referred to in Article 117(1) of the Act of Accession,
    - Annex VIII List referred to in Article 128 of the Act of Accession,
    - Annex   IX List referred to in Article 142(1) of the Act of Accession,
    - Annex   X List referred to in Article 142(2) of the Act of Accession,
    - Annex   XI List referred to in Article 144 of the Act of Accession,
    - Annex XII List referred to in Article 145 of the Act of Accession;
  - B. Protocol No. 1 on the Statute of the European Investment Bank,
    - Protocol No. 2 on the definition of the basic duty for matches falling within heading No. 36.06 of the Common Customs Tariff,
    - Protocol No. 3 on the granting by the Hellenic Republic of exemption of customs duties on the import of certain goods,
    - Protocol No. 4 on cotton,
    - Protocol No. 5 on the participation of the Hellenic Republic in the funds of the European Coal and Steel Community,
    - Protocol No. 6 on the Exchange of Information with the Hellenic Republic in the field of nuclear energy,
    - Protocol No. 7 on the Economic and Industrial Development of Greece;
  - C. The texts of the Treaty establishing the European Economic Community and of the Treaty establishing the European Atomic Energy Community, together with the Treaties amending or supplementing them, including the Treaty concerning the Accession of the Kingdom of Denmark, Ireland and the United Kingdom of Great Britain and Northern Ireland to the European Economic Community and to the European Atomic Energy Community, in the Greek language.

The Plenipotentiaries have taken note of the Decision of the Council of the European Communities of May 24, 1979, concerning the accession of the Hellenic Republic to the European Coal and Steel Community.

Furthermore the Plenipotentiaries and the Council have adopted the Declarations listed below and annexed to this Final Act:
1. Joint Declaration on the free movement of workers.
2. Joint Declaration on particular transitional measures which might be required in relations between Greece and Spain and Portugal after accession of the latter States,
3. Joint Declaration concerning protocols to be concluded with certain third countries according to Article 118,

4. Joint Declaration concerning Mount Athos.
5. Joint Declaration on the procedure for the joint examination of national aids granted by the Hellenic Republic in the field of agriculture during the period prior to accession,
6. Joint Declaration on the joint examination procedure of the annual changes in prices of agricultural products in Greece during the period prior to accession,
7. Joint Declaration on sugar, milk products, olive oil and products processed from fruit and vegetables,
8. Joint Declaration concerning the First Council Directive of December 12, 1977, on the co-ordination of laws, regulations and administrative provisions relating to the taking up and pursuit of the business of credit institutions.

The Plenipotentiaries and the Council have also taken note of the following Declaration to this Final Act:

1. Declaration by the Government of the Federal Republic of Germany on the application to Berlin of the Decision concerning Accession to the European Coal and Steel Community and of the Treaty of Accession to the European Economic Community and to the European Atomic Energy Community.
2. Declaration by the Government of the Federal Republic of Germany on the definition of the term "nationals".

The Plenipotentiaries and the Council have also taken note of the arrangement regarding the procedure for adopting certain decisions and other measures to be taken during the period preceding accession which has been reached within the Conference between the European Communities and the Hellenic Republic and which is annexed to this Final Act.

Finally, the following Declarations have been made and are annexed to this Final Act:

1. Declaration of the European Economic Community on Greek workers taking up and pursuing paid employment in the present Member States,
2. Declaration of the European Economic Community on the European Regional Development Fund,
3. Declaration by the Hellenic Republic on monetary questions.

In witness whereof the undersigned Plenipotentiaries have signed this Final Act.

Done at Athens on the twenty-eighth day of May in the year one thousand nine hundred and seventy-nine.

Declarations

JOINT DECLARATION ON THE FREE MOVEMENT OF WORKERS

The enlargement of the Community could give rise to certain difficulties for the social situation in one or more Member States as regards the application of the provisions relating to the free movement of workers.

The Member States declare that they reserve the right, should difficulties of that nature arise, to bring the matter before the institutions of the Community in order to obtain a solution to this problem in accordance with the provisions of the Treaties establishing the European Communities and the provisions adopted in application thereof.

JOINT DECLARATION ON PARTICULAR TRANSITIONAL MEASURES WHICH MIGHT BE REQUIRED IN RELATIONS BETWEEN GREECE AND SPAIN AND PORTUGAL AFTER ACCESSION OF THE LATTER STATES

The accession of Spain and Portugal to the Communities before the expiry of the transitional measures laid down in Article 9 of the Act could require particular transitional measures on relations between these countries and Greece.

These transitional measures would have to be determined in the instruments of accession with Spain and Portugal.

JOINT DECLARATION CONCERNING THE FIRST COUNCIL DIRECTIVE OF 12 DECEMBER 1977 ON THE CO-ORDINATION OF THE LAWS, REGULATIONS AND ADMINISTRATIVE PROVISIONS RELATING TO THE TAKING UP AND PURSUIT OF THE BUSINESS OF CREDIT INSTITUTIONS

On the occasion of the amendment to Article 2(2) of the Directive in question, it is stated that the Council will decide to exclude "Ταχυδρομικοῦ Ταμιευτηρίου" (Post Office Savings Bank) from the list of institutions given in this provision
—if the statutes of the Post Office Savings Bank are amended; or
—if this body's share of the Greek market, with respect either to deposits, credits or assets, increases by more than 1.5 per cent as compared with the situation existing on November 30 1978.

DECLARATION BY THE GOVERNMENT OF THE FEDERAL REPUBLIC OF GERMANY ON THE APPLICATION TO BERLIN OF THE DECISION CONCERNING ACCESSION TO THE EUROPEAN COAL AND STEEL COMMUNITY AND OF THE TREATY OF ACCESSION TO THE EUROPEAN ECONOMIC COMMUNITY AND TO THE EUROPEAN ATOMIC ENERGY COMMUNITY

The Government of the Federal Republic of Germany reserves the right to declare, when the accession of the Hellenic Republic to the European Coal and Steel Community takes effect and upon depositing its instrument of ratification of the Treaty concerning the accession of this country to the European Economic Community and to the European Atomic Energy Community, that the Decision of the Council of May 24 1979 concerning accession to the European Coal and Steel Community and the Treaty referred to above shall equally apply to Land Berlin.

DECLARATION BY THE GOVERNMENT OF THE FEDERAL REPUBLIC OF GERMANY ON THE DEFINITION OF THE TERM "NATIONALS"

As to the Federal Republic of Germany, the term "nationals", wherever used in the Act of Accession and in the Annexes thereto, is to be understood to refer to "Germans as defined in the Basic Law of the Federal Republic of Germany".

DECLARATION OF THE EUROPEAN ECONOMIC COMMUNITY ON GREEK WORKERS TAKING UP AND PURSUING PAID EMPLOYMENT IN THE PRESENT MEMBER STATES

Under the transitional provisions on the exercise of the right of freedom of movement, the present Member States shall, when they have recourse to labour originating in third countries, which do not belong to their regular labour market, in order to satisfy their labour requirements, grant Hellenic nationals the same priority as nationals of the other Member States.

DECLARATION OF THE EUROPEAN ECONOMIC COMMUNITY ON THE EUROPEAN REGIONAL DEVELOPMENT FUND

If, in the context of the re-examination provided for in Article 22 of Regulation (EEC) No. 724/75, as amended by Regulation (EEC) No. 214/79, the Council will not have succeeded in making amendments, in good time, setting out the participation of the Hellenic Republic in the resources of the Fund as from January 1, 1981, the provisions of Article 2 (3) (*a*) will be amended upon accession, following the procedure applicable for the adoption of this Regulation, with a view to ensuring that the Hellenic Republic will share in the benefit of these provisions.

DECLARATION BY THE HELLENIC REPUBLIC ON MONETARY QUESTIONS

In order that the movement of the real rate of the Greek drachma, particularly in relation to the currencies of the present Member States, may be followed on foreign exchange markets, the Hellenic Republic will, before accession to the Community:
—set up a foreign exchange market in Athens,
—take the necessary measures in order to ensure that in at least one of the foreign exchange markets of the Community as at present constituted, the drachma is the subject of an official quotation, where such quotation exists, or of a quotation of similar type.

Part VI
EUROPEAN COMMUNITIES ACT

European Communities Act 1972

(1972 c. 68)

An Act to make provision in connection with the enlargement of the European Communities to include the United Kingdom, together with (for certain purposes) the Channel Islands, the Isle of Man and Gibraltar.

[17th October 1972]

PART I

GENERAL PROVISIONS

Short title and interpretation

1.—(1) This Act may be cited as the European Communities Act 1972.

(2) In this Act [. . .]—

"the Communities" means the European Economic Community, the European Coal and Steel Community and the European Atomic Energy Community;

"the Treaties" or "the Community Treaties" means, subject to sub-section (3) below, the pre-accession treaties, that is to say, those described in Part I of Schedule I to this Act, taken with—

   (*a*) the treaty relating to the accession of the United Kingdom to the European Economic Community and to the European Atomic Energy Community, signed at Brussels on January 22nd 1972; and

389

(b) the decision, of the same date, of the Council of the European Communities relating to the accession of the United Kingdom to the European Coal and Steel Community;

and any other treaty entered into by any of the Communities, with or without any of the member States, or entered into, as a treaty ancillary to any of the Treaties, by the United Kingdom;

and any expression defined in Schedule 1 to this Act has the meaning there given to it.

(3) If Her Majesty by Order in Council declares that a treaty specified in the Order is to be regarded as one of the Community Treaties as herein defined, the Order shall be conclusive that it is to be so regarded; but a treaty entered into by the United Kingdom after January 22nd 1972, other than a pre-accession treaty to which the United Kingdom accedes on terms settled on or before that date, shall not be so regarded unless it is so specified, nor be so specified unless a draft of the Order in Council has been approved by resolution of each House of Parliament.

(4) For purposes of subsections (2) and (3) above, "treaty" includes any international agreement, and any protocol or annex to a treaty or international agreement.

AMENDMENTS
   In subs. (2) the words omitted were repealed by the Interpretation Act 1978 (c.30), Sched. 3.

General Implementation of Treaties
   2.—(1) All such rights, powers, liabilities, obligations and restrictions from time to time created or arising by or under the Treaties, and all such remedies and procedures from time to time provided for by or under the Treaties, as in accordance with the Treaties are without further enactment to be given legal effect or used in the United Kingdom shall be recognised and available in law, and be enforced, allowed and followed accordingly; and the expression "enforceable Community right" and similar expressions shall be read as referring to one to which this subsection applies.

(2) Subject to Schedule 2 to this Act, at any time after its passing Her Majesty may by Order in Council, and any designated Minister or department may by regulations, make provision—

(a) for the purpose of implementing any Community obligation of the United Kingdom, or enabling any such obligation to be implemented, or of enabling any rights enjoyed or to be enjoyed by the United Kingdom under or by virtue of the Treaties to be exercised; or

(b) for the purpose of dealing with matters arising out of or related to any such obligation or rights or the coming into force, or the operation from time to time, of subsection (1) above;

and in the exercise of any statutory power or duty, including any power to give directions or to legislate by means of orders, rules, regulations or other subordinate instrument, the person entrusted with the power or duty may have regard to the objects of the Communities and to any such obligation or rights as aforesaid.

In this subsection "designated Minister or department" means such Minister of the Crown or government department as may from time to time be designated by Order in Council in relation to any matter or for any purpose, but subject to such restrictions or conditions (if any) as may be specified by the Order in Council.

(3) There shall be charged on an issued out of the Consolidated Fund or, if so determined by the Treasury, the National Loans Fund the amounts required to meet any Community obligation to make payments to any of the Communities or member States, or any Community obligation in respect of contributions to the capital or reserves of the European Investment Bank or in respect of loans to the Bank, or to redeem any notes or obligations issued or created in respect of any such Community obligation; and, except as otherwise provided by or under any enactment,—

(*a*) any other expenses incurred under or by virtue of the Treaties or this Act by any Minister of the Crown or government department may be paid out of moneys provided by Parliament; and

(*b*) any sums received under or by virtue of the Treaties or this Act by any Minister of the Crown or government department, save for such sums as may be required for disbursements permitted by any other enactment, shall be paid into the Consolidated Fund or, if so determined by the Treasury, the National Loans Fund.

(4) The provision that may be made under subsection (2) above includes, subject to Schedule 2 to this Act, any such provision (of any such extent) as might be made by Act of Parliament, and any enactment passed or to be passed, other than one contained in this Part of this Act, shall be construed and have effect subject to the foregoing provisions of this section; but, except as may be provided by any Act passed after this Act, Schedule 2 shall have effect in connection with the powers conferred by this and the following sections of this Act to make Orders in Council and regulations.

(5) [. . .]; and the references in that subsection to a Minister of the Crown or government department and to a statutory power or duty shall include a Minister or department of the Government of Northern Ireland and a power or duty arising under or by virtue of an Act of the Parliament of Northern Ireland.

(6) A law passed by the legislature of any of the Channel Islands or of the Isle of Man, or a colonial law (within the meaning of the Colonial Laws Validity Act 1865) passed or made for Gibraltar, if expressed to be passed or made in the implementation of the Treaties and of the obligations of the United Kingdom thereunder, shall not be void or inoperative by reason of any inconsistency with or repugnancy to an Act of Parliament, passed or to be passed, that extends to the Island or Gibraltar or any provision having the force and effect of an Act there (but not including this section), nor by reason of its having some operation outside the Island or Gibraltar; and any such Act or provision that extends to the Island or Gibraltar shall be construed and have effect subject to the provisions of any such law.

AMENDMENTS

In subs. (5) the words omitted were repealed by the Northern Ireland Constitution Act 1973 (c. 36), s. 41 and Sched. 6, Pt. I. The subsection referred to is subs. (2) of this section.

Decisions on, and proof of, Treaties and Community Instruments etc.

3.—(1) For the purposes of all legal proceedings any question as to the meaning or effect of any of the Treaties, or as to the validity, meaning or effect of any Community instrument, shall be treated as a question of law (and, if not referred to the European Court, be for determination as such in accordance with the principles laid down by and any relevant decision of the European Court).

(2) Judicial notice shall be taken of the Treaties, of the Official Journal of the Communities and of any decision of, or expression of opinion by, the European Court on any such question as aforesaid; and the Official Journal shall be admissible as evidence of any instrument or other act thereby communicated of any of the Communities or of any Community institution.

(3) Evidence of any instrument issued by a Community institution, including any judgment or order of the European Court, or of any document in the custody of a Community institution, or any entry in or extract from such a document, may be given in any legal proceedings by production of a copy certified as a true copy by an official of that institution; and any document purporting to be such a copy shall be received in evidence without proof of the official position or handwriting of the person signing the certificate.

(4) Evidence of any Community instrument may also be given in any legal proceedings—

> (a) by production of a copy purporting to be printed by the Queen's Printer;
>
> (b) where the instrument is in the custody of a government department (including a department of the Government of Northern Ireland), by production of a copy certified on behalf of the department to be a true copy by an officer of the department generally or specially authorised so to do;

and any document purporting to be such a copy as is mentioned in paragraph (b) above of an instrument in the custody of a department shall be received in evidence without proof of the official position or handwriting of the person signing the certificate, or of his authority to do so, or of the document being in the custody of the department.

(5) In any legal proceedings in Scotland evidence of any matter given in a manner authorised by this section shall be sufficient evidence of it.

PART II

AMENDMENT OF LAW

General provision for repeal and amendment

4.—(1) The enactments mentioned in Schedule 3 to this Act (being enactments that are superseded or to be superseded by reason of Community obligations and of the provision made by this Act in relation thereto or are not compatible with Community obligations) are hereby repealed, to the extent specified in column 3 of the Schedule, with effect from the entry date or other date mentioned in the Schedule; and in the enactments mentioned in Schedule 4 to this Act there shall, subject to any transitional provision there included, be made the amendments provided for by that Schedule.

(2) Where in any Part of Schedule 3 to this Act it is provided that repeals made by that Part are to take effect from a date appointed by order, the orders shall be made by statutory instrument, and an order may appoint different dates for the repeal of different provisions to take effect, or for the repeal of the same provision to take effect for different purposes; and an order appointing a date for a repeal to take effect may include transitional and other supplementary provisions arising out of that repeal, including provisions adapting the operation of other enactments included for repeal but not yet repealed by that Schedule, and may amend or revoke any such provisions included in a previous order.

3. Where any of the following sections of this Act, or any paragraph of Schedule 4 to this Act, affects or is construed as one with an Act or Part of an Act similar in purpose to provisions having effect only in Northern Ireland, then—

(*a*) unless otherwise provided by Act of the Parliament of Northern Ireland, the Governor of Northern Ireland may by Order in Council make provision corresponding to any made by the section or paragraph, and amend or revoke any provision so made;

(*b*) [. . .]

(4) Where Schedule 3 or 4 to this Act provides for the repeal or amendment of an enactment that extends or is capable of being extended to any of the Channel Islands or the Isle of Man, the repeal or amendment shall in like manner extend or be capable of being extended thereto.

AMENDMENTS

In subs. (3), para. (*b*) was repealed by the Northern Ireland Constitution Act 1973 (c. 36), s. 41 and Sched. 6, Pt. I.

Customs duties

5.—(1) Subject to subsection (2) below, on and after the relevant date there shall be charged, levied, collected and paid on goods imported into the United Kingdom such Community customs duty, if any, as is for the time being applicable in accordance with the Treaties or, if the goods are not within the common customs tariff of the Economic Community and the duties chargeable are not otherwise fixed by any directly applicable Community provision, such duty of customs, if any, as the Treasury, on the recommendation of the Secretary of State, may by order specify.

For this purpose "the relevant date", in relation to any goods, is the date on and after which the duties of customs that may be charged thereon are no longer affected under the Treaties by any temporary provision made on or with reference to the accession of the United Kingdom to the Communities.

(2) Where as regards goods imported into the United Kingdom provision may, in accordance with the Treaties, be made in derogation of the common customs tariff or of the exclusion of customs duties as between member States, the Treasury may by order make such provision as to the customs duties chargeable on the goods, or as to exempting the goods from any customs duty, as the Treasury may on the recommendation of the Secretary of State determine.

(3) [Schedule 2 to this Act shall also have effect in connection with the powers to make orders conferred by subsections (1) and (2) above.]

(4) [. . .]

(5) [. . .]

(6) [. . .]

(6A) [. . .]

(7) [. . .]

(8) [. . .]

(9) [. . .]

AMENDMENTS

Subs. (3) was replaced by the Customs and Excise Duties (General Reliefs) Act 1979 (c. 3), Sched. 2, para. 3.

Subs. (4) was repealed by the Customs and Excise Management Act 1979 (c. 2), Sched. 6, Pt. I.

Subs. (5) was repealed by the Customs and Excise Duties (General Reliefs) Act 1979 (c. 3), Sched. 3, Pt. I.

Subs. (6) was repealed by the Customs and Excise Duties (General Reliefs) Act 1979 (c. 3), Sched. 3, Pt. I.

Subs. (6A) was repealed by the Customs and Excise Duties (General Reliefs) Act 1979 (c. 3), Sched. 3, Pt. I.

Subs. (7) was repealed by the Customs and Excise Management Act 1979 (c. 2), Sched. 6, Pt. I.

Subs. (8) was repealed by the Customs and Excise Management Act 1979 (c. 2), Sched. 6, Pt. I.

Subs. (9) was repealed by the Customs and Excise Management Act 1979 (c. 2), Sched. 6, Pt. I.

The common agricultural policy

6.—(1) There shall be a Board in charge of a government department, which shall be appointed by and responsible to the Ministers, and shall be by the name of the Intervention Board for Agricultural Produce a body corporate (but not subject as a statutory corporation to restrictions on its corporate capacity); and the Board (in addition to any other functions that may be entrusted to it) shall be charged, subject to the direction and control of the Ministers, with such functions as they may from time to time determine in connection with the carrying out of the obligations of the United Kingdom under the common agricultural policy of the Economic Community.

(2) Her Majesty may by Order in council make further provision as to the constitution and membership of the Board, and the remuneration (including pensions) of members of the Board or any committee thereof, and for regulating or facilitating the discharge of the Board's functions, including provision for the Board to arrange for its functions to be performed by other bodies on its behalf and any such provision as was made by Schedule 1 to the Ministers of the Crown Act 1964 in relation to a Minister to whom that Schedule applied; and the Ministers—

(a) may, after consultation with any body created by a statutory provision and concerned with agriculture or agricultural produce, by regulations modify or add to the constitution or powers of the body so as to enable it to act for the Board, or by written directions given to the body require it to discontinue or modify any activity appearing to the Ministers to be prejudicial to the proper discharge of the Board's functions; and

(b) may by regulations provide for the charging of fees in connection with the discharge of any functions of the Board.

(3) Sections 5 and 7 of the Agriculture Act 1957 (which make provision for the support of arrangements under section 1 of that Act for providing guaranteed prices or assured markets) shall apply in relation to any Community arrangements for or related to the regulation of the market for any agricultural produce as if references, in whatever terms, to payments made by virtue of section 1 were references to payments made by virtue of the Community arrangements by or on behalf of the Board and as if in section 5 (1) (d) the reference to the Minister included the Board.

(4) Agricultural levies of the Economic Community, so far as they are charged on goods exported from the United Kingdom or shipped as stores, shall be paid to and recoverable by the Board; and the power of the Ministers to make orders under section 5 of the Agriculture Act 1957, as extended by this section, shall include power to make such provision supplementary to any directly applicable Community provision as the Ministers consider necessary for securing the payment of any agricultural levies so charged, including provision for the making of declarations or the giving of other information in respect of goods exported, shipped as stores, warehoused or otherwise dealt with.

(5) Except as otherwise provided by or under any enactment, agricultural levies of the Economic Community, so far as they are charged on goods imported into the United Kingdom, shall be levied, collected and paid, and the proceeds shall be dealt with, as if they were Community customs duties, and in relation to those levies the following enactments shall apply as they would apply in relation to Community customs duties, that is to say:—

(a) [The Customs and Excise Management Act 1979 (as for the time being amended by any later Act) and any other statutory provisions for the time being in force relating generally to customs or excise duties on imported goods; and]

(b) sections 5, 6, 7, 10 and 13 of the Import Duties Act 1958, but so that in those sections (and in Schedule 3 to the Act), as amended by this Act, references to the Secretary of State shall include the Ministers;

and if, in connection with any such Community arrangements as aforesaid, the Commissioners of Customs and Excise are charged with the performance, on behalf of the Board or otherwise, of any duties in relation to the payment of refunds or allowances on goods exported or to be exported from the United Kingdom, then in relation to any such refund or allowance [section 133 (except subsection (3) and the reference to that subsection in subsection (2) and section 159 of the Customs and Excise Management Act 1979 shall apply as they apply in relation to a drawback of excise duties], and other provisions of that Act shall have effect accordingly.

(6) The enactments applied by subsection (5) (a) above shall apply subject to such exceptions and modifications, if any, as the Commissioners of Customs and Excise may by regulations prescribe, and shall be taken to include section 10 of the Finance Act 1901 (which relates to changes in customs import duties in their effect on contracts), but shall not include [section 126 of the Customs and Excise Management Act 1979] (charge of duty on manufactured or composite articles).

(7) Where it appears to the Ministers, having regard to any such Community arrangements as aforesaid (and any obligations of the United Kingdom in relation thereto), that section I of the Agriculture Act 1957 should cease to apply to produce of any description mentioned in Schedule I to that Act, they may by order made by statutory instrument, which shall be subject to annulment in pursuance of a resolution of either House of Parliament, provide that as from such date as may be prescribed by the order (but subject to such savings and transitional provisions as may be so prescribed) the Act shall have effect as if produce of that description were omitted from Schedule I.

(8) Expressions used in this section shall be construed as if contained in Part I of the Agriculture Act 1957; and in this section "agricultural levy" shall include any tax not being a customs duty, but of equivalent effect, that may be chargeable in accordance with any such Community arrangements as aforesaid, and "statutory provision" includes any provision having effect by virtue of any enactment and, in subsection (2), any enactment of the Parliament of Northern Ireland or provision having effect by virtue of such an enactment.

AMENDMENTS

Subs. (5) (a) was replaced by the Customs and Excise Management Act 1979 (c. 2), Sched. 4, Pt. I.

In subs. (5) (b) the words in square brackets were substituted by the Customs and Excise Management Act 1979 (c. 2), Sched. 4, Pt. I.

In subs. (6) the words in square brackets were substituted by the Customs and Excise Management Act 1979 (c. 2), Sched. 4, Pt. I.

Sugar

  7.—(1) [. . .]

  (2) [. . .]

  (3) If as regards the home-grown beet crop for the year 1973 or any subsequent year it is made to appear to the Ministers by the processors of home-grown beet or by a body which is in their opinion substantially representative of the growers of home-grown beet that the processors and that body are unable to agree on the prices and other terms and conditions for the purchase of home-grown beet by the processors, the Ministers may determine or designate a person to determine those prices, terms and conditions; and any purchase by processors for which prices, terms and conditions have been so determined, or contract for such a purchase, shall take effect as a purchase or contract for purchase at those prices and on those terms and conditions.

  (4) This section shall be construed as one with the Sugar Act 1956; and in this section, as in that Act, "the Minister" means the Minister of Agriculture, Fisheries and Food, and "the Ministers" means the Minister and the [the Secretary of State for Scotland and the Secretary of State for Wales] acting jointly.

AMENDMENTS

  Subs. (1) was repealed by the Agriculture (Miscellaneous Provisions) Act 1976 (c. 55), Sched. 4, Pt. I.

  Subs. (2) was repealed by the Agriculture (Miscellaneous Provisions) Act 1976 (c. 55), Sched. 4, Pt. I.

  In subs. (4) the words in square brackets were substituted by the Transfer of Functions (Wales) (No. 1) Order 1978 (S.I. 1978 No. 272).

Cinematograph films

  8.—(1) On and after the entry date Community films shall be registered under the Films Act 1960 to 1970 as a class distinct from other foreign films, and be registered as quota films, and the register shall be kept accordingly; and—

    (*a*) references in those Acts to a foreign film, except in sections 11 and 17 of the Films Act 1960 (which relate to registration) shall have effect as references to a foreign film other than a Community film; and

    (*b*) references to a British film shall in the following provisions of the Films Act 1960 have effect as references to a British or Community film, that is to say, in sections 1 (1), 2 (2) (as set out in section 10 (1) of the Films Act 1970), 30 (3) (*b*), 32 (1) (*b*) and 44 (1) (*b*).

In this subsection and in subsection (2) below "Community film" means any such film as in accordance with any relevant Community instrument is to be regarded as a film of a member State.

  (2) Where a film which on the entry date is registered under the Films Act 1960 as a foreign film is a Community film, a person who has the right to distribute the film or is in a position to confer that right may apply for the register to be amended by registering the film as a Community film; and if the application is accompanied by the requisite particulars and evidence to show the film is a Community film, and by such fee as may be prescribed for this purpose under section 44 of the Act, the register shall be amended accordingly and there shall be issued to the applicant, in substitution for any certificate of registration previously issued, a certificate of registration specifying the particulars of the film as recorded in the register after the amendment.

In relation to a film registered as a Community film by virtue of this subsection, section 2 of the Films Act 1960 (disregard of old films for quota purposes) shall have effect as if in subsection (2), whether as originally enacted or as set out in section 10 (1) of the Films Act 1970, the reference to a film being first registered as a British film were a reference to its being first registered.

(3) The requirements for the registration of a film as a British film under section 17 of the Films Act 1960 shall be modified, with effect from the entry date, by inserting after the words "of the Republic of Ireland", wherever those words occur in section 17 (2) (*a*) and (3), the words "or of any country that is a member State".

(4) If, on the application of an exhibitor in respect of a cinema, the Secretary of State is satisfied that during the year 1973 or any later year it is proposed to exhibit at the cinema no films other than foreign language films, he may (after consultation with the Cinematograph Films Council) direct that section 1 of the Films Act 1960 shall not apply to the exhibition of films at that cinema during that year; but secion I shall nevertheless apply as if no such direction had been given—

> (*a*) where during the year any film other than a foreign language film is exhibited at the cinema; and
>
> (*b*) where, on the application of an exhibitor who exhibits films at the cinema, the Secretary of State substitutes for the direction a direction under section 4 (1) of the Act.

In this subsection "foreign language film" means a film in which the dialogue is mainly in a foreign language.

(5) This section shall be construed as one with the Films Act 1960.

Companies

9.—(1) In favour of a person dealing with a company in good faith, any transaction decided on by the directors shall be deemed to be one which it is within the capacity of the company to enter into, and the power of the directors to bind the company shall be deemed to be free of any limitation under the memorandum or articles of association; and a party to a transaction so decided on shall not be bound to enquire as to the capacity of the company to enter into it or as to any such limitation on the powers of the directors, and shall be presumed to have acted in good faith unless the contrary is proved.

(2) Where a contract purports to be made by a company, or by a person as agent for a company, at a time when the company has not been formed, then subject to any agreement to the contrary the contract shall have effect as a contract entered into by the person purporting to act for the company or as agent for it, and he shall be personally liable on the contract accordingly.

(3) The registrar of companies shall cause to be published in the Gazette notice of the issue or receipt by him of documents of any of the following descriptions (stating in the notice the name of the company, the description of document and the date of issue or receipt), that is to say—

> (*a*) any certificate of incorporation of a company;
>
> (*b*) any document making or evidencing an alteration in the memorandum or articles of association of a company;
>
> (*c*) [any notification of a change among the directors of a company];
>
> (*d*) [any documents delivered by a company in pursuance of section 1 (7) of the Companies Act 1976];
>
> (*e*) [any notice of a change in the situation of a company's registered office];

    (*f*) any copy of a winding-up order in respect of a company;

    (*g*) any order for the dissolution of a company on a winding up;

    (*h*) any return by a liquidator of the final meeting of a company on a winding up;

and in the following provisions of this section "official notification" means, in relation to anything stated in a document of any of the above descriptions, the notification of that document in the Gazette under this section and, in relation to the appointment of a liquidator in a voluntary winding up, the notification thereof in the Gazette under section 305 of the Companies Act 1948, and "officially notified" shall be construed accordingly.

    (4) A company shall not be entitled to rely against other persons on the happening of any of the following events, that is to say—

    (*a*) the making of a winding-up order in respect of the company, or the appointment of a liquidator in a voluntary winding up of the company; or

    (*b*) any alteration of the company's memorandum or articles of association; or

    (*c*) any change among the company's directors; or

    (*d*) (as regards service of any document on the company) any change in the situation of the company's registered office;

if the event had not been officially notified at the material time and is not shown by the company to have been known at that time to the person concerned, or if the material time fell on or before the fifteenth day after the date of official notification (or, where the fifteenth day was a non-business day, on or before the next day that was not) and it is shown that the person concerned was unavoidably prevented from knowing of the event at that time.

    For this purpose "non-business day" means a Saturday or Sunday, Christmas Day, Good Friday and any other day which, in the part of Great Britain where the company is registered, is a bank holiday under the Banking and Financial Dealings Act 1971.

    (5) Where any alteration is made in a company's memorandum or articles of association by any statutory provision, whether contained in an Act of Parliament or in an instrument made under an Act, a printed copy of the Act or instrument shall not later than fifteen days after that provision comes into force be forwarded to the registrar of companies and recorded by him; and where a company is required by this section or otherwise to send to the registrar any document making or evidencing an alteration in the company's memorandum or articles of association (other than a special resolution under section 5 of the Companies Act 1948), the company shall send with it a printed copy of the memorandum or articles as altered.

    If a company fails to comply with this subsection, the company and any officer of the company who is in default shall be liable to a default fine.

    (6) Where before the coming into force of this subsection—

    (*a*) an alteration has been made in a company's memorandum or articles of association by any statutory provision, and a printed copy of the relevant Act or instrument has not been sent to the registrar of companies; or

    (*b*) an alteration has been made in a company's memorandum or articles of association in any manner, and a printed copy of the memorandum or articles as altered has not been sent to him;

such a copy shall be sent to him within one month after the coming into force of this subsection.

If a company fails to comply with this subsection, the company and any officer of the company who is in default shall be liable to a default fine.

(7) Every company shall have the following particulars mentioned in legible characters in all business letters and order forms of the company, that is to say,—

[(a) whether the company has its principal office in England, Wales or Scotland, as the case may be, and the number which has been allocated to the company by the registrar of companies;

(b) the address of its principal office; and

(c) the manner in which it was incorporated and, if it is a limited company, that fact;]

and, if in the case of a company having a share capital there is on the stationery used for any such letters or on the order forms a reference to the amount of the share capital, the reference shall be to paid-up share capital.

If a company fails to comply with this subsection, the company shall be liable to a fine not exceeding £50; and if an officer of a company or any person on its behalf issues or authorises the issue of any business letter or order form not complying with this subsection, he shall be liable to a fine not exceeding £50.

(8) This section shall be construed as one with the Companies Act 1948; and section 435 of that Act (which enables certain provisions of it to be extended to unregistered companies) shall have effect as if this section were among those mentioned in Schedule 14 to that Act with an entry in column 3 of that Schedule to the effect that this section is to apply so far only as may be specified by regulations under section 435 and to such bodies corporate as may be so specified, and as if sections 107 (registered office) and 437 (service of documents) were so mentioned (and section 437 were not included in the last entry in the Schedule).

The modifications of this section that may be made by regulations under section 435 shall include the extension of subsections (3), (5) and (6) to additional matters (and in particular to the instruments constituting or regulating a company as well as to alterations thereof).

(9) This section shall not come into force until the entry date (except to authorise the making with effect from that date of regulations by virtue of subsection (8) above).

AMENDMENTS

In subs. (3) para. (c) was substituted by the Companies Act 1976 (c. 69), s.22 (3), para. (d) was substituted by the Companies Act 1976 (c. 69), s.1 (10), and para. (e) was substituted by the Companies Act 1976 (c. 69), s.23 (6).

In subs. (7) the words in square brackets were substituted by the Companies (Unregistered Companies) Regulations 1975 (S.I. 1975 No. 597, reg. 6 (f)). It is thought that the words added in square brackets apply to all companies to which s. 9 applies, and not only to unregistered companies. The wording of reg. 6 (f) of the 1975 Regulations is in no way restricted and another interpretation would raise difficulties with respect to companies (other than unregistered companies) which state that they are registered in England or Wales, without stating the seat of the Companies Registration Office which is now in Cardiff, and no longer in London.

Restrictive trade practices

10. [*This section was repealed by the Restrictive Trade Practices Act* 1976, (*c.* 34), *Sched.* 6.]

Community offences

11.—(1) A person who, in sworn evidence before the European Court, makes any statement which he knows to be false or does not believe to be true shall, whether he is a British subject or not, be guilty of an offence and may be proceeded against and punished—

  (*a*) in England and Wales as for an offence against section 1 (1) of the Perjury Act 1911; or

  (*b*) in Scotland as for an offence against section 1 of the False Oaths (Scotland) Act 1933; or

  (*c*) in Northern Ireland as for an offence against section 1 (1) of the Perjury Act (Northern Ireland) 1946.

Where a report is made as to any such offence under the authority of the European Court, then a bill of indictment for the offence may, in England or Wales or in Northern Ireland, be preferred as in a case where a prosecution is ordered under section 9 of the Perjury Act 1911 or section 8 of the Perjury Act (Northern Ireland) 1946, but the report shall not be given in evidence on a person's trial for the offence.

 (2) Where a person (whether a British subject or not) owing either—

  (*a*) to his duties as a member of any Euratom institution or committee, or as an officer or servant of Euratom; or

  (*b*) to his dealings in any capacity (official or unofficial) with any Euratom institution or installation or with any Euratom joint enterprise;

has occasion to acquire, or obtain cognisance of, any classified information, he shall be guilty of a misdemeanour if, knowing or having reason to believe that it is classified information, he communicates it to any unauthorised person or makes any public disclosure of it, whether in the United Kingdom or elsewhere and whether before or after the termination of those duties or dealings; and for this purpose "classified information" means any facts, information, knowledge, documents or objects that are subject to the security rules of a member State or of any Euratom institution.

This subsection shall be construed, and the Official Secrets Acts 1911 to 1939 shall have effect, as if this subsection were contained in the Official Secrets Act 1911, but so that in that Act sections 10 and 11, except section 10 (4), shall not apply.

 (3) This section shall not come into force until the entry date.

Furnishing of Information to Communities

 12. Estimates, returns and information that may under section 9 of the Statistics of Trade Act 1947 or section 80 of the Agriculture Act 1947 be disclosed to a government department or Minister in charge of a government department may, in like manner, be disclosed in pursuance of a Community obligation to a Community institution.

SCHEDULES

SCHEDULE 1

Section 1   Definitions relating to Communities

PART I

The Pre-Accession Treaties

 1. The "E.C.S.C. Treaty", that is to say, the Treaty establishing the European Coal and Steel Community, signed at Paris on the 18th April 1951.

 2. The "E.E.C. Treaty", that is to say, the Treaty establishing the European Economic Community, signed at Rome on the 25th March 1957.

 3. The "Euratom Treaty", that is to say, the Treaty establishing the European Atomic Energy Community, signed at Rome on the 25th March 1957.

4. The Convention on certain Institutions common to the European Communities, signed at Rome on the 25th March 1957.

5. The Treaty establishing a single Council and a single Commission of the European Communities, signed at Brussels on the 8th April 1965.

6. The Treaty amending certain Budgetary Provisions of the Treaties establishing the European Communities and of the Treaty establishing a single Council and a single Commission of the European Communities, signed at Luxembourg on the 22nd April 1970.

7. Any treaty entered into before the 22nd January 1972 by any of the Communities (with or without any of the member States) or, as a treaty ancillary to any treaty included in this Part of this Schedule, by the member States (with or without any other country).

PART II

OTHER DEFINITIONS

"Economic Community", "Coal and Steel Community" and "Euratom" mean respectively the European Economic Community, the European Coal and Steel Community and the European Atomic Energy Community.

"Community customs duty" means, in relation to any goods, such duty of customs as may from time to time be fixed for those goods by directly applicable Community provision as the duty chargeable on importation into member States.

"Community institution" means any institution of any of the Communities or common to the Communities; and any reference to an institution of a particular Community shall include one common to the Communities when it acts for that Community, and similarly with references to a committee, officer or servant of a particular Community.

"Community instrument" means any instrument issued by a Community institution.

"Community obligation" means any obligation created or arising by or under the Treaties, whether an enforceable Community obligation or not.

"Enforceable Community right" and similar expressions shall be construed in accordance with Section 2 (1) of this Act.

"Entry date" means the date on which the United Kingdom becomes a member of the Communities.

"European Court" means the Court of Justice of the European Communities.

"Member", in the expression "member State", refers to membership of the Communities.

Section 2   SCHEDULE 2

PROVISIONS AS TO SUBORDINATE LEGISLATION

1.—(1) The powers conferred by section 2 (2) of this Act to make provision for the purposes mentioned in section 2 (2) (a) and (b) shall not include power—
  (a) to make any provision imposing or increasing taxation; or
  (b) to make any provision taking effect from a date earlier than that of the making of the instrument containing the provision; or
  (c) to confer any power to legislate by means of orders, rules, regulations or other subordinate instrument, other than rules of procedure for any court or tribunal; or
  (d) to create any new criminal offence punishable with imprisonment for more than two years or punishable on summary conviction with imprisonment for more than three months or with a fine of more than £400 (if not calculated on a daily basis) or with a fine of more than [£100 a day].

(2) Sub-paragraph (1) (c) above shall not be taken to preclude the modification of a power to legislate conferred otherwise than under section 2 (2), or the extension of any such power to purposes of the like nature as those for which it was conferred; and a power to give directions as to matters of administration is not to be regarded as a power to legislate within the meaning of sub-paragraph (1) (c).

2.—(1) Subject to paragraph 3 below, where a provision contained in any section of this Act confers power to make regulations (otherwise than by modification or extension of an existing power), the power shall be exercisable by statutory instrument.

(2) Any statutory instrument containing an Order in Council or regulations made in the exercise of a power so conferred, if made without a draft having been approved by resolution of each House of Parliament, shall be subject to annulment in pursuance of a resolution of either House.

3. Nothing in paragraph 2 above shall apply to any Order in Council made by the Governor of Northern Ireland or to any regulations made by a Minister or department of the Government of Northern Ireland; but where a provision contained in any section of this Act confers power to make such an Order in Council or regulations, then any Order in Council or regulations made in the exercise of that power, if made without a draft having been approved by resolution of each House of the Parliament of Northern Ireland, shall be subject to negative resolution within the meaning of section 41 (6) of the Interpretation Act (Northern Ireland) 1954 as if the Order or regulations were a statutory instrument within the meaning of that Act.

AMENDMENTS
In para. 1 (1) (*d*) the words in square brackets were substituted by the Criminal Law Act 1977 (c. 45), s.32 (3).

Section 4

SCHEDULE 3

REPEALS

PART I

CUSTOMS TARIFF

Chapter	Short Title	Extent of Repeal
6 & 7 Eliz. 2. c. 6	The Import Duties Act 1958.	The whole Act, except— section 4; Part II, including Schedules 3 to 5; in section 12 (4) the words "fish, whales or other natural produce of the sea, or goods produced or manufactured therefrom at sea, if brought direct to the United Kingdom, are", and paragraphs (*a*) and (*b*); and sections 13, 15 and 16 (1) and (2). In Part II, section 5 (2), (3), (5) and (6), section 7 (1) (*c*) with the preceding "and", section 9 (4) and section 9 (5) from "and" onwards. In Schedule 4, paragraph 1.
8 & 9 Eliz. 2. c. 19.	The European Free Trade Association Act 1960.	The whole Act.
1965 c. 65.	The Finance Act 1965.	Section 2, except subsection (5).
1966 c. 18.	The Finance Act 1966.	In section 1, in subsection (1) the words between "1958" and "chargeable", and subsection (6). Section 9.
[...]	[...]	[...]
1971 c. 68.	The Finance Act 1971.	Section 1 (1) to (3).

The repeals in this Part of this Schedule shall take effect from such date as the Secretary of State may by order appoint.

PART II

SUGAR

Chapter	Short Title	Extent of Repeal
4 & 5 Eliz. 2. c. 48.	The Sugar Act 1956.	In section 3, subsection (1) from "including" onwards and subsection (2) (b). Section 4 (2) and (3). Section 5, except as regards advances made before this repeal takes effect. Sections 7 to 17. Sections 18 (3) and (4). Sections 19 and 20. Sections 21 and 22, except as regards advances made and guarantees given before this repeal takes effect. Section 23, but without prejudice to the modification made by subsection (2) in the articles of association of the British Sugar Corporation. Sections 24 to 32. In section 33, in subsection (1) the words "regulations or", in subsection (2) the words from the beginning to "subsection", subsection (3) and subsection (5). In section 34, the words "or the Commissioners". In section 35, in subsection (2) all the definitions except those of "the Corporation", "financial year of the Sugar Board", "functions", "the Government", "home-grown beet" and "pension", in subsection (3) the words "or of the Corporation" and subsections (4) to (7). Section 36 (2). In Schedule 3, paragraphs 2, 3 and 4. Schedule 4.
5 & 6 Eliz. 2. c. 57.	The Agriculture Act 1957.	Section 4 (*application of provisions ensuring relative stability of guaranteed prices to sugar beet prices*). In section 36 (2) the words "and to sugar beet".
10 & 11 Eliz. 2. c. 23.	The South Africa Act 1962.	In Schedule 2, paragraph 5.
10 & 11 Eliz. 2. c. 44.	The Finance Act 1962.	In section 3 (6) the words from "the Sugar Act 1956" onwards. Part II of Schedule 5.
1963 c. 11.	The Agriculture (Miscellaneous Provisions) Act 1963.	Section 25.
1964 c. 49.	The Finance Act 1964.	Section 22.
1966 c. 18.	The Finance Act 1966.	Section 52.
1968 c. 13.	The National Loans Act 1968.	In Schedule 1, the entry for the Sugar Act 1956, except as regards advances made before this repeal takes effect.
1968 c. 44.	The Finance Act 1968.	Section 58.

The repeals in this Part of this Schedule shall take effect from such date as the Minister of Agriculture, Fisheries and Food and the Secretary of State acting jointly may by order appoint.

PART III

SEEDS

Chapter	Short Title	Extent of Repeal
1964 c. 14	The Plant Varieties and Seeds Act 1964.	Section 5 (3). Sections 20 to 23A. Section 25 (8) (*b*) and the word "and" preceding it. Section 32. In section 34 (2) the words from "or in the Index" to "into force", and the words "or fact". Schedule 5.
1968 c. 29.	The Trade Descriptions Act 1968.	Section 2 (4) (*a*).
1968 c. 34	The Agriculture (Miscellaneous Provisions) Act 1968.	Schedule 7, except amendments of section 1 of or Schedule 1 or 2 to the Plant Varieties and Seeds Act 1964.

The repeals in this Part of this Schedule shall take effect from such date as the Minister of Agriculture, Fisheries and Food and the Secretary of State acting jointly may by order appoint.

PART IV

MISCELLANEOUS

Chapter	Short Title	Extent of Repeal
9 & 10 Geo. 6. c. 59.	The Coal Industry Nationalisation Act 1946.	In section 4, in its application to the Industrial Coal Consumers' Council, subsections (1) to (8); and in its application to the Domestic Coal Consumers' Council, in subsection (2) the words "to represent the Board and", in subsection (3) (as applied by subsection (4)) the words from "and where" in paragraph (*a*) onwards and subsection (5) Section 4 (9), (10) and (11).
10 & 11 Geo. 6. c. 48.	The Agriculture Act 1947.	Section 2 (2).
15 & 16 Geo. 6. and 1 Eliz. 2. c. 44.	The Customs and Excise Act 1952.	Schedule 6, except for cases in which the value of goods falls to be determined as at a time before the entry date.
1 & 2 Eliz. 2. c. 15.	The Iron and Steel Act 1953.	Section 29.
5 & 6 Eliz. 2. c. 57.	The Agriculture Act 1957.	Section 2 (6) (*b*), with the preceding "or". Section 3. Section 8 (1), and in section 8 (2) the words "and subsection (1) of section 3". In section 11 the words "and 'special review' " and the words "or special review".
10 & 11 Eliz. 2. c. 22.	The Coal Consumers' Councils (Northern Irish Interests) Act 1962.	Section 1 (1) and (2), in so far as they apply to the Industrial Coal Consumers Council.
1963 c. 11.	The Agriculture Miscellaneous Provisions) Act 1963.	Section 9 (8).

MISCELLANEOUS—*continued*

Chapter	Short Title	Extent of Repeal
1967 c. 17	The Iron and Steel Act 1967.	Sections 8, 15 and 30. Section 48 (2) (*b*). In Schedule 3, the entries relating to section 6 of the Iron and Steel Act 1949. In Schedule 4, section 6 of the Iron and Steel Act 1949 as there set out.
1967 c. 22.	The Agriculture Act 1967.	Section 61 (7). Section 64 (6). Section 65 (5).
1968 c. 48.	The International Organisations Act 1968.	Section 3. In section 4, the words "other than the Commission of the European Communities".
1970 c. 24.	The Finance Act 1970.	In Schedule 2, paragraph 5 (1) from "Where, by virtue" onwards, and paragraph 5 (2) (*b*) and (*c*), except for cases in which the value of goods falls to be determined as at a time before the entry date.
1970 c. 40.	The Agriculture Act 1970.	Section 106 (5).

AMENDMENTS

In Pt. I the words omitted were repealed by the Finance Act 1978 (c. 42), Sched. 13, Pt. I.

SCHEDULE 4

ENACTMENTS AMENDED

A: *Customs Duties*

A (i) *Import Duty Reliefs etc.*

1.—[*Repealed by the Customs and Excise Duties (General Reliefs) Act* 1979 (*c.* 3), *Sched.* 3, *Pt.* I.]

A (ii) *Customs and Excise Act* 1952

2.—(1) [*Repealed by the Customs and Excise Management Act* 1979 (*c.* 2), *Sched.* 6, *Pt.* I.]
(2) [*Repealed by the Finance Act* 1976 (*c.* 40), *Sched.* 15, *Pt.* I.]
(3) [*Repealed by the Customs and Excise Management Act* 1979 (*c.* 2), *Sched.* 6, *Pt.* I.]
(4) [*Repealed by the Finance Act* 1978 (*c.* 42), *Sched.* 13, *Pt.* I.]
(5) [*Omitted by the Customs and Excise (Warehouse) Regulations* 1978 (*S.*1 1978 *No.* 1603.]
(6) [*Repealed by the Finance (No.* 2) *Act* 1975 (*c.* 45) *s.* 75 *and Sched.* 14, *Pt.* I.]
(7) [*Repealed by the Customs and Excise Management Act* 1979 (*c.* 2), *Sched.* 6, *Pt.* I.]
(8) [*Repealed by the Customs and Excise Management Act* 1979 (*c.* 2), *Sched.* 6, *Pt.* I.]

B: *Food*

3.—(1) In the Food and Drugs Act 1955 ("the Act of 1955"), and in the Food and Drugs (Scotland) Act 1956 ("the Act of 1956"), there shall be inserted in section 4 (1) (regulations as to composition of food etc.) after the words "protection of the public" the words "or to be called for by any Community obligation".

(2) (*a*) after section 123 of the Act of 1955 there shall be inserted as section 123A the following section:—

"(1) The Ministers may, as respects any directly applicable Community provision relating to food for which, in their opinion, it is appropriate to make provision under this Act, by regulations make such provision as they consider necessary or expedient for the purpose of securing that the Community provision is administered, executed and enforced under this

Act, and may apply such of the provisions of this Act as may be specified in the regulations in relation to the Community provision with such modifications, if any, as may be so specified.

(2) For the purpose of complying with any Community obligation, or for conformity with any provision made for that purpose, the Ministers may by regulations make provision as to—

(a) the manner of simplying any food specified in the regulations, and the manner in which samples are to be dealt with; and

(b) the method to be used in analysing, testing or examining samples of any food so specified;

and regulations made by the Ministers for that purpose, or for conformity with any provision so made, may modify or exclude any provision of this Act relating to the procuring or analysis of, or dealing with, samples or to evidence of the results of an analysis or test";

and in section 124 (2) of the Act of 1955 (statutory instruments subject to annulment), in paragraph (a) after the words "eighty-nine" there shall be inserted the words "or section 123A".

(b) After section 56 of the Act of 1956 there shall be inserted as section 56A the same section as is set out in paragraph (a) above but with the substitution for the words "the Ministers", "their opinion" and "they consider" of the words "the Secretary of State", "his opinion" and "he considers" respectively.

(c) In section 22 (2) of the Trade Descriptions Act 1968 (admissibility of evidence of analysis where offence is one under both that Act and food and drugs laws) after the words "123" there shall be inserted the words "or 123A" and after the word "56" there shall be inserted the words "or 56A".

(3) As from the end of the year 1975, or any earlier date which, for any provision, the Minister of Agriculture, Fisheries and Food and the Secretary of State acting jointly may by order made by statutory instrument appoint, there shall be omitted the following provisions of the Act of 1955 or the Act of 1956, that is to say,—

(a) section 32 (2) of the Act of 1955 and section 17 (1) (b) of the Act of 1956, and the words "any separated milk, or" in section 32 (4) of the Act of 1955 and in section 17 (2) of the Act of 1956;

(b) section 33 of the Act of 1955, together with the words from "(being" to "Act)" in section 29 (1) (l) of that Act, and in section 16 of the Act of 1956 subsection (1), together with the words from "(being" to "subsection)" in subsection (2).

C: *Grading etc. of Horticultural Produce*

4.—(1) Part III of the Agriculture and Horticulture Act 1964 (grading and transport of fresh horticultural produce) shall be amended as follows:—

(a) in section 11 (power to prescribe grades) there shall be added at the end as a new subsection (3)—

"(3) Regulations under subsection (1) above shall not apply to produce of any description for the time being subject to Community grading rules; but in relation to any such produce the Ministers may by regulations—

(a) make additional provision as to the form of any label required for the purpose of those rules or as to the inclusion in any such label of additional particulars (not affecting the grading of the produce);

(b) provide for the application, subject to any modification specified in the regulations, of all or any of the following provisions of this Part of this Act as if the produce were regulated produce and as if the standards of quality established by those rules were prescribed grades.";

(b) at the end of section 22 (3) (which provides against the grading etc. of produce by agricultural marketing boards otherwise than in conformity with regulations under section 11 (1) or 21 or, in Northern Ireland, any corresponding provisions for the time being in force there) there shall be added—

"This subsection shall apply in relation to Community grading rules as it applies in relation to regulations under section 11 (1) or 21 of this Act or, as regards Northern Ireland, under any corresponding provisions.";

(c) in section 24 (interpretation of Part III) there shall be inserted after the definition of "authorised officer" the following definition:—

"Community grading rules" means any directly applicable Community provisions establishing standards of quality for fresh horticultural produce.

(2) In section 2 (4) of the Trade Descriptions Act 1968 (which provides that certain statutory descriptions and markings are to be deemed not to be trade descriptions) after the words "the Agriculture and Horticulture Act 1964" there shall be inserted the words "or any Community grading rules within the meaning of Part III of that Act".

D: *Seeds and other propagating Material*

5.—(1) In the Plant Varieties and Seeds Act 1964 there shall be made the amendments provided for by sub-paragraphs (2) to (5) below.

(2) In section 16 (1) (*c*) (preventing spread of plant disease by the sale of seeds) for the words "the sale" there shall be substituted the word "means", and after section 16 (1) there shall be inserted as subsection (1A):—

"(1A) Seeds regulations may further make provision for regulating the marketing, or the importation or exportation, of seeds or any related activities (whether by reference to officially published lists of permitted varieties or other wise), any may in that connection include provision—

(*a*) for the registration or licensing of persons engaged in the seeds industry or related activities;

(*b*) for ensuring that seeds on any official list remain true to variety;

(*c*) for the keeping and inspection of records and the giving of information;

(*d*) for conferring rights of appeal to the Tribunal;

(*e*) for excluding, extending or modifying, in relation to or in connection with any provision of the regulations, the operation of any provision made by the following sections of this Part of this Act or of Part IV of this Act, and for the charging of fees";

and the provisions relating to offences connected with seeds regulations shall be amended as follows:—

(*a*) in section 16 for the words from "which concerns" in subsection (7) (*b*) to the end of subsection (8) there shall be substituted the words "he shall be liable on summary conviction to a fine not exceeding £400"; and

(*b*) in section 18 (2) for the words from "for an offence" in paragraph (*b*) to the end of paragraph (*c*) there shall be substituted the words "for any other offence"; and

(*c*) in section 25 (7) for paragraphs (*a*) and (*b*) there shall be substituted the words "to a fine not exceeding one hundred pounds".

(3) At the end of section 16 there shall be added a subsection (8)—

"(8) The Ministers acting jointly may make seeds regulations for the whole of Great Britain".

(4) In section 29 (which extends Part II to seed potatoes) after the words "seed potatoes", in both places, there shall be inserted the words "to any other vegetative propagating material and to silvicultural planting material" and at the end of that section there shall be added as subsections (2) and (3)—

"(2) The Forestry Commissioners may establish and maintain an official seed testing station for silvicultural propagating and planting material, and seeds regulations may confer on those Commissioners any functions the regulations may confer on a Minister, and the Commissioners may charge or authorise the charging of fees for services given at any such station or in connection with any such functions; and accordingly—

(*a*) references in this Part of this Act to an authorised officer shall include an officer of those Commissioners; and

(*b*) in section 25 above the references in subsections (3) (4) and (6) to a person duly authorised by the Minister shall include a person duly authorised by the Commissioners.

Any expenses incurred or fees received by the Commissioners by virtue of this subsection shall be paid out of or into the Forestry Fund.

(3) In relation to matters concerning silvicultural propagating or planting material or concerning the Forestry Commissioners, 'the Minister' shall in this Part of this Act mean, in relation to Wales and Monmouthshire, the Secretary of State, and the reference in section 16 (8) to the Ministers shall be construed accordingly."

Accordingly in section 30 (1) in the definition of "official testing station" there shall be omitted the words "by the Minister or Ministers", and in section 38 (1) in the definition of "the Minister" after the word "means" there shall be inserted the words "(subject to section 29 (3))".

(5) In section 10 (1) for the name "Plant Variety Rights Tribunal" there shall be substituted the name "Plant Varieties and Seeds Tribunal", and in paragraph 5 (1) of Schedule 4 there shall be added at the end of Paragraph (*b*) (which sets up, to furnish members of the Tribunal, a panel of persons with specialised knowledge) the words "or of the seeds industry".

(6) In Part II of Schedule 1 to the House of Commons Disqualification Act 1957, as amended by the Plant Varieties and Seeds Act 1964 (both for the Parliament of the United Kingdom and for the Parliament of Northern Ireland), and in Schedule 1 to the Tribunals and Inquiries Act 1971, for the name 'Plant Variety Rights Tribunal' there shall be substituted in each place the name 'Plant Varieties and Seeds Tribunal'."

E: *Fertilisers and Feeding Stuffs*

6. After section 74 of the Agriculture Act 1970 there shall be inserted as a new section 74A—

"74A.—(1) Regulations under this Part of this Act, with a view to controlling in the public interest the composition or content of fertilisers and of material intended for the feeding of animals, may make provision—

(a) prohibiting or restricting, by reference to its composition or content, the importation into and exportation from the United Kingdom, the sale or possession with a view to sale, or the use, of any prescribed material;

(b) regulating the marking, labelling and packaging of prescribed material and the marks to be applied to any container or vehicle in which any prescribed material is enclosed or conveyed.

(2) Regulations made under subsection (1) above with respect to any material may include provision excluding or modifying the operation in relation to that material of any other provision of this Part of this Act; but, subject to any provision so made, references in this Part of this Act to feeding stuffs shall apply to all material which is intended for the feeding of animals and with respect to which regulations are for the time being in force under that subsection.

(3) Any person who contravenes any prohibition or restriction imposed by regulations under subsection (1) above, or fails to comply with any other provision of the regulations, shall be liable on summary conviction to a fine not exceeding £400 or, on a second or subsequent conviction, to a fine not exceeding £400 or to imprisonment for a term not exceeding three months, or to both.

(4) With a view to implementing or supplementing any Community instrument relating to fertilisers or to material intended for the feeding of animals, regulations may provide for the application, in relation to any material specified in the regulations, of all or any of the provisions of this Part of this Act, subject to any modifications which may be so specified."

F: *Animal Health*

7.—(1) In the Diseases of Animals Act 1950 there shall be made, with effect from the entry date, the amendments provided for by the following sub-paragraphs.

(2) [*Repealed by the Diseases of Animals Act 1975 (c. 40), Sched. 2.*]

(3) After section 36 (*export quarantine stations*) there shall be inserted a new section 36A—

"36A. The Minister may by order make provision in the interests of animal health or of human health, for regulating the exportation from Great Britain to a member State of animals or poultry or carcases thereof, and in particular for prohibiting exportation without such certificate or licence as may be prescribed by the order, and as to the circumstances in which and conditions on which a certificate or licence may be obtained".

(4) [*Repealed by the Diseases of Animals Act 1975 (c. 40), Sched. 2.*]

(5) [*Repealed by the Diseases of Animals Act 1975 (c. 40), Sched. 2.*]

G: *Plant Health*

8.—(1) In the Plant Health Act 1967 there shall be made, with effect from the entry date, the amendments provided for by the following sub-paragraphs.

(2) In section 1 (1) (by which the Act has effect for the control in Great Britain of plant pests and diseases) the words "in Great Britain" shall be omitted; and—

(a) in section 2 (1) and section 3 (1) (orders for control of pests) after the words "thinks expedient" there shall be inserted the words "or called for by any Community obligation";

(b) at the end of section 3 (1), after the words "preventing the spread of pests in Great Britain", there shall be added the words "or the conveyance of pests by articles exported from Great Britain";

(c) in section 3 (5) (which extends the time limit for summary prosecutions of certain offences) there shall be omitted the words "where the offence is one in connection with the movement, sale, consignment or planting of potatoes".

(3) In section 3 (2) (a) (which provides for the removal or destruction of infected crops etc.) there shall be inserted after the word "removal" the word "treatment" and after the words "any seed, plant or part thereof" the words "or any container, wrapping or other article", and in section 3 (2) (b) (which provides for entry on land for those and other purposes) there shall be inserted after the word "removal" the word "treatment" and after the word "land" the words "or elsewhere"; and the words "or elsewhere" shall also be inserted after the word "land" in section 4 (1) (b) (which also relates to entry).

(4) At the end of section 6 (1) there shall be added the words "or, in the case of an order prohibiting or regulating the landing in or exportation from Great Britain of any articles, shall be subject to annulment in pursuance of a resolution of either House of Parliament".

H: *Road Vehicles (Driving under Age, and Drivers' Hours)*

9.—(1) In section 4 (4) of the Road Traffic Act 1972 (offence of driving below the permitted age) there shall be added at the end the words "and this subsection shall apply to a contravention in Breat Britain of any directly applicable Community provision relating to the driving of road vehicles on international journeys, being a provision as to the minimum age for driving a vehicle of any description, as it applies to a contravention of the provisions of this section".

(2) In Part VI of the Transport Act 1968, in section 103 (1), after the definition of "employer" there shall be inserted the words " 'the international rules' means any directly applicable Community provision relating to the driving of road vehicles on international journeys"; and—

(*a*) after section 96 (11) there shall be inserted as subsection (11A)—

"(11A) Where, in the case of a driver or member of the crew of a motor vehicle, there is in Great Britain a contravention of any requirement of the international rules as to periods of driving, or distance driven, or periods on or off duty, then the offender and any other person (being the offender's employer or a person to whose orders the offender was subject) who caused or permitted the contravention shall be liable on summary conviction to a fine not exceeding £200";

and in section 98 (4) (failure to comply with regulations as to keeping of records etc.) after the words "regulations made under this section" there shall be inserted the words "or any requirement as to books or records of the international rules", in section 98 (5) after the words "of regulations under this section" there shall be inserted the words "or of the international rules", and in section 99 (5) (falsification of records) after the words "regulations under section 98 thereof" there shall be inserted the words "or the international rules";

(*b*) in section 99 (1) (power of enforcement officer to inspect records and other documents) there shall be inserted after paragraph (*c*)—

"(*d*) any corresponding book, register or document required by the international rules or which the officer may reasonably require to inspect for the purpose of ascertaining whether the requirements of the international rules have been complied with";

and in section 99 (3) after the words "subsection (1) (*a*)" there shall be inserted "or (*d*)";

(*c*) in section 98 (2) (power to make provision supplementary and incidental to the provision made under section 98 (1) as to the keeping of books and records) there shall be inserted after the words "supplementary and incidental provisions" the words "including provisions supplementary and incidental to the requirements of the international rules as to books and records", and after the words "for the purpose of the regulations" in paragraph (*a*) the words "or of the international rules".

(3) [*Repealed by the Road Traffic (Drivers Ages and Hours of Work) Act* 1976 (*c.* 3), *Sched.* 3, *Pt.* II.]

(4) In the following provisions as amended by the Transport Act 1968 (which, as so amended, allow records kept under Part VI of that Act to be inspected), that is to say, in section 11 (1) (*a*) of the Road Haulage Wages Act 1938 [. . .] after the words "Part VI of the Transport Act 1968" there shall be inserted the words "or of the international rules within the meaning of the said Part VI"; and in Schedule 2 to the Road Traffic (Foreign Vehicles) Act 1972, in the entry relating to sections 96 to 98 of the Transport Act 1968 and regulations and orders thereunder, there shall be added at the end of the words in the first column the words "and the international rules within the meaning of Part VI of that Act".

AMENDMENTS

In sub-para. (4) the words omitted were repealed by the Wages Council Act 1979 (c. 12), Sched. 12.

I: *Road Transport (International Passenger Services)*

10. In section 160 (1) of the Road Traffiic Act 1960 (regulations with respect to licensing of public service vehicles), in paragraph (*k*) after the word "vehicles" there shall be inserted the words "registered elsewhere than in Great Britain or" and the following shall be added at the end of the subsection:—

"(*l*) exempting vehicles from the requirement of a road service licence when used under an authorisation granted in pursuance of any directly applicable Community provision regulating the provision of international passenger-carrying road transport services;

(*m*) requiring documents of any prescribed description relevant to the administration or enforcement of any such Community provision to be kept and produced on demand for the inspection of a prescribed person;

(*n*) prescribing persons to act as authorised inspection officers for the purposes of any such Community provision;"

and at the end of section 239 of that Act (penalty for contravention of regulations) there shall be inserted the words "and where any such directly applicable Community provision as is referred to in section 160 (1) (*l*) of this Act requires the keeping or production of any document, any person who contravenes that requirement shall be guilty of an offence under this section."